I0815400

ALTERNATIVE FOR THE MASSES

ALTERI

FOR THE

THE '90s ALT-RO

AN ORAL

★ GREG

NATIVE MASSES

CK REVOLUTION

HISTORY

PRATO ★

CONT

ENTS

INTROD

It seems like most articles or documentaries about '90s alt-rock would like to have you believe that Nirvana came out of nowhere in 1991, unleashed *Nevermind*, and suddenly the direction of mainstream rock and culture shifted. Heck, at the time I am writing this little old intro, Nirvana seems to be the most popular they've ever been, judging by the number of shirts featuring the band's infamous smiley face logo being worn and their songs still heard not only on the radio but also played on social media platforms, blasted at sporting events, sung on talent-search TV programs, and the like.

But as a gentleman who was lucky enough to witness events unfold as they happened beginning in the late '80s and continuing throughout the '90s, I can honestly say that while Nirvana certainly played an enormous role in the great alt-rock uprising of the early '90s, countless other artists helped set the stage for the massive success of *Nevermind* and, at the same time, offered music just as compelling, original, and great as that of Cobain and Co. Quite a few were just as (or nearly as) popular.

MTV and its specialty shows *120 Minutes* and *Alternative Nation* (plus alt-rock-based magazines) certainly helped introduce me and most rock enthusiasts of the era to countless

UCTION

artists throughout the decade. Sadly, quite a few of those artists seem to have been overlooked, or, completely forgotten over time. However, I listened to many of these unsung artists and albums just as much as the better-known ones . . . and have continued to do so over the years.

Having already penned books focused solely on the great grunge bands (*Grunge Is Dead: The Oral History of Seattle Rock Music* and its follow-up, *I Love Grunge: 'Grunge Is Dead' Outtakes*, plus additional books that focused on specific grunge artists), I decided the time was right to shed some light on the outstanding non-grunge alt-rock bands of the same era that shared the airwaves and media space. So, as a disclaimer, I didn't dig as deeply into some of the grungers of the period as you might expect in a book about '90s rock, as I already told their stories back in 2009 and 2023 (in addition to the aforementioned books about specific artists).

As with many of my previous offerings, the decision to write this book arose from the belief that if there's a musical artist or movement that I feel deserves more attention or credit, why not use the power of my noggin and laptop computer to pay tribute in literary form—and, in this case, to speak to many of the top contributors to '90s alt-rock so we get the entire story straight from the horses' mouths?

Hopefully this book will remind you of—in my humble opinion—rock's last truly great movement. Or, better yet, introduces (or reintroduces) you to some truly exceptional artists, albums, and songs.

Here we go!
Greg Prato

P.S. Questions? Comments? Feel free to email me at gregprato@yahoo.com.

CAST OF CHARACTERS

John Agnello:
Producer/engineer (Dinosaur Jr., Mark Lanegan, The Breeders)

Steve Albini:
Producer (Nirvana, Bush, PJ Harvey)

Art Alexakis:
Everclear singer/guitarist

Fred Armisen:
Actor/comedian (*Portlandia*, *Documentary Now!*, *Saturday Night Live*), Trenchmouth drummer

Lori Barbero:
Babes in Toyland drummer

Lou Barlow:
Sebadoh singer/guitarist, Dinosaur Jr. bassist (1984–1989, 2005–present)

Miki Berenyi:
Lush singer/guitarist

Frank Black:
Pixies singer/guitarist and solo artist

Tracy Bonham:
Solo singer/violinist/pianist/guitarist

Gerald Casale:
Devo singer/bassist, music video director (Foo Fighters, Soundgarden, Silverchair)

Les Claypool:
Primus singer/bassist

Dana Colley:
Morphine saxophonist

Evan Dando:
The Lemonheads singer/guitarist

Robert DeLeo:
Stone Temple Pilots bassist

Vinnie Dombroski:
Sponge singer

Tanya Donelly:
Belly/The Breeders/Throwing Muses singer/guitarist

Mike Edwards:
Jesus Jones singer/guitarist/keyboardist

Fat Mike:
NOFX singer/bassist

John Flansburgh:
They Might Be Giants singer/guitarist

Jimmy Flemion:
The Frogs singer/guitarist

All left to right. Row 1: Frank Black, Page Hamilton, Miki Berenyi; Row 2: Johnette Napolitano, Moby, Fred Armisen; Row 3: Ian MacKaye, Tanya Donelly, Angelo Moore; Row 4: Jennifer Herrema, Corey Glover, Matt Pinfield; Row 5: Craig Wedren, Art Alexakis, Mike Watt

Corey Glover:
Living Colour singer

Bill Gould:
Faith No More bassist

Page Hamilton:
Helmet singer/guitarist

Chris Haskett:
Rollins Band guitarist

The Reverend Horton Heat:
Singer/guitarist

Jennifer Herrema:
Royal Trux singer

Kristin Hersh:
Throwing Muses singer/guitarist

Darren Jessee:
Ben Folds Five drummer

Matt Johnson:
Jeff Buckley drummer

Mike Johnson:
Dinosaur Jr. bassist (1991–1997), Mark Lanegan multi-instrumentalist, solo artist

Al Jourgensen:
Ministry singer/guitarist

Kennedy:
MTV VJ, host of *Alternative Nation*

Cris Kirkwood:
Meat Puppets bassist

Mark Kohr:
Music video director (Green Day, No Doubt, Alanis Morissette)

Paul Q. Kolderie:
Producer (Dinosaur Jr., Radiohead, Hole, Morphine)

Eric Kretz:
Stone Temple Pilots drummer

Fergal Lawler:
The Cranberries drummer

Paul Leary:
Butthole Surfers guitarist, producer (Meat Puppets, Sublime, Daniel Johnston)

Vaden Todd Lewis:
Toadies singer/guitarist

Scott Lucas:
Local H singer/guitarist

Ian MacKaye:
Minor Threat singer, Fugazi singer/guitarist, co-owner of Dischord Records

Roger Joseph Manning Jr.:
Jellyfish multi-instrumentalist/singer

Dave Markey:
Director of *1991: The Year Punk Broke* and music videos (Sonic Youth, Meat Puppets, fIREHOSE)

Kevin Martin:
Candlebox singer

Moby:
Solo artist/DJ/remixer

Angelo Moore:
Fishbone singer/saxophonist

Bob Mould:
Hüsker Dü/Sugar singer/guitarist, solo artist

Johnette Napolitano:
Concrete Blonde singer/bassist

David Pajo:
Slint guitarist, Tortoise bassist

Richard Patrick:
Filter singer/guitarist, ex-Nine Inch Nails guitarist

Mark Pellington:
Music video director (Pearl Jam, U2, Foo Fighters)

Jonn Penney:
Ned's Atomic Dustbin singer

Jason Pettigrew:
Alternative Press magazine writer and editor

Matt Pinfield:
MTV VJ, host of *120 Minutes*

Poe:
Solo artist

Lee Ranaldo:
Sonic Youth guitarist

Rudeboy Remington:
Urban Dance Squad rapper

Eddie "King" Roeser:
Urge Overkill singer/bassist

Gavin Rossdale:
Bush singer/guitarist

Danny Saber:
Black Grape multi-instrumentalist/producer, producer/remixer (Marilyn Manson, David Bowie, U2)

Joey Santiago:
Pixies guitarist

Fred Schneider:
The B-52s singer

Speech:
Arrested Development rapper

Rogers Stevens:
Blind Melon guitarist

Matt Sweeney:
Chavez singer/guitarist

Chad Taylor:
Live guitarist

Johnny Temple:
Girls Against Boys bassist

Mary Timony:
Helium singer/guitarist

Butch Vig:
Producer (Nirvana, Smashing Pumpkins, Sonic Youth), Garbage drummer

Mike Watt:
Minutemen/fIREHOSE singer/bassist, Porno for Pyros bassist, solo artist

Craig Wedren:
Shudder to Think singer/guitarist

Eric Wilson:
Sublime bassist

Naoko Yamano:
Shonen Knife singer/guitarist

1 SETTING THE STAGE

"A change in the atmosphere"

The end of the '80s and dawn of the '90s seemed like quite a promising time for alternative rock. But how did we get there? Which locations contributed and/or had scenes? Let's let those who witnessed it firsthand set the stage, shall we?

MIKE WATT (Minutemen/fIREHOSE singer/bassist, Porno for Pyros bassist, solo artist): It's not beats per minute or even funny stage names, haircuts, and clothes. I really think the movement was about anti-arena rock. Because, helping the Stooges guys out for 126 months [Watt provided bass for a reunited Stooges from 2003 to 2016], I found out [that] in the '60s there was a huge underground club scene, garage bands, and little labels.

FRED SCHNEIDER (The B-52s singer): I'm more of a funkster. When I was a kid, I was "Mr. Motown." Then grew to like everything from the Velvet Underground to Yoko Ono. Hanging around in Athens [Georgia], we all had a lot of common likes that ran the gamut from Pérez Prado to Karlheinz Stockhausen. I'm pretty eclectic—I had stopped listening to the radio pretty much in the '70s. But what I listened to was the Velvet Underground . . . and I still like my old '60s stuff. And we got the singles for Devo and the Ramones and Patti Smith. And getting real popular in New York City—because I'm from New Jersey originally—it seemed like it was on its way. And [the B-52s] were pretty "punk" when we started out because we had attitude. People don't realize that now, but I have a bit of punkiness at heart, *still*.

R.E.M., 1987. Left to right: Michael Stipe, Bill Berry, Peter Buck, and Mike Mills. "There was no college radio for punk in the movement in the early days. It was R.E.M. that opened that up."—Mike Watt *Chris Carroll/Corbis Historical/Getty Images*

MOBY (solo artist/DJ/remixer): We can even go back to the '70s and start with the Modern Lovers. The Modern Lovers *invented* alternative rock. It was the first time that oddball nerds with guitars started writing songs about oddball nerd issues. And that led to the Talking Heads—which were also the godfathers of modern alternative rock.

THE REVEREND HORTON HEAT (singer/guitarist): In the '70s, at least in Texas—and it was probably this way in a lot of places—if you had a rock band and you played gigs, you could not play original music or they would not have you back. But they knew it was a catch-22—they knew to get a record deal and to have a future and career as a recording artist, you had to play your own original music. So, they'd let you play one song. Then new wave came in in the '80s and the punk rock thing really obliterated that idea. And all of a sudden, all the clubs and the bands were more of their own music.

MIKE WATT: Starting with me, D. Boon, and Georgie [George Hurley], we graduated from San Pedro High in '76 at just the right time. And we get into this scene. And those times—late '70s/early '80s—you could know almost all of the bands in the scene because of the fanzines. We had our own parallel world—the fanzines were kind of the fabric that connected us all. Because a lot of the more mersh [commercial] shit, they wanted this thing to die. They created this thing called "new wave," which was actually something used for French films ten or fifteen years before that. There was some success—the Cars, the Knack. But how close were we, the Germs, and Screamers to the Knack? Even though it was the same town—Hollywood.

CRIS KIRKWOOD (Meat Puppets bassist): Our first tour that went out East was in '82, and I met a lot of people that I still know on that tour. The first show we did east of Arizona was in Lawrence, Kansas; and we met this opening band that was all into stuff—they had smoke machines and were goofy, fun, young guys—called the Flaming Lips. And then I met [Hüsker Dü's] Grant Hart on that tour—in extremely cold Minneapolis—and he took us to a hamburger shop that they don't have in Arizona called White Castle. It was such a personal thing we were doing—the kind of art that we were making. I personally wasn't trying to be like a . . . *musician*. It was incidental. I thought I was doing dentistry.

As it grew through the '80s, there was something definitely bitchin' going on. It wasn't as widespread as, say, the generation before us—the hippies. But it was definitely underground, and it was healthy and alive. And it got to be this thing where we kept trying to push the bar a little higher every night, where it would be like, "*Damn.*" And some nights it wouldn't quite get there, and we'd be like, "Okay. Next time." We were saying what we wanted to say about what it is to be. And had people there to go along with that evening's version of expression and creation.

BOB MOULD (Hüsker Dü/Sugar singer/guitarist, solo artist): Mid-tempo, super-pop catchy guitars with super-depressing lyrics. *[Laughs]* That's sort of my specialty, I guess.

MOBY: And then in the '80s, it splintered . . . but it was always very gentle. Modern rock and alternative rock in the '80s was R.E.M., the Cure, New Order, Echo and the Bunnymen. It was music by and for nerds who liked going for long walks and listening to sad songs. Or cuddling with their high school girlfriend on the couch, listening to New Order or the Cure.

EVAN DANDO (The Lemonheads singer/guitarist): The '80s set it up—Mission of Burma, Sonic Youth, the Wipers. Without these '70s and '80s influences, we wouldn't have had any '90s worth speaking about. The Gun Club—all that stuff that was bubbling under the surface.

MIKE WATT: There was no college radio for punk in the movement in the early days. It was R.E.M. that opened that up. And this is what . . . '83–'84? I know this because I'm working at SST [Records] and Greg Ginn's got me calling radio stations up, trying to get [Black Flag's] "Nervous Breakdown" onto college radio. Their playlists . . . it's all Journey and shit! It's all guys looking for jobs after college. D. Boon's name for them was "corporate pawns." So, they're playing things that they expect the guys that are going to hire them will like. Then when R.E.M. opens it up, all of a sudden, every DJ has their own show; and they'll play the most weird shit ever.

And talking to Kurt [Cobain], he wanted to be in the Germs! He talked to me about this kind of stuff, like, "I was born at the wrong time, Mike." And I was like, "Well, you're born when you're born." [*Laughs*] Any kind of thing is like that with the arts—"I wish I would have been there with Vincent van Gogh." Y'know, Vincent ends up selling *one* painting [during his lifetime], right? And his paintings go for all the money now. It's weird how you can see these parallels.

But R.E.M. really helped us with the college radio. I know, because I was calling up. Greg used to have me call up and he'd say, "Don't let them know you're in the Minutemen." So, I came up with this name Spaceman. "Hey, it's Spaceman! Would you play 'Nervous Breakdown'?" "No. We're playing Journey." [*Laughs*]

LOU BARLOW (Sebadoh singer/guitarist, Dinosaur Jr. bassist [1984–1989, 2005 present]): Under R.E.M., there was a whole scene of bands that were not playing hard rock. This is starting in the early '80s, really. There were a lot of bands that were influenced by '60s garage rock that were happening, and then there was this whole post-punk scene that has been brewing since the late '70s—Gang of Four, and into the Birthday Party, the Cure, Joy Division, Cocteau Twins.

But when I was a kid, for me to get ahold of [Motörhead's] *No Sleep 'til Hammersmith* was equal to getting ahold of a New Order record. These two things existed at the same time for me. And then, really, post-hardcore—'83/'84/'85—that's when the underground speed metal scene really started to happen. I was in a really cool space where I saw all these things happening, and I loved all of it.

College radio formed everything that I listened to. Everything that I discovered—into the early '90s. I listened every day. It completely changed my life. And I found radio stations that were close to me and would send them tapes, call them up, and request shit. J Mascis had a college radio show when he was in high school! He played all these amazing UK hardcore records he was getting at the time—Discharge, GBH—on Sunday morning. I heard him as a DJ before I met him—WMUA, University of Massachusetts. The Replacements had a song called "Left of the Dial."

BOB MOULD: There were a lot of radio stations that had been around. College stations, and then stations like WLIR in New York. So, that was all part of building the firmament, as well. It was a long process. It didn't just happen out of thin air. And WBCN, and Matt Pinfield was DJing down in South Jersey.

EVAN DANDO: I came into it like, 1984. I saw Flipper, and it was like, "Okay. Now I know what I want to do with my life." And then my friends were like, "Evan, you play guitar really well. You should start a punk band." I was like, "*Alright.*"

DAVE MARKEY (director of *1991: The Year Punk Broke* and music videos [Sonic Youth, Meat Puppets, fIREHOSE]): A band like fIREHOSE were road dogs—bands that would record an album and tour for the rest of the year on that album. Then come home, record another album, and then the next year, go out for a tour on that album. These are bands that are in a van, they're driving across the US, they're playing the same punk circuit that was established in the early to mid-'80s paved road that SST Records made happen.

There was this underground touring network that really was popped out of necessity, which was very much carved out by bands like the Minutemen, the Meat Puppets, and Hüsker Dü. These guys were like the foot soldiers that were laying the groundwork for all the stuff that was to happen in the '90s. I don't think there would have been a Nirvana had there not been all this stuff going on underground in the '80s. These were certainly the artists that Kurt Cobain was formed by.

PAUL Q. KOLDERIE (producer [Dinosaur Jr., Radiohead, Hole, Morphine]): We had some talks with Kurt, and through Courtney Love [while Kolderie was co-producing Hole's album *Live Through This*] also, about the things that he was into. And he was into the Pixies and another Boston band called the Lyres. There's an LP that [producer] Rick Harte did [1984's *On Fyre*] that's a big touchstone. It's kind of second generation because the Lyres were completely influenced by '60s bands. I think that influenced Kurt a lot—the sound of them, the attack of it. The influence is pretty direct, because people were going back to things that were a little more raw. Like, the Stooges started to get popular.

MIKE WATT: Of course, every time has good stuff. So, I'm not saying those were the lamest years. But there was kind of this "clown car ride" going on. And the thing about that, a farmer will tell you, "If you want a good crop, use a lot of manure." Here's my reaction: R.E.M. came out of this really square-john college town. Athens, Georgia. And Wuxtry was this record store—maybe all of them worked there—and they knew what was up.

COREY GLOVER (Living Colour singer): [CBGB in the mid-to-late '80s] was the mecca for that. You could hear bands that you would probably, for the most part, never hear of again. On any night, you would be privy to some brilliance in the form of a klezmer band or a band that was fronted by somebody with an accordion . . . and super-genius/proficient on all of it. And songwriting on par with anything that you could think of. So, CBGB's, particularly in the '80s—Hilly [Kristal] and Louise [Staley]—booked what they liked and what they thought was interesting. And it was oftentimes *transcendent*.

JOHN FLANSBURGH (They Might Be Giants singer/guitarist): When John [Linnell] and I first started, we started playing at a number of venues in New York City. With the exception of CBGB's—which is a much more knowable rock venue with its own venerable history—we played an East Village circuit which were like performance art spaces. There was the Pyramid Club, which was like a 1980s version of the club in *Cabaret*. Very decadent, very fun. Between 9 p.m. and 4 a.m., it was seven hours of different entertainment on different floors. But it was an extremely "adult" place—most of the people in it seemed older than me and John. And we really formed a lot of the ideas of the band in these venues—8BC, Darinka, Pyramid Club. And the people who were in the club encouraged us to do original material.

PAGE HAMILTON (Helmet singer/guitarist): We would meet all these different bands [in New York City]. There were the bands that came a little before us: Sonic Youth, Live Skull, Rat at Rat R, Swans, stuff like that. And then a bunch of bands started to pop up: Helmet, Cop Shoot Cop, Surgery, Unsane, Jon Spencer had Pussy Galore, Boss Hog, and then Blues Explosion was a little later. There was kind of a friendly competition, but we would all go see each other. It felt pretty supportive. People were trying to get the headlining slot at CBGB's—the midnight slot would be the prime slot, and then there was a closing band after everybody split.

We played with Nirvana actually the first time they played New York. It was the day after they became a three-piece—they had just kicked out Jason Everman in Boston the night before. We were playing the Pyramid, and they were already kind of a big deal in the indie world. Their album [*Bleach*] was out; our album was not out yet. But I remember that show at the Pyramid, and I talked to Thurston Moore years later when we were playing with Sonic Youth in Australia, and he said, "Man, I saw you guys when you opened for Nirvana at the Pyramid." It was like the "who's who of New York." Iggy Pop was there, Marc Ribot, and Sonic Youth. And Thurston said, "Man, it was just fuckin' too loud and too intense. I didn't get it." I think we were kind of scaring people—we were very loud and very heavy. The detuned guitar stuff compared to jangly and out-of-tune guitar stuff.

MATT JOHNSON (Jeff Buckley drummer): In the late '80s, I had moved to New York from Houston. Eventually, I became a working drummer playing in local bands. I had a short internship at the Looking Glass, which is Philip Glass's studio on Lower Broadway. I met some various musicians, and I remember this guy, John Moran, walked by outside—I was in a bar on Avenue A and First Street. And he was with Rebecca Moore—I believe Jeff Buckley's girlfriend at that exact time.

So, I ran out there to say hi to John, and that's where I met Rebecca. And then John mentioned to Rebecca that I was a drummer, and she said, "Let me get your number." And lo and behold, I got a phone call from Jeff a day or two later on my answering machine. I met Jeff at Context Studios [in Williamsburg, Brooklyn]. We played together, and I believe at that time we started to create what eventually became "Dream Brother"—probably at that first rehearsal/audition.

CHAD TAYLOR (Live guitarist): There were a handful of worthy artists and bands [near York, Pennsylvania]—all featured performers at the Chameleon Club. Suddenly, Tammy! was amongst my favorites, along with Innocence Mission. The band Ocean Blue was also from our region and did well.

CRAIG WEDREN (Shudder to Think singer/guitarist): The late '80s and early '90s were pretty fascinating to me in terms of what was going on in the D.C. underground music scene. Dischord had started in the early '80s. I was living in Cleveland at the time . . . I was only vaguely aware of Minor Threat and Bad Brains. I moved there in '85, at the end of what would be termed "revolution summer," which was Rites of Spring and the second wave of D.C. hardcore. And it was more impressionistic and a little more . . . not overtly psychedelic, but there was an experimentation to it. And everybody was growing up—it was a bunch of kids who were in their early teens in the early '80s and were now getting into their late teens in the mid-to-late '80s. The older you got, the more omnivorous you get. It was okay to admit you loved the Beatles. Whereas that was verboten before. So, this sort of expansive creativity or attitude toward experimentation in the D.C. underground really kicked in in the Dischord world at that point.

In Cleveland, you took whatever you could get. There weren't enough weirdos to be strict about "Well, I'm into hardcore." "Well, I'm into ska." "Well, I'm into noise." It was just one bunch of freaks. So, when I joined Shudder to Think, it was during that phase of D.C. music that was already starting to open up. The minute we started playing together, it was very clear that there was something different happening—the combination of sensibilities, the sounds, my voice, and lyric style. And fortunately, everybody in the band agreed that originality and inventiveness would be a premium. And I think there was a lot of that mentality happening in young bands in D.C. in the late '80s. So, by 1990, there were so many different types of bands in D.C. and in the Dischord stable between Shudder to Think, Jawbox, and Fugazi. That's a pretty wide variety of music right there already.

IAN MacKAYE (Minor Threat singer, Fugazi singer/guitarist, co-owner of Dischord Records): Dischord Records largely exists in our own zone. In the forty-plus years since we put out our first record, we've never used contracts and never had a lawyer. And Fugazi . . . I don't think any other bands operated like us. As a result, I think I have a really weird perspective on the music business. Fugazi never had a manager or relied on a booking agent; we never toured on a bus and never used setlists. We were a weird fuckin' band.

CRAIG WEDREN: We were close—and still are—with Dave Grohl because he was part of the D.C. scene. He played in the band Scream; he had a band called Dain Bramage. And we were the same age—he was dating a girl in my class, and we went to the prom together. We were all buds. And I would go see any band he was playing in just to watch him play drums, because it was *so* electric.

JASON PETTIGREW (*Alternative Press* magazine writer and editor): Being in Cleveland [where *Alternative Press* was based], you weren't commercial enough for L.A., you weren't cool enough for New York. We generally wrote about stuff that was different. And hopefully, we could pull somebody away from their parents' classic rock records long enough to get them hooked on something else.

PAGE HAMILTON: Madison [Wisconsin] had—because of Smart Studios—a cool part of the world, too. There were little pockets like Chicago, Madison, Minneapolis, New York, and Seattle—where there were scenes.

BILL GOULD (Faith No More bassist): I grew up in Hollywood in the late '70s/early '80s. And it was like mods and rockers. There were hair bands and there were punks. And I was on the side of the punks. So, on a very cultural level, I always saw the hair bands as "the other." Kind of the enemy. Those were the guys that drove the pickup trucks and would kick our ass.

FAT MIKE (NOFX singer/bassist): Los Angeles was the most violent music scene of all time. There were punk gangs: there was the Suicidal Tendencies gang; there was FFF, the L.A. Death Squad, and Burbank Punk Organization. The main reason I left L.A. is because I went to see the Dickies at a nightclub in Santa Monica, and I knew some Suicidals, and my friend got stabbed in the lung at the show. They didn't know him—they just knew he wasn't from Venice. My friends got beat up with golf clubs. Y'know, *punk rockers beating other punk rockers*.

And the cops would mace us. I got arrested—only once, in Hollywood—but for nothing. But that was *every* punk show. It wasn't until the late '80s when Fugazi and Bad Religion came out. Bad Religion put out the best-selling record that year in punk [*No Control*]. Do you know how many it sold? *Ten thousand.* And we couldn't believe they sold ten thousand because NOFX sold two thousand in '89. So, what was the punk scene like in L.A.? It was the most horrific, violent scene. I moved to San Francisco after my friend got stabbed.

MATT PINFIELD (MTV VJ, host of *120 Minutes*): [Drummer] Matt Sorum found Tori Amos playing by the LAX Airport in a hotel. He heard her, and he was so blown away by her piano playing that he was like, "Hey, we need to start a band together!" And basically, they started the band Y Kant Tori Read. That record [1988's self-titled] didn't really do anything, but Jason Flom ended up signing her to Atlantic—by telling her that he didn't want the whole band, he wanted her to do her own thing. And then, *Little Earthquakes* came next.

MOBY: And then overnight, we realized there were these nerdy alternative rockers in Seattle—who also had been listening to Black Sabbath.

KEVIN MARTIN (Candlebox singer): I moved to Seattle in 1984. My dad took a job up there. It was right when all the grunge music was starting to happen. Chris Cornell was still playing drums when I saw Soundgarden—they were a three-piece.

BILL GOULD: When we played in Seattle, I think the first time was 1985/1986 at the Central Tavern. It was us, Skin Yard—Jack Endino's band—and Soundgarden. *There were only like thirty people there.* We went with Soundgarden to play Ellensburg, Washington, and I think that the guys from Screaming Trees came to that show and started a band after that. It wasn't like a movement—they were just friends of ours up there that we'd play with. And things gathered steam. I remember the first time I heard Nirvana; Nirvana seemed like kids coming from that world, basically.

CHRIS HASKETT (Rollins Band guitarist): Soundgarden were the first of "us" to get signed. They got signed to a major label [A&M] in, like, 1988. We were all like, "Whoa! How did *that* happen?" That kind of put them in a different world.

COREY GLOVER: We did a show in Albany, New York, once; and Soundgarden opened. And it was the most amazing shit I've ever seen in my life. I thought that Chris Cornell was amazing. I thought the band was *overly* talented—too talented for the room.

FRED ARMISEN (actor/comedian [*Portlandia*, *Documentary Now!*, *Saturday Night Live*], Trenchmouth drummer): I think when I saw Mudhoney's records—that looked like a different movement was happening. It didn't seem like the same kind of "college rock/alternative" bands that were coming out. Even without hearing them, I could tell there was something happening. Then of course, there were these other genres starting to happen in the late '80s.

I feel like industrial had its own look—the Wax Trax! scene and all that. That seemed like something different than college/alternative. What I mean by "college/alternative" is the Smithereens, 10,000 Maniacs, and maybe even the Sugarcubes—somewhere in there, that's what seemed like alternative. Aside from the jangle of the sound, I would say that the Smithereens also had a distorted sound. Which at the time, was not being played on every radio station. I see them as less jangly and a little harder than that. I loved it all, but Mudhoney caught my eye as, "Oh . . . what's happening *here*?"

EDDIE "KING" ROESER (Urge Overkill singer/bassist): We formed in a microcosm, where I kind of showed up on the campus of Northwestern from a small town in Minnesota. I was unaware of the scene in Minneapolis—at the time, the Replacements and Hüsker Dü were thriving. And I lived far away, and there was no place to even get a fanzine where I grew up. So, I grew up almost unaware of any underground punk rock thing. A pal of mine had things that were more public—I was aware of the Sex Pistols and things like that.

The main thing in my life that was happening was that I became aware of Big Black, as there was this sort of raconteur on campus who wrote for *The Daily Northwestern* and was a known figure as being an outspokenly public asshole. The first person that I was aware of being publicly against the grain. By the time I showed up there, *Steve Albini* was on his way out, and I ended up at this tiny on-campus place where I saw a version of Urge Overkill. It was their last show, basically. And Big Black played one of their first shows—I think it was Steve and a drum machine.

I can't even say what was happening in Chicago, but through meeting [Urge Overkill bandmate] Nash [Kato] and Steve, I was aware of stuff like Naked Raygun. And Ministry—I think Al Jourgensen was a guy that Steve actually played music with a couple of times. It was sort of a nascent scene in Chicago, and while I was there, I was able to see a few things that were important to me—I saw Naked Raygun open for the Replacements, and I think there were about twenty people there.

Steve was the guy who said, "You can actually rent a studio and make a record." We recorded a record that Steve helped finance. It was recorded in 1984—it came out on Steve's label, Ruthless [1986's *Strange, I . . .*]. He was an entrepreneur in the world of punk rock. Everybody else was not capable of being able to pay attention and see a project through. Steve was the guy who did that.

Corey Rusk started the label Touch and Go in Detroit, and his presence on the scene was very important. And somehow, Steve hooked up with them. I don't know how they met the Butthole Surfers, but that was in the mix as well. So, we're talking mid-'80s. It was a very tiny world of misfits and dreamers. It's basically a bunch of Asperger's patients who didn't know how to have fun and had very antisocial tendencies. I mean, Touch and Go parties at the time, people would grill a bunch of meat and you could probably count the words said among people in the hundreds, because no one knew how to communicate or have fun.

And then these freaks from Texas showed up. Scratch Acid were in the mix. Those guys came to Chicago, and Jesus Lizard was a later thing. But Steve left the campus area, bought a house, and decided he wanted to become a professional recordist and blaze his own trail. And because we were in the mix early enough and we were all pals, one of our first tours, Steve rented a van and played in Kentucky and had Squirrel Bait play, and the first version of Urge went along with them. This was our entire world: the nascent Touch and Go scene.

The biggest band on earth to me at the time was Sonic Youth. And Steve had a relationship with them. When they came to town, we went to the park and had a barbecue. But there was no intimation that anything involved with punk rock would become something that anybody was going to care about. It was the place to go if you were a loser or a misfit. It was for its own entertainment.

We recorded a version of "Wichita Lineman" with Steve. And Steve got it to Corey, and he's like, "I would like to put this single out." We couldn't even believe that we had a label that wasn't Steve. Nash, his real interest was arts and graphic design. He designed the Touch and Go logo.

TANYA DONELLY (Belly, The Breeders, and Throwing Muses singer/guitarist): At that point, there were so many bands [in Boston] from the late '80s to the early '90s—Pixies, Throwing Muses, Uzi, the Neats. Any given bill on any given night would have been *wildly* eclectic. And it was a joyful thing. It would be the Blake Babies and Dinosaur Jr., and Throwing Muses and Pixies played together quite a lot. But then there were the "Mission of Burma breakout bands" like Birdsongs of the Mesozoic.

At the time, I know this sounds naïve, but we weren't focused on being female in music. But when I look back now, I'm like, "There was a healthy percentage of women driving the scene at the time." And that is something also that I think was unique to that era—and specifically to Boston and London at the time. There were pockets everywhere, obviously; but Boston was *so* female-rich. I feel that that was something that I sort of took for granted at the time. It was easily 50/50 at that time.

PAUL Q. KOLDERIE: When Fort Apache Studios started, we were just a local eight-track studio in Boston. It was starting at ground zero from nothing. All of us were musicians and people who played in bands and knew a lot of people in town. But the thing that made people like going there is that it was grungy. It was in an old warehouse that had been a commercial laundry. And it was like a city block—it was an enormous empty warehouse, with old industrial bathrooms and old beat-up wood floors. So, our studio was carved out of the second floor of that building. We didn't have the whole floor, but a lot of times at night, we'd use it—we'd drag mics out there. A lot of screaming vocals on the Pixies' *Come on Pilgrim* were recorded out there.

And word of mouth was so important. Back then, there was a very achievable thing you could do: You could go into a studio, book time, record songs, and make a quarter-inch reel-to-reel tape that you could take to college radio stations and a few commercial alternative stations that would potentially play that tape. Y'know, it was the local ghetto show on Sunday night, but if it was really successful, you would graduate over into actually being added to the rotation. And nobody was paying payola either—it was very meritocracy-based. It was never a question of having to bribe someone or slipping a hundred-dollar bill in with a tape. They listened to it, and if they liked it, they'd play it.

The first real commercial success we had was Treat Her Right—Mark Sandman's band before Morphine. They scored a local hit that actually became a national hit ["I Think She Likes Me"], and they signed to RCA Records. All of a sudden, that really put us on the map. Because once people start to think there's a lucky convenience store where they sell lottery tickets that come in, people are like, "How can I get in there?" And then after that, the Pixies. Gary [Smith] brought in the Pixies and produced *Come on Pilgrim*, and I engineered it. We all kind of teamed up on it. Man, that was a real Fort Apache early golden era. People were sleeping in the other room, and we were mixing around the clock. That record really blew a lot of doors open. And at one point, WFNX put out their "Top 50 Local Songs of the Year"; and we had like thirty-eight of them!

We went up the ladder from 8-track to 16-track to 24-track to two 24-track studios. And then eventually we had our own production deal with a label. We were pretty proactive about going after bands that we wanted to record, especially in the early days. Like, I went to the Rat [the Rathskeller club] with Gary, and we saw the Pixies. We went backstage and talked to them and said, "Let's make a record." That didn't always work. But it did in that case.

After *Come on Pilgrim* came out—which I engineered—I went to Las Vegas, and I was hanging out with some people. And they said, "You're an engineer? Well . . . what did you do?" And I said [*Come on Pilgrim*], and they were like, "Wow, really? You did that?" They knew about it instantly—it had only been out a few weeks. It spread like wildfire, the equivalent of going viral.

DAVID PAJO (Slint guitarist, Tortoise bassist): I remember when we were recording *Tweez*, [drummer] Britt [Walford] asked [Steve Albini], "Do you think Slint will ever be popular?" And Steve—really wisely—said, "I don't think Slint will ever be popular . . . *but they'll be influential*." And then he said that we were "the sound of the '90s." Which, in 1987, it sounded like the far-off future. But he was so spot-on.

FERGAL LAWLER (Cranberries drummer): There wasn't really many [alt-rock bands in Ireland]. It was more further afield where we looked—either to the UK or the US—for those kind of bands. In Ireland, there were lots of smaller bands that we used to go and see . . . which would have been a little bit alternative. There were a few bands in Limerick. One was They Do It with Mirrors, who were great, quirky, almost like the Cure at times. And then there were a couple of Dublin bands. There was one called the Pale, which had three guys in the band. And An Emotional Fish—they were a good band back then.

There were nighttime DJs that would be on the radio, and we'd tune in to them to find out who the new alternative acts were or what new singles were coming out. Stuff you'd never hear on daytime radio. There were "pirate radio stations." They were basically a guy in his bedroom who had a broadcast thing and played whatever alternative stuff was around.

We were actually Cure-heads. We had the hair back-combed and everything like that. Actually, when I first met [guitarist] Noel [Hogan] and [bassist] Mike [Hogan], we were

Pixies, at Pinkpop Festival, Landgraaf, Netherlands, May 15, 1989. Left to right: David Lovering, Frank Black, Joey Santiago, and Kim Deal. "That record [*Come on Pilgrim*] really blew a lot of doors open."—Paul Q. Kolderie *Gie Knaeps/Hulton Archive/Getty Images*

breakdancers! So, it would have been '83 or '84. After a few years, we got into more alternative stuff like the Cure, Joy Division, the Smiths, Depeche Mode, Stone Roses. It was always that kind of left-field kind of music. We went to see the Cure as one of our first concerts—they were playing in Dublin. It was amazing to see them live.

MIKE EDWARDS (Jesus Jones singer/guitarist/keyboardist): There was a watershed point [in England]—in the late '80s, we had this kind of Jesus and Mary Chain/introverted/noisy kind of thing. Which gave way to a rebirth or renewal of heavier rock sounds. A lot of bands were looking toward the Stooges, MC5, stuff like that. And an awful lot of Velvet Underground–influenced bands. Shortly after the likes of the Shamen and Pop Will Eat Itself, we started using more dance music in our music. There was a shift toward more groove-orientated sounds—even if bands didn't really use the technology that we were using, they kind of changed the feel of the beats and groove.

JONN PENNEY (Ned's Atomic Dustbin singer): One of the key things that occurred at the time was live guitar music made its massive comeback. There were a lot of guitar gigs going on in the UK. Which meant bands like ourselves were coming through with influences from the '80s—like the Cure, Echo and the Bunnymen, the Teardrop Explodes, Killing Joke. An absolute *plethora* of fantastic punk-rock-ethic music that was trying to be of its own. The thing for us was there were a lot of gigs to go and play.

There would be a gig every other week you'd want to go to of a UK guitar band. There was Manchester—"Madchester"—going on. We felt a little bit of an antidote to Manchester when we came through—there was a lot of dancey, "baggy" stuff going on. We felt a bit less groovy and a bit more in your face. But I think from where I'm looking, the popularity of the guitar gigs grew and grew during those early '90s years.

And there were a lot of great live bands that have gone under the radar since. But not bands that are similar in genre, necessarily. If you look at the three bands that came out of Stourbridge, we're not a million miles from the way the Wonder Stuff sounded. But we're a bit more punk rock, we had two bass guitars, and I'm certainly not the troubadour that Miles Hunt is. And then you've got Pop Will Eat Itself, who are like a British Beastie Boys. It's not similar music, necessarily, but the ethic certainly was a common thread amongst all the music that was coming through at the time—amongst all the British bands that were touring. You had bands like Jesus Jones, the Senseless Things, Mega City Four.

FERGAL LAWLER: Our first band was called the Cranberry Saw Us. A friend of ours who played in another band called the Hitchers, Niall Quinn, wanted to do a side project. Myself, Noel, and Mike played together, rehearsing instrumental music. We were trying to find a singer, and he said, "I heard you guys are looking for a singer. I'm doing this side project." So, we did that with him for about six months, but it wasn't really what we wanted to do.

And then the girl he was going out with was in school with Dolores [O'Riordan]. And she said to Dolores, "I heard this band is looking for a singer, and they play original stuff." Because she had been looking for bands and she had been to a few auditions, but most of them were doing cover versions and she wanted to do original material. It was through Niall that we met Dolores. She came up to rehearsal and spoke about the music she was into. And she was into the Smiths and Depeche Mode—similar stuff to us. We went in to record our demo in the studio—we could really hear her clearly and went, "*She can really sing.*"

LOU BARLOW: And from Australia, there were these incredible bands like the Eastern Dark and the Scientists. Fucking amazing, powerful garage rock bands.

CHRIS HASKETT: When I first started touring with Rollins, the other bands that would be out at that point would be the Swans, Sonic Youth, Scratch Acid, Jawbox, Bullet LaVolta, the Butthole Surfers, the Big Boys, and Tuxedomoon. There was this whole other world of people doing radically different things from each other. You think about how incredibly influential a band like Sonic Youth was.

FRED ARMISEN: Before *Nevermind*, I would say the real change in everything happening was Fugazi's first EP [1988's self-titled]. Mudhoney was kind of like, "Oh . . . what's going on over there?" And then Fugazi was a real breaking point of, "Ah, *now* this is a solid movement. This is a real thing happening." I don't know how charts work or how they count all that stuff, but "Waiting Room" is what I consider to be a "hit song." Fugazi was the breaking point of "things are happening."

BOB MOULD: If I look at '89/'90—*Workbook* and *Black Sheets of Rain* [Mould's first two solo albums]—*Workbook* was definitely a statement of intent. "I am not just the guy from Hüsker Dü." *Black Sheets* to me was sort of a reimagining of what [bassist] Tony Maimone and the late [drummer] Anton Fier brought to *Workbook*, and what all the touring from *Workbook* got us to this heavier, louder version. And that was *Black Sheets*.

FAT MIKE: Faith No More kind of did it before Nirvana. "Epic" was different—it was awesome. They weren't hair metal, but they made it out of that scene, kinda. But they played all the punk warehouses in Oakland. I saw them with their first singer, Chuck [Mosley]; and there were fifteen people at a warehouse. And the piano chords at the end of "Epic" are so beautiful. And Mike Patton could *really* sing. That whole record, *The Real Thing*, was amazing.

BILL GOULD: There was still hair metal bands; there was still this tour called Monsters of Rock that had Whitesnake, Aerosmith—that was very popular. Metallica was in full swing. Guns N' Roses were in ascendance. Our little scene that we were in, there was still a bit of a thrash thing—bands like Nuclear Assault. Soundgarden and us were playing. It would also be the era of *RIP Magazine*, and there was a music conference that was going on in New York around that time: *CMJ* [*College Music Journal*].

ROGER JOSEPH MANNING JR. (Jellyfish multi-instrumentalist/singer): I was front row and center, because the first Jellyfish album [*Bellybutton*] came out at the height of what was left over of hair metal and MTV pushing that. That was 1990. The Guns N' Roses album [*Appetite for Destruction*] hit in 1988, so that's what everything was. We took great pride of being so unique at the time. In fact, we were amazed that any record company—major labels in this case, with Virgin and Atlantic—were willing to take a shot on us, considering we had nothing to do with either the metal scene that was happening at the time or the pop/R&B sound that's always on the radio, no matter what decade you're in.

So, late '80s/early '90s is this bizarre period, because you literally have the twenty-somethings making their "rock rebellion statement," but you've still got Bad Company, ZZ Top, AC/DC, and all these groups you'd associate with '70s and '80s classic rock, they're still hitting it. And you've got the students of that going, "No. This is a new movement. We're going to rebel against that." That's what always happens with art movements—you're always commenting on the establishment. And whether those bands knew it or not, they were the establishment. Even Queen, Judas Priest, Led Zeppelin—there was a reverence for that stuff growing up, but it was also kind of like, "Hey, you old guys. Time to leave the room. *We youngsters have something to say.*"

LES CLAYPOOL (Primus singer/bassist): Alternative was the alternative to what was popular, and for us it was all those hairball bands. *That's* what we were rebelling against. I think once these bands started gaining some traction, it was like anything that was different from all the hairball bands that were dominating the airwaves and MTV were starting to get juice—like us, the Chili Peppers, Nirvana, Soundgarden.

COREY GLOVER: There was a change in the atmosphere for a lot of bands that didn't want to be these commercial hair bands.

DANA COLLEY (Morphine saxophonist): I'm trying to picture Morphine playing in the '80s, and I'm not sure we had the hair or the lapels for it.

JENNIFER HERREMA (Royal Trux singer): People started taking themselves more seriously and were like, "We're *not* dressing up. We're *not* doing our hair. We're serious about this guitar thing."

KRISTIN HERSH (Throwing Muses singer/guitarist): In our subculture, we were pretty clear that there was a corporate attempt at top-down popular culture happening that was really goofy; so we ignored it . . . figured that anything real was gonna happen down here on the ground in bars and basements, bedrooms, and garages. It was cooler there because life was hard, and we were the soundtrack to that.

FRANK BLACK (Pixies singer/guitarist and solo artist): The compact disc had certainly taken over, and vinyl was completely dead at that moment. But artists were still involved in very traditional kinds of relationships with record companies. And when I say "traditional," I mean in terms of the financial connections.

EVAN DANDO: It was '89, and I was in Berlin. I had a girlfriend over there, and I was staying for Christmas. And the Wall was coming down—New Year's Eve into 1990. And it's like, "Alright . . . *this looks like it could be quite a decade.*"

Jane's Addiction in Chicago, Illinois, November 1988. Left to right: Perry Farrell, Dave Navarro, Stephen Perkins, and Eric Avery. "Jane's Addiction need to be credited as *the* most important."—Matt Pinfield *Paul Natkin/Getty Images*

2 JANE'S ADDICTION AND LOLLAPALOOZA

"Dangerous and crazier"

The importance of Jane's Addiction's 1990–1991 infiltration of the mainstream cannot be overstated. And the same can be said about the inaugural edition of the traveling North American festival Lollapalooza, which JA's frontman, Perry Farrell, co-founded.

MATT PINFIELD: The great thing about bands like Jane's Addiction was it had a dangerous side to it. Like, what Guns N' Roses had opened the door for on that end of things, it started that whole wave of people being more dangerous and crazier. More confrontational.

JASON PETTIGREW: There was a big article in *Rolling Stone* ["Local Heroes," October 22, 1987, issue]. And there was an article on Jane's Addiction—which was cool, because it was hard rock with a weird, atmospheric, psychedelic thing to it. And the other one was Tommy Conwell and the Young Rumblers. I was reading it, and it was all that heartfelt, oh-so-earnest, Midwest rock . . . like, if a Hallmark card had 110-decibel amps. I thought,

"This is more of the same. I can't stand it." And Perry Farrell was making all sorts of crazy proclamations. And I'm like, "He's so out of his mind! I love it!"

Because you were so used to a status quo where it was either Springsteen or that horrible AOR. The fact that Perry Farrell was making all these brash comments . . . but he had the freak-itude to back it up. I mean, if you don't get "Ocean Size," I'm sorry—I'm walking away from the table. There was *so much* power there, yet it really sounded alien. Plus, they looked like opiates and funhouse mirrors—it was wild to look at and go see them do that wild percussion jam in the middle of their sets. *There was something happening.*

MOBY: In the world of punk rock but also alternative rock, there were always the bands that you liked . . . but you were a little suspicious of. Like, in the world of hardcore punk, it was bands like DRI, Corrosion of Conformity, or Suicidal Tendencies, where you were like, "I really like them. But they seem like 'heavy metal guys.'" Like, "Uh oh. Are they part of my 'nerd tribe' . . . or are they actually the guys who know about sports?" And Jane's Addiction was the first time the underground alternative rockers sounded like—and looked like—*rock stars*. I remember seeing them at the Cat Club in Manhattan, and I was like, "Huh? I don't know what this is. Are they a rock band? Are they alternative?"

MATT PINFIELD: Jane's Addiction need to be credited as *the* most important. I met resistance when I wanted to get behind Jane's Addiction at the radio station—when I wanted to play the *Nothing's Shocking* album. But I did anyway, and they allowed me to do it. But I was like, "This is an important band and an important record. It's taking what's artistic about all the alternative stuff that's out now in the arts community and lacing it with Led Zeppelin and a lot of hard rock." Because Stephen Perkins had that history of being in bands that were on the Strip and Dave Navarro played with that "heavy metal/hair metal rock fury" that was happening.

But at the same exact time, Perry Farrell and Eric Avery were part of this arts community that came out of Venice; and then there was this whole other thing happening that they were exposed to and introduced to in Los Angeles. So, it was a melting pot of those two scenes that made Jane's Addiction what they were. And having someone as original and as absolutely confrontational and fearless as Perry Farrell as your frontman was life-changing for the music scene. And I will tell you this for a fact: I would hear from other people that some of the bands that were more on the "jangly" side of the bands disliked Jane's Addiction very much because of the way they incorporated the hard rock and metal thing. But I saw it as something that was really important and "the future."

COREY GLOVER: Jane's Addiction seemed like a mix of a whole bunch of stuff. And that was due to the members of the band. Eric was a straight-ahead jazz player, Dave was really into the glam rock thing, Stephen at the time was embracing a New Orleans second line aesthetic, and all that made Perry do what he did. They were influential in the fact that they were unapologetic about what they were doing. The ambiguity was a feature, not a bug.

"HOW MUCH WILL IT TAKE TO REPLACE THAT WINDOW, STEVE?"

Johnette Napolitano negotiates the "Joey" video budget.

Bloodletting was an important record not just to us, but it was the first release under the new distribution deal between I.R.S. and EMI. This was good for us—the relationship was fresh. I.R.S.'s office in London was in a very old building—Victorian or Edwardian—with an ornate stained-glass window in front, called "Bugle House."

I knew that, contractually, we had a video budget for the record that wasn't huge but Andy Lee, having made the Sugarcubes video ["Birthday"] for £200, would be happy with $60,000. So, I arranged a meeting with Steve Tannett, the guy that ran the UK office, to get our money in order to get going with the "Joey" video, since they'd already picked that as the single.

I'm sitting in the office with Steve, whose back was to the window, and he's telling me that they're not going to give me the money to shoot the video. I was pissed, because I knew they owed it to us contractually; and, of course, we needed a damn video. A lot of us signed to I.R.S. often wondered if they were actually a real label at all or a front for something else, given Miles Copeland's CIA DNA.

Anyway, Steve's telling me this BS, and I'm not in the mood. So, I pick up a stapler—a heavy metal one—and said, "How much will it take to replace that window, Steve?" I fully intended to hurl that thing through that priceless antique stained-glass window. Steve knew I wasn't kidding and opened a drawer in the desk real quick, looked down for a minute, slid it closed, and said, "*Yes, yes, you're right. $60,000*"—as if the contract was in the drawer and he'd just checked. And that's how we got our money.

[The "Joey" video] had class, atmosphere, and visually [was] a beautiful video. The story was great, and *The Third Man* is an old film that inspired Andy—he cast Joey, who was a Scottish guy. That was kind of strange to me, because this character was a person now. If you see the video for "Candy" by Kate Pierson and Iggy Pop, it looks almost exactly like the "Joey" video.

JOHNETTE NAPOLITANO (Concrete Blonde singer/bassist): In L.A. at the time, the weirder you were and the more extreme you were, the cooler you were.

MIKE WATT: I look at it now as like, "Oh, this is like when Jane's Addiction goes up and plays in Seattle." Because you know what Seattle bands were like before that, right? They were like Gang of Four bands.

ANGELO MOORE (Fishbone singer/saxophonist): They were more like "rock psychedelia."

JONN PENNEY: There's a story about them playing a really small place in Birmingham [England], where the place was absolutely rammed out. And the crowd refused to go home. So, Jane's—who had broken down all their gear—sat around on the dancefloor and they were drumming on the drum cases and having a sing-song with the audience.

To me, it felt like Jane's had a massive impact quite a while before Nirvana did. Nirvana were not on my radar at all until the latter years of our success. But we were open to welcoming that kind of music over here. There was a great love of the potency of it. And in fairness, not a great deal of our guitar bands had got quite that "rock sensibility" about them. That kind of "chunkiness" of sound, it took a while to develop. But I do believe that people like Jane's Addiction and Smashing Pumpkins coming over, those kind of sounds did influence our music as well.

LES CLAYPOOL: Watching them perform "Three Days" was just absolutely spectacular [Primus opened for Jane's Addiction in 1990–1991]. The whole soundscape of it. Obviously, there is the visual element; but there was a contrast between dirty and beauty with Jane's Addiction. Because they all were dreaded and there was some dark drug use at the time . . . but there was also this beauty to it all, with Perry's voice and the way they would texture it with the delays and the way Stephen attacks his drums and the way Eric played his bass. Eric did a lot of drone-y, whole note-y octave and third stuff. I was won over very quickly.

And then we wound up going to Europe with them. Smoking hash under the Peter Pan statue in Nottingham at two in the morning. [*Laughs*] The Pixies were on that tour, too. So, the whole night was this spectacular contrast in sounds between us and a lot of angular elements to it, the Pixies being this driving force, and then Jane's Addiction with this swirling contrast between heaviness and beauty.

FRED ARMISEN: Mudhoney was a little underground. Whereas Jane's Addiction, I had heard them on the radio a little more.

MOBY: The song that really turned my friends and I into fans was "Been Caught Stealing." Because we were like, "Okay. *We get it.* They are borrowing from rock traditions, but there's also definitely a punk rock ethos here."

KENNEDY (MTV VJ, host of *Alternative Nation*): It's funny, because Dave Navarro doesn't look good in that video [for "Been Caught Stealing"] . . . but he's *so* hot. Like, to this day he's so hot. And I think if they had really objectified him appropriately, that would have helped things.

CRAIG WEDREN: If you look at the *Billboard* charts from then, they're just *so* fucked up and confused. And really boring—with strange weirdos occasionally popping through. So, there was this feeling of, "There could be a 'strange weirdo' that pops through." I remember going to see Jane's Addiction, and it was the first alt-rock show that I had seen in an arena that wasn't Peter Gabriel or U2. I went to see Jane's Addiction on the Ritual de lo Habitual Tour at Madison Square Garden [on April 24, 1991].

I remember thinking beforehand, "How are they going to sell out the Garden? The Garden is for the Rolling Stones." I went, and not only was it sold out, *it was a real event*. It felt like a tribal gathering. So, that was sort of the first moment for me that I glimpsed how it might be possible for this "secret music" that we had all been nursing for most of our teens to break through—for better or worse.

JOHNETTE NAPOLITANO: I have a lot of respect for Jane's Addiction and appreciate a lot of the originality, but I never could warm up to Perry Farrell's voice. However, having said that, I've seen a couple of acoustic performances; and he holds his own really well. So, I think he improved a lot over time. And I'm a big Dave Navarro fan—his Deconstruction album [1994's self-titled] is one of the best albums I've ever heard.

JOHNNY TEMPLE (Girls Against Boys bassist): I think a lot of it had to do with Perry Farrell's psycho/gender-bendy/brilliant poetics. His lyrics were incredible. And really moody—like Sonic Youth. Almost like a more structured, more commercial version of some of the dynamics in Sonic Youth songs. But adding this more urgent electricity to it. I almost think of, musically, *Nothing's Shocking* being more of a predecessor to *Nevermind* than even Sonic Youth. *Ritual de lo Habitual* got them further commercially, but I think that their biggest triumph is *Nothing's Shocking*.

KENNEDY: People kind of forget the cool artistic side of L.A. music. And that's the amazing thing about L.A.: It's never just one thing. And Jane's Addiction never was just one thing. But there was so much intensity, I don't know if they could have gone forward in the way that they were. And it's utterly impossible to see that not only is something going to hit, but it's going to be a complete paradigm shift. I know how much they inspired people that came out of that "Soundgarden/Nirvana/Pearl Jam/Mudhoney wave."

MIKE WATT: Perry was really influenced by what Stuart Swezey did [as the impetus for Lollapalooza]. You know about *Desolation Center*, that documentary? Stuart was booking clubs and said, "If you're going to be wild with the music, why not with the place you play the gigs?" And a lot of those things were at bars because the rock 'n' rollers hated the movement. So, you'd find a bar where, "You keep the beer money and let me have the door money." And then that became a little predictable, so he said, "Hey, let's get a generator and rent some school buses and go to a dry lake bed out in the Mojave." Perry picked up on this—he had a band then called Psi Com. He helped build the stage there. I think that helped inform his thing, too.

CHRIS HASKETT: Jane's Addiction—this must have been 1990—were taking out the coolest bands that they came across and giving them like a week each as a support slot. Bands you would not necessarily see right in front of their audience. We got a week, and somebody had to drop out, and we got an extra week. And at the end of the two weeks, the idea got mooted: "We're putting together a big festival of six bands, and they want to add you guys and make it seven." I think originally the Butthole Surfers were supposed to be the "strange first band on," and then we became the "strange first band on."

Crowd at Lollapalooza, Waterloo Village, New Jersey, August 14, 1991. "All of a sudden, we were playing these big outdoor venues with tons of people—it was eye-opening."—Paul Leary *Ebet Roberts/Redferns/Getty Images*

JESUS JONES' 2X UK CHART DISAPPOINTMENT

Mike Edwards recalls the underwhelming chart performance of their most recognizable single.

["Right Here, Right Now"] was released in 1990 in the UK, and it got to number thirty-one, which was our worst chart position in a year or so. And we were very disappointed in that. Fortunately, it got picked up by a bunch of American radio DJs on a trip over to the UK, and it built up over there. When it became a success in the US, the record company in the UK said, "Hey! Here we go! Let's release it again!" It got to number thirty-one for a second time. [*Laughs*] The thing that I find interesting is that it was one of our worst-performing singles in the UK—twice. As the years have gone by, even in the UK it has become our most popular song. It shows the influence that America has had on the UK in that time. "International Bright Young Thing" was the highest-charting single, "The Devil You Know" charted very high, "Real, Real, Real" sold more than any other single that we released. But it's still "Right Here, Right Now"—the worst performer out of all of those—that is the one, even in the UK, that we're most known for.

One thing I just wanted to stress is how absolutely cool an idea it was, how generous it was of Ted Gardner and Perry and the people from the agency [Marc Geiger and Don Muller] to put that together and make it so welcoming. They wanted to do a cool thing—and that filtered down into the bands.

PAUL LEARY (Butthole Surfers guitarist, producer [Meat Puppets, Sublime, Daniel Johnston]): The bass player for Jane's Addiction wanted us—he was a Butthole Surfers fan. So, we were on the bill. It was quite an eye-opening experience for us. Up until that point, we'd been traveling around and setting up our own equipment and tearing it down at the end of the night and driving ourselves around. Suddenly, we had a bus and someone to do all the work for us, and we were playing early shows in the late afternoon—which left us plenty of time after that to get drunk and be stupid. We'd never experienced that kind of "rock experience" before, where everybody else was doing all the work and we were just doing all the playing around.

CHRIS HASKETT: It did have the sense or feeling of a traveling circus.

COREY GLOVER: As soon as you saw the Butthole Surfers, you were like, "*This is different.*" To go from Butthole Surfers to Siouxsie and the Banshees to Body Count, it was like, "This is amazing. I love this. I love the fact that it's just like, 'Let's shake it up and throw it on a board and see what happens.'"

CHRIS HASKETT: There was a little bit of shoulder jostling between the Body Count guys and the Living Colour guys—at least initially. Just because I think Living Colour's political stance was somewhat weary of the presentation of Body Count and the kind of gang thing and lyrical content. But everybody got along. Me and [Body Count guitarist] Ernie C played with Living Colour in Denver.

PAUL LEARY: It was like a big family. Everybody was hanging out with everybody else and getting up onstage with everybody else. It was a whole lot of fun.

CHRIS HASKETT: We went to Disney World together! When the tour got to Florida, somebody found a large quantity of LSD. So, a very large number of people from Lollapalooza went to Disney World—*tripping their brains out*.

PAUL LEARY: Jane's Addiction were amazing. I really wasn't that into Jane's Addiction that much prior to that tour, but seeing them live changed my mind on that. They put on a really good visual display behind their set. They were *fabulous* live.

CHRIS HASKETT: Nine Inch Nails were the breakout stars. They were a world unto themselves because they were a heavy party band at that point, so they kind of gravitated more toward the Butthole Surfers. There's also a certain hubris of when you know you're great and you know you're going somewhere; you've got a bit of swagger. And Nine Inch Nails were great, and they were definitely going somewhere . . . whereas we were just the "hungry little indie band."

We couldn't afford a bus—we were on a bus with Nine Inch Nails' crew. That was the first time I ever toured on a bus. At that point, I think Trent [Reznor] was a fairly volatile artist—they broke a lot of gear during their set every day. And their guitar tech had to put these things together every night—he had to rebuild these guitars that had been smashed. Back then, they did not treat their crew terribly well; and that did not make me really want to hang out that much with them.

PAUL LEARY: Most of the big outdoor festivals we'd done were in Europe and maybe some radio shows here in the States. And they're all kind of the same—they're big, there's a tall stage, and you're separated from the audience. That's kind of a weird experience. We were used to playing in clubs where people were right in your face. All of a sudden, we were playing these big outdoor venues with tons of people—it was eye-opening. And then to come home and find out that we were sharing equally in the merchandise sales—we got a nice check.

BILL GOULD: That was huge. That first Lollapalooza I think was really *a statement*. And the fact that it went over well and was a success really made people take stuff that was a little left of center more seriously.

LES CLAYPOOL: Lollapalooza really helped the whole notion of being unique and different from what was the norm *becoming* the norm.

PAUL LEARY: Once it was a big success, then the doors were open—that's what people started doing.

GERALD CASALE (Devo singer/bassist, music video director [Foo Fighters, Soundgarden, Silverchair]): I have to use the cliché of de-evolution. I saw it was devolving, but what was happening was the germ of new genres were popping up. Jane's Addiction and Nine Inch Nails were their own world. And I liked both of them a lot early on because I could tell something new was happening there. I mean, Jane's Addiction . . . what was that? It was dark and nasty, but pop at the same time. And of course, by the time we get to [Nine Inch Nails'] *Downward Spiral*, that's a masterpiece.

MIKE WATT: All of a sudden, with Dave Navarro's big lead guitar and Perry singing, you had all these . . . I don't want to hurt anyone's feelings, but you had Smashing Pumpkins. Here's another example: Little Richard sold many less copies of "Tutti Frutti" than Pat Boone. He had a great way of answering it: "Well, his version was for the living room . . . *mine was for the bedroom*."

DITCHING COLLEGE

Chad Taylor and his Live bandmates make a case for choosing rock over education.

I recall the immense pressure I placed on myself to "be something" after graduating high school and electing to pursue music over a college degree. The cassette copies of our first album, *The Death of a Dictionary* [by Public Affection, before being renamed Live], were ready for pickup from the manufacturing facility on the day we graduated. When every other student was off to a graduation party, all I could think about was getting the physical cassette in my hands. The first real recording of my art was a chance to showcase that our collective talents warranted and justified the gamble to step outside the norm. Making *Dictionary* would eventually lead to our gigs at CBGB and our discovery by artist manager and label founder Gary Kurfirst.

LOU BARLOW: When they came out, I thought they were kind of a glam version of the Butthole Surfers. *Which is not a bad thing.* But I saw them last week in Italy for the first time ever . . . and they were awesome. I went back in my mind and did this whole rewind—to me, they were a natural progression of what was going on in the underground.

JASON PETTIGREW: You can't deny what Jane's Addiction did for underground music.

KENNEDY: I think it would have been completely different [if Jane's Addiction didn't split in 1991, after the conclusion of the first Lollapalooza]—they would have been Beyoncé to this year's Taylor Swift. It's like, Beyoncé is still huge—she's the queen. But Taylor Swift is the empress. Taylor Swift is the paradigm shift, and that's really what Nirvana was.

3 NIRVANA AND *NEVERMIND*

"Wow, Metallica wrote a really good song this time"

Although several albums set the stage, there is no denying that it was Nirvana's sophomore full-length that finally put alt-rock over the top.

FAT MIKE: There was no hope of making it in punk rock—until Nirvana. It changed everything.

JOEY SANTIAGO (Pixies guitarist): I had no idea it was going to blow up that much, considering the music that Nirvana put out wasn't in a commercial pigeonhole at the time. In that sense, it became a surprise.

CHRIS HASKETT: There's a kind of historical moment of "Before *Nevermind*" and "After *Nevermind*." It's not just that people think about "Before Nirvana"—they forget that Nirvana was actually a band before *Nevermind*. My favorite Nirvana is actually *Bleach*. I wish *Bleach* had the production quality of *Nevermind* and *In Utero*.

CRAIG WEDREN: I remember going to a party soon after *Bleach* had come out. Somebody was spinning the vinyl of *Bleach* really loud. It was a dorm party. And it was so fucking good. It just ripped. It had a kind of punk rock–era pedigree of Washington State—almost like '60s garage punk—with great tunes. But I was like, "How and why would this be more popular than Dinosaur Jr.?"

TANYA DONELLY: They were already huge to all of us. Nirvana and the Pixies were the big breakouts of the time. And that was *Bleach*—to me, *that* was like a massively successful album at the time. It felt like they were already "the shit." Our expectations were so different then.

Nirvana before filming the "Smells Like Teen Spirit" video at GMT Studios, Culver City, California, August 17, 1991. Left to right: Krist Novoselic, Kurt Cobain, and Dave Grohl. "There was no hope of making it in punk rock—until Nirvana. It changed everything."—Fat Mike
Kevin Estrada/MediaPunch/Alamy

DAVID PAJO: Nirvana were just one of many bands around at the time. Mudhoney were part of that, Railroad Jerk—there were all these bands that I kind of lumped Nirvana in. They were all cool, and I liked them all for different reasons. I didn't think any of it was accessible.

MIKE EDWARDS: I bought the *Bleach* album when it came out, and they had champions like John Peel, who was playing them on the radio [in England]. He was kind of a figurehead of the British music scene. In today's terms, he'd be an "influencer."

JASON PETTIGREW: There was one woman who worked at *Alternative Press*, and it was the first time I ever saw a Nirvana T-shirt—the one with the rings of hell on it, and the back of it said, "FUDGE PACKIN, CRACK SMOKIN, SATAN WORSHIPIN MOTHERFUCKERS." I'm like, "Wow. There's a commentary. *I better go listen to these guys.*" And I remember really liking "Negative Creep."

MATT PINFIELD: I know that when I was helping run that radio station, WHTG, and I took over as music director, I was playing the "Sliver" single early because I had heard from friends and I was paying attention to the Seattle scene, and those bands were coming through New Jersey. I was an early supporter of Nirvana.

EVAN DANDO: I remember when I first heard "Sliver." I was like, "Oh, fuck. Someone's got my back here. Someone's doing music that speaks to me, that's what I'm into, too—with melodies and hard guitar and stuff." "Sliver" was the one for me.

DAVE MARKEY: Soundgarden had much more radio-friendly music. AOR. I even thought Mudhoney was going to hit before Nirvana. I was exposed to Nirvana through Sonic Youth—before that '91 tour. Sonic Youth's closest call with the mainstream was the *Goo* album in 1990 on Geffen—they're doing arena tours supporting Neil Young. It seemed like they were being exposed to a whole new audience. It didn't really work out for them, but I think the *Goo* album is an important thing to talk about before *Nevermind*.

Because that's another thing that changed the underground scene—that really shifted everything. It seemed like there were new possibilities that were there that weren't there a year or two before. That was the first changing of the guard. And the minute that happened, [Sonic Youth's] Thurston Moore especially was really pushing for Nirvana to DGC Records, saying, "You guys really got to check this band out," and of course, made possible their signing.

Sonic Youth had Nirvana open up a series of shows on the West Coast that I caught back in 1990 . . . the year *before* punk broke. [*Laughs*] At that point, they had not secured Dave Grohl yet—they had Dale Crover from the Melvins filling in. I saw them at the Palladium, and then I traveled with Sonic Youth and Nirvana to Las Vegas to see the shows there. But again, Grohl hadn't joined yet.

DAVID PAJO: Nirvana were just one of many bands around at the time. There's definitely something to be said about the addition of Grohl in that band. He solidified it in a way. I mean, Dale Crover is a phenomenal drummer, but there was something about Grohl's fit into Nirvana at that time that was just perfect. And really changed their sound. You look at them with previous drummers—Dan Peters, or Chad Channing on *Bleach*—again, cool drummers. But I don't think *Nevermind* would have happened with Chad.

Those shows they did in '90 were great, and I saw that audiences *really* dug them. There was an indication that Nirvana would be huge. But again, huge on this "underground level." We never had a band from our scene go quadruple platinum overnight. Whatever term you want to use—post-punk, alternative, underground, whatever—*there was no band*. Hüsker Dü and the Replacements—they were the close contenders. But still, no one ever imagined those bands knocking Michael Jackson out of the number-one spot. That was just a crazy thought.

BOB MOULD: Well, I had the demos because I was in contention for producing the record [that became *Nevermind*]. I did not have the demo of "Teen Spirit"—I don't know if there was one, and I don't know if anybody got it, if there was. But I remember sitting with Gary Gersh at Geffen, and it came up. History went the way it did, and it was absolutely the right way. Butch Vig [who would produce *Nevermind*] was somebody that I worked with back in '84. Butch is amazing. And it was a perfect fit for what the songs on *Nevermind* were. And everything went exactly as it should. [*Laughs*] Y'know, Butch does that, they blow up, and then it's sort of like, "Oh, now I've got this E-ZPass for the toll road I may have had a hand in building." [*Laughs*]

CRAIG WEDREN: I remember hearing that Dave Grohl had joined Nirvana. And I was like, "*Lucky for fuckin' Nirvana.*" And it became the irresistible force.

IAN MacKAYE: Nirvana were a popular band. A lot of people really loved *Bleach*. But to give you some context, *Bleach* came out in '89; and I think it initially sold something like forty thousand copies, which is pretty incredible. Later that same year, [Fugazi's] *Repeater* came out and sold well over one hundred thousand copies; so I think at the time it would be safe to say that we were a much bigger band.

Dave [Grohl] was a part of the D.C. scene, and I've known him since he was sixteen, and I remember Kurt and Krist asked him to join. It wasn't exactly a surprise that they would; I'd seen him drumming and knew that he was a powerhouse. Anyway, Dave came home at some point after he joined the band and stopped by to say hello. He told me about their recording session and asked if I wanted to hear some of the tracks. I remember going into Joe Lally's room here at Dischord House and listening to what turned out to be "Teen Spirit."

I was pretty stunned and said something to the effect of, "Wow! That's going to be a hit!" Of course, all I was thinking of was that it was going to go over well with the independent set, you know, like, *Alternative Press* is going to write about it or something. I certainly wasn't thinking at all that it would be some massive, universal commercial hit. I just recognized it was a good song and thought it was catchy.

JASON PETTIGREW: There was one small piece on Nirvana [in *Alternative Press*] . . . because everybody thought that the big thing out of Sub Pop was going to be Mudhoney. And then, Kim Gordon and Thurston Moore blew it all for us, and said, "No! You should really sign *Nirvana*, DGC."

DAVE MARKEY: It was Sonic Youth and Nirvana traveling together as a pair [in the summer of 1991 throughout Europe]. It was a lot of festival dates, and we met up with a lot of bands that Sonic Youth had relationships with—Dinosaur Jr., Babes in Toyland, Gumball. Sonic Youth was really responsible for bringing Nirvana along on that tour. It was prior to *Nevermind*. Nirvana had toured Europe previously, but I think that was the first time they were on huge festival stages—and they were thrilled. I remember that tour being such a blast. It was really like a summer vacation—it didn't really seem like business at all. It was certainly geared more toward the pleasure part of the experience.

All those shows on that tour were *pre-fame* Nirvana. They had recorded *Nevermind*, they had shot the video for "Smells Like Teen Spirit" the day before we left, and I met them at LAX to board the flight to Heathrow to begin the European tour. So, there was a lot of excitement in the air. I remember thinking at the time, "Nirvana's going to be huge." But the "huge" that I was thinking was defined "Before *Nevermind*" huge, which meant being huge was you sold one hundred thousand or two hundred thousand units and you were getting airplay on *120 Minutes* and you were hitting it big on college radio. But mainstream radio was staying away.

I remember coming back from Ireland after the first show, which was a small club show in Cork, Ireland. And I think we did a show the next night in Dublin at a theater, the Top Hat. It was maybe 1,500 seats. We regrouped back to London, and then I ended up hanging with Nirvana on the day off, and they were doing a day of press. They had tons of interviews lined up.

If it was anywhere that Nirvana had a buzz, it was in London at that time. Because I think London had received *Bleach* almost better than anywhere else. So, as far as the press goes—I'm talking about *Sounds* and *NME*—there were plenty of people that were looking to talk to the band and talk about their major label signing and this tour with Sonic Youth.

In the downtime on that tour, I really got to know the guys individually, talking about music and realizing we were coming from the same place—the same 1980s underground-informed music scene that happened in the US. I was a musician, too. I was touring and playing in a band called Painted Willie. We did a six-month tour in 1986 with Black Flag and got to see the continental US in great detail. And in '87, we opened shows for bands like the Butthole Surfers.

I remember really bonding with Kurt on our love for the Butthole Surfers and also, diversely, Devo. I was like, "Wow. It's so great to meet someone that has shared interests in music, and we can talk about these bands at length." We had a history in many cases playing shows with these bands back in the '80s. And also just being fans.

CRIS KIRKWOOD: A cool musical thing happened: the They Might Be Giants album with "Put a little bee in your bonnet" ["Birdhouse in Your Soul" from *Flood*] and *Nevermind*. We were back East doing some radio thing, and I heard both those records. And both of them were like, "Goddamn, those are catchy." I could almost sing both albums all the way through.

EDDIE "KING" ROESER: After Nirvana were signed, we were on tour with them in the Midwest. They were pretty decent-sized shows. But the first show was just a normal rock show: Stache's in Columbus [on October 9, 1991]. A couple of hundred people there. Three weeks later, "Teen Spirit" hit MTV. There were guys with baseball hats at the show. *Hundreds of people.* The bands would go around with maybe a suitcase of T-shirts. And in the span of three weeks, Nirvana became this juggernaut that was *way* bigger.

PAUL LEARY: I remember going to see the Dicks play one night in Austin, at Liberty Lunch. I went down one night, and there was a line around the block—like twice. I was like, "What the hell? When did the Dicks get popular?" And then I found out, "Oh. *They're opening for this band called Nirvana.*"

CRAIG WEDREN: There was so much buzz prior to when *Nevermind* was released. I think *Nevermind*, *Loveless* by My Bloody Valentine, *Blood Sugar Sex Magik* by the Red Hot Chili Peppers, and *The Black Album* by Metallica all came out around the same time. So, there was this real sense that something was going to break. *Really break.* But there had been, I don't know, twenty years of that kind of "ghetto mentality." Of "Well, the Ramones couldn't do it." R.E.M. was pretty huge by then, and U2 was huge. But I personally was skeptical about the whole Nirvana thing.

STEVE ALBINI (producer [Nirvana, Bush, PJ Harvey]): Nobody in the underground had any expectation that underground music was going to become big. So, when it happens, it's always a weird "lightning strike moment." It's some random thing that happens that makes somebody popular. And no one could predict it. I mean, Nirvana were a great band. But there are *lots* of great bands. The fact that they became super popular is a fluke more than something that could have been anticipated or engineered.

FAT MIKE: Books are important, and paintings; but they don't bring back that memory like the first time you heard "Smells Like Teen Spirit." Most people remember exactly where

Kurt Cobain at the Roxy in Hollywood, California, August 15, 1991. "Nirvana was kind of like the Beatles going on *Ed Sullivan*."—Eddie "King" Roeser *Kevin Estrada/MediaPunch/Alamy*

they were when they heard that song. Like, "Holy shit. *This is amazing.*" I was in my Volvo with [Lagwagon singer] Joey Cape, and he goes, "You've got to hear this song." I said, "Pull over." We knew that this was going to change music. It would have happened anyway, but Kurt Cobain gave all our bands a career.

RUDEBOY REMINGTON (Urban Dance Squad rapper): I remember I was in a club in New Orleans, and it was pitch black. I was with two or three girls that picked me up from my show at Tipitina's. I was staring at the speakers, and I heard the riff from Cobain and I saw these people dancing—especially this girl, who was a dancer. And I started getting scared because I knew from that moment, there was no competition against this song. *None.*

MIKE JOHNSON (Dinosaur Jr. bassist [1991–1997], Mark Lanegan multi-instrumentalist, solo artist): I remember getting it when it came out, or getting promos—J [Mascis] got one or something—listening to it, and it seemed like it had been radio-compressed a little bit on purpose. But it was an instant classic with so many great songs. And a lot of those songs, people in Seattle had already heard an earlier version of "In Bloom" and a couple of those songs; so they knew there were these killer songs already in the pipeline. But "Smells Like Teen Spirit" was kind of bizarre because that was *such* an instant anthem. It was always on. It was this ever-present sound. It was such an instant mega-hit.

MIKI BERENYI (Lush singer/guitarist): It was our manager, Howard [Gough]—I remember him putting it on in his office and saying, "Have a listen to this Nirvana record . . . they totally ripped off the Pixies." [*Laughs*] Because Nirvana prior to that would get coverage, but they didn't even get coverage in things like the *Melody Maker* and *NME*. They were a "*Sounds* band." And *Sounds* was another weekly magazine, but it was much more garage music and slightly more niche. Not as glamorous and not as hip. So, it was kind of mad when that album became so big. And that was imported as sort of this "grunge explosion."

FRANK BLACK: ["Smells Like Teen Spirit"] certainly was very popular. It was catchy. I don't really get involved in so-called discussion or whatever [about the Pixies' influence on Cobain], because from my point of view, it's just band stuff. Some musicians or some bands say, "They were influential on me." Sometimes you can hear it, sometimes you can't, but that's just the way it works.

It's not a big mystery. At the end of the day, everyone is just a musician. We're all just working musicians. We all play different styles. That's who we are—we're just a bunch of music geeks. Or proactive music listeners that are so proactive we actually feel the need to do it ourselves.

LOU BARLOW: When I first heard "Smells Like Teen Spirit," my first thought was, "Wow, Metallica wrote a *really* good song this time." I was convinced it was Metallica. As much as Nirvana breaking through was a moment where you could say people were ready to accept heavy music that was not accompanied with the residue of glam rock . . . that was also not because of Nirvana. *That was because of Metallica.* It had a lot to do with these two things coalescing.

It was almost like the real hard speed-metal scene and also the indie rock scene kind of coalescing. Because both sides were not really commercial things. But Nirvana came at this perfect point where people were ready for heavy music that was melodic—but it was also angst-driven. Because the speed-metal thing was also anti-glam, so there was already a movement within heavy metal that was saying, "*No false metal!*"

I equate it to my own Dinosaur Jr. experience. When we did *You're Living All Over Me*, we focused the band's sound. And I think Nirvana focused the sound and put some really great songs together.

IAN MacKAYE: *Nevermind* came out in September 1991, and it came out within a few weeks of Fugazi's record, *Steady Diet of Nothing*, which was a follow-up to *Repeater*. That record was sort of a sleeper for us. We were touring in Australia, and everywhere we went, they were playing *Nevermind* over the PA. It was *crazy*. But it really was an interesting juxtaposition. *Steady Diet* was decidedly not sparkly. And the Nirvana record was *fully* sparkly. It certainly wasn't a competition, but it was proof, again, of the "magic fairy dust" that major labels can put on stuff—it's about compression and radio play.

But this isn't calling into question the songs—the songs are great. In fact, if you ask me personally, I find the record does a *disservice* to the songs. Because I actually think the production is too loud—I can hear the commercial application. But who cares what I think? People love that record. It's great.

MOBY: I remember thinking, "*A punk rock record is breaking through?*" Because at that point, the charts were metal and Michael Jackson. It was banal pop music and the end of hair metal, and no one expected pop charts to ever be interesting. You just sort of accepted "There's alternative music, there's underground dance music, and then there's incredibly banal, overproduced major label pop." And when Nirvana started breaking through, it really felt like, all of a sudden, the punk rock kids were taking over—for better or worse.

EDDIE "KING" ROESER: Nirvana was kind of like the Beatles going on *Ed Sullivan*. It wasn't unusual music to us, but everybody thought they were somehow from a different planet, because they were grunge. It just sounds like rock music to me, pretty much.

ART ALEXAKIS (Everclear singer/guitarist): When *Nevermind* came out, boom, "grunge" became a word that people were actually using as a thing. Grunge wasn't really *a thing*—musicians didn't use the word "grunge." No one did. Only the guys at record labels and the press used the word "grunge." No one said, "Hey. I want to start a grunge band." Later I think bands started saying that, especially in the Midwest and South, but not in the Northwest.

TANYA DONELLY: There were no expectations for a platinum album, for God's sake. *Not even close.*

MATT PINFIELD: I don't think anybody could have predicted—and if they say they did, they're lying—that that was going to explode the way that it did. Certainly, the band had no idea. Neither did the record company—there weren't even enough records, CDs, and cassettes pressed to deal with the explosion that came from "Smells Like Teen Spirit" being played on commercial alternative radio. And the fact that MTV was playing that video, and it was a seismic shift for the next generation of younger brothers and sisters that were under the age of the stuff that had just been popular—young people who were looking for their own thing that would speak to the latchkey kids of the generation.

GERALD CASALE: I could hear that it was serious and the craft of the songwriting was great. But it was the sounds and the way Kurt sang was taking me a while to want to get into it . . . but it was like, "Okay. Who is this gravelly voiced, whiny guy complaining?" *Then I got it.* It took a while.

FRED SCHNEIDER: I sure didn't [see Nirvana's success coming], because I thought funk was going to come back and hot pants and miniskirts. [*Laughs*] So, we did *Good Stuff*—which is pretty funky. We missed that boat! It definitely *totally* took over alternative.

BILL GOULD: I thought it was really good, but I just thought it was a rock band. It didn't really blow my mind. But I thought it was solid. There's no doubt that Kurt was a great songwriter and they played it really well. I can't really say anything bad about them—they just didn't blow my mind.

CRAIG WEDREN: I put it on and was like, "This is great. Super catchy. Super rocking. Half slick . . . and half still in the garage." But I was like, "Yeah, I don't hear how this is going to crack Janet Jackson." So, I was skeptical, and I was cynical—and then I was completely wrong. Ten billion percent.

ANGELO MOORE: When you compare Nirvana and Guns N' Roses, to me Nirvana had more edge and more nerve. Not even really knowing what a lot of the lyrics were about in-depthly because I never really got that far. But when I'd hear it overall, it would be a lot more edge in the music.

NAOKO YAMANO (Shonen Knife singer/guitarist): We were invited to [Nirvana's] UK tour in November 1991. We got the information that Kurt Cobain and Nirvana were fans of us. Kurt said that he came to our Los Angeles show in August 1991. He also listened to our music, which was released on K Records in Olympia, Washington, on cassette.

When we supported Nirvana on the tour, Kurt was always watching our show from the side of the stage. Our dressing room was always cold, and he invited us to their warm dressing room. One day, he was eating a peanut butter and strawberry jam sandwich in the dressing room, and he offered it to me. He wanted to cover Shonen Knife's song "Twist Barbie" at their secret gig [on December 1, 1991, at the Southern Bar in Edinburgh] and asked for the guitar chords. He learned it very quickly . . . then we had a food fight in the dressing room.

IAN MacKAYE: I find *Nevermind* is a "polestar"—something that becomes the thing that everything spins around. And it does a disservice to the band and to the record because it gives it *too much* cultural impact.

JOEY SANTIAGO: For me, it started probably with the Beatles, and then Lou Reed. It just strung along and then came to us—and then Nirvana blew up. It was just a perfect storm for them. Everything started getting accepted as that. It was truly alternative at the time.

CHRIS HASKETT: One thing that is true in pre- and post-Nirvana, when we, the Swans, Sonic Youth, and the Butthole Surfers got started, there was nowhere to go. We were never going to be rich, we were never going to be famous, we were never going to be popular. We were doing it because we were determined to do something great that we believed in. Why else would you do that? Why would you put yourself through that? And there was freedom in that—there was no reason to do anything other than what you absolutely believe in and what you absolutely want to make great.

After that becomes commercially viable, everything changes. It doesn't mean you don't want to be great, but all of a sudden, there is an extra burden. But in '90/'91/'92, we had a tremendous amount of "non-asshole pride." We were proud, and justifiably, because it was a great band. For all of us, it was about going out and being undeniably as good as we could be. Destroying mediocrity. And showing mediocrity up for what it was. So, that was the driving force not just for Henry—but when you see us out there, it's "Fuck you, world." Not "Fuck you, people." "*Fuck you, world.*"

BUTCH VIG (producer [Nirvana, Smashing Pumpkins, Sonic Youth], Garbage drummer): Well, that record changed my life. I didn't talk about it for a while, especially when I started Garbage, because I got tired, quite frankly, of people asking, "What was it like to work with Kurt Cobain?" And then a couple of years ago we started working on the twentieth-anniversary *Nevermind* box set.

I'm good friends with Dave Grohl, and we started going through a lot of the archives and finding unreleased tracks and rehearsal tapes and alternate mixes and things like that. And Dave and Krist [Novoselic] and I did a lot of press for it when it came out. It was really cool to go back and revisit the record, especially going through photos and a lot of the different tracks. It was a pleasure to work on the box set.

When we went on this tour for the last year in Garbage, I did a lot of press for Garbage, but almost every time we would do a meet and greet, there would be a lot of fans that would bring Nirvana CDs or vinyl to sign. And I have no problem signing that because I'm really proud of that record. It fundamentally changed my life.

LES CLAYPOOL: I remember right around the time *Nevermind* was coming out, our agent said, "I've got a great idea: Let's do a co-bill with Nirvana and Primus." And I was like, "Nah, I don't want to do that. We want to do our own tour." Because we had been opening for Jane's Addiction and Public Enemy, where we only played for thirty to forty-five minutes. We didn't do it. *And it's probably something we should have done.* [*Laughs*]

FRED ARMISEN: It's been so documented as a turning point for music. I was excited for it because I really do see Nirvana as a punk band—in every single way. When they started going up the charts, I felt like it represented an actual *band*.

MOBY: No one can question Nirvana's integrity, songwriting, and ability to make *phenomenal* records.

Sonic Youth in the Netherlands, August 1991. Front to back: Thurston Moore, Kim Gordon, and Lee Ranaldo. “I think [Moore] thought it was something that would be a cool VHS video that Sonic Youth could sell at their merch booth at their shows.”—Dave Markey *Gie Knaeps/Hulton Archive/Getty Images*

4 1991: THE YEAR PUNK BROKE

"It was like a dividing line in music"

The title of Dave Markey's documentary concerning a Sonic Youth/Nirvana tour in the summer of 1991 seems to be a neat summary of the time *Nevermind* hit . . . or not?

DAVE MARKEY: I did come up with the title. We didn't even know it was going to be called that. It was on the very first date of the tour, and we had flown in from Heathrow, got the equipment in London, traveled from London to Ireland—which meant us getting in a bus to a ferry and taking the ferry up over to Ireland. And then the next day, everyone is jetlagged and tired.

I was rooming with Lee Ranaldo from Sonic Youth, and we had MTV on. And what should we see? Mötley Crüe, performing the Sex Pistols' "Anarchy in the UK." I said, "Wow. *1991 is the year punk broke.*" Here's this band performing this song in front of fifty thousand to one hundred thousand people screaming . . . how many of those people knew it was a Sex Pistols song? The title was sort of a toss-off, sarcastic comment. I come from L.A. and watched Mötley Crüe's rise in the '80s. And they were just a glam rock band—they never struck me as "punk" at all. But obviously, there was something in the air at that time.

At that point, how many years were we away from '77? Fourteen years? It was kind of a joke. Punk rock never went mainstream in the US. Some bands had *some* mainstream success that were sort of considered "punk/new wave"—Talking Heads, Devo, B-52s. All bands I loved as a kid and was happy to see them break through with the occasional hit. But that was a decade before '91. There was a ten-year period where it was clear that that was as good as it was going to get. By the time of the late '80s/early '90s, it didn't seem like there was a *whiff* of true punk left. It was gone. Even in the underground, it sort of had run its course.

To see Mötley Crüe pull out a Pistols track was *stunning* at the time. Of course, in retrospect, it doesn't seem like much. In retrospect, the Sex Pistols just sound like rock 'n' roll at this point—I could hear the Sex Pistols alongside Aerosmith and not flinch. But you've got to remember at the time, it was a different world. In the '70s, it sounded different. By the time the '90s rolled around . . . I think the world had changed. The music didn't change, but *the world* changed.

I think Thurston Moore had an idea that it was going to be a special time. I think he thought it was something that would be a cool VHS video that Sonic Youth could sell at their merch booth at their shows. Never thought it was going to get a theatrical release [in 1992]. Never thought there would be this attention toward it.

MIKE WATT: That was a joke. I think when it breaks is an individual experience. For us, it broke in 1976. For some people, maybe. Because it didn't "break"—there were guys that were doing that for fifteen years. We just wanted to rub their face in that name. Y'know, "punk" was a very bad word—it was a guy who got fucked in jail for cigarettes. Why would you call your music this?

ROGER JOSEPH MANNING JR.: That statement ["The Year That Punk Broke"] has so much information attached to it. And if you were of that era, you would understand what that statement meant—the upside and horrible downside of that, potentially.

BILL GOULD: The whole thing about that—even the title of it—turns me off. It sounds like a journalist's interpretation of things that happened, and it just never interested me. This goes way back. I played with MC50—they were celebrating the MC5's fiftieth-year anniversary. And they were these grungy punks of 1968/1969.

And I got to know [MC5 guitarist] Wayne Kramer, and we talked about our shared histories—being in bands when we were kids—and it was a very similar experience, dealing with the same kinds of people. It's almost like a continuum of people who were independent under the surface expressing themselves. And then when it becomes recognized by the business, it becomes something else.

But it doesn't just go back to the '80s—it goes back further than that. I mean, look at the band Sparks. Sparks is another one of these bands that never really fit into anything. They came from the Pacific Palisades area of L.A., which would be surfers, Jackson Browne, and Crosby, Stills & Nash. And they're these two weird guys [Ron and Russell Mael] that didn't fit into the times *at all*. And I think that that's always going to happen.

FRED ARMISEN: I like that they have the title—it's good for the movie. I understand it, and I don't disagree with the idea that that's what's called punk. But that's *not* when punk broke. Punk broke in 1981 with the Go-Go's. That was the first punk Top 10 album: *Beauty and the Beat*. It's not even up for discussion: The Go-Go's were part of that L.A. punk scene, and that was a real hit record. *A number-one record.* So, I think that's the year punk broke.

GERALD CASALE: To be honest, I probably didn't at the time [see any comparisons between early '90s alt-rock and '70s punk/new wave]. And then with the benefit of history and retrospection, I understand now what was going on there that was as primal/angst-driven as what was happening with Devo in the '70s—reacting to the bullshit of the mainstream music business. And just the terrible nature of music that was on the Top 40 charts.

So, stylistically if you listen to Devo and to the outgoing meta lyrics that we were creating, we weren't talking about ourselves in, "Oh, my dad didn't love me, my mom didn't love me. Woe is me." *It was about the world.* Whereas the '90s was about the breakdown of family and personal angst—real serious developmental problems that people were going through because of the generation they were growing up in, having different dynamics than when I grew up. And now, I realize all that.

PAUL LEARY: I didn't know what was going on. I sort of figured that the Butthole Surfers would be relegated to this hole in the ground for the rest of our careers and we'd be underground. We were kind of at that point where we drawing 1,000 or 1,500 a night in the big cities. Maybe 600 in the smaller cities. And that almost seemed like a ceiling for us. We never saw ourselves as being able to fill the big venues on our own.

COREY GLOVER: It was like a large population of people that decided to buck the system.

BOB MOULD: So, that late '80s through '91/'92, all of that was critical infrastructure, as well. It's just funny—you know this and I know this—but there's sort of a "mainstream history," like, "There was all this hair metal, and then *Nevermind* came, and it changed." There was a lot of people who did a lot of work to get to that point.

ROGER JOSEPH MANNING JR.: Hair metal was the soundtrack of rebelling against your parents—coming of age. And then literally in a nine-month window, it swaps with grunge. And then *that* becomes "Fuck you, Mom and Dad" soundtrack music. And every generation's got one.

Bill Gould in England with Faith No More, 1992. "The whole thing about [*The Year That Punk Broke*]—even the title of it—turns me off. It sounds like a journalist's interpretation of things that happened."—Bill Gould *Ian Dickson/Redferns/Getty Images*

CRIS KIRKWOOD: Suddenly, the shift happened. And it was Nirvana that did it. Some of the people going from Mötley Crüe to Nirvana. Like, a change in what clothing is hip.

MIKE WATT: I don't know if hair metal was dead. I think Mötley Crüe was selling some records, and Guns N' Roses. In fact, the only thing stopping Guns N' Roses from selling records and tickets was themselves—the guy [Axl Rose] goes on five hours late and was shooting *himself* in the foot!

CRAIG WEDREN: *Use Your Illusion* . . . I love early Guns N' Roses. But *Use Your Illusion* was such a bloated dud. There was probably a great single album there. Who knows? So clearly, that was over, which was great, as far as I was concerned. And I don't mean to lump GN'R with hair metal strictly, but that whole era of retrograde/L.A./Aqua Net rock was a bummer. Because the first half of the '80s were *so* promising—I think because of MTV—which gave the pop charts kind of a progressive trajectory until it got flattened by hair metal and pop. So, I think partly for that reason, it was hard to imagine any music that we were listening to actually cracking through.

DAVID PAJO: I'm so glad that movement happened, because the hair metal stuff was getting pretty out of control. But hair metal had also evolved into like, the "Pantera route," where the hair metal dudes became extreme metal.

COREY GLOVER: [Hair metal] was too rigid. There was a hierarchy to that sort of thing that a lot of people didn't want to live up to, they didn't want to be a part of. The reason you decided to play metal music in particular was to be somewhat rebellious and not follow the trend. You can't deny a riff. A riff is a riff. But it's like, if Miles Davis had a riff that you could pitch, it would be a completely different thing.

JONN PENNEY: I'm not sure hair metal was quite so big over here [in England]. TV and the live circuit, sometimes they kind of reflected each other, and sometimes they didn't. I don't remember seeing a lot of hair metal on TV. But then of course, music TV or such in this country was pretty limited compared with the States. And MTV took some time to be established over here.

MIKE JOHNSON: When grunge or alternative hit, all the metal bands were like, "What the fuck's with *these* guys? They're not as good musicians as us!"

KENNEDY: My favorite part of the early '90s was Metallica's identity crisis! It was just sink or swim. They didn't want to be the next Warrant, so they all got bobs. I remember when they got bobs, I'm like, "*What a bunch of fucking sellouts.*" It was really funny. I love Metallica, but they are at the absolute top of their game . . . and there's this terror that what they think are these total Northwest soy boys are going to take over music, and metal is just going to be left in the graveyard. I get that they were trying to "go along to get along," but I also think there's obviously natural tension in any band, and that's what makes Metallica so great. But the dark side won that one.

FERGAL LAWLER: There was a healthy enough scene in Ireland, but because it's a small country, there's a small number of bands. Whereas the States, there were so many bands and so many places to play. We were kind of limited in Limerick—there were only one or two venues. And then one in Dublin, one in Cork. And that was it. Whereas every state [in the US] had a couple of different clubs you could play in—it was amazing to see. On our days off, we'd try to see gigs locally of whoever was playing. And the first tour we did in the States was opening for The The. We got to see Grant Lee Buffalo one night in Minneapolis. They were fantastic. We ended up doing a tour with them a few years later.

NAOKO YAMANO: Many grunge and alt-rock bands came to Japan for shows. When Nirvana came to Osaka, I took them out to dinner. They came to our show after their show in Osaka. Dave Grohl announced onstage that they will go to our show after their show. Many Nirvana fans followed them and came to our venue. The neighbors of our venue got angry because of all the people on the street. We had a contract with MCA Victor Japan at that time. I was invited to many labelmates' shows, like Smashing Pumpkins, Bush, and Urge Overkill. I also went to see Mudhoney and Fugazi.

MIKE WATT: fIREHOSE had many more people we were playing for than Minutemen did because the movement was at a different stage. Y'know that Germs song, "What We Do Is Secret"? *That's what it was.* So, it was a little less secret when it's on television. But, at the same time, it wasn't like I was going to play more mersh shit. Like with R.E.M., that last tour Minutemen did with them, I meet cats still to this day—that's the first time they saw us. Even though people were booing us. I remember [R.E.M. vocalist] Mike Stipe coming out and yelling at his own crowd, "You give those people respect! That was bullshit what you did!" But these cats, that was the first time they saw us.

But opening for Black Flag, we had cups of piss, sacks of shit, and vomit thrown at us. I was used to negative kind of things. [*Laughs*] Batteries . . . *they hurt.* I remember at one of these gigs, someone throwing money and getting hit, and picking up a quarter, and of course I hit the guy next to him who was into the gig. I never threw money back again after that. Negative receptions, sometimes that's what happens when there's a bigger audience.

Opening for Primus and getting hit with dirt clods—and it wasn't Les's fault. Beastie Boys, the same thing. This is opening up, so you're playing in front of other people's crowds. But you're only there because they wanted you. And Adam Horovitz and Mike D come out and play with us, and they're looking at us like, "Oh . . . you actually know these guys?"

FAT MIKE: Mike Watt is a fucking *punk rocker*. He used to ride on our bus on the Warped Tour—he went on the Warped Tour with no clothes! Just a jacket and some habanero sauce. That's the difference between "college rock" and "punk rock."

FRED ARMISEN: Venues were a little more open to the idea of a band that wasn't well known. The concept of "Let's take a risk" was a little better.

IAN MacKAYE: We were a popular band—we were playing big shows—and, as a result, I got to know larger booking agents. Occasionally they would call me and say something like, "Hey, we've got this 'baby band' [who just got signed on a major label]. Can they open for you?" In 1993, Jawbox had left Dischord to sign with Atlantic, and they played with us at the Roseland in New York City. It occurred to us around this time that it was weird having major label bands opening for us, and we decided that Jawbox would be the last. Our thinking was that, given that we were drawing so many people, any band opening for us would get a fair amount of exposure. Bands that had signed to majors were given access to the promotional machinery and exposure that those labels specialized in. On the other hand, there were all of these independent bands that didn't have the same access to that level of promotion. I'm talking about bands that had remained committed to the underground and other bands that could really only exist in the underground because they were so quirky or weird. We made the political and philosophical decision to only have independent bands opening for us with the idea of hopefully getting them in front of more people.

We did a show in L.A. at the Palladium [on January 24, 1992]. It was a Rock for Choice Benefit show that had been organized by our friends in L7. The bill initially was Fugazi, L7, and the Lunachicks from New York City; but at some point, L7 asked if this new band from Seattle could open. That band ended up being Pearl Jam. The backstage scene was really strange. There seemed to be a lot of action down by the Pearl Jam dressing room, people with cameras, etc. But down on our end of the hallway, you would find the four Fugazi members quietly drinking tea and reading books!

One of the ways Fugazi was able to keep our ticket prices so low was being really tight about production costs. We usually traveled with our own lights or, barring that, would just ask for simple white lights on stage, meaning that we didn't need to pay a lighting director. But Pearl Jam's label, Epic, paid for a spotlight for those guys! They played second, I think, and it was a full production for them. I don't doubt that the people in the band were sincere about their commitment to the cause, and I'm actually very close friends with Eddie [Vedder]—he's a lovely guy. But I'll tell you this: The label was thinking, "This is a great way to get our guys in front of a lot of eyes!" That night was a real lesson for us. We had to think about, "To the degree that we have illumination, what do we do with it? How do we use it?"

CHRIS HASKETT: That was the transition where we went from van touring to bus touring, which made it a lot easier to tour harder. Because if you don't have to sleep on somebody's floor and then drive to the next gig the next morning—or drive and not have any sleep—that's still very different from having a shower, having dinner, getting on the bus, going to sleep, waking up, and being able to do a gig. So, you ended up doing more gigs that way.

BOB MOULD: I did not foresee being the beneficiary of, y'know, I guess the wave of grunge that really picked up steam when *Nevermind* came out. And I think, sort of "reverse engineering" why that record was successful—it would take you to the Pixies, that would take you to Hüsker Dü. As like, just a small percentage of what made that record great. I think the roads were already paved in a way.

I did not see the instant success of Sugar as it was happening. I mean, the moment I guess I knew, was we did a couple shows in London in late July/early August of '92, and one of them was at ULU—the University of London Student Union Building. And it was just a completely unhinged, insane show. Parts of the PA falling into the crowd, nutty stage diving—just madness that I hadn't seen in years. And I could sort of feel it—"This is taking off, and we haven't even put the record out." So that was pretty exciting.

AL JOURGENSEN (Ministry singer/guitarist): It's very cyclical—as it's been throughout musical history. At least since the '50s—or '30s, even—if you can't beat it, buy it. So, that scene in Seattle that was going on was really getting popular. And then the companies swooped in and signed everybody that sounded like that and incorporated it. And put their "corporate stamp" on it—corporate approval—and made a bunch of money, and then wait for the next thing. We've seen this with rap, we've seen this with country, we've seen it with everything, man. Like I said, "If you can't beat it, buy it." And the corporate overlords will make sure that money is flowing into their wallets.

You know where I really get my thrills? It's when I meet authors or directors or filmmakers—things I don't know how it's done. So, I learn from them. I know how to make a Pearl Jam record or a Soundgarden record. They do it well . . . or they *did* it well. And I was appreciative of it—and they're good bands. And we know how to do what we do. But at that point, I was living with Timothy Leary and hanging out with William Burroughs, and that was much more my gig than checking out bands, or "What's going on musically?" and "What's the new scene?"

DAVID PAJO: It seemed like once grunge and all that stuff hit, it pushed me further into older music, like folk music and singer-songwriter stuff. I felt like there was so much old music to discover, I sort of felt like my music had been taken away by the rest of the world.

MOBY: It seemed like after Nirvana, there was this magic period where alternative rock could be loud and aggressive but also smart and thoughtful. It was like, the nerds finally discovered distortion pedals. But they were still writing smart songs.

EVAN DANDO: Nirvana did it *so* perfect. They nailed it right on the head. It was kind of what I was trying to do for a long time. And then I was like, "Okay, I'm going to go against that now. I'm going to go back. I'm going to do something quieter." I did that stuff before—if you listen to a song like "Mad," we did it. It wasn't really where I was at. Like, "Let's see what would happen if I put out an AM radio pop record, with a lot of acoustic guitars—instead of all bluesy."

FAT MIKE: Do you know why alternative music and Nirvana got big? I have a record label [Fat Wreck Chords], and when CDs were invented, records we used to sell wholesale for $3.25. Remember when albums were $4.98 and $5.98 in stores? What that meant is that when Kiss went double platinum, the record label only made $2 million off that. And the band made less. *That's double platinum.* When CDs came out, they were cheaper to make—they cost 75 cents to make—and you'd sell them wholesale for $7.25. Retail, they were $16.

So now, you can take chances—"Oh . . . maybe this will hit." You couldn't get signed [earlier]. I mean, *Joan Jett couldn't get signed.* Twenty-three labels turned her down. She put out her *I Love Rock 'n' Roll* record on her own Blackheart Records. It was *really* hard to get signed. The album made it possible for major labels to take chances. And what did they do? They signed every piece-of-shit band. Any band from Seattle. And what happened was the world realized that punk rock is so awesome. They'd never heard it before—there was no distribution, there was no radio play. But now, you had a major label pushing Nirvana.

CRIS KIRKWOOD: It's a question of, does it matter that people like it that much? Does it mean that it's good art? *People like fuckin' McDonald's.* That speaks volumes to me, in terms of the importance of people's tastes. But, definitely, I think the door was opened to that. I think *Nevermind* is fuckin' great—cool music gets out there. R.E.M. is great. Sometimes people like stuff that is really bitchin', and sometimes they don't like it until the artist is long dead, like van Gogh or something. Does it mean it's not good art because people don't like it? It better not—because nobody likes me, that's for goddamned sure . . . and I think I'm fuckin' completely fantastic.

BOB MOULD: I think I saw it when Sugar got really big. I was like, "Oh yeah, we did this." [*Laughs*] At the risk of the sound of me patting myself on the back being louder than my voice. And I mean Mudhoney, Meat Puppets . . . there's so many things that got into *Nevermind*, right? But yeah, I think I knew, by the time Sugar was blowing up, that if I had any doubts about what maybe had happened in the past, then I think that was sort of like, "Oh yeah. That's right."

MATT PINFIELD: Once things really exploded out of Seattle, guitars and harder rock crossed into the alternative music format. The thing that was so beautiful about the artists that came out in the '90s was that it was one of those eras where "anything goes." It had

MADONNA GOES GRUNGE

Candlebox singer Kevin Martin tells how the band signed with Maverick Records.

Guy Oseary [A&R for Madonna's Maverick Records] saw us and wanted to sign us. The day we actually signed the contracts with Maverick, our attorney called us with three other offers. Geffen Records offered like 1.5 million dollars, I believe Atlantic Records had offered 1.25 million, and Warner Bros., to keep us in the family, offered us like 750,000. But we ended up signing to Maverick, I believe for 125,000. We had made the record [1993's *Candlebox*] for 10,000, so we recouped immediately. It was certainly strategic for us to go that route—we knew that we would get the Warner Bros. family. But if we had Maverick Records, we would have *all* the attention. And we were the first signing to that label.

We met Madonna in New York—I believe we were playing Madison Square Garden with Rush. She took us out to dinner. I think she thought [alt-rock] was cool. I don't think she "got it." I mean, it's not like she wanted to hang out with Kurt Cobain—but she certainly wanted to sign Courtney Love. But Madonna loved the "dance side" of things. That's why the Prodigy signed with Maverick. But she certainly came to see the shows, and she was cool and fun to be around. She was a great boss. She brought us back to her apartment after dinner, and she took us into her library. She's like, "You should really read more—to help with lyrics." And I was like, "What book in here did you read to write 'Like a Virgin'?"

been a while since the '60s and the '70s, where people were so open to so many different styles of music.

FRED SCHNEIDER: They had to [create a category for "Best Alternative Music Album" at the Grammys, starting in 1991]. I guess they want to keep up with the times. I call them the "Grannys." At least we lost to somebody who really deserved it—who had never gotten a Grammy before [in 1993, the B-52s lost to Tom Waits]. I mean, talk about a long career. I used to introduce us as "*three-time Grammy losers . . . the B-52s.*"

LORI BARBERO (Babes in Toyland drummer): We worked really, really hard. It wasn't like anything was just given to us on a silver platter. But the payback was really damned great.

GERALD CASALE: '91, my God . . . that was like a shot across the bow. It was like a dividing line in music.

The Reverend Horton Heat and Jimbo Wallace in California, September 3, 2003. "The '90s was when, finally, the original music got opened up into all sorts of other creative type of areas."—The Reverend Horton Heat *Anthony Pidgeon/MediaPunch/Alamy*

5 ORIGINALITY

"Everybody had a different take on things"

It's uncanny how many of the alt-rock bands that hit in the early '90s put their own unique spin on things musically—especially when compared to the largely same-sounding rock artists at the time of this book's release. Here, we get to the bottom of exactly what made these artists stand out.

ROGER JOSEPH MANNING JR.: Bands like R.E.M., the Replacements, Hüsker Dü, the Pixies always championed that—"success on our own terms." Sometimes that panned out to large numbers, and sometimes it didn't. But that was also the beauty of that generation. So many groups that I grew up with in the '70s and '80s, it was all about you could tell when the band suddenly . . . "Oh, now there's disco songs on their record." Well, clearly that was a commercial decision based on commerce. And some cases are more obvious than others. But they lost me and a lot of other fans in the process.

KRISTIN HERSH: We'd play in Boston with five other bands who were our audience, then we'd become the audience for the next few bands—none of us headlining—and we all celebrated our unique voices and sonic vocabularies.

LORI BARBERO: The unique-ism of not just our band, but if a band—even if you don't like it—you hear them and you know exactly who it is, I think it's very creative. There's bands I can think of that I can't stand—maybe the person's voice—but I know that it's them.

MIKE JOHNSON: It seemed like everybody had a different take on things. And not many of the bands sounded the same—that's why I guess people laughed about the labels. Because Nirvana doesn't sound like Screaming Trees doesn't sound like Dinosaur Jr. doesn't sound like Soundgarden. They're all "hard rock bands" I guess, but they all have a very different spin on what their sound is and what they were doing.

DANA COLLEY: The actual configurations didn't differ that much—you had drums, bass, guitars, and the same three chords. So, there wasn't a lot of differentiation in the actual fundamental music and makeups of the bands. Where those differences sort of surfaced was more around the nuanced aspect of that. And you really have to be a listener to understand what that means. The difference between Smashing Pumpkins and Screaming Trees—there's a flavor there that you have to savor to understand. Like a wine. All red wines may look the same, but you can certainly taste the differences and nuance of the grape.

Mark Sandman and Dana Colley of Morphine at the Glastonbury Festival in England, June 22, 1995. "All red wines may look the same, but you can certainly taste the differences and nuance of the grape."—Dana Colley *Rob Watkins/Alamy*

CRIS KIRKWOOD: We used to get spit on and shit thrown at us because of being the band we are—not easy to figure out and not being really obvious about our intentions. We had a pretty "broad palate," if you will. And that's commercial death. That was our sound—the sound was whatever noises we happened to make. But the idea is hit upon something, make it obvious enough, and if you listen to it, it's the sound of *us*. But it's all still guitar music, by and large. Musically, it's all been done . . . and it's all been done hundreds of years ago. Rock 'n' roll wasn't a musical revolution—it was a sociological revolution. So, as far as what music we were doing? It wasn't the point. *We were trying to make the sound of turds being baked up in your guts with our guitars.*

JOHN FLANSBURGH: We worked as a duo starting in '82–'83 until '92. Immediately after that, we were going to tour the world and then we realized we didn't want to go out with the same show we had a year before. How can we change it up? Almost provisionally, we took on a live [backup] band. And that was really the end of our "duo years." I'm glad we did, because we would have become a much more anachronistic act. I'm not sure when Milli Vanilli happened, but anything with a track or a drum machine suddenly had this bad vibe around it.

We played onstage with a tape recorder between us—it wasn't like we were hiding anything. And we were playing so close to people, there was no mistaking what was a drum machine. When we worked with a drum machine, I felt quite sincerely as a musician that there was nothing lacking. I could have been in AC/DC—in my head, I was like, "We are the most rocking, full bore, loudest, screamiest band in the world. We're doing it in a totally different way than other bands have done it before."

JENNIFER HERREMA: At the time, Royal Trux just being myself and Neil, we worked best that way. But I guess we were considered "a band" because on the first album [1988's self-titled], it was more than just voice and guitar—we would play different instruments. We bounced [tracks]. Kind of filling out the picture or the band, as it were, and all the different instruments that were played. But it was just the two of us. Then when we would go to play live, nobody understood when we would have a machine playing the backing tracks.

FRED SCHNEIDER: I'd done a basement tape with [B-52s drummer/guitarist] Keith [Strickland], which was basically reciting poetry. I never really sang in high school or college. Instead of singing, I would more recite the lyrics I wrote melodically, rather than singing [a vocal style also known as *sprechgesang*]. [B-52s vocalist] Kate [Pierson] was in other bands and could play piano and guitar and could really sing. And [B-52s vocalist] Cindy [Wilson] could really sing—and they'd harmonize. But I basically talk/sang the lyrics I wrote. And gradually started singing more, of course. I can't just do that all the time. But I didn't realize that people were so amazed by it. Because I want to sing like Wilson Pickett . . . but I can't. So, I'm stuck doing what I do.

John Linnell and John Flansburgh of They Might Be Giants in New York City, 1988. "We played onstage with a tape recorder between us—it wasn't like we were hiding anything."—John Flansburgh *Ebet Roberts/Redferns/Getty Images*

ANGELO MOORE: Fishbone was going through the whole racial thing of like, "We're an all-black band playing rock music." And stereotypically, rock music is supposed to be meant for white people; funk and R&B are supposed to be meant for black people. If you're playing reggae, then you've got dreadlocks; if you're Latino, you're playing salsa. All these barriers. The record companies and businesses, they need sections to work with in order for them to be able to put the music out there. They need to have a genre to describe a certain style of music: country, R&B, reggae.

THE REVEREND HORTON HEAT: I took rockabilly and decided to get more aggressive and "turned up." A lot of fast, high-energy songs, and it fit in. We kind of bounced around and played various different types of venues and various different types of crowds. But we still played shows where there was a mosh pit. That's kind of the reason that we got embraced—it was a little bit of a backlash against the "shoegazer/doom and gloom" of grunge. Here comes these guys that smile and are zany and high-energy.

MIKE EDWARDS: There was a genesis starting with people like Age of Chance in 1986, who were using the technology of dance music—and that was the crucial thing, using the really primitive samplers. Then, you had bands like Pop Will Eat Itself, who looked very much to hip-hop and weren't afraid using the technology of that, even though their contemporaries were very much rock bands. It was about the technology, because that allowed a musical leap forward.

A huge influence on us was the Shamen. I used to go and see them play in places in London. The way they were using technology was fascinating and gave me, as a struggling musician, a clear route ahead. So, I did what I thought was emulating the Shamen. Then we were kind of perceived as part of a new way of making music. I wasn't happy with the very Velvet Underground, '60s-based sound that typified a lot of alternative bands at the time. I wanted to reflect the kind of acid house scene that was going on, the hip-hop scene, the burgeoning new beat and techno scene. I wanted to reflect that through the medium of a rock band.

JONN PENNEY: I remember when we got signed to Sony: They were courting us, and what Muff Winwood said to us was we really need to get rid of our "'Deacon Blue' image." And I think what he was talking about was it was just all very sanitized and there was no danger in there. "What on earth are Ned's Atomic Dustbin going to do next?"

MIKE EDWARDS: Samplers, the Akai S900 was the groundbreaking machine. Although looking to the Chicago house musicians, there was a lot of the Roland stuff—like the TB-303 Bass Line, which was at the heart of acid house. And the 808 and 909 drum machines. But I think also the rise of sequencers within computer programmers—Cubase is the one that comes to mind. And the birth of Logic.

That was a thing that as a songwriter, it was really useful not to have to rely to do things on tape all the time but to program stuff and to have it come back at you straightaway. The storyboarding aspect of songwriting was hugely improved by putting an idea down and having it played back to you immediately. I was just a guitarist, but I could arrange strings and I could play drums and have all sorts of sounds come in. To have sequencing and sampling, those two things really changed rock music.

JONN PENNEY: Had a few gigs with Alex [Griffin] in his previous band. I was pretty intrigued by his style of bass playing—it was based on Peter Hook's [of Joy Division] style of chord playing and riffing, and higher up the neck and higher strings. A very melodic style of playing. So, when he was interested in forming a band with me, I thought, "This is great."

Matt [Cheslin], the other bass player, only picked up a bass when we began. So, he never played any kind of guitar at all. The beauty of it for us was it was that way from the word go. So, these two guys learned to play together organically and naturally from the start. It was never a discussion about "What kind of bass playing are you going to do? What kind of bass playing am I going to do?" Alex played what came natural to him in that style that he was playing. Matt learned to play the bass to accompany and go with that.

And I suppose the very first instance that I would have thought, "We actually do sound different than other bands," is when I heard Alex come into rehearsals with these riffs and these chord progressions that he was doing on the bass. And that was for me a massive appeal. That was the reason for being in a band—wanting to sound different.

MIKE EDWARDS: In the early days of our success, a lot of people were comparing us with bands like Ministry and Nine Inch Nails. And I found that interesting, because, yeah, the technology was being used there but it was a very different feel. For me, that kind of stuff didn't have the swing of the dance music I was listening to. It was very rigid. It kind of drew from bands like Front 242. So, there was a different take on the technology of the dance music in the US. Whereas in the UK, because we had that acid house revolution—which really was a massive deal—you felt like it was going to be punk all over again. But because you didn't have that in America, I think it gave rise to two different kinds of scenes, although technology was broadly the same.

RUDEBOY REMINGTON: Back in the day, what was considered R&B, these people didn't like rappers. They thought it was music for children. Then they figured there is money involved, and certain producers came with this R&B thing—because it was selling—and that changed rap in general completely.

We knew what happened internationally. You had some collaborations—Run-DMC and Aerosmith ["Walk This Way"]. But the fact is, they never did it live like a statement to the world, like, "We are *this kind* of group of people that make *this type* of music all the way live." Urban Dance Squad jumped in that, and we were the first.

You hear nowadays people try to get the history on their side, but the fact is they weren't an all-out statement as a group toward people, saying, "The DJ is a traditional instrumentalist, just like a guitar player. And the MC is a frontman and basically like a vocalist. One hundred percent." There was no gimmickry going on there; there was no joke. It was the real deal. So, in my point of view, we were the first [to merge hip-hop and rock on a full-time basis].

SPEECH (Arrested Development rapper): There are positives to being groundbreaking. As a hip-hop group, we were able to tour with Primus, Fishbone, and Rage Against the Machine. We did a lot of gigging in areas that a lot of our peers in hip-hop weren't doing yet. We were gigging overseas a lot—all throughout Europe, Africa, Australia, New Zealand—when a lot of our peers were just doing the States.

DANA COLLEY: Mark [Sandman] was working with Treat Her Right when I first met him, and he was interested in a stripped-down kind of idea in general. He had invented this one-string bass and had invited me over to jam one day. It was kind of immediate, really, because as soon as the baritone and the one-string combined, it seemed like a very compatible sound. And then along with Mark's vocals, it formed this triad. So, it had a "eureka moment" from the start.

He was inspired by a few different places. The idea of a one-string [bass] was not uncommon in the Delta as . . . from that came the idea of taking a piano string and nailing it to the support beam of a porch and stretching it, nailing it down, and giving it a little bridge, and then playing that string that was part of the architecture of the front porch. The idea of a unitar sprung out of that.

And then there's this other song called "Cherokee Dance" by Bob Landers, this singer who is singing with almost like a frog-like voice, hence his nickname ["Froggy"]. Apparently, he had died from throat cancer not long after the recording was made, unfortunately. But there was a one-string solo in this particular song that was very inspirational for Sandman. The idea kind of sprung out of that. I think Mark was looking for something that would free him up a little bit. He didn't have to pay attention to what the frets were doing—he could feel it and find it. And the slide and a one-string gave him a lot of fluidity in terms of accessing the scale.

DARREN JESSEE (Ben Folds Five drummer): Ben Folds Five, we knew it was going to be a piano trio with no guitar. We had a clear idea of what we were hoping to accomplish musically. So, that in a way was something to lean into. We practiced for a while and discovered our sound with the fuzz bass and lots of low end going on with a baby grand piano and over-the-top drumming. Once we had a blueprint for what we thought we could take into clubs and turn into really a working band, that actually made it easier because we knew what we were going for.

We wanted to accomplish all the musical ideas as a trio. We weren't going into the studio and overdubbing pedal steels and keyboards and stuff. It was pretty honest, and we tried to arrange the music to fit in the format of the trio. So, the background vocals remained the finishing touch—the harmonies and stuff. It was instantly pretty obvious what we were trying to do. Then it became, "Can we take this into clubs and festivals with big rock bands and pull this off?" So, we found a way to do that.

Ben Folds Five was always kind of an island. But we didn't really feel like we were total outsiders. We weren't playing jazz—*we were breaking stuff*. But because it didn't have a guitar player, it really was just an island. When I first met Ben, I remember us talking, and him saying in 1992 that there was a window of opportunity for us—he sensed that the times were ready for that band. And he had been looking for the right people to create a sound that would get people's attention and would be exciting. And Robert [Sledge] and I were somehow able to do that.

TRACY BONHAM (solo singer/violinist/pianist/guitarist): I started playing violin at age nine, so I was classically trained; and I even went to university thinking I was going to maybe have a job in a symphony someday. But when I turned the corner and I started writing my own songs and it was reflecting of what I was listening to at that time—which was the Pixies and the Buzzcocks—the violin was still with me . . . but it was on the back burner.

It wasn't until I heard a track by PJ Harvey ["Yuri-G"], she played the violin, which I was really impressed. And in the early '90s, I would go see bands in Boston—I used to go see the Dambuilders. And the Dambuilders had Joan Wasser in it—she's "Joan as Police Woman" now—and she would get up onstage and she had this sparkly, gold violin, and she would plug into a Marshall stack and rock on the violin and sing at the same time. I was like, "Okay. Now I understand." That's when I started to incorporate violin into my stuff. It just seemed like a perfect combination of who I was at the time.

VINNIE DOMBROSKI (Sponge singer): The audiences demanded it [that most alt-rock artists wrote their own songs, without the aid of outside songwriters]. We had groups like Journey and stuff like that, and then all of a sudden you got bands signed to major labels, where you're like, "*Primus* is signed to a major label? *Sonic Youth* is signed to a major label? *The Flaming Lips?*" They're making big records and huge news. Who else could write that kind of music? *Nobody.*

Jane's Addiction, you just sit and go, "Who else could write that stuff? That stuff is not written with a group of people and they're thinking about, 'Three minutes and where does the chorus come in? What template do we grab it from?'" Some bands write from templates—they take somebody else's song and break it apart. To truly write something that people were interested in back then that was considered alternative, nobody could write that but people coming out from the underground.

GAVIN ROSSDALE (Bush singer/guitarist): I like that sort of Ginsberg-y, stream-of-consciousness approach to words, rather than, say, country songwriting where there are narratives and stories and places and names and descriptions. That's a specific approach, and I've never related to that because for me, it tied things down too much. I like broader stories. It doesn't always have to be time and place and descriptions. It's just a tool. It's a decision and approach you can take. I like things that sort of float more and have more schizoid elements to them.

THE REVEREND HORTON HEAT: In the '90s, you had bands like the Toadies doing music in very odd time signatures . . . but it was still danceable; it still had a groove for days. Another band that did odd time signatures was Soundgarden, but it still had this groove; it still was danceable. Before that, you'd say, "A dance song has to be in 4/4." Nobody wanted to dance to a 3/4—that's a waltz. But all of a sudden the Toadies and Soundgarden are doing songs in 6/4, 7/4, 7/8—*crazy* stuff like that. But it had a groove.

MIKI BERENYI: The fact that we could tour with Babes in Toyland or the Flaming Lips or Weezer or all these bands that sound completely different, and we would all have some kind of camaraderie between us. It wasn't like we've got some band on tour like Babes in Toyland and we're like, "We're *only* interested in touring with the Birthday Party" or something. It wasn't like that. There are *death metal bands* that like Lush. And equally, our drummer was into oi! punk. The whole point of that alternative scene was that people took their inspirations from . . . it was a world of music.

ANGELO MOORE: That's where you have the most diversity: in the underground alternative scene.

AL JOURGENSEN: It's funny . . . I always mention that back in the day, there was very little technology . . . and everyone sounded different. Nowadays there's all this technology, and oddly enough, everyone sounds the fuckin' same.

6 BEYOND THE MUSIC

"The art sort of reflected life, and life sort of reflected art"

Throughout the course of history, the arrival of specific musical movements seemed to affect and influence not only music but also fashion, politics, and even audiences' behavior at concerts, among other things. Cases in point: the '60s hippie/psychedelic movement, the '70s punk movement, and certainly the '90s alt-rock movement.

COREY GLOVER: All these people were around the same age when this stuff was happening. So, the art sort of reflected life, and life sort of reflected art.

MIKE JOHNSON: Especially with Nirvana—they had a more progressive worldview. Coming out of a DIY/punk scene originally made sense. More inclusive, I'd say.

KRISTIN HERSH: Rock misogyny and homophobia were always embarrassing, and finally the old guard was embarrassed—though you didn't find it everywhere. Meaning that the shit that will be anachronistic is always considered stupid by smart people.

JIMMY FLEMION (The Frogs singer/guitarist): There were songs, but we didn't set out to start a movement [with the Frogs' 1989 gay-themed album, *It's Only Right and Natural*]. But when you look back, it was a predecessor compared to all the people now with "I Kissed a Girl" [by Katy Perry] or whatever. It was *way* before that. We never had a proper conversation with Kurt Cobain to know how he felt about that stuff, but I know that's part of all that "God is gay" [a lyric from Nirvana's "Stay Away"] and Sonic Youth's "God is gay and you were right" [the song "Androgynous Mind"].

Jimmy Flemion with the Frogs at the South by Southwest Music Festival in Austin, Texas, March 17, 2000. "When we did release [*It's Only Right and Natural*], there was a guy who had worked with us on mastering it, and he said, 'You know you guys will never be able to run for president after this' or something."—Jimmy Flemion *John Anderson/Archive Photos/Getty Images*

It woke up people a little bit. And there was a lot of positivity with LGBTQ back then. When we did release it, there was a guy who had worked with us on mastering it, and he said, "You know you guys will never be able to run for president after this" or something. We didn't think anything of it. We knew that when we'd recorded it and we played it amongst our friends it had a reaction, one way or the other. I don't know if it was something we were seeking or that it was something in the future that would foretell all this. It was ahead of its time.

There was no backlash or anything like that. But we did play Milwaukee one time, and we did play a certain song off the record and some jocks threw a chair at the stage while we were performing. They weren't open to the material. But whatever—that's part of life. The world is a big zoo, and there's lots of different people.

Eddie "King" Roeser with Urge Overkill at The Venue in New Cross, London, April 12, 1991. "Who would bother with their clothes?"—Eddie "King" Roeser *Andrew Turner/Alamy*

FRED SCHNEIDER: I wasn't aware of that [Cobain mentioning "kissing Chris and Dave on *Saturday Night Live* just to spite the homophobes" in the liner notes of Nirvana's *Incesticide*]. But boy, that's great. I know he was pro-gay. Good for him. Any major artist—and they were *major*—to be supportive is a big deal.

COREY GLOVER: You can say it in the music, that's one thing. But to say it out loud and have someone really champion those ideas of being against what felt like, and still feels like, the status quo, was always welcome.

EDDIE "KING" ROESER: It was kind of a non-fashion style. It's funny that people made it *into* a style. It was more like, "Who would bother with their clothes?"

BILL GOULD: There was this place, Urban Outfitters. I remember walking in there and seeing all plaid everywhere! "The Seattle look." And I realized it was affecting society. Definitely things like politics. I personally thought it was a step in a positive direction if you think of where it was coming from. To me, hair metal is like the 1950s—it feels like it's from an era that happened a long time ago that's very "retro" to how I always thought about things. So, I felt like going away from that with popular culture was a positive thing.

CHRIS HASKETT: You get this thing where Kmart is selling flannel shirts. There's the saying, "Whatever you throw at capitalism, it will find a way to sell it back to you."

GERALD CASALE: I did see it. And once again to me, it was off-putting because it was so dumpy looking and the lumberjack plaid shirts. And the shoegazing, like, "We're not here to perform for you. We're not trying to get you off. Fuck you—we're looking down." It took me a while to understand why they were doing that. Visually, I thought, "*What am I looking at here?*"

LORI BARBERO: I think that people started admiring different kinds of folks that weren't really ever in the limelight before. They had holes in their jeans, and they had uncombed hair, and they didn't shave all the time. Even with women—women are always supposed to shave their legs and their armpits. And they realized, "Oh . . . you can use a Sears guitar that isn't the greatest-sounding guitar, but it makes this *sound*." Kurt made that kind of famous. So, people started realizing you could just do what you want to do—you can have more of a musical and spiritual freedom.

DARREN JESSEE: In the '90s, the clothes you bought had to be from the thrift store. You couldn't buy anything off the rack that would fit you, first of all. Even if you went to the Gap, you would come home with ridiculously oversized clothes. So, that fed into it, too, because the only way to have a look was to buy stuff at thrift stores. It was a hard time to buy clothes, honestly!

KENNEDY: I faked my first eye exam in fifth grade and wore glasses ever since. I was very happy because when I got the job at MTV, they let me wear my glasses. Because I wore my glasses at KROQ, I wore my glasses everywhere. And I didn't want to not wear them. So, they let me. And "geek chic" was very big. I remember one time I went over to Dave Navarro's house, and I was wearing a pair of sage green sailor pants and a pink rose photo print agnès b. top. And he was like, "Oh, my God, you look like Billy Corgan . . . and that's not a compliment." [*Laughs*] I was like, "Oh, no. I'm geek chic! *Help me!*" I thought I looked so good.

I wore a lot of Air Walks and super-baggy shorts and little, tiny T-shirts. And for a long time, I was wearing wrestling shoes. Looking back, there were some very questionable choices. But I always felt great—that's because my mom gave me an overinflated sense of self-confidence. Especially with my style.

I had Jean Paul Gaultier on *Alternative Nation* one night, when he first launched his perfume in 1994. And I wore a bunch of his outfits and did a fake fashion catwalk on the sidewalk and rolled around on taxicabs and was kind of making fun of him. And he loved it so much that he asked me to fly to Paris to be in his fashion show! So, I was in a Jean Paul Gaultier fashion show with Isabella Rossellini and Madonna. There are things like that that you could never replicate. The stars had to align in a specific way.

LORI BARBERO: I met [Babes in Toyland singer/guitarist] Kat [Bjelland] in 1985, and she was wearing that before we were even in a band together—she just liked vintage dresses. She had closets *full* of them, and that's just what she wore. That was her style: dresses with big collars, buttons, heels [a fashion style known as "kinderwhore"]. I was never a heel person, really—I'm a "boot girl." And then girls would come to the show, and they'd be wearing dresses like Kat—and then it was this thing that kind of snowballed.

MIKI BERENYI: Hair dye was Poppy Red Manic Panic—although it was branded Directions in the UK—and I'd buy it from Kensington Market. Most of my visits to hairdressers were a bit disastrous, so I just cut/bleached/dyed my own hair. To be honest, I wasn't very savvy about clothes/image—just shopped what was available at market stalls and charity shops. It was very much a DIY culture, and I could hand-sew a bit to modify any clothes I bought.

My rather scrappy efforts were made more stylish by the influence of our makeup artist, Sarita; manager Howard, at least in pointing me toward slightly higher-end shops; and boyfriend, John Best, who was half of the PR team Savidge & Best, who bought me the Pam Hogg body-map dress on the book cover [Berenyi's 2022 autobiography, *Fingers Crossed: How Music Saved Me from Success*].

MATT PINFIELD: It was out of necessity for some of us that were losing our hair and receding [concerning the "bald look" that such alt-rock gentlemen as Michael Stipe, Billy Corgan, Ed Kowalczyk, Craig Wedren, and Pinfield embraced]. But I also feel it made it acceptable because people cared about the music more than the look.

Lush at Gassy Jacks Pub in Cardiff, Wales, January 1996. Left to right: Miki Berenyi, Emma Anderson, Phil King, and Chris Acland. "Hair dye was Poppy Red Manic Panic—although it was branded Directions in the UK—and I'd buy it from Kensington Market. Most of my visits to hairdressers were a bit disastrous, so I just cut/bleached/dyed my own hair."—Miki Berenyi *Rob Watkins/Alamy*

ROGER JOSEPH MANNING JR.: I always enjoyed fashion to whatever degree—even though music always prevailed. So, by the time Jellyfish is being created and evolving out of late-'80s San Francisco, my bandmates and I were very much interested in thrift-store chic and having fun expressing ourselves that way. By the time we get to *Spilt Milk*, we toned down some of the color—earth tones were more what I was feeling at the time.

EDDIE "KING" ROESER: The guys who definitely got it were Nirvana. They did their kind of "Ed Sullivan thing," where they show up in the suits [for the "In Bloom" video]. They understood the showbiz part of it. But nobody saw what we were kind of doing was more of an R&B thing—where you would see the guys with the tailored suits. Consciously going against the anti-showbusiness aspect of the Touch and Go aesthetic. Jeans and flannel shirts was sort of the "uniform." What could be less fun than that? And that's always part of the deal: to have some swagger and fun.

We definitely started wearing the suits and the medallions when people [were dressing down]. A lot of people that we were in the scene with had no sense of musical history—that this is what you do if you're going to take a stage. You want to use all the tools that you can. That's what we were trying to do. It wasn't a gimmick as much as it was part of a tradition that we thought was very cool and very "Chicago" and "soul." A band should have a flair that's like a fantasy world.

RADIOHEAD'S "SCOTT WALKER SONG"

Producer Paul Q. Kolderie recounts the circumstances behind a classic '90s alt-rock anthem.

We weren't supposed to do "Creep." They asked the group if they wanted to have us try out recording with them, and they said sure. I did the Pixies, and that was [Radiohead guitarist] Jonny Greenwood's favorite band. They brought us to England and gave us these two songs ["Inside My Head" and "Million Dollar Question"] to work with. And they were *not* good songs. Probably the worst songs I've ever heard Thom [Yorke] write.

We were like, "Fuck . . . *these songs suck*. What are we going to do?" They had played "Creep" at rehearsal a couple of nights before, and they said it was "their Scott Walker song." And I thought they said it was "a Scott Walker song." And I don't know all those Scott Walker records—there's a lot of them. We walked out of the rehearsal, and [Kolderie's production partner Sean Slade] said, "It's too bad the best song is a cover."

So, I grabbed that song out of my brain: "Okay. That song was good. Play that one!" And there is only one take of it. They did one take, and I said, "Okay. You guys go have lunch. I'm going to edit this." Then I called the label and said, "Well, we did this other song." And they were very suspicious. They were like, "Oh, you just want to get paid for another song." I said, "Just come out and listen to it, and you tell me what you think." The guy [Keith Wozencroft] came out, listened, and said, "Well, it's not a hit. But you can finish it." *One and a half billion streams later . . .*

JIMMY FLEMION: We didn't set out that we were going to show up in our leather jackets. We observed and enjoyed showbiz all along the way, and it gravitated toward the "glam look" where people seemed to be louder looking. It was more attractive to me. In 1983 is when we first came out with the wings. Over the years, there was black, brown, red, silver, gold, green, leopard skin, and then black sparkly ones. At that time [in the '90s], we were doing the silver ones. Now, it seems like everybody is getting dressed up or they're doing something onstage. Back then, we were one of the few ones that got dressed up at Lollapalooza. So, we were looked at as weird back then. And we never thought twice about it. The first time we played Minneapolis, we came out with the wings, and [Soul Asylum's] Dave Pirner was cross-legged on the ground, watching us.

JOHNNY TEMPLE: I always liked that punk venues were a place where society's rules were relaxed. Y'know, stage diving being a perfect example of that sort of thing.

JOHN FLANSBURGH: I was seventeen in 1977. I would go to the Rat in Boston. I also visited England—specifically London—in the summer of 1977. So, I had seen the first wave of punk rock firsthand. And was very familiar with moshing and pogoing and all the trappings of that first wave of punk rock. It was a little like seeing bell-bottoms come back—you kind of can't believe people are believing in it [when moshing and crowd-surfing became commonplace at alt-rock shows in the '90s].

ANGELO MOORE: At a point we started having *a lot* of mosh pits and crowd-surfing. It started in the mid-'80s and it stayed that way. It takes a community to engage in crowd-surfing or mosh pits, and people are together. Even though it's an aggressive and sometimes violent dance culture, still, everybody had to partake in it together. Like, when somebody would fall, somebody would pick you up and you're still in it. Or, it takes a crowd of people to hold up somebody who's crowd-surfing. It's a community effort.

I was caught up in the moment, man [in response to being asked if he was ever scared diving off balconies, which Moore was known to do back in the day]! The music would inspire me. A couple times I got dropped. You jump out there, sometimes somebody might not be underneath you that you thought they were. You roll over to a part of the crowd where there's a hole.

THE REVEREND HORTON HEAT: I don't like stage diving—that's disrespectful to the music. The moshing, that's fine if they want to do it—as long as nobody gets hurt.

CHRIS HASKETT: I really hate being distracted while I'm playing. When I'm playing, I'm playing with the people onstage. That's what's going on. Anybody else . . . that's why I hate stage divers.

POE (solo artist): I had a thing for stage diving, and I'd wear these skirts with these biker shorts. And everyone was like, "Isn't everyone trying to grab you?" And it's crazy—it happened once that someone tried to put their hand up my pants. But the audience removed him. I think that culture really considered the art and the music sacred.

LORI BARBERO: Thurston Moore said he remembers the first time he ever met me. He told me exactly what I was wearing, and he said, "You were stage diving at 7th Street Entry [in Minneapolis]." I also stage dove at Nirvana when they played in St. Paul, and Kim Deal said she had never stage dove. We were back by the amps, and I said, "All you do is just run and you dive . . . and they'll catch you." I think that was her first stage dive. I was always up in the front with all the guys because I liked being in the front—that's where I could feel the music bouncing off me. I was always the first to be dancing. We've had to stop our set a few times because it was getting too crazy or someone was hurt.

ROGERS STEVENS (Blind Melon guitarist): We were from the country. We thought that was crazy—"You're going to break your damned neck up there!" I can't really blame the youth—they're going to do what they're going to do. So, I didn't really care one way or the other to be honest, as long as people didn't get hurt. The whole thing at that point had become ridiculous in the sense that the size of the crowd . . . it wasn't really an "organic event" anymore. I guess it was expected behavior. If you consider ten years before, you didn't see that on MTV. I remember going to concerts when I was a teenager, and no one kicked me in the head—and it was jam-packed.

CHRIS HASKETT: It's what people saw on MTV and in the videos: stage diving, the flannels, and the drop-D tuning.

FRED ARMISEN: In the '90s, aside from a couple of haircuts, striped shirts, and I guess skateboards, I don't remember seeing any TV shows where there was like . . . a grunge band depicted. Or a Dischord band depicted. It didn't really come up, and that might have to do with the fact that MTV existed—so, therefore, that's where it all lived. But I don't remember seeing parodies of it that much. Like whereas *Love Boat* had an episode with glam rock or Kiss, *Quincy* had a punk band, and I think *CHiPs* even had a punk band.

JOHNNY TEMPLE: It was popping up in Kevin Smith's movies, Richard Linklater.

MARK KOHR (music video director [Green Day, No Doubt, Alanis Morissette]): Films like *Clerks*, it had that low-budget black-and-white thing that's raw and real. And that came out of a lot of the music video work that was low-budget, fun, and had a lot of energy. But still, it was difficult for music video directors to work in film.

LOU BARLOW: There were really big Hollywood films like *Reality Bites* and *Singles*. And you'd see underground music popping up in films. It made sense to me in context of underground film—what they were doing. I thought *Kids* was sort of sensationalistic—they really wanted to shock people. Because not only was *Kids* an arty film, but they wanted it to be this lurid movie. I talked to [director] Larry Clark and [screenwriter] Harmony Korine—we hung out when the movie was first being casted. They wanted me to get a feel for the set and what they were doing [Barlow's music was featured on the film's soundtrack]. Harmony was a *total* punk—I was really impressed. They had this whole manifestation shit going on: "We're going to win the Oscars with this one! We're going to walk down the aisle at the Oscars listening to 'Good Morning, Captain' by Slint!"

JOHNNY TEMPLE: Books . . . *High Fidelity* [by Nick Hornby, published in 1995] comes to mind. I feel like I see alternative's impact on books more now than back then—there's so many people from punk or alternative backgrounds that are now either writing books or publishing books. Henry Rollins was a huge inspiration for me and Akashic Books [Rollins has his own publishing company, 2.13.61]. In fact, when I started Akashic, the first person I turned to was Henry; and he put me in touch with the people from his staff and they shared so much valuable information. It really moved me, because this spirit of community and a cultural understanding led to Henry and his team sharing information with us. We got going through the generosity of 2.13.61.

And the range of books they were publishing also inspired me—they weren't just publishing Henry Rollins books or punk rock books. They were also publishing Hubert Selby Jr. and other great writers. I liked the way 2.13.61 defined underground culture really broadly—not just literally punk rock but rebel spirits, rebel books, rebel music. *Get in the Van: On the Road with Black Flag* is the one that comes to mind [as a standout 2.13.61 title, published in 1994]. We used to listen to the audiobook of that on tour. Also, *Black Coffee Blues* [published in 1992]. 2.13.61 was, to me, punk rock's first foray into book publishing.

MOBY: In the alternative rock world, the only outspoken animal rights person was Morrissey. But in the hardcore and punk rock world—I even made a movie about it: *Punk Rock Vegan Movie*—everybody from the Cro-Mags to the Bad Brains to the Damned to Crass to Gorilla Biscuits . . . even later on, Sepultura, Earth Crisis, on and on. There's *so much* punk rock animal rights–oriented music.

TANYA DONELLY: I feel like every five years, music impacts the culture—aesthetically and politically. Whether or not that political influence actually impacts in terms of the language being used and the way people function politically, I do think music has a massive impact.

"AMERICA'S FASTEST-GROWING SPORT"

The time Matt Sweeney's Chavez bandmate made Bill Boggs an alt-rock analyst.

MATT SWEENEY (**Chavez singer/guitarist**): Clay [Tarver] from Chavez made a promo video called *What's Up Matador* that I highly recommend because it's making fun of the whole indie rock explosion in real time. He must have done this in 1993 or something. It's presented as a children's show, and he got [television journalist] Bill Boggs to be the host! Bill Boggs just took the job for what it was—"I'm explaining this record label and what happens, to kids." Like, Clay called indie rock "America's fastest-growing sport." It was pretty funny. I'm sure it's the same thing as '60s stuff, like if you were conservative and all of a sudden you wanted to be in a band and decided to grow your hair long. So, it was kind of embarrassing in a way.

LORI BARBERO: It's because of bad politics it made a lot of good music. There's always something good that comes out of bad things.

KENNEDY: It did influence politics. It was MTV that swayed the election [in 1992]. Of course you could say, "If Ross Perot would have won, there never would have been a Clinton presidency." Well, that didn't matter, because there were a lot of eighteen-year-olds voting for the first time who were put off by the Reagan/Bush era and they wanted to vote for someone new. And that was enough in a lot of places to get Bill Clinton into the White House. And that ushered in a completely different political era. And MTV was very liberal—there were a lot of liberal Democrats that worked there. And I was the self-proclaimed Republican. I know for a while they treated me with curiosity, but they just wanted to be careful because they wanted to make sure that whatever they were amplifying was in line with their politics.

IAN MacKAYE: It's arguable that MTV's advocacy helped elect Bill Clinton. And you know who else helped elect Bill Clinton? George H. W. Bush and Ronald Reagan—by creating circumstances that were diabolical and fucked up. And I think people were like, "Well . . . let's try the other team for a while—to see how *they* fuck things up."

PAGE HAMILTON: I was born in Portland, Oregon, and Proposition 9 was trying to ban gay teachers in the state of Oregon. Nirvana was doing a benefit at Portland Meadows Raceway [on September 10, 1992]. We were direct support, and there were a bunch of other bands—Poison Idea, Fitz of Depression. It was a big day because of this ridiculous law. We played with them that day and two nights later in Seattle at the Coliseum.

AL JOURGENSEN: We work with various voting organizations—you can always register to vote at a Ministry concert. No matter where we're at. Well, I take that back—when we work with Rob Zombie and Alice Cooper [on tour], they don't want any part of that. But when we're doing our own tours, there's always some voter registration by the merch booth.

KENNEDY: It was an issue [concerning whether MTV ever asked Kennedy not to discuss politics]. Not necessarily in the context of my show, *Alternative Nation*. The only people I've really got into it about politics were Rage Against the Machine because they were so self-serious and I disagreed with them philosophically. And they always assumed if people liked their music, they also liked their politics—which was not necessarily true. [Republican Wisconsin Congressman] Paul Ryan was a huge Rage Against the Machine fan, and he would listen to Rage Against the Machine while he was doing workouts in Congress. And they asked him to "stop listening to my music, man." It's like, "*You don't get to choose who you inspire.*" When you put your art out there, it is consumed.

But they did have a problem with me going on and doing political analysis on other shows. So, one time John McLaughlin—y'know, *The McLaughlin Group*—he had a one-on-one interview show on CNBC, and I had met him at the 1993 Clinton inauguration, and I lifted up my dress to show him my Republican elephant tattoo on my hip. And he was like, "Ohhh, my goodness! Ohhh, my goodness!" And then he went and told that story on *The Tonight Show*.

And then *The Tonight Show* invited me on—I was on twice—in 1993. And I was *so* nervous, I completely bombed. But then John McLaughlin had me on his CNBC show, and they sent Doug Herzog, who was just under Judy McGrath—he went on to run Comedy Central and MTV Networks—with me so I "wouldn't embarrass the network talking about my politics." Which I thought was stupid. I love Doug. But he came off very dry, and I came off very fun. I was having a great time—I was there to party.

TANYA DONELLY: In terms of social politics, music is unchallenged in importance of how culture moves forward. I do think literature, too, obviously. But in terms of first-line cultural shifts, music in the last century has always been *so* important.

THE STORY BEHIND A PECULIAR ALT-ROCK BAND NAME

Lou Barlow uncovers the "gross" truth.

I had a bunch of nonsense words I'd made up when I first started writing songs when I was a teenager. Because when I first started writing songs, I didn't want to write lyrics, so I wrote nonsense words to the songs. And "Sebadoh" was one. "Sentridoh" was another. I had a few other phrases I came up with that I would use in songs. Speaking of "slacker," I was averse to putting any kind of meaning to some things. So, I thought, "*Sebadoh.* That doesn't mean anything." It is what it is—it looks like "Play-Doh." I wanted to combine like, *Sesame Street* with . . . something kind of gross. [*Laughs*] A gross *Sesame Street*.

7 THE SHADOW OF THE '70s

"My generation taking the best moments of previous eras"

It turns out that the '70s certainly seemed to have left its musical mark on quite a few alt-rockers of the '90s.

JOHNNY TEMPLE: In the '80s, people were like, "Fuck everything that came before us!" But by the '90s, maybe there was a maturation process and people realizing you can still have outsider attitudes or punk attitudes, but it doesn't mean that you have to burn your predecessors.

NAOKO YAMANO: I actually like '60s and '70s rock music very much.

MARY TIMONY (Helium singer/guitarist): We all grew up in the '70s. It's still my favorite era of music. That was the music of the people who were in their twenties then. It was their childhood. It's the golden era of rock music.

JENNIFER HERREMA: Our main thing was listening to records and thinking, "These are so amazing, so great." We don't want to *do* that, but we want to do something as extra-special and our own as that. It was always based on guitar.

STEVE ALBINI: That was the distinction between the "punk era" and then the "'90s alternative or underground rock era"—people stopped being embarrassed to like heavy metal. In the punk era, heavy metal was just "idiot music." No one wanted to pay any attention to it because all the associations with it were morbid and sexist and crass and commercial. Then, as all of that context stuff got stripped away and people were just listening to it, there are some *smoking* things in the hard rock and heavy metal era—really great and invigorating music. And people were able to appreciate that as separate from the sociological construction around it.

Smashing Pumpkins in Chicago, Illinois, May 1991. Left to right: D'arcy Wretzky, Billy Corgan, James Iha, and Jimmy Chamberlin. "People stopped being embarrassed to like heavy metal."—Steve Albini *Paul Natkin/Getty Images*

LOU BARLOW: The thing that changed with us was when we breached hardcore and came out of that, we were like, "Everything is open. *Absolutely everything.* Nothing is off-limits, nothing is uncool." Like, Dinosaur Jr. covered a Peter Frampton song, "Show Me the Way." And that's *not* a sarcastic take on the song. That's like, "We love the song. And we're going to play it." Still to this day, such a tremendous respect for '70s hard rock. We kind of gave up on our guilty favorites. And especially J [Mascis]'s tastes were like, "Yes. *Everything.*" And I think even J naming the band "Dinosaur"—he kind of understood. He also brought back a lot of vintage instruments that a lot of people were not playing at the time. He wanted us to have stacks behind us like we were at fuckin' Woodstock.

JOHNETTE NAPOLITANO: They used to call it "dinosaur rock," and now they call it "classic rock." That's what the *dudes* were into. I was really into Queen and Bowie. Thin Lizzy was Irish, and one of the reasons I liked Thin Lizzy was because they had that double edge—Phil Lynott had a tenderness about him. They were very tough, and that was no act—if you've ever been to Belfast, that's a tough part of the country. It's not the nice/easy place that Dublin is. And Phil grew up tough. But, man, when he got tender and sweet . . . he was tender and sweet. And that's why I related to that. [Note: Concrete Blonde covered Thin Lizzy's "It's Only Money" on 1989's *Free*.] That's what I liked about us, too: We could rock out, but we could also pull out something that was very soft and tender.

LORI BARBERO: I think the music is pretty similar, just sped up. I listened to Queen and Alice Cooper when I was young, and to me, Queen is the best band. I got to see them in the '70s when I went to high school in New York. There's so many bands that love Queen, but no one can really imitate them. It's kind of like Prince, David Bowie, Devo, or Led Zeppelin—you can't hold a match to them because they were so above anything that ever happened before.

ROGER JOSEPH MANNING JR.: What I really liked was my generation taking the best moments of previous eras. So, psychedelia, which we typically associate with the '60s. Glitter rock you usually associate with the early '70s. And heavy blues rock—Zeppelin, Sabbath. All this stuff was reemerging—Cheap Trick—in new and fresh ways. And that was terribly exciting for me. Because in the case of psychedelia, most of us were too young to have experienced that in full effect—we kind of got the aftermath of that, and all the drug influence.

To this day, *Ritual de lo Habitual* from Jane's Addiction—that's one of my favorite psych-rock records. But it's also got a lot of goth/post-punk energy in it. That's a really definitive example of what my generation was bringing together. And then come up with original music that I think is as good as any of its predecessors. It's a very demonstrative example of nostalgia coming back and repurposed in the best possible ways.

MATT SWEENEY: Chavez, we were into Cheap Trick and Aerosmith, and the weirder, spookier, more intense parts of '70s rock was what we were into and fucking with. And also bands like Amon Düül II we *really* liked.

EVAN DANDO: I got back into my K-tel shit, like [Paul Nicholas's] "Heaven on the 7th Floor" or [McFadden & Whitehead's] "Ain't No Stoppin' Us Now." I listened to disco a lot, and Earth, Wind & Fire. But let's talk about Joe Walsh and the James Gang. They're "white Meters." Granted—they're like, "We like the Meters, but we're white boys and we can play." [*Sings the guitar riff at twenty-seven seconds into "Funk #49," which sounds similar to the Meters song "Cissy Strut."*] I fucking *love* Joe Walsh and his whole approach. And Cheap Trick—they were punk rock in their own way. Really in your face. For me, Pearl Jam sounds like Lynyrd Skynyrd. Pearl Jam weren't afraid to embrace the '70s completely.

Jellyfish at the Metro in Chicago, Illinois, November 1990. Left to right: Roger Joseph Manning Jr., Andy Sturmer, Jason Falkner, and Chris Manning. "What I really liked was my generation taking the best moments of previous eras."—Roger Joseph Manning Jr. *Paul Natkin/Getty Images*

JENNIFER HERREMA: We considered ourselves normal people who loved rock 'n' roll. Like James Gang and Joe Walsh. During that time of *Twin Infinitives*, I really thought we were just making the next King Crimson album or Blue Öyster Cult album. Or something that was so far out there . . . but sat right there in the guitar rock world.

ROGERS STEVENS: I remember at the time thinking that the Cult record that they did with Rick Rubin [1987's *Electric*] sounded incredible—and it still does. I listened to it incessantly for two years when it came out. It sounds more like an AC/DC record with Bon Scott. It's *super* dry. We liked that and definitely more natural-sounding recordings that you would hear in the late '60s. Performance-based recordings, like the Band, or something like that.

EDDIE "KING" ROESER: Certainly, a lot of songs from the '70s I never need to hear again—that I've heard too many times to even enjoy. But there was extra effort into the singing, the crafting, and the recording—the sound—of that music. I think maybe because hardcore was a big undercurrent when we were coming up, it was our way of countering what the prevailing winds were—*anti-'70s*. That was our thing to say, "Fuck you." It's another way for us to go against the grain.

[Urge Overkill] certainly didn't want to be retro, but we wanted our stuff to sound good—we wanted to use the good mics and great-sounding traditions of the time. I think it goes without saying now that everybody is more aware of everything that has been recorded. Back then, because it was a little bit more verboten to do something that was considered "retro," drove us to do that more. Which is exactly why we would have gravitated toward Neil Diamond. And we've been proven to be prescient in that judgment, I believe.

ROGER JOSEPH MANNING JR.: One of the things that I loved—and credit them with inspiring me at the time—was Redd Kross. Because they were like, "If this song is catchy and has something of value to us, we're either going to reference that, or we're going to flat-out do a cover in our set." I learned about all kinds of deep cuts and B-sides from them. And celebrating great moments in our formative years of childhood, they would cover TV themes. They covered one of my favorite songs from *Jesus Christ Superstar* ["I Don't Know How to Love Him"].

JOHNNY TEMPLE: It's amazing to me that Neil Young is not more commonly cited. I see Neil Young's influence all over the place: the sound of his guitar, the guitar solos. Neil Young could do the best one-note solo of anybody! [Note: In reference to the solo in the song "Cinnamon Girl."]

EVAN DANDO: Big Star. Our teacher in high school, in tenth grade, he had *Radio City*. And no one else had it. We were like, "What is this?! It's like the Beatles!" In our high school, everyone knew that *Radio City* record. We didn't even get that first one until later. One other thing about the '70s: Our friend Bill Whelan, who played bass in Bullet LaVolta, he put the

Nick Drake song ["Pink Moon"] in that Volkswagen commercial that "made" Nick Drake. I was proud of myself because I copied that Ozzy "Yeah!" thing before anyone else did on a major label. You go, "Yeah!" into the next thing. Even if it's "no"—"I really can't do that, sorry . . . *yeah!*"

DARREN JESSEE: I grew up in the '70s and '80s, and music seeped in and influences us without us really even knowing. There were so many great recordings from that time. The Carpenters were a *huge* influence—the mastery of those compositions and those arrangements. Some of those songs are really sparse—they're just so beautifully put together.

I think we all admired Todd Rundgren and especially the track "I Saw the Light." But there wasn't a lot of discussion about him being an influence. I think Ben was more into a little more twisted lyrical perspective—like, Randy Newman might have been a bigger influence than Todd Rundgren.

All the guys in Ben Folds Five, when we were growing up, we were listening to the stuff on the radio and it was big '70s tracks. Even a band like Fleetwood Mac was the soundtrack to my childhood. I guess I'm trying to say we didn't look to borrow ideas—we felt like we knew what we were doing. But we would listen to the Carpenters sometimes in the studio and flip out over how beautiful the recording was.

MIKE JOHNSON: A lot of the Seattle bands and early '90s bands, they definitely had an influence from things like the first Zeppelin record [1969's *Led Zeppelin*], which was supposedly what punk was reacting to. It really is a full-circle type of thing—it isn't as big a change as it seems. Maybe a lot of it is just the sound and the image. Especially Sabbath and Zeppelin and the guitar sounds, too.

People didn't feel as doctrinaire about the music anymore, too. Because the punk scene at one point was very much a reaction to that, and then people were like, "Yeah, but I like these records." Even the Ramones are talking about how much they like Zeppelin. So, it's like, "Wait a minute . . . we don't have to be reactionary about *everything*."

TRACY BONHAM: In the '80s, it was synthesizers and digital. But when the '90s came around, people were kind of going back to tape and more organic sounds—more analog. And the focus on an album. And even the style.

EVAN DANDO: '70s doesn't round off as well as '60s and '90s numerically. People's brains work in funny ways. I think they'd rather compare us to '60s and '90s because they're upside down of each other.

JOHN AGNELLO (producer/engineer [Dinosaur Jr., Mark Lanegan, The Breeders]): Every twenty-five years a certain genre comes back. People forget about it and then kids go back and listen to Big Star, or fast-forward twenty-five years and they listen to Teenage Fanclub.

EDDIE VEDDER GOES DUMPSTER DIVING

Mike Watt remembers the Pearl Jam frontman's critical role in his solo debut *Ball-Hog or Tugboat?*.

Here's what's a trip about Ed singing that song ["Against the '70s"]. He comes to Cherokee [Studios], and in the alley . . . Ed likes surfing. And in the garbage, there's a wet suit. He digs this wet suit out and puts that fucking thing on to sing this song! First, we were going to do a cover of Captain Beefheart's "Dirty Blue Gene." I could just hear Ed's voice singing . . . Captain Beefheart is doing Howlin' Wolf, so it's like Ed doing Howlin' Wolf through Captain Beefheart. And Ed wrote it all out on this paper and charted it all out—did all the homework, all prepared. And then I thought, "Ed, why don't you do this other song that I wrote?" He just went for it and did such a bitchin' job that I said, "Don't worry about that one. I like the way you did this one here."

How well do you know *Tommy* by the Who? Do you know "Christmas"? I didn't do it on purpose, but when I listen back, I was like, "Y'know, that sounds like 'Christmas'!" Ed really was earnest about it—when he sings, "Garbage vendors against true defenders of the craft." His grandfather I think was a Freemason and [Eddie] gave me his belt buckle . . . Ed was so straight about that, looked me in the eyes, he was beautiful and sincere about it.

And the song is about Little Richard not selling as much "Tutti Frutti" as Pat Boone. It was about when that TV show *Happy Days* came over—my father told me, "I was making $95 a month as third-class seaman. Those were *not* happy days." Nostalgia is always bullshit. It's airbrushed and about jive. That's why I wrote it. I think the way Ed sang that thing, he sang it like he almost wrote it. And then Dave Grohl's drums . . . *oh, my God*. And Gary Lee Conner from the Screaming Trees does that one-note solo! And Krist Novoselic played the organ.

The thing that changed with us was when we breached hardcore and came out of that, we were like, 'Everything is open. Absolutely everything. Nothing is off-limits, nothing is uncool.' Like, Dinosaur Jr. covered a Peter Frampton song, 'Show Me the Way.' And that's not a sarcastic take on the song. That's like, 'We love the song. And we're going to play it.'

LOU BARLOW

8 THE PRODUCERS

"They can't make me add reverb to the snare"

As a result of alt-rock's re-appreciation of '70s sounds, the production and sonics of recordings started hearkening back to yesteryear. In other words, the sound of a band playing live in a room together, without a lot of post-recording fiddling. And a handful of producers seemed to play a major role in some of the decade's standout albums.

CRAIG WEDREN: That '80s era of mixing rock records was a little bit funky. There were a lot of unnecessary effects on drums. It took a few years for people to relax and remember you could just record a sound well and let it be.

MATT PINFIELD: There was something about that era [the '90s], where you *feel* the bottom of the music in those songs and productions. It moved away from some of the stuff in the '80s that was super-clean and super-light and using Simmons electronic drums. It was getting back to the core of the sound of live music.

BILL GOULD: It's funny, because a lot of these bands came from demo tapes—in the punk rock world, where production value wasn't such a big deal, and arrangements were more simple. So, there wasn't a lot of "larger than life arena sound spaces" like you'd hear in the '80s. Bands like a Whitesnake, for example—these huge, monstrous snare drums. You got to where things were more stripped down.

Rick Rubin had a thing where he said he didn't like reverb at all, and he was just using room compression to give ambience to the recording. So, that was popular at the time. And we went to that because that felt more alive and direct and stripped down.

Steve Albini in Chicago, Illinois, July 2014. "You just put microphones up and go."—Steve Albini *Brian Cassella/Chicago Tribune/TNS/Alamy*

I remember Quiet Riot wanted to do some recordings, and they asked me if I wanted to mix something to give it a "new, fresh sound." I remember thinking, "Wow. Just using less reverb and stuff like that is, I guess, 'a thing.' It's an aesthetic."

EVAN DANDO: When we started recording in '87, we knew we had to bring it all the way back because there were a million snakes [cables] in the board and you'd pull them all out and it would sound way better. It's like, "Dudes, just record the music without all this bullshit—limiters, gates, and negative gates." I was so relieved when who comes to the rescue, but the unlikely Danzig with the Rick Rubin record [1988's self-titled] . . . and the Cult [*Electric*], even more unlikely. But they showed the way with a nice snare sound. It was in my contract initially! It says, "They can't make me add reverb to the snare."

FRED ARMISEN: I didn't have an ear for discerning sound in a recording studio. There are things that worked out well in my life, and there are things that I enjoy doing. I love drumming. But hearing mixes in a recording studio, my ear gets fatigued too quickly. So, I sit in the control room in front of the mixing board, and they're playing songs over and over, and I cannot tell the difference. Really quickly, I'm like, "I have no idea." So, it was like those guys [Trenchmouth's Damon Locks and Wayne Montana], really, in the studio. I was like, "Are my drums loud enough?" And then that was it. I learned to respect all those engineers and producers enough to where I was like, "I'll just be quiet. As long as you can hear the drums."

PAUL Q. KOLDERIE: I grew up on '70s rock, and one of my favorite records was Humble Pie: *Rockin' the Fillmore*, which is literally a live record. I recommend it—it's awesome. [*Laughs*] That, to me, was rock 'n' roll. *That's* what I wanted to do.

MIKE JOHNSON: Most of those guys ['90s alt-rock producers] are also musicians or band guys. So, I think it does have a certain similarity . . . like with Jack Endino and Steve Albini, probably.

STEVE ALBINI: A lot of things are cyclical. And in the '80s, there were some technological developments, with things like sequencers, samplers, drum machines, and synthesized instruments that empowered engineers and producers to take more authorial control over the sounds of the records. And in an era where that was being politically indulged by the power structures of the record label system, those engineers and producers made a name for themselves by using these new and cutting-edge sounds. And in so doing, they were able to justify rather exorbitant fees.

So, a lot of that was driven by a general music industry trend to seek power toward the administrative part of the music business—and I would include producers in that. And then there's also a technological fascination that producers and engineers have, where something new comes in and they want to try it out. Then it becomes popular, and then it runs like a rash through all the records of that era. In the '90s in the underground music scene, there was a reaction against that kind of stylized and gussied-up production aesthetic—that was spearheaded by the punk and underground bands. And then that translated into a simpler, more organic kind of recording.

Mercifully, a lot of that more naturalistic recording is also less expensive to conduct, because you don't need to spend a lot of time working with the technical stuff—you just put microphones up and go. So, it suited budget-conscious and independent bands to have a simplistic recording. A lot of the bands from that era, their best records were their earliest ones—before they had any funding and before they were enmeshed in the system that would do this lavish and elaborate stuff pro forma.

PAUL Q. KOLDERIE: I certainly admired Albini for his uncompromising attitude. I'm more impressed if a guy has a sonic signature, and you say, "Oh. *That sounds like Albini.*" Even though it's kind of a "service business," so a lot of people start out like, "I'll do whatever you say. You tell me what you want." I like to see people step out.

But there was another duo, Rob Schnapf and Tom Rothrock, and they produced Beck and stuff like that—they were West Coast guys. People used to compare them to us [Kolderie and Sean Slade], and I thought we were kind of working on the same level. I remember having a conversation with Sean, "Who's out there that we're competing with?" And he's like, "Well, *there's the Butch Vig guy*." At the time, Butch was just a guy in Madison, Wisconsin, who had done some Killdozer records [at Smart Studios]. And then Nirvana redefined what a lot of rock sounded like, because that was so raw and guitar heavy.

EDDIE "KING" ROESER: We did work with Steve first, then we worked with Butch, and then went back with Steve. Butch was more of a guy who had been in a band that was on a major label called Spooner, so he was not an "industry outsider"—the way Steve was. He had been part of the establishment. He sort of understood you could do certain things to streamline. Like, one reason we didn't keep doing our records with Steve was because he hated vocals! I mean, I'm not a fan of vocals, either. Nobody in any of these bands wanted to sing. And Steve didn't want to work on vocals or turn them up in the mix. That was part of the aesthetic—that that wasn't important. And we sort of got to the point where, "Well, we want something that's more intelligible and more pop."

Butch had been working with this Touch and Go band, Killdozer. I thought they were brilliant, but their songs were really slow, and no one was going to mistake them for being a pop band. But when you played a Killdozer record, you could *hear* those vocals, and they had this incredible sheen and power to it. And I think this was the part of it that Nirvana wanted in their music. Even though it was punk, you could tell that Butch cared about vocals and he had more of a willingness to say he's not top of the list at making avant-garde music.

Whereas with Steve, it's like, he was more interested in the total sound—however sludgy it might be or however incomprehensible. I think Butch came from more of a traditional "rock" background. Steve was the first person who would say that he hated anything before

Butch Vig in England, February 2009. "And Butch, obviously with the *Nevermind* stuff—that was the record that blew up, so everybody referenced it."—John Agnello *Hayley Madden/ Redferns/Getty Images*

1976. He would maybe make an exception for the Stooges or a few things here or there. We didn't have the confidence to go for the fader and say, "We want the vocals to be up like *this*." So, [Touch and Go owner] Corey [Rusk] had worked with Butch, and Killdozer had called him because he was the first studio in Madison they could get on the phone. I think Butch Vig is a very lucky guy—that these freaks happened to call him and said, "We hear that you have this recording studio . . ." And they did some records that were very important.

PAUL Q. KOLDERIE: Butch Vig is just a pro. He can handle all the technical stuff, but he's also inspired to do cool things—his stuff always sounds *big*. A lot of those vocals on the Nirvana record, for instance, are four takes. Once Butch demonstrated that the John Lennon thing was a doubled vocal . . . the thing is if you do four vocals right, it sounds really good and big. And that's what those vocals sound like: four matched-up tracks. But again, Butch had to do a certain amount of editing in Pro Tools to make that happen. There's always going to be little things that are off, but you can make them tighter if you push them around. He's kind of a perfectionist, but in a relaxed way.

DAVID PAJO: I always loved the sound of the Big Black records [produced by Albini]. They sounded horrible live—which Steve would say onstage, "The sound does not matter." But the studio sounds were *so* cool—the guitars didn't sound like guitars; nobody really used drum machines and tried to make them sound big. And then as an engineer for other bands, when we heard that first Pixies record that he did [1988's *Surfer Rosa*], it became clear that he got really amazing drum sounds. And that his aesthetic that we heard in Big Black fit into his production. There is a "Steve Albini drum sound" and "bass sound," I think. Part of the sound is that he delays the room mics a little bit—milliseconds—so it gives it a more expansive room sound.

JOHN AGNELLO: In the '90s, Butch Vig was kind of legendary . . . and Steve Albini—for different reasons. Steve was anti-production, so that was always controversial. But he always made really great-sounding records. And Butch, obviously with the *Nevermind* stuff—that was the record that blew up, so everybody referenced it.

PAUL Q. KOLDERIE: What people don't realize, *Nevermind* was one of the first heavily Pro Tools–edited records. Even though it sounds very live, Butch was right in there early on, realizing you could record things in a raw way; but then you can make them more perfect by editing aggressively with digital. Like drum tracks and things like that. So, he jumped right in on that.

Nobody ever really talks about it much, but you can hear vocals being repeated, bits of choruses that are the same flown in. Because you could do that stuff on tape, but it took forever and it was hard. But on digital, it becomes quite easy. I think to do *Nevermind*, he used a pretty primitive eight-track system. It was a really early version of Pro Tools. I know they mastered that album for six days. It's heavily EQ'd in the master. So, it was a collaborative effort.

STEVE ALBINI: The setting of it was really nice [Pachyderm Studios, where Nirvana recorded *In Utero*]—it was out in the country, about fifty miles from Minneapolis. So, you could be very productive there. There weren't a lot of distractions there—there wasn't a bar down the street, there weren't people dropping in, there weren't shows to go to on the weekends. And I think that was a contributing factor. It was a freshly built studio that was very well executed. The acoustics in the studio were very good. The main live room had a lovely live character. The isolation rooms were nothing special, but access to them was very convenient. The tape machines and the console were professionally installed and in really great shape.

CHRIS HASKETT: We'd never worked with an external producer before. In fact, we were really against it. Andy Wallace had an excellent engineering ear. I don't think he got to do much with us [for 1992's *The End of Silence* by the Rollins Band]—and by that, I don't mean in a negative sense. I mean we were too intractable. And in hindsight, I regret this.

But you look at his other work—listen to *Grace* by Jeff Buckley. That's just fucking genius . . . and that's partially production genius. He got excellent sounds. He had a good intuitive sense for when a take was done. Back then, I was like, "It's got a minor flaw! We have to redo it!" He's like, "*Nah.*" He was able to take takes away from me—which was good. And he flew in part of a solo from one take into another, which I'd never seen before.

ROGERS STEVENS: Andy was very meticulous. He was a real brilliant engineer. He knew how to set up stuff the way he wanted it to be very specifically. And that was at Kingsway [where Blind Melon recorded their 1995 album, *Soup*], which is not a proper recording studio. That's an old mansion with a bunch of weird, different rooms and different ambience. So, there's a lot of opportunities there. I think that's what [Kingsway owner] Daniel Lanois saw in that place—you could do all kinds of things in there.

We set up in one medium-sized room on the second floor and never left it in terms of the live tracking—that's where we had the drums set up, and that's the most important part. That was an incredible experience to see him work. There were a lot of mics on the drum kit—for it to end up sounding like it did. If you listen to the Led Zeppelin records, those are three mics on the drums.

We pushed both of those guys [Wallace and Rick Parashar, producer of the band's 1992 debut] to go further in that direction of a '70s-style production than they normally would have. I remember being with Rick and telling him all the time, "We don't want any fake reverb on the record. We'll use room mics." Which, now, is kind of dumb, I realize.

But there were certain things that were used, like the Eventide Harmonizer is on that record—I'm pretty sure that's the vocal effect on "No Rain." But that record and the console that Rick had at London Bridge was really a treasure—it was an old Neve console. And we recorded to two-inch tape, which people don't do anymore. I mean, they *do*, but they don't do it all the time—that was the only way to do it back then.

ERIC KRETZ (Stone Temple Pilots drummer): Brendan O'Brien's records have such a good focus on the midrange, which is how Zeppelin made records as well. Especially by the time we got to *Purple*, our second album, Brendan was like, "Oh . . . that would be *this* kind of amp." He'd pull out all little amps, and would say, "Jimmy [Page] would use this on this kind of song, and Jimmy would use this on that kind of song." Because the first record [1992's *Core*], we were just so excited to be making a record that we kind of had somewhat of a grasp on our equipment; but by the time we made our second record, everybody was buying gear left and right. So, we couldn't wait to try out new tones. And of course, all those tones basically harken back to what Zeppelin were putting together.

JOHN AGNELLO: Scott Litt was great. His records sounded really great and clear on the radio—the R.E.M. stuff sounded great, *In Utero* sounded great [which Litt mixed two songs on]. He captured what he captured really great. The vocals sit perfectly. It's that thing where certain people have a certain style, and it works all the time.

JASON PETTIGREW: What *does* Flood bring to those records [*Achtung Baby, Zooropa, The Downward Spiral, To Bring You My Love, Mellon Collie and the Infinite Sadness*, etc.]? I don't mean that as a flippant comment. It just seemed like whoever he was working with, he brought something to it that's not the same thing. I think Flood brought a sense of presence to it: "Don't make the middling thing. Stand behind everything and just run to it." I thought he brought a great sense of animation to everybody's work. There was no idea that was too "out there."

IAN MacKAYE: Ted Niceley worked with me, Brendan, and Guy at a record shop called Yesterday and Today. Ted was a friend and someone that we respected, so we asked him to help us by refereeing the mixing process of what would become our first record [1988's *7 Songs*]. Up to that point, I had been the person producing most of the records on Dischord and started to slip into that role with the Fugazi session, but it quickly became clear that I needed to be more of a band member at that time. That's what led us to ask Ted to come in and I think he really helped. His ideas about sound were great!

MATT PINFIELD: What made Ric Ocasek unique as a producer was he loved music and had an ear for it. Ric and I had a conversation once: He said he took everything he learned in the studio working on those first two Cars albums [1978's self-titled and 1979's *Candy-O*, produced by Roy Thomas Baker], but he didn't believe everything needed to have a hundred layers of vocals on it. What he wanted to do with the bands he produced [Bad Brains, Weezer, Bad Religion, etc.] was give the best representation of what the band was at its core.

Also, Michael Beinhorn is a great producer and was instrumental in bringing the Chili Peppers and Soundgarden to a new level on *Mothers Milk* and *Superunknown*. He wasn't afraid to push the artist and challenge them to take chances and, at the same time, let them be and remain themselves.

JOHN AGNELLO: I learned a lot from Don Fleming—it was a good relationship because I was technical, so he didn't have to worry about any of that stuff. I just made it sound good, and everybody liked it—it was easy. He was a super-great musician. I met him and J [Mascis] at the same time—it was right before *Green Mind*, when Dinosaur Jr. was looking to sign with a bigger label. I was doing a lot of recording in the late '80s for Columbia, and Columbia was pitching to sign them.

There was a meeting in their offices, and they wanted to bring a younger, long-haired engineer to work with them. So, they presented me as, "We'll sign you to a major label deal, and you can work with John." Then they signed with Warners, and they were doing *Green Mind* and I got a call from the A&R guy, and he said, "J is not happy with the mixes. He remembers you, and he'd love for you to mix the record." And then a while later I got a call saying, "J wants to work with you on the next record," and that was *Where You Been*.

ROGER JOSEPH MANNING JR.: As far as [Jellyfish co-founder] Andy [Sturmer] and I were concerned—overseeing the songwriting and production—we were still enamored with more of a sophisticated, intricate, hi-fi production sound of the '70s in particular . . . and into the '80s. That is where we leaned most of the time. We loved a good Seeds/'60s/garage band sound as much as anybody. But our writing was not hanging out in that world. Our writing was more interested in different levels of architecture—with both sound and arrangement.

There's roughly twenty-two, twenty-three songs between the two albums [1990's *Bellybutton* and 1993's *Spilt Milk*]. We didn't feel we had much time to say what we wanted to say, and we were trying to get everything in there that we could—that was important to us. And often, that had to do with a level of production that we were enamored by. In a lot of ways, it had a lot more to do with a Steely Dan or Earth, Wind & Fire or Quincy Jones/Michael Jackson than what Soundgarden was doing—even though *Superunknown* is one of my favorite records of that time and its own production masterpiece [co-produced by Michael Beinhorn and the band].

PAUL Q. KOLDERIE: There were effects you could use, but the idea of constructing songs the way the Dust Brothers [Michael Simpson and John King] did with samples, like *Paul's Boutique*, where every song is made up of a chain of samples . . . there's *no way* we could have attempted that. No one thought of it. So, they came along and made that happen, and I thought it was great. Obviously, it created a lot of chaos in the business—which is not a bad thing, necessarily.

ROGER JOSEPH MANNING JR.: I had spent almost the entirety of my touring years in Imperial Drag listening in the back with headphones to *Odelay* and marveling at what Beck and the Dust Brothers team had done together. Because the three of them made that record. And I was in awe of what they were doing with technology.

Now, there were all these things you could do with samplers and computers that you couldn't do in the '80s. I kind of got a slap in the face when I heard *Odelay*, Marilyn Manson, and Portishead. I hadn't noticed this new freedom technology is allowing. And when I listen to this music—if it's done well, by people who know how to write songs—the technology doesn't get in the way.

JOHN AGNELLO: When people would say to me, "Oh, my God. The guitars you record jump out of the speaker!" I'd say to them, "It's because there's no air between the sound and the microphone." It was three microphones on one speaker—up to the speaker. Whereas if you put in room mics that are far away, you're not going to get that direct impact.

STEVE ALBINI: I think the best approach is to start by making a naturalistic recording of what's happening organically. That is, to try to make an accurate representation of what's happening in the studio so that the band can at least hear themselves as they truly are—before they start stylizing things according to their aesthetic. On one hand, conceptually it's simple to do a naturalistic recording—you just get good microphones, put them in a place that's flattering, and then listen to the results. But it does require a lot of attention to detail.

PAUL Q. KOLDERIE: Once again, we were working with pretty primitive equipment. As the '90s went on and we did more major label records, we started working in studios that had fancy Neumann microphones and all that jazz. But really, the first Pixies thing, we had a couple of good microphones, but we used a lot of 57s and cheap microphones. It's just putting a mic out in the room and mix it in.

JOHN AGNELLO: I would make sure I had a really good tube mic—an old tube mic. Like a Neumann 67 or a 48. We'd set 'em up, and you had a pop screen. Years later, I started doing weird things with other singers just to have fun. But with Mark Lanegan, it was very traditional. *It was his voice.* I always used to joke, "Mark could read a phone book, and it would be riveting." And he also knew his dynamics. He knew when to hit harder. It was an emotional experience recording with him because of the sound of his voice, how much I loved him as a person, what a nut he was, and how scary he could be.

STEVE ALBINI: We did have a PZM microphone as an ambient microphone in the room [for the recording of the Pixies' *Surfer Rosa*], but there's nothing special about that mic—it's just a good choice for an ambient microphone. I've used dozens of different microphones in that same application, and there's nothing magical about the PZM. PZMs, when they first came on the scene, they were a relatively inexpensive mic that had pretty good ambient or sort of area pickup, so they sounded good as a room mic or as an ambient microphone.

BUTCH VIG: Well, Kurt [Cobain] had no patience for doing anything more than a couple of times. Contrary to the slacker mentality, he wanted to make a great-sounding record. When we finished *Nevermind*, he loved it. He later had to kind of diss it because you can't really retain your punk roots or your punk authenticity and say, "Man, I'm glad we sold ten million records." So, he had to start to diss the record. But when we finished it, he loved it. And then both Dave and Krist Novoselic confirmed that when we were doing all the interviews for the *Nevermind* twentieth [anniversary].

Kurt wanted to make a very ambitious record, but I'd be lucky to get a couple of vocal takes and get him to go back and double-track his guitar. If you didn't get it in a couple of takes, he would put the guitar down in frustration. Billy [Corgan], on the other hand, is more of a perfectionist. He would work on a section of a song for hours or a solo section or whatever. He didn't care; he would just do whatever it took. I really respected that, because I always wanted to work with someone who wanted to get things as close to being perfect as you can. There's no such thing, really, as "perfection" in a performance; but there is a way to get a feel that just feels so good you know you've got it right. I totally loved and respected Billy's work ethic.

HOW URGE OVERKILL LANDED THE *PULP FICTION* SOUNDTRACK

Eddie "King" Roeser relates how he believes Quentin Tarantino really came across UO's Neil Diamond cover.

Had we not been familiar with *Reservoir Dogs* . . . it was not normal to share your music with anything that would be considered "advertising." They had to talk us into that. They had to fly us out to see the movie and to get the permission to do that. I think before *Pulp Fiction*, soundtracks had been out of the mainstream for a while. That was the one that kind of brought it back into music and movies being this important . . . Tarantino used songs to elevate the scenes. That kind of started with Tarantino. After that, it was a no-brainer. But that was an unexpected thing to us. I would say that when we saw the movie, we were like, "This is a great movie," but we had no concept that it would turn into this *juggernaut*. Like, this was going to be a classic, world-dominating movie and soundtrack. It was like, "This is a kickass movie. Yeah, you can have the song."

It seemed like in hindsight, there was some aspect of every other song on that soundtrack is actually a period song. We were the only current song. I believe they did ask for Neil Diamond's original, and because the scene had to do with drugs, Neil was like, "I don't want my song playing during an OD scene." So, I think somebody figured out that there was almost an exact cover of the song—and then they tracked us down. Even though Tarantino claims that he discovered our song in a used-record bin. We found out later that I believe what happened is they wanted the Neil Diamond version, and he *could afford* to not give his song to anybody. In the end, we were very lucky to be on there, because there are no other current bands.

JIMMY FLEMION: We were doing our takes out there, and [Billy Corgan, who produced the Frogs' *Starjob*] says, "One more take," and you figure that he's not paying attention—he's reading a magazine in the studio, he's not even watching. But he's listening and *really* paying attention. It's quick because he's done it so many times. He knows how to layer things—like Jimmy Page layers the guitars. We didn't do that, but that's kind of his thing. I write songs and know how to deliver them, but I know nothing about amps or lead guitar or pickups. And Billy's totally a tech-head that way.

PAUL Q. KOLDERIE: The most important thing you can do as a producer of Radiohead is interact with Thom [Yorke] . . . and all of them—and their ideas. They have a lot of ideas, and they don't want to be produced in the sense of David Foster would come in and produce a Chicago record or something. They don't want to be told what to do. They need someone who will magically make their ideas happen—that's not uncommon.

But I think Nigel [Godrich] is really good at that—he's a tremendous engineer. Gets great sounds and is able to interact with them and get what they want out of it. The sounds on *OK Computer* . . . it's not just the sound; it's how it's manipulated and the guitars that sound kind of "diseased."

PAUL LEARY: I always tell people, "Don't be afraid to work for free." Because I owe everything to working for free. Had I never worked for free, I would have never produced anything. And then Sublime came along, and they liked [the Meat Puppets'] *Too High to Die*. They'd been working with David Kahne, and he produced "What I Got." They worked in the studio with him, and David Kahne liked to work with drum loops. That song turned out great.

I remember they asked me to do the album [Sublime's self-titled release from 1996], and I said yes. So, they sent me a cassette tape to listen to, and I thought it was just going to be a demo—but it was the stuff they had done with David Kahne. When I first heard that, I was like, "God, you guys are nuts. Whatever you're doing here, you just need to continue doing that. Because it's great." And they're like, "No. David Kahne likes drum loops, and we want to be *a live band*."

STEVE ALBINI: The one that comes to mind [as one of the best-sounding '90s alt-rock albums] is *Spiderland* by Slint. Brian Paulson did that—it's an absolutely *impeccable* recording. It's really a beautiful representation of a truly odd band. That's a benchmark. If you can make a record that sounds as much like the real presence of the band as that, then you've done a great job.

DAVID PAJO: Slint is just all private jokes—or in-jokes. And a "Derd Niffer" was a term that Britt [Walford] invented, which means someone who nuzzles their nose on someone's dingleberries. [*Laughs*] It's really specific. Albini thought it was really funny, and he wasn't into the idea of adding "Produced by Steve Albini" on the album [1989's *Tweez*]. Because in his mind, he was just engineering and was not a producer. Which is right—he was just pushing the buttons. But he was getting the sounds that he liked. So, that was the joke we did: "Produced by Some Fuckin Derd Niffer."

MARY TIMONY: A lot of music that was recorded in the early '90s could have sounded better. People were starting to record more on their own—in their own basement studios with their shitty equipment. A lot of it was you could put out your own record easily—you didn't have to get signed to a major label, so you'd record cheap and put it out cheaply.

JOHN AGNELLO: The difference with the '80s records was with Cyndi Lauper [Agnello was assistant engineer on 1983's *She's So Unusual*], maybe we were in the studio on and off for four or five months. Whereas Redd Kross, we did the record [1993's *Phaseshifter*] in *a month*. It was, "You got to get in, you got to get out. There's no dicking around." And honestly, as my career progressed from the '80s to the '90s to the '00s, I noticed people didn't party much. When you went into the studio, *you worked*.

DARREN JESSEE: The CD was a great format to have a nice dynamic range. I think if you're a young person listening to something directly from your phone streaming it, there are certain frequencies that don't sound that good. And a lot of '90s music doesn't sound good just streaming through your phone because all the low and middle, it doesn't come through. Like, all that stuff where there's tons of information and all the emotional stuff exists, it doesn't come through. The stuff that sounds good streaming on your phone is when it's kind of sparse in the middle and has this nice vocal. But bands were playing with a lot of fire back then.

In the ’90s in the underground music scene, there was a reaction against that kind of stylized and gussied-up production aesthetic—that was spearheaded by the punk and underground bands. And then that translated into a simpler, more organic kind of recording.

STEVE ALBINI

Moby at Matterley Bowl, Winchester, Hampshire, England, May 27, 2000. "'Electronica' is one of those words that I've never heard used by anyone who makes electronic music."—Moby *Edd Westmacott/Alamy*

SUBGENRES

"They can call us whatever they want to"

There were seemingly countless subgenres tied to alt-rock throughout the '90s—grunge, industrial, shoegaze, lo-fi, Britpop, etc. Here, many of these offshoots are discussed.

JOHN AGNELLO: My analogy with baseball is, "If everybody liked the Yankees, baseball would be boring." If everybody liked whatever type of hi-fi music, it would be boring. You need to have guys with elbows knocking shit around.

MIKE JOHNSON: The whole grunge thing—nobody ever thought of themselves as "grunge" or "alternative." Both of those labels seemed like marketing words, or they were made up. So, it was a big joke to everybody.

BILL GOULD: I think what a lot of what is called "grunge music," a lot of it just sounds like bad rock 'n' roll to me.

PAGE HAMILTON: I remember talking to Steve Turner from Mudhoney once—we toured Australia together—and he said, "We were just playing Stooges songs and slowing them down or speeding them up."

ROGER JOSEPH MANNING JR.: Grunge had dethroned hair metal, and now it was going full speed ahead and, again, we had nothing to do with that world. But we were very excited and happy that a lot of people we knew were having success in that arena, and we liked a lot of it. I was a huge Soundgarden fan. It was my generation giving us some "Alice Cooper" through another filter, but very much that same childhood energy we grew up with in a hard rock setting.

AL JOURGENSEN: I don't know what "industrial" is. I just write music that fits me. To me, industrial is the early Einstürzende Neubauten records. And we incorporated some of the self-sampling stuff—like going out to railyards with a Sony recorder and adding that to the music, and this and that. But Billy Gibbons and ZZ Top use samples . . . are they an industrial band? What does that term mean exactly? It's either "good music" or "bad music." It's the journalists' job—you guys come up with the catchy catchphrases. We just write fuckin' stuff.

JASON PETTIGREW: I know that a lot of the people on the *Alternative Press* staff were really into the Wax Trax! stuff because they were in clubs and it was dance music to them, but it was more harder-edged and also noisier. There always seemed to be this weird "cold war" between the electronic European new wave coming into Chicago via Wax Trax! Records—the record store. Because [label founders] Jim Nash and Dannie Flesher were aficionados of that stuff, amongst many other genres. That really set the stage that would come along.

I mean, Depeche Mode was synthesizer-driven, and it was cute and "Just Can't Get Enough." But you hear those Front 242 records, which were done on cheap sequencers . . . they sound very militaristic, forceful, and driving. It wasn't like listening to your typical college rock band that somebody had a remix of that ended up in clubs. Wax Trax! was helping cultivate that sound into something much bigger than what it could possibly be.

MIKI BERENYI: "Shoegaze" was termed as an insult by a guy named Andy Ross, who was the head of Food Records, which was Blur's label, and Voice of the Beehive's. But the point is, he was at a Moose gig, and I think he was just slagging off the genre, because his bands were very different and there's a lot of infighting and bitchiness in the British music scene. So, he was literally next to a journalist, going, "Oh, these fucking bands and their boring music, staring at their shoes. I'm going to call it 'shoegaze.'" And then it got picked up. But it was literally coined as a term of insult or derision.

It was quite hard to go to America with Ride that first tour and have interviewers going, "Oh, so you're a shoegaze band." You take it as an insult. But in a funny way, it's a term that has been reclaimed, like, being a lesbian and calling yourself a "dyke"—it was originally meant as an insult, but I think it's become a term that nobody questions. So, as a name, I wasn't particularly enamored of it.

ROGER JOSEPH MANNING JR.: I didn't even know that "Britpop" was a scene or a term because I had been following Blur ever since they were a Manchester "dancey-dance" band.

I thought it was strong material. And *Modern Life Is Rubbish* is another masterpiece. So, I was already on board with that camp. Then Oasis dropped, and I was not terribly excited—I didn't see what all the hoopla was about. I believe one of their first singles was a song called "Live Forever," which I adore to this day—it's one of my favorite songs they've ever done. And I don't dislike them—the music's fine. Frankly, it's a lot more straightforward, simple, plain average to me, while their competitors were pulling out all the stops.

Meaning, Blur—taking all these chances stylistically, they're bringing in synthesizers at a time where I'm like, "Nobody does that! What are you guys doing?" And I couldn't tell if they were just a bunch of stoners sitting around, taking drugs, and they would stumble onto these brilliant things, or if they were these art-school intellectuals. A great combination of all that stuff is happening. And they're doing a great job of bringing in obvious influences like Bowie, but in a completely fresh way.

MIKE EDWARDS: Britpop was a low point, I think. It took me ten years really to get back to listen to rock music after that, because I thought, "This is kind of depressing and tedious. It's got nothing of interest for me."

MARY TIMONY: The other thing that totally influenced music in the '90s was people recording cheaply. The whole lo-fi thing—Guided by Voices making whole records on four-track cassette is kind of crazy. But that really was a huge part of it. It became an aesthetic and a limitation that people liked.

JOHN AGNELLO: *Bee Thousand*, the Guided by Voices record, is one of my favorite records ever. *Super* lo-fi. Like, thirty-five two-minute songs. Probably recorded with one mic.

JIMMY FLEMION: The Frogs started recording our written songs around the house way back in 1982. We came upon what is described as "lo-fi" in 1986 when we started recording *It's Only Right and Natural*. We became known for that—we did that from '86 to '96 when we did that made-up stuff. And some of it was termed lo-fi because working at home and doing your own recording, we weren't in a proper recording studio—it was my brother with two or three mics, drums, and guitar. And that was it. I don't know when that became "a thing."

The *It's Only Right and Natural* stuff—that was just stuff we did at home for our own enjoyment while we were knocking out the first album [1988's self-titled] in the studio. And that one had all the production on it and all the money spent behind it. We got a phone call in the midst of recording that record from Gerard Cosloy at Homestead Records, who had heard the lo-fi recordings. We thought he was interested in the record we were working on in the studio, but he was interested in *that*. So, that set us on that road.

PAUL Q. KOLDERIE: I've always been a sucker for "alt-country," personally. I played in bands that were leaning a little bit toward the bluegrass side, sometimes. And I was a fan of Gram Parsons and [the Byrds'] *Sweetheart of the Rodeo*, where people like Gram were trying to bring country music and rock 'n' roll together. Like the Flying Burrito Brothers. And I liked the Eagles' first three records—*On the Border* is a pretty rockin' record. I was the kind of guy who would be interested in that—Jason and the Scorchers were playing it, the Georgia Satellites. There were all these different takes on it. And I thought Uncle Tupelo was a *really* cool take on it—to play amped-up country music.

I'm not sure where that phrase "alt-country" came in—sometime in the '90s, I guess. It's one of those things where things are fresh at first, then they get a little ossified. It got so I'd go see a band and it would be so obviously alt-country, and they'd only use E, C, G, and maybe E minor in their songs. There was a certain "sameness."

THE REVEREND HORTON HEAT: If people ask, "What type of music are you?" I say, "Rock 'n' roll. We're '50s rockabilly–influenced, but we play our own original music. A lot of it is fast, high-energy music, so a lot of the kids think we're punk rock." When I'm speaking to somebody at the grocery store or something, that's what I'll say. I don't like to say we're "psychobilly," but we fit into that—we play a lot of psychobilly shows and festivals. We're definitely a part of that scene, but we do a lot of stuff that psychobilly bands don't do—we get bluesy, we get country, and we can get more alternative.

And one thing about Reverend Horton Heat, we were so desperate to make this work that we played all sorts of different types of venues. Especially in the early years around Texas—

Les Claypool with Primus at Shoreline Amphitheater in Mountain View, California, July 7, 1991. "I always cringed when the word 'funk' was attached to Primus."—Les Claypool *Tim Mosenfelder/Hulton Archive/Getty Images*

we would play a country bar, and we'd still be playing my songs, but we would just make it more country. And then the next night, we'd play a heavy metal club, and it would still be my songs, but we'd make it more our heavy metal type stuff. And then the next night, it would be a punk rock place, and then a blues place, and then a dinner club. To this day, we're like that. And the reason why we're like that is out of desperation, basically.

DARREN JESSEE: I thought "alt-pop" was okay. Ben coined the term "punk rock for sissies" that ended up being everywhere. Ben Folds Five was just a piano-rock band—during a time of alternative music.

DANA COLLEY: When you're doing interviews, people ask you, "How do you describe your music? How would you categorize it?" So, I think Mark, in an attempt to head off that question, sort of said, "low rock"—that was our genre.

ANGELO MOORE: The first thing I think of [concerning "ska-punk"] is the Specials, the Selecter, Madness—that whole era of ska is what I grew up on. English invasion of ska. After that, I got hip to the Jamaican ska, which is the original form of ska. Then came a lot of the punk rock—all that good alternative rock stuff. All of it seemed like it was within the same alternative genre or subculture.

LES CLAYPOOL: I always cringed when the word "funk" was attached to Primus. Mainly, because it would embarrass me for George Clinton to go, "Oh, what's this? I hear it's funk." And he listens to it and goes, "*What the hell is this?!*" People who I respect in the funk world—whether it's Larry Graham, George, or Bernie Worrell. Because I was the only one in Primus that had *any* soul or funk background. I used to play four sets a night, five nights a week, in Hells Angels biker bars all around Northern California, playing old R&B. So, it always bothered me when the term "funk" was related to Primus. Because Herb [Alexander] is not a funk drummer, Ler [LaLonde] is not a funk guitar player.

SPEECH: To me, "alternative hip-hop" was way more experimentative, and it was way more expressive—in every way. Some of the groups I remember were Disposable Heroes of Hiphoprisy with Michael Franti, Me Phi Me, Basehead, and of course A Tribe Called Quest, Jungle Brothers, De La Soul. I mean, De La Soul's *Three Feet High and Rising* album was so groundbreaking for hip-hop. And not just that whole album, but even their singles prior to it were groundbreaking in numerous ways.

I feel like it was the heart and soul of what hip-hop is and should be—which is experimentation, expression, and yet, holding on to the pillars of what hip-hop is. So, I thought it was extremely vibrant and great times. Public Enemy, KRS-One . . . there were quite a lot of artists that I loved a lot. But the way I see it, they were pushing boundaries as well and yet were called alternative hip-hop.

RUDEBOY REMINGTON: We questioned the fact that even the United States didn't have an answer on this [merging hip-hop with rock] back in the day, when [Urban Dance Squad] got signed. We said it in many interviews, "We're surprised that you guys didn't come up with stuff like that." But we did. And we had the guts to do so. People give you flak for being colored and doing this, people give you flak for being white and doing that. And we figured we all came from different backgrounds, ethnicity-wise. So, for us it wasn't a problem. Also musically, we had so many influences that we were listening to as individuals—you take that with you, as a person, as soon as you start expressing yourself in music. For us, it was no big deal. For other people, it obviously was.

SPEECH: I think gangsta rap really had a place in the late '80s. Because take away [N.W.A's] "Fuck tha Police," for instance, or "Colors" with Ice-T—a lot of people wouldn't have known how serious gangs were on the West Coast. Back in those days, we saw the West Coast as gorgeous palm trees, bikini-clad women in oceans . . . basically, *Baywatch* is what we're thinking of L.A. And [gangsta rap] painted a picture of, "No. There's this police brutality. There are gangs that are killing one another over blue scarves or red scarves." It's like, "*What?!*" We had no idea. So, it was very useful, initially.

And as what can happen usually with things that become successful, it started to become a caricature of itself. Where instead of it informing and allowing us to see inside of a world that we never saw, it started to become like it was glorifying this violence, and it was sort of like "shock rock" in a sense—where it lost a lot of its legitimate purpose, and it became just shocking music for the sake of shocking music. And at that point, I felt it was deeply destructive.

I sided with some of the elders. There was a woman at the time, C. Delores Tucker, who is misinterpreted as being against hip-hop. She wasn't. I studied her very seriously back then, and she loved hip-hop, she loved creativity, she loved the youth. But she fought hard to try to basically censor lyrics that were deeply demeaning toward women—black women, in particular. And also deeply destructive against black men—a lot of times talking about killing each other and killing black men. These things were just deeply destructive, and she was talking against it.

There was another guy from New York, Reverend Calvin Butts. He was a pastor, and he was also speaking out against it. And again, not against hip-hop but against this ultraviolent [version], and you couldn't really find anything constructive within its type of lyrics that were against women, black women in particular, and black men against black men. I agreed with them, because if we were to talk about killing a gay person or killing a Jewish person, it would not have went over well at all. It would have been looked at for what it was—which is, it's gone too far. So, that's what I felt gangsta hip-hop had started to become.

LOU BARLOW: In the late '80s, LL Cool J was amazing, and the rise of Def Jam. Early rap to me existed on the same plane as what industrial music was: sort of sparse, harsh dance music. Minimal. I love Snoop Dogg. N.W.A was huge. The first Cypress Hill album [1991's self-titled] was crazy. And it was also at the same time as *Nevermind*. Rap music was a *huge* deal for me. And then Wu-Tang Clan kicked in, and I'm like, "*Oh, God.*" I was obviously engaged in rock because I was playing it, but as far as what I listened to, I was really excited about the rise of rap. Rap, shoegaze, and trip-hop—those were my '90s peaks.

KENNEDY: I loved going to see trip-hop bands live. Oftentimes, I was with people who were on psychedelics and a lot of ecstasy. And I never did that. I was completely sober and straight-edge in the '90s, and I can tell you as a sober person, it still had the same effect. I remember going and seeing Primal Scream, and I understood why people did psychedelics—although I never had any desire to do them myself. But it threw the enhanced experience, where you could just dive into a part of your brain that needed jostling. It was very effective and worthwhile. I'm a fan. It's not what I listen to all the time, but I really appreciate it. I did go through a big Portishead phase . . . but I had to pull myself back with some mindless California punk rock.

DANNY SABER (Black Grape multi-instrumentalist/producer, producer/remixer [Marilyn Manson, David Bowie, U2]): If you really think about the Happy Mondays, mixing dance culture—both technically and just from a vibe standpoint—and bringing rock 'n' roll into that equation and guitar-driven stuff, they're one of the first bands to really do that ["alt-dance"]. To where we are now—where *anything* goes. I remember going over there and meeting Shaun [Ryder] for the first time, and it was so liberating because musicians tend to be really uptight and straight.

With Shaun and a lot of those British musicians of that time . . . the charts aren't segregated there. If it felt right and it sounded good, we went with it. Shaun was super into the Geto Boys, so all we listened to was hip-hop. And that was the golden age of hip-hop, in my opinion, especially from a production standpoint with Dr. Dre—*The Chronic* had just come out. I'd put that in the top five records of all time, sonically. It's the cornerstone of a whole genre. So, the Mondays had a huge contribution.

GERALD CASALE: I loved it [techno and EDM]. I'd become friends with Timothy Leary and his wife, Barbara; and they had a son, Zach. And Zach was totally into the rave scene in L.A., where there would be this temporary space where everybody had to find out where it was and go there. And it didn't have permits. And I loved the music. I thought, "This is exciting. This is a relief if this is going on." When I heard it, I thought, "*This is what Devo should be embracing.*"

Again, they were long riffs that people could take drugs and dance. It wasn't song structure, really. And there wasn't some featured singer or anything. And I thought, "All you've got to do is take these sounds and this energy and structure them into a song and put our Devo spin on it with our content, substance, and narrative, and this would be perfect." But at the time, it fell on deaf ears.

MOBY: "Electronica" is one of those words that I've never heard used by anyone who makes electronic music. It seemed like there was a moment in the mid-'90s, where a bunch of music journalists from New York went to a festival in the Netherlands . . . and took ecstasy and danced to techno. And all of a sudden, were like, "Oh. *This is a real thing.*" Because journalists in the '90s didn't trust electronic music. It wasn't very artist-oriented; it wasn't very album-oriented.

JOHNNY TEMPLE: Post-hardcore, post-punk, noise rock . . . for Girls Against Boys, I always preferred "noise rock." Certainly, we came from a punk rock background, so post-hardcore or post-punk . . . maybe I prefer post-punk to post-hardcore, because Girls Against Boys doesn't really sound like a hardcore band at all. I'd say there are more punk elements than hardcore. But then on the other hand, hardcore is part of our roots.

JENNIFER HERREMA: With Royal Trux, I just recently noticed [press] in the UK talking about us as "scuzz rock." I don't even know what that is! I think "noise rock" would be coming from the *Twin Infinitives* record, specifically, because people couldn't get their heads around it. We never were intentionally obtuse to be obtuse—we were always intentionally trying our best to be music that people could connect with. We were never making music for other people—we were making it for ourselves.

MARY TIMONY: I grew up in D.C., so I was around the punk scene here and was in this all-girl band in 1990 called Autoclave here. And then the riot grrrls came to town because Bikini Kill and Bratmobile moved . . . some of Bratmobile were from here but had gone off to Olympia [Washington] to go to school. Then they came back here, and Bikini Kill met Nation of Ulysses on tour and decided to move here one summer. It was happening here because those two bands did the fanzine and started the meetings. It came from the fanzine that Tobi Vail or somebody from Bikini Kill had called *riot grrrl*. It was inspiring. I was kind of part of that scene. There was a lot of energy.

KENNEDY: Emo is a real thing. Just don't even try to run away from the tag, because we all know emo people. And of course, I'd rather see somebody pour their feelings into music than their politics. Let the rational STEM world be for technology, and let the emo writers sit in their feelings and produce life-changing music.

MATT SWEENEY: David Kleiler from the Volcano Suns, who were a cool Boston band, was a friend of ours. And prior to Chavez, I was in a band called Wider that had a lot of difficult music. And David Kleiler, to make fun of it, would call it "math rock." And when we'd play, after a song, he would pretend to be tapping something into a calculator. It was a total diss—he was totally making fun of it. One hundred percent David Kleiler came up with "math rock" as saying, "No girls are going to like this. This music is up its own ass and is brainy and overly complicated." With Chavez, it doesn't sound complicated to me. It sounds intense, I guess.

CHRIS HASKETT: Metal stayed huge. When you listen to something like [Alice in Chains'] "Man in the Box" . . . I think it's genius. In the same way that "Kashmir" is genius in the simplicity of it and making it so powerful. But "Man in the Box" would work perfectly as a metal song. You could hear that on a metal station, and you would not blink. There was more of a psychological difference in certain situations. The same with Jane's Addiction—in places of "Pigs in Zen," you could almost hear that on a metal station.

PAGE HAMILTON: We were dropping off seven-inches at Bleecker Bob's and Sounds on St. Mark's—we had done "Born Annoying." They put it on, and one guy said, "This is like . . . industrial metal, or something." Then it became "alternative metal."

KEVIN MARTIN: "Post-grunge" would be kind of where we [Candlebox] fit. Nirvana, the Melvins, and Blood Circus and that kind of movement from Seattle is what I would consider to be punk rock—not even grunge. So, I really felt like it was an odd term when I first heard it. But I think that if that is what you have to label us as so people understand where we come from in a generation of the music scene, then so be it.

VADEN TODD LEWIS (Toadies singer/guitarist): I see stuff coming up now that I like that's considered post-grunge. I'm like, "Okay. Whatever you want to call it. I like guitars, so keep those coming."

VINNIE DOMBROSKI: It's like time stopped after grunge, right? Now, we're the post-people! Stone Temple Pilots . . . what are they? Are they a rock band? Grunge? Post-grunge? They're none of that shit, man. I just go, "Okay, call it what you want. And we'll just keep making music and doing gigs."

MATT PINFIELD: "Pop-punk" was fitting because Green Day and Blink-182 inspired so many bands to come. But it all goes back to the Buzzcocks in the late '70s and the Descendents in the early '80s . . . and '70s power pop.

THE REVEREND HORTON HEAT: It's kind of like the old thing, "If they're saying something bad about you, be grateful they're saying *something* about you." I don't really like the labels that much, but at the end of the day, it doesn't really matter—except for the fact that it promotes us. I know what it's like to have somebody *not* writing about you. [*Laughs*]

JOHNNY TEMPLE: I think it's hard for any artist of any medium to be grouped in a genre. From the artists' side, it's awkward because you think of your music as being really unique and not part of a group of people doing the same thing. So, it's hard for musicians to be categorized.

FRED ARMISEN: There's another book to be written just on the genres alone—how many there were.

COREY GLOVER: They can call us whatever they want to. As long as they're listening, *it's fine*.

Björk and PJ Harvey at the Alexandria Palace in London, February 14, 1994. "The emphasis was not on your wardrobe and your stage production. It was on the originality of the playing and the lyrics."—Jennifer Herrema *JMEnternational/Hulton Archive/Getty Images*

10 ♀

"We all empowered each other"

For female rockers in the '80s, it seemed as though how you looked mattered as much as—or more than—your music. That appeared to change with '90s alt-rock, as the focus was more on songwriting and lyrical message.

KENNEDY: There weren't a ton of female rockers in the '80s. I know I'm going to miss people, but obviously [Heart's] Ann and Nancy Wilson, and Lita Ford. So finally, the dudes wanted parity and equality with the women. It wasn't "cock rock"—it was way more emotional and democratic. I remember looking around at L7, Kim Gordon, Courtney Love, Veruca Salt, Bikini Kill, Juliana Hatfield, Liz Phair, and thinking, "This is so cool. Women are totally taking charge of their path and their lyrics." There was so much confidence, so much to look up to, and so much to look forward to.

And it wasn't this condescending quota system like, "Aw, isn't she adorable? She can play guitar." There were women that were creating this insane music, but they were still able to incorporate all the visual elements that women for so long were relegated to because they had mastered their instruments, and their artistry was on par with anything the dudes had been cranking out at that point. And it was a really special time because the music was *so* strong, it was *so* inspiring. And PJ Harvey and Björk . . . it had this incredible poetry and quirkiness and rage and all the things that had been previously assumed to be in the "male domain."

MARY TIMONY: There was definitely not as many women playing music in rock bands as now. It felt like a political statement to just be doing it at the time. People were definitely a little more sexist and just assumed that you were at a show because your boyfriend was there. It felt like you were a female cab driver or something that people didn't expect.

JOHNETTE NAPOLITANO: I don't think it changed at all. I remember Miles Copeland—who was the head of our label—really wanted me to dress up. He really wanted me to do the "girl thing." And it wasn't that I didn't want to do that—it's just that's not who I am. I was like, "Never mind a wardrobe budget . . . *pay our royalties*." [*Laughs*] I was happy to look pretty in videos.

FERGAL LAWLER: I really admired that about [Cranberries singer] Dolores [O'Riordan]: She wouldn't put up with photographers trying to say, "Can you take the shoulder off your jumper?" or something like that. She would say, "Look, it's all about the music. *That's* not important." She was always against that whole "sex symbol thing" because she wanted to be taken seriously as an artist. She stood up for her rights and her right to be viewed as another artist rather than a "sexy frontwoman."

IAN MacKAYE: From my point of view, it wasn't hair metal bands; it was *society* that was having a problem with women. I mean, hair metal bands were an extreme example of it. But that's what you come to expect from bozos—they're going to be clowns. I was more shocked, frankly, by the behavior of some of the so-called "punk bands." Just *appalled* by some of the shit that I saw people doing at that time in terms of how they treated women. It was disgusting to me. I was like, "I thought that's what we *weren't* doing?"

But also, I was a kid growing up, and early punk, all the boys and girls in D.C. who were slowly becoming men and women, were trying to figure out what we were and how things worked. So, we were going through that process. And certainly, there was immaturity going on, and also we were opening our minds to looking at the world differently.

So, by '83 or '84, we started to really think about the larger world—society—it wasn't just about our tight clique. And women who were in our scene, they had a lot on their mind. And they were teaching us a fuck of a lot. There was a lot of dialogue going on. They weren't scolding us, necessarily—they were talking about their experiences in a society where women are being treated terribly. That women are scared of being killed for being women—that's a reality. We had friends who were attacked in the street and friends who had been raped. It was so upsetting, but it was such a difficult subject to write about. But to me, that's exactly what punk is supposed to do: It's supposed to tackle these difficult things.

So, I do think that the early punk scene, coming out of that, we were given the tools to address things the way we did. And I'd like to think that it also exploded the form—the lockdown that the rock scene had been under before—to allow anybody to become part of it. The increasing number of women who are playing music and playing different instruments, that seemed to me to be a logical result of the foundational destruction the punk scene was doing. Just breaking it open. At least creating a different world where different ideas can be presented.

SPEECH: For me, it's probably one of the main things we wanted to accomplish as a group: Lift up women in the music and also in the actual group—we had women and men coexisting in the same group. Which, in hip-hop, hadn't happened before us, except for a group called Funky 4 + 1. So, it was quite a rare thing to happen in hip-hop. And then a lot of our song lyrics—whether it's "Mama's Always on Stage," "Natural," or "Dawn of the Dreads"—followed the same suit of just lifting up women and their power.

For me, it was a no-brainer because I had some of the most influential people in my life be women—my mother, who was a poster child for strong and resilient, but beautiful and feminine and just incredible in all these ways. And my grandmother was one of the most pivotal people in my entire life. So, for me, it made sense to tell the truth about the amazing experiences that probably most people have had with women in their life.

MIKI BERENYI: In terms of women . . . America is *so* different to Britain. People think we're really similar because we speak the same language, but it's very, very different. I think when I went on tour in America, women were maybe more comfortable with their sexuality. Britain in the '90s . . . it was before Britpop. Alternative music and independent music was quite anti-establishment. So, even if you look at punk rock, you've got Siouxsie Sioux onstage with no top on, or you've got the Slits—there's a sexual kind of side to that. But it is so *not* sexy in a way that is "mainstream friendly." It's incredibly aggressive and disruptive and designed to be anti-establishment.

And I think the music that I came up in—whether that's My Bloody Valentine or Slowdive—was very "anti-star." Bilinda [Butcher] from the Valentines, all the indie boys are kind of wetting themselves over how lovely she is. But she's not on that stage trying to be some sort of "sexy queen." I think that shoegaze scene we came up with, you're not going to pretend you're not a woman, but you were aware of the traps that were being laid for you and you rejected them.

Once you get in the mainstream, all of those things get blunted and either you're encouraged to chip away a little bit or play the game a bit more. It's hard to withstand that, because if you don't go along with it to some extent, then you're deemed as "difficult" and they won't work with you, either. And at the end of the day, we all have to make a living.

Dolores O'Riordan with the Cranberries, August 3, 1995. "She stood up for her rights and her right to be viewed as another artist rather than a 'sexy frontwoman.'"—Fergal Lawler *John Atashian/Alamy*

I never got asked to get my clothes off or anything. But it's a very weird thing to have what you are become marketable. It's like, playing on what is an inborn quality feels quite strange—rather than the music. Like, the music you make, great; but I think women have always been marketed in that way. Where it's like, "Alright, you're Kate Bush. Let's push the kind of 'kooky angle,'" even though the music is quite serious. Whatever you think of each of these musicians, it's this public persona that's pushed—that I think is quite lazy. It's sort of fetishized. It's almost impossible to escape that, personally, as a woman. And I'm sure it's the same if you're black or gay, or whatever thing—someone at some record company is going to think, "This is a great way to market it."

TANYA DONELLY: I felt whatever pressure there was to present yourself a certain way, I also felt very strongly that the pushback was accepted. And maybe because I was coming from "underground indie world"—they didn't really know quite how to market us or what to do with us or what boxes or packages to put us in. Which gave us the freedom to say, "Nah, I'm not going to wear that" and "No, I'm not going to be in this uncomfortable position that you want to put me in." Also at that time, there was an increasing amount of women on the industry side. So, every single public relations A&R person—with the exception of a couple—have been female and strongly on the side of the female voice.

LORI BARBERO: We started in '87, so it was the '80s . . . we were the ones that were the all-female band that wrote our own songs instead of covers. A lot of those bands did cover songs or had the guys play the music and they just sang in front—the frontwomen. So, we didn't care—we didn't care if our hair was curled and we weren't wearing pretty dresses or makeup. It was kind of like, "Well, I guess my jeans are torn . . . and so are my tights. We don't care."

It's kind of that thing where we never discussed, "Oh, are we going to change what we're going to wear? What we're going to look like?" When we signed to Warner Bros., we made sure our lawyer had in the contract that "You don't get to tell us how we're supposed to look or what we're supposed to do. We get to do whatever we want." Because it was kind of weird—these women that were like, "What you see is what you get. Like us or leave us—I don't care."

I guess people found Kat's lyrics—and I wrote some songs, too, and sang them—really offensive, because people weren't supposed to sing those words or talk about that stuff. But I think we were like, "Things need to change. I'm sick of the breathy singing and, 'We're so fragile.' We're *not* fragile—we're going to tell it as it is." But some people found it cathartic, and we were full-frontal-assault music.

JOHNETTE NAPOLITANO: I'm feminine enough, and I love being a female—make no mistake—but I felt a certain segment of the riot grrrl thing was overcompensating to me.

JENNIFER HERREMA: And then it became the riot grrrl thing. And that to this day rubs me the wrong way. I felt they were being regressive and just finding a new platform in which to showcase their femaleness.

JOHNETTE NAPOLITANO: When we started touring, I had the pressure of, "Hire a woman." Whenever I've hired a woman just because she's a woman, it has always bitten me in the ass. So, I don't buy into that. Whoever does the gig, does the gig—whether it's male or female. And I thought a lot of women were overcompensating with that—having to be too tough and having no vulnerability and coming off too hard and just too much. Y'know, the girls in Heart were very feminine, but they played and sang their asses off. There's nothing wrong with being a woman and maintaining your femininity. But there was definitely that pressure to do "the sexy thing."

JENNIFER HERREMA: The whole riot grrrl thing, they made it very obvious: "We're females, and we aren't wearing any clothes." Which is also fine—but it was counter to their thesis, as it were.

IAN MacKAYE: Riot grrrl was really exciting, interesting, and made a lot of sense. But this was all part and parcel of questioning everything in society. There was a lot of discussion of what people spent their money on, what people ate, race issues, homophobia, the political stuff—everything was up for a discussion. And when the discussion came to the role of women in the music scene, it was clearly out of balance. I don't think it was simply a matter of the boys in the scene not letting the girls get on stage, it also had a lot to do with the tendency that mainstream society has to discourage girls from participating in just about anything. At some point, I think a lot of us in the DC scene would have recognized it as a rule that society had imposed, and we would have thought it was fucked-up, and said..."Let's break it."

JENNIFER HERREMA: The emphasis was not on your wardrobe and your stage production. It was on the originality of the playing and the lyrics. As far as females go, at the time, we knew the people we knew—Sonic Youth, Live Skull, White Zombie, Pussy Galore. There were females in all of those bands. Sylvia Juncosa was a huge inspiration on me. I remember seeing her at CBGB's—I didn't know if she was a male or female—and just watching her *shred*.

KRISTIN HERSH: My heroines were women like Exene Cervenka and Lynda Barry—hardworking, funny, smart humans. I see women as people, and I ignore the ones trying to knock each other down to objectify themselves no matter what decade it is.

FRED ARMISEN: You can find examples of people with a message going back to Joan Baez. So, I don't know that one decade had a message that was any more important than the other. And in a way, what is a message? Does that mean lyrics? Because in a way, the Supremes are a message—that's like a *revolutionary* message. I don't think it changes by decade or genre.

WAS A GOO GOO DOLL GAGA OVER AN MTV VJ?

Kennedy recalls the origins of the hit single "Name."

I was a huge Goo Goo Dolls fan. And when they came to the MTV studio, Johnny Rzeznik had seen my show; and he had seen me give bands a hard time—screwing around with them. So, he was worried that I was going to make fun of them. And I didn't. I was like, "I love you guys so much." And he was like, "I love *you* so much!" And then we hung out a few times—but he was married. So, one night, we went out to dinner, and we were hanging out at my apartment . . . and he kissed me. And I was like, "We can't do this." And he was like, "Okay. Then just put your head on my lap, lay here, and let's watch TV." And that's where the lyric, "You can hide beside me maybe for a while," came from. And then he thanked me on the album as "Lisa Montgomery"—which, I thought that was really funny.

I didn't talk to him for a while after that, and then I saw them I think at CMJ in New York, and he handed me a tape of that album, *A Boy Named Goo*. I heard that song, and I knew *exactly* what it was about. I knew with every fiber of my being that it was about that moment. So, I called him and I was like, "Hey, what's up with that song?" And he's like, "What do you mean?" And I'm like, "Come on, man." He's like, "Yes. *It is about you.*" There are some very personal lines in there, and I knew exactly what he was saying. And some of them weren't very sweet, and they came from some of the conversations we had. And then I interviewed him for my book [2013's *The Kennedy Chronicles: The Golden Age of MTV Through Rose-Colored Glasses*], and I was like, "You have to go on record and say that you wrote that about me." And he's like, "I did. That's the only song I've ever written about just a moment in time."

WHAT DID BELLY, *SEINFELD*, AND *THE WIZARD OF OZ* HAVE IN COMMON?

Tanya Donelly explains three degrees of separation between Belly and . . . *Seinfeld*.

The photo session [when Belly appeared on the cover of the April 20, 1995, issue of *Rolling Stone*], it's one of those things we might have handled differently now—with the luxury of time and experience behind us. Mark Seliger did the shoot—and he's an amazing photographer. He wanted it to be a *Wizard of Oz*–themed photo shoot—that I would be Dorothy and the other three would pick whatever "cohorts" they wanted to be. I think we came back and said, "If we can do a 'dark version' of that, then maybe we would talk about that." That didn't work. We didn't want to get dressed up. We just wanted to show up and "Take our photo, please." But that was not the vibe. He's a pro . . . and we were not. [*Laughs*] I do like that cover, and I'm happy with it. But then, a while later [the May 28, 1998, issue, to be exact], the cast of *Seinfeld* was on the cover of *Rolling Stone* as the *Wizard of Oz*! He found the people to dive into that . . .

POE: There was a character that I wrote into short stories in high school called "Angry Johnny." He was like an archetype of the angry guy that lived inside every guy. I wrote a lot of stories about him. Years later, when I was signed to Atlantic and started to make the album [1995's *Hello*], I had the chorus running through my head, "Johnny, Angry Johnny, this is Jezebel in Hell." It was still pretty early in the game when it came to the empowerment of women.

The first women allowed into my college graduated only a decade before I attended. There were not a lot of examples of swag for women back then—all of the women in my life would apologize for anything they did well. Like, my mom would ace my dad on a public court playing tennis—and she'd apologize. But then I was getting this education that was telling me I could go off and do anything . . . but I didn't have the attitude to go with it. There was this attitude of, "I'm sorry for everything."

Women in my generation had to invent that attitude—invent a character to figure out, "How do I advocate for myself and feel good about it? How do I ask for equal pay?" I don't like politicizing things, but you didn't even know how—you'd be like, "I'm so sorry. I'll do everything for free." So, who is this part of me that's emerging that can advocate and say what I want on every level—sexually, at work, in life? Can I actually rise to the level of expressing all of that desire? And not apologize?

I remember I had this image in my head of racing a boyfriend on a motorcycle and being able to say, "I'm going to kill you"—like, "I'm going to win." And that's okay. And then it's an even bigger power grab if you're also not required to ditch your feminine wiles. So, you have all this sexual power as a young woman, and you now have an education and this power in the workplace. "Angry Johnny" was the ultimate female power grab. Literally, I can be sexy and completely fuck with your head, and I can beat you at this race. And, I can also profoundly care about you. Because at the very end, it says, "I want to kill you, every part of you that doesn't feel okay." Every part of you that isn't okay with me being a complete person, that's afraid of my power.

KENNEDY: In terms of being a VJ . . . Judy McGrath, who was the president of MTV at the time, told me, "Now, you've given other women who come after you on MTV a way to be completely themselves. Because no one has ever quite looked like you on MTV." And that was true—they were pretty much all hot chicks. It's like, I had had wild hair, blue lipstick, and was having a great time—and that's what the women in alternative music were doing. They were doing everything on *their* terms—they had been working as hard as the boys for so long, and they finally had this incredibly perfect storm. This moment where all the elements—artistic, cultural, and political—came together, and they really defined themselves in a beautiful time.

My heroines were women like Exene Cervenka and Lynda Barry—hardworking, funny, smart humans. I see women as people, and I ignore the ones trying to knock each other down to objectify themselves no matter what decade it is.

KRISTIN HERSH

TRACY BONHAM: MTV, we saw Madonna. And there were more alternative bands like Siouxsie and the Banshees. I feel like the creativity that they could express visually was pretty amazing, and they were free to express themselves in ways that bands like Heart maybe was different—maybe a little more mainstream. But when the '90s came along, I don't think it changed where the pressure to look a certain way had gone away. I think for women, it maybe will always be the case—that there's this pressure to look a certain way.

Also in the '90s, we saw things like Britney Spears and all of that crap—there's a lot of the industry trying to categorize and put women in boxes. So, it was like, "Here's the scruffy alternative chick, here's the angry young woman . . . and here's the Britney Spears/sexpot kind of thing." I feel as though they were trying to fit *me* into a box. And you only had a certain amount of women who could fit in that box, too.

So, when I came along, I had started right as Alanis Morissette was breaking. And I was *constantly* compared to Alanis. I didn't like being compared to her musically. But I feel as though I was constantly battling the way that I was perceived—it was very limiting. And I will say later in the '90s when things were changing drastically, the pendulum started swinging back to, "You've got to look sexy"—maybe because also, my label changed. I was lost in the shuffle when all of a sudden, I'm doing Island/Def Jam. And the pressure to look a certain way was really strong. Really "sexy"—or nothing.

JENNIFER HERREMA: There's always some angle to play. And females play those angles just as much as anybody else. I feel like everything is the same. And it's not bad, it's not good—*it just is*.

TANYA DONELLY: We all did things where we were like, "*Ah, shit . . .* " But *we* did it. I made every decision in every moment—whether or not I can stand by that comfortably now.

POE: It felt as though it was about the music, the songwriting, and the creative solutions. The identity issues were not taking mainstage—the *art* was. So, even though you may be working through a power struggle with your identity as a woman—like I discussed with "Angry Johnny"—you were finding those solutions by finishing that song.

Interestingly enough, I didn't play Lilith Fair because I thought it was sexist. I was like, "Be the women that produce the festival and win at that." Be great producers. But don't turn around and say, "Men can't be in our show." Be the tastemakers who choose the music. *That's* where you're going to find your power.

LORI BARBERO: We were all friends back then because all of us women pretty much stuck together a lot. We all empowered each other.

11 CATCHPHRASES AND BUZZWORDS

"I'm proud of being part of Generation X"

It seems like what is now known as "alternative rock" first went by two other names: "college rock" and "indie rock."

LOU BARLOW: The first time I ever heard any reference to indie rock was in the English music tabloids—*NME*, *Sounds*, *Melody Maker*. They had an "indie list." In the '80s, they made the distinction between labels that were independent and major labels.

PAGE HAMILTON: What back then we called "indie rock"—it wasn't mainstream. Meaning, it wasn't the main stuff on pop radio at the time.

FRED ARMISEN: Indie rock sort of covers a lot of other genres. We [Trenchmouth] were on an independent label, so sure. I think we considered ourselves more along the lines of Dischord bands and post-punk and Gang of Four. Or bands like Bow Wow Wow. But who knows—there was something we were trying to achieve. It's fine with me whatever anyone wanted to call it.

MIKE JOHNSON: There was the "college rock" scene. R.E.M. was the big thing there for a while. And they actually seemed underground. And the SST scene was more popular than people maybe remember it—like as far as hipster musicians like me, or my friends.

Tanya Donelly with Gail Greenwood and Belly in England, 1993. "I think 'college rock' is 100 percent accurate—the most accurate description of what I was a part of in the '80s and early '90s."—Tanya Donelly *Martyn Goodacre/Hulton Archive/Getty Images*

MATT SWEENEY: People kind of forget that college rock was "a thing." That was described more in the late '80s. A station like WFMU—that's where I first heard Can; that's where I first heard hardcore. And WFMU was a nonprofit thing. And the biggest music festival was called *CMJ—College Music Journal*, for fuck's sake. Essentially, South by Southwest started as an alternative to *CMJ* because *CMJ* was so commercial.

MATT PINFIELD: College rock radio was *absolutely* important at that time. Because in the late '80s and early '90s—before Nirvana exploded—that was the way that you found out about music, besides *120 Minutes* when Dave Kendall was on. I came up in college radio and started in the early '80s. At that point and up until the early '90s, there were probably about thirteen or fourteen commercial alternative radio stations. I continued to do a show on college radio [Rutgers University's WRSU]—literally until I became music director at WHTG. I also spun in the alternative nightclubs. And I'm not going to say that college radio isn't still important, but it was *essential* for the alternative music scene back then.

CRIS KIRKWOOD: We got played some—some places, sometimes. But not very much. We were not that good of a band, we're singing about really horrible things, and our main intention is, first, to make ourselves feel bad, and then, everybody else.

TANYA DONELLY: I think "college rock" is 100 percent accurate—the most accurate description of what I was a part of in the '80s and early '90s. Because that was the network at the time, that was the internet—college radio. And the *CMJ* showcase every year was kind of the culmination of that network. But it was a time when college radio stations were extremely involved in the local venues and clubs. And that network was really like a "Ma Bell" kind of situation. You would get into a city or a town, and everyone would be ready because they had already been in communication with the last town you came from on tour.

Now, we take a look at two phrases that seemed to appear in just about every article or news story about alt-rock in the '90s describing young people at the time: "Generation X" and "slacker."

MIKE WATT: It's trippy, especially when people are trying to talk about it—they want to make it like Generation X and Y and Z. They make things all convenient like in the chain stores with records. In the old days of the movement, [Minutemen would] be in the import section. Yeah, *imported from Lawndale!* [*Laughs*]

EVAN DANDO: I really liked "Generation X" . . . but it was Billy Idol's band!

MATT SWEENEY: "Generation X" was just a marketing term, because they were like, "What do we call these people that aren't buying heavy metal records anymore?" There's always a name for Millennials or whatever. It's all marketing; it's all money. "Who's buying what between the ages of eighteen to twenty-five?" At the time, it was cringey when people would say "Gen X." There's kind of two things: people trying to make money off of music, and then there are these musicians or people in bands. And the meeting points are weird.

KENNEDY: That was from Douglas Coupland [who penned the book *Generation X: Tales for an Accelerated Culture* in 1991]. But Gen X were like a generation that kind of had PTSD [post-traumatic stress disorder] from the Cold War era—and the idea of nuclear annihilation at any time. So, it kind of gave way to this apathy and this apathetic individualism.

But I still think that Gen X is the greatest generation, because we are bookended by two of the most selfish generations that have ever existed [Baby Boomers and Millennials]. And we really just wanted to be left alone to do our own thing and live interesting lives . . . and work hard. Baby Boomers were the "me generation"—they were all about themselves. Bill Clinton is a prototypical Baby Boomer: annoying, narcissistic. And then you have Millennials and even Gen Z, and they're all about self-care, feelings, and "I don't want to work too hard."

It's funny, because Gen X moms are now the premium in the workplace because their kids are older, they want to work their asses off, they don't want to retire, and they're not going to take a bunch of days off. A lot of headhunters are looking for Gen X moms now.

FRED ARMISEN: I'm proud of being part of Generation X.

LOU BARLOW: I thought "slacker" was pretty accurate for us. And certainly for the people that I knew that were involved. I wouldn't say that it necessarily represents *me*, because I want to create and produce as much as I can and make as much "contact" as I can. My reference is more hardcore, which was *not* slacker. But I do think that the slacker thing was a vibe at that time—you don't want to seem like you're trying too hard. You want to come off like everything is effortless. And certainly, J [Mascis] did that. Even the early shoegazer stuff like Jesus and Mary Chain, that was a huge influence on us—and they looked like they didn't give a fuck.

To me, that slacker thing was more residue from punk rock. It was, "*We don't care*"—a less angry Johnny Rotten, where the anger has receded into apathy. To me, it's definitely an accurate representation of how the bands performed. Pussy Galore, not so much Sonic Youth, but there was definitely a feeling of, "You get what you get. *This is it.*" And the Meat Puppets, they were putting out sloppy records, which we loved. And the Replacements, they were *the ultimate* slackers—they're playing these absolutely stellar pop songs, but Paul Westerberg could barely remember the lyrics, and they were notorious for these really loose shows.

MARY TIMONY: I think the indie rock aesthetic was this sort of slacker mentality. Like, people would play with broken gear and not mind not practicing. Their emphasis was on being authentic rather than being a perfect musician. Raw voices were appreciated more—people who didn't know how to sing. There was an amateurism thing that was valued. And messiness and not being a pro.

Superchunk has that song "Slack Motherfucker," which I think of as the anthem of that generation. But a band like Polvo really sums that up to me, because they, on one hand, have this super-genius songwriting and chordal structure; but then they're pretty slack about how to record and practice. It gets a little obscured—the messiness of not being a perfect musician and practicing a ton.

TRACY BONHAM: It was relevant in that a lot of bands wanted to be perceived as not selling out. So, they're going to look like they just got out of bed and they're still hungover—and that was perceived as "cool." They didn't want to seem as though they were trying too hard. I think probably Kurt got a little mixed up in that world—too much pressure to be a certain thing. When Beck came out with "Loser," I remember, before I really understood Beck, I was judgmental on that. It was like the slacker, the loser, and it seemed contrived. Of course, they *all* wanted success—so I felt like it was a mask.

EVAN DANDO: Slacker didn't mean that they weren't busy and working hard, but maybe they were doing bongs all day and taking speed and drawing and writing and sometimes getting crazy about exercise—not *planned* exercise.

Evan Dando with the Lemonheads at the Reading Festival in England, August 22, 1997. "It was pretty funny being called a slacker—I'm like the last one up, I'm the first one up, and I'm always doing shit. It's a pose, and you go along with it."—Evan Dando *Rob Watkins/Alamy*

Fred Schneider with the B-52s at Chastain Park Amphitheatre in Atlanta, Georgia, August 11, 2001. "It was an alternative to a lot of boring crap."—Fred Schneider *MediaPunch/Alamy*

I think it was more like being an adventurer—you didn't go to work every day, you didn't cut your hair short, you didn't wear a uniform. So, it might have looked like you were relaxing. But you might not have been. I certainly wasn't—I've always had terrible problems with relaxation. It was pretty funny being called a slacker—I'm like the last one up, I'm the first one up, and I'm always doing shit. It's a pose, and you go along with it.

Oh sure, yeah, yeah, yeah! [In response to the observation that his description of a "slacker" sounds similar to the character "The Dude" from *The Big Lebowski*] It's almost quasi-Buddhist if you go that way with it. You have an inner peace. Like, the bowling is a Buddhism analogy in a way—something to concentrate on. It's almost like he's a monk or something. I think it's more of a refusal to see what you're doing and not worry if it might look like you're not doing much. It's something you have to do to block shit out.

Finally, what did some of the people interviewed for this book think of the most commonly used term to describe the music they specialized in: "alternative"?

JASON PETTIGREW: It seemed that "college rock" phased out and everything was "alternative"—probably in the late '80s.

FRED SCHNEIDER: It *was* an alternative—it was an alternative to a lot of boring crap. I found a list of the Abrams stations, and they told the DJs what to play. And it started out like, "If you play the Eagles, Linda Ronstadt, and Billy Joel, you appeal to people that drive Mercedes." And it went down, and at the bottom, it said, "If you play the B-52s, Talking Heads, and Devo, you appeal to people who borrow their friend's car." [*Laughs*] So, it was sort of a badge to be "alternative."

ANGELO MOORE: The record label's excuse was always, "We don't know what to do with you because you're playing too much different shit." And then when the term "alternative" came into the picture, then they had a category to fit us in.

IAN MacKAYE: I appreciate the dictionary version of alternative—being alternative is something that is not mainstream. I wasn't as much of a fan of the word "alternative" as a marketing device. That is obviously sort of a paradox, because the people who were marketing it were major labels for the most part. Y'know, "alternative rock"—it was another card in a racking display. Like most of those things, it loses meaning. It doesn't really have *any* meaning. The same is true for rock or jazz or punk or hip-hop or any of the other genres—at some point, there may well have been an articulated point of term and [it] may have remained relevant on a regional level. But at some point, it doesn't have any real definition.

JASON PETTIGREW: I know that Mike Shea did not name his magazine *Alternative Press* because it was going to be a buzzword. He was rebelling against the music press structure of Cleveland—where your daily newspaper is not going to care about it unless it's got some "hit value" to it. Nobody was going to cover the punk rock bands he loved, the hardcore bands he loved, the British imports or the dance music he was listening to. So, this was an alternative to all the news outlets in Cleveland or MTV or *Rolling Stone* that would not write about the music that he wanted to hear about. And he felt that there were a lot of people.

MIKE WATT: I was suspicious of that word. Because number one, what is the alternative to music? Silence? And number two, look at it now—these motherfucking right-wing assholes use "alt-right." That's a dangerous term. I didn't know that it was going to get abused like that.

KRISTIN HERSH: Indie, meaning "independent," was valid, as we weren't playing the corporate game. "College" meant college radio, which was also valid because they weren't told what to play. "Alternative" we considered an insult . . . alternative to what? Can't rock change? All the other genres do. Just more goofiness to laugh at really. We didn't take it personally.

JOHNETTE NAPOLITANO: I walked into a music store, and "alternative" had more records than any other bin. Right away, that cancels out the entire concept of "alternative." It may have started out as something, but it quickly became just another label to sell records.

ART ALEXAKIS: I don't really know what's "alternative" about us. We're a rock 'n' roll band . . . a *guitar* rock 'n' roll band. When you talk about Cake and some of the other bands that were really inventive, I guess they can be considered alternative. But I was happy that guitars were on the radio again.

SPEECH: I never liked it. And it's because, while our music was an alternative to some aspects of hip-hop that were existing, to make a new genre out of it, I always felt like it placed us on an island in a sense—of our own. And that was never our intention. We knew that we were making music that expanded the boundaries of hip-hop, definitely. But we also didn't intend to not be included in the hip-hop legacy that existed already—we wanted to expand it and be known as trendsetters within it.

KENNEDY: It has changed and morphed over time, and whenever something like that becomes co-opted, you have to come up with new words. But at the time, you knew *exactly* what it meant. And before Nirvana and the grunge explosion . . . I think I hate the word "grunge" more than I hate the word "alternative." Because it was an alternative to popular music. And for bands, they had to come up with alternative ways to market their shows, and they didn't get any sort of mainstream push. [*Adopts old person voice*] "*It was the era before the internet.*" You knew what you were talking about when you used that term. But like everything else, every generation comes up with their own words—like they should.

ANGELO MOORE: I'm glad they actually made up a label to describe alternative, rather than saying, "Fishbone plays ska, reggae, funk, jazz, punk." *We're just alternative.*

Jeff Buckley at the Fleece and Firkin in Bristol, England, January 15, 1995. "I knew Jeff Buckley personally, and he was hauntingly beautiful the way he sang." —Corey Glover *Rob Watkins/Alamy*

12 SINGERS

"The soulfulness was the way they put the feeling across"

Alt-rock in the '90s gave us an impressive number of original and instantly identifiable singers—perhaps more so than any other rock era past or present. Who were the top vocalists, and what made them so special?

MATT JOHNSON: You couldn't fake it back in those days [as a singer]. There were no in-ear monitors. There really was no Melodyne; there was no Auto-Tune. On the live side, you had monitors that, if you turned them up really hot, they're going to feedback. So, you had to sing out more. And I think singers had to go through a very difficult phase of development—where they had to learn how to open up their voice sufficiently to where they could sing with limited and lower-tech monitor gear. And also, the bands were louder.

You had less of the studio conditions that you would associate with being in a recording studio on a stage. Now when you go see a band with in-ears, there may not be any speakers onstage, and everybody has their own independent monitor mixes. And you can possibly get away with having a singer get up and almost *whisper* into the microphone—and sound great, even.

The barrier to entry for a singer thirty years ago was, "Well, for starters, you're going to have to be able to be heard over a loud band," and bad technology by today's standards. That's a huge part of it to me. And I think that eliminated a lot of people—who, these days, would no longer be eliminated from the possible cast of characters that are going to be branded as singers. It's not that I think singers have necessarily gotten worse, but I think more and more unlikely singers are making it into the professional domain of "singer."

CHRIS HASKETT: Most rock singers are not great "singers" in a classic sense. That doesn't mean they're not great. I just mean that, more often than not, they're working with a small palette of tonal color and timbral/dynamic options and making the most of it. That's part of what makes them great and unique. Conversely, it's really uncommon for people that have really rich singing voices to be convincing rock singers.

KEVIN MARTIN: They were looking for real, raw talent. Chris Cornell was incredibly good looking, but [other singers of the era were] not the best-looking guys. Weird, androgynous—the "David Bowie element" of things that were allowed in the late '60s/early '70s were being allowed again. There were so many guys hiding in the shadows that had these great voices that never would have had an opportunity in the '80s to be successful.

It was when that Nirvana train peaked over that hill and started to come down, it opened the world up to great talent—not just great singers. There are so many great bands that came out of the '90s. One of my favorites is the Smashing Pumpkins, and Billy Corgan is one of the most original "nasally" singers ever—that has written some of the greatest songs of all time.

COREY GLOVER: This is all about expression and how people chose to express themselves. I think Eddie Vedder is in that pantheon—they're really compelling storytellers. *All of them.* Chris Cornell was a very compelling storyteller. It wasn't their ability to sing but what they said and how it resonated with people. "Jeremy" was *a story*—with a beginning, middle, and end. As nutty as "Spoonman" is as a song, you got it because Chris gave you the story—and you understood the story.

GERALD CASALE: Chris Cornell almost hearkened back . . . he was like a guy who was time traveling. He could have almost been a blues guy if he wanted to. I would have loved to hear him do hardcore rural blues—but in his style. He had an amazing voice. Powerful. And controlled. He could croon if he wanted to croon.

JOHNNY TEMPLE: Perry Farrell's singing style is *so* unhinged and artful.

LORI BARBERO: There's great frontpeople, but Mike Patton apparently has the widest range of singing—pitch perfect.

MATT PINFIELD: Mike Patton obviously was not comfortable with the overnight admiration and success of "Epic." But his ability to transform into different styles—and truly alternative forms of expression with Mr. Bungle and Peeping Tom, just to name two—showed his talent and range. Covering the Commodores' "Easy" and making it cool for a judgmental alternative audience . . . only *he* could have gotten away with at that time.

TRACY BONHAM: Björk could really go for these notes in such a way that was edgy but not harsh. I really loved that. She could also sing beautifully and quietly and expressive—even veer into this almost jazz . . . I don't even know what to call it. I know a lot of singers right after her tried to emulate her sound. It was jazzy; it was punk in its energy. I didn't care about whether it was proper technique at all. It was more the expressiveness of it. It was compelling.

MATT PINFIELD: Tori Amos was unique as a singer and had a beautiful delivery. It was so passionate and so honest. She addressed a lot of things that weren't always as pretty as other singers—she had a deeper soul and looked into things that maybe weren't as comfortable. There was a lot of pain involved in a lot of those songs. But also beauty.

VINNIE DOMBROSKI: *Nothing* sounded like Layne Staley back in the "rock days"—Peter Wolf, Brian Johnson. Who sounded like Eddie Vedder back in the '80s? Really nobody. I think what was a great singer was redefined. Would Kurt Cobain have been chosen as the singer of a band in 1980? You were looking for the "castrati dudes." And that was what people thought of as a "great singer."

Any one of us can sit down and sing an Alice in Chains song. But not like *that*. That's coming from a whole different planet, man. It's like Mark Lanegan—Lanegan wouldn't have been that guy in the '80s that was "I need you for a band." But there's something *so* special about that voice. You can't imitate it. I'm happy that we consider these people and these voices great singers today, because they deserve it.

JOHN AGNELLO: Mark Lanegan was a special singer. In my career for forty years, he is one of my favorite singers I've had the pleasure to record. He had many sides and styles to his delivery. He could sing soft songs of the soul or torch-song style. He could belt a rocker like few others. And sometimes, he could do both in the same song—as he did in the Screaming Trees classic "Dollar Bill." He could give you chills while delivering his solo classic "House a Home." His choice of melodies and wonderful lyrics added to the emotive quality. He was literally one in a million. Mark sang like his personality—really strong at times, really delicate and vulnerable at times. Because Mark as a person, that's how he was—he'd either be in your face and beat the shit out of you or he could be vulnerable.

J Mascis is himself—he's very wistful. If you talk to him, he's like [*talks in soft-spoken voice*], "*Well . . . I don't know.* " And his vocalizations are an extension of that. He's not really pushing more, as he's questioning. It is his character, though. If you go through technical singers, yes, he's not the greatest singer ever. But he's got a real *style*. When you hear Dinosaur Jr., you know he's singing. But he also has real character. Even the beginning of "Start Choppin'"—he's putting it out there. He is fun in a way because of the way he sings.

When a Dinosaur Jr. song comes on, you know it's J Mascis. Not many other people sound like that. If you're listening to a Dinosaur Jr. song, imagine the singer having a question mark over his head! That's J's style—he's not pushy; he's not in your face. He gets that shit out in his guitar playing—he doesn't get that shit out in his vocals. And that's the difference between him and Mark. Mark didn't play much guitar, so he had to really express himself with the vocal. J does it with the Jazzmaster.

CHRIS HASKETT: Corey Glover is one of the exceedingly rare frontmen that has an enormous tonal, dynamic, and timbral range, and still totally brings it home as a rock singer. People with *that* much power and control often sound like their technique is driving their aesthetic—whereas with Corey fronting Living Colour, there's not even a nanosecond that he's not coming from the heart. *Always.* Listen to the range he covers between the Middle Eastern opening and closing of "This Is the Life"—one of my fave songs, by the way—and the soaring, roaring soul cry of the end chorus. Or contrast the commanding force of "Never Satisfied" with the bittersweet gentleness of "Nothingness."

Corey Glover with Living Colour at the Paradiso in Amsterdam, Netherlands, February 15, 1993. "Corey Glover is one of the exceedingly rare frontmen that has an enormous tonal, dynamic, and timbral range, and still totally brings it home as a rock singer."—Chris Haskett *Frans Schellekens/Redferns/Getty Images*

KEVIN MARTIN: Shannon Hoon had an incredible voice. Again, *so* original. I can't think of anybody that sounds like him—even to this day. I remember I was working in Christopher Thorn's studio when he first moved to Seattle, and I helped him build his studio in his basement. And Shannon used to call and leave him voicemails on his answering machine with songs—and one ended up on the *Nico* record ["Letters from a Porcupine"]. Just hearing him sing through the phone, I was like, "Man, what is it like being in a band with him?" And Christopher's like, "He's fuckin' out of his mind . . . *but every night is amazing*." And what a brilliant lyricist Shannon was. "Vernie" and "Galaxie" and all of those songs on *Soup* are ten times what the first album is—it's a brilliant album.

MATT PINFIELD: The thing that made Scott Weiland so special as a singer and frontman was his vocal range, his undeniable swagger, and this chameleon-like personality onstage. Even when he was struggling with his personal demons and not 100 percent, he was still a better performer than most people who fronted bands in that era.

MIKE JOHNSON: From the first time I heard Kurt's voice, I thought, "This is a voice that should be on radio."

FAT MIKE: Kurt Cobain not only sang in pitch, but his emotion was incredible. *You felt it.* Kurt sang his heart.

EDDIE "KING" ROESER: I do have to say I was fortunate enough to see Nirvana play, and I think Kurt Cobain probably had the most engaging vocal thing. I mean, that guy *really* had something that he worked on—to make it really consistent. And he really knew what he was doing—without really trying too hard. That was one of the things where you didn't see a lot of people who had any sort of compelling vocal style. Anybody could play guitar or do a drumbeat. But to really have that voice *that pierces you to the core* . . . I mean, Chris Cornell, same thing. You didn't see guys like that. And they really deserved to have that stage.

COREY GLOVER: I knew Jeff Buckley personally, and he was hauntingly beautiful the way he sang. And I think Jeff had the potential to become so . . . I would have hoped that he would have gone beyond where he was at the time before he passed [on May 29, 1997, at the age of thirty].

CRAIG WEDREN: The minute Andy Wallace played us [Jeff Buckley's] "Mojo Pin," it was like, "Oh. *This is generational.*" We were fiercely competitive and into our own thing, but it didn't change the fact that when you hear beauty at *that* level, that combination of gifted technical, transcendent . . . I've known a lot of really great singers and great composers and musicians, and he was the best of all those things.

Like, I went to college with Anohni—an extraordinary singer and artist. Just beautiful—even when she was eighteen. She'd open up her mouth, and out would pour Nina Simone–level gorgeousness. I toured with Chris Cornell, and we were friends, and that "instrument" is . . . there are only a couple of those. But Jeff somehow transcended all of it—the era, the genre, the instrument, the humor, the intelligence, the sensuality, the musicality. It was a gift.

MATT JOHNSON: [Jeff Buckley's] use of vibrato to me—and his use of falsetto—I didn't know how to place it when I first heard it. It really took me by surprise. I think the time when his voice most strongly affected me was, we were playing a gig at [New York City club] the Fez, and I remember some part of a song we were in and some part of his voice—the way he used his voice—caused an effect in my body that I can only describe as your whole internal environment of your mind and your body and the way your whole being feels, it's almost like it got a shock of electricity through it. It moved like a wave throughout my whole body. And it was associated with the music that we were making at that time. I associate it with me having a very kinetic, physical, psychological, and emotional connection to music. A truly incredible feeling.

COREY GLOVER: The soulfulness was the way they put the feeling across. The way that they put the emotional aspect of the song into their performances. And that sort of resonated with people.

ROBERT DeLEO (Stone Temple Pilots bassist): I think people had a lot to say. And it was timing. Things were going a certain way, and there was a reaction. And sometimes when there's a reaction, something that is really explosive comes out of that; and I think it was the time for that to happen. There were a lot of very talented . . . and I hate to use the word "was." A lot of those people are gone, and it's a shame, but it was a great time for music. It really was.

"I'M A TOTAL POSTER BOY ASSHOLE"

Lemonhead Evan Dando wrestles with his fame.

All of a sudden, there were, like, *a thousand girls*; and they were all freaking out. It was quite a test for your restraints. But you do that for a while and you go, "Well, that's not the answer. It doesn't really work. A different girl every night, it's no fun." I mean, it's fun *for a little while*. We went over the top in this bullshit of me being handsome or whatever. It worked . . . and I got stung exactly in the cliché way—I'm a total poster boy asshole. I went along with it. I guess it was my "jujitsu move," like, "Okay. I use their power against me and go that way instead and roll over." I ended up in a trailer as a junkie for five years, but that was all part of the recovery, I guess. Because luckily, this girl Antonia came up to the Vineyard and saved my life—and brought me to Brazil.

But I cut my hair off just to piss people off. I did it after Kurt Cobain first tried to kill himself, on March 4 [1994, in Rome]—thanks, Kurt, on my birthday! I cut my hair because my friend used to say it's the best thing to do if you're in shiva—or potentially—you cut your hair off when someone dies. So, I did. And I was high. I was testing the loyalty of the fanbase. But I tried not to be precious—my whole career I tried not to be fussy. I totally understand with people seeing me as, "Oh, fuck . . . *that guy*." At that same time when something like *Die Evan Dando Die* [the title of a zine from 1994] comes out, my friends were all like, "You're doing *something* right."

13 GUITAR

"I never was in it for the gymnastics"

The role of guitar in '90s alt-rock was the polar opposite of its role in late-'80s mainstream rock. Suddenly, shredding on your pointy, high-priced instrument was usurped by bashing your secondhand/pawnshop guitar. Also, the importance of the almighty riff once again proved crucial.

DAVID PAJO: As a kid in the '80s, I practiced a ton, and I learned to shred pretty fast. It's crazy how fast I picked up guitar. I could do all the Yngwie Malmsteen stuff, and I'd figure out Van Halen records note for note. I still remember how to play most of those albums.

When [pre-Slint band] Maurice transitioned to Slint, I was losing interest in shredding and was getting more interested in people like Thurston Moore—who were putting drumsticks under their strings. Or Steve Albini—screaming into his pickup. Stuff that was not shredding but was super-cool approaches to guitar. It didn't follow any rules.

So, I started doing more stuff like that—getting into not playing the guitar normal but not shredding, either. I think at some point, I completely stopped shredding. I still have that attitude of, "I love to solo and do all the show-off stuff, but I like to do the anti-solos." Sometimes, doing the opposite of what you want to do is the best thing.

ROGERS STEVENS: I never was in it for the gymnastics. I couldn't get there anyway. I remember trying to do that in high school. You're learning to play, and here's [Van Halen's] "Eruption." Which is a masterpiece—it's got it all. I could *never* do that. I'd get kind of close on *some* things—that lickety-split playing.

J Mascis with Dinosaur Jr. at Cardiff University Terminal in Cardiff, Wales, February 26, 1993. "J was really unique because, to be brutally honest, I don't think anybody approached what J was doing with his pedals."—Lou Barlow
Rob Watkins/Alamy

Thurston Moore of Sonic Youth, 1991. "I was losing interest in shredding and was getting more interested in people like Thurston Moore—who were putting drumsticks under their strings."—David Pajo *Gary Malerba/Corbis Entertainment/Getty Images*

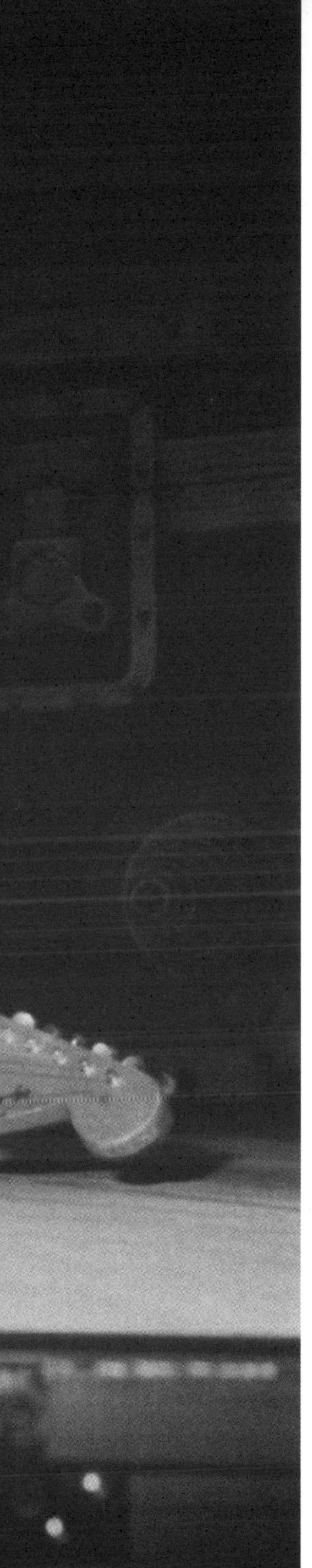

THE REVEREND HORTON HEAT: I'm kind of a shredder. It's not like I'm as great as Dimebag Darrell or Randy Rhoads—that's not my style. But I was one of those guitarists that did that wild guitar playing that a lot of the grunge bands didn't. When Kurt Cobain soloed on quite a few songs, it was like all he did was step on a boost pedal and start playing the same melody that he sang. Except his guitar may be an octave lower, or he might have added a few little things to it—a trill or hammer-on or hammer-off thing. But it was basically the melody . . . and that is *so* powerful.

There's a story about Chet Atkins producing somebody, but a guitar player was saying, "Gosh, I can't figure out what to do for a solo on this song." And Chet Atkins said, "Well, *you can always just play the melody*." It's powerful—it reinforces the melody in the listener's ear. It's heartfelt, it's good, and kind of throws the shredders aside and "Instead of showboating, I'm just going to really establish the importance of this melody."

PAGE HAMILTON: I've got a degree in classical guitar and jazz guitar at Oregon and then went to Manhattan School of Music and got my master's in jazz. So, I always had this weird kind of background. I had given up on rock music when the radio was playing Journey and Foreigner and that kind of thing.

When I played with Band of Susans with Robert Poss, he's like, "Look. I'm putting a Rat pedal in front of another Rat pedal and getting this distortion. And I can get the guitar to feedback and do this and that." He kind of got me going on feedback. And Robert was mathematical about how he put the Band of Susans stuff together—he had simplified harmonic stuff, but he would layer things.

I remember going in and recording *Strap It On*. And the song "Repetition," I was playing a solo. I'd go in and listen to it and go, "God. This sucks. I'm playing cheap pentatonic rock licks." That's not what our music was about. And [producer] Wharton [Tiers] said, "Stop thinking so much." So, I got the idea to put two distortion pedals together—like

Robert Poss had talked about. The guitar became this vibrating . . . I had to half wrestle it and half play it to keep the feedback under control and sculpt the sound. Or as I once said to David Bowie about my guitar playing, "I'm not really a guitar player. *I'm a shit sculpturer.*" He cracked up.

MARY TIMONY: The feeling that came from punk was, "You don't have to be showy. You don't really need to learn that stuff." I did go to this arts high school and practiced guitar a lot. And then I suddenly was like, "Ah, *fuck it*. I'm just going to play punk music." I think it was more about good songs mattered and you don't have to be a pro.

CHRIS HASKETT: You also get the absence or deliberate avoidance of a certain level and style of musicianship. So, in metal you get the opposite—you get these people that go off on this weird Yngwie tangent, where they all want to show a certain style of completely soulless virtuosity. Which comes out of an absolute misunderstanding of what Eddie Van Halen does. People grab just one component of that and then run with it. *It becomes a shtick.*

KRISTIN HERSH: Anything that pulls us away from jerking off in public is good, right? [*Laughs*] I prefer shame to showing off if somebody's gonna stand onstage trying to get people to look at them. Real songs are beautiful that way. They chew up the musician and spit them out in public.

PAUL LEARY: I always thought of myself as a hack. I started playing guitar at age five, and I took lessons all through high school and tried my best to be a good guitar player. And I'm not talented. I have no talent. So, I worked with what I had. I was always trying to make the worst guitar solo and the worst guitar part because I found it amusing. I think I read an interview with a guitar player in a band much bigger than ours; he said he liked my guitar playing because it "sounded like I was hanging upside down in a barn."

MIKI BERENYI: Alternative music, you can say that [Gang of Four's] Andy Gill was one of the greatest guitarists ever . . . even though he wasn't playing heavy metal solos. He wasn't trying to play as many notes as possible in one riff just to prove how proficient he was. It was about a sonic impact of this jarring, clanging, rhythmic noise that he would produce. And I think a lot of that punk rock thing was working with what you've got and moving the window to where, "*This* is proficient. *That* is boring and bland."

I remember with me and [Lush guitarist] Emma [Anderson]—even very early on—writing songs, and someone who actually did know about music and was well trained, going, "Yeah, but you can't do that. You can't play those two chords together." And I was like, "Well . . . *I can.* Because it sounds alright." It's sort of interesting, because if you're musically trained, it would jar on you to do that. And a lot of Emma's things, she would just put two fingers on two strings and you'd have to draw the boxes so we could tell each other how to play the song because we didn't even know the names of the chords—you're just making it up.

MARY TIMONY: It didn't sound like blues rock. The chord progressions . . . there would be a lot of weird notes in there. A lot of dissonant notes. People were trying to make up their own thing a little bit more.

PAGE HAMILTON: I was also determined to be the anti-songwriter. There was this whole movement of the kind of folk-rock thing, the singer-songwriter stuff. And I kind of liked it, but everybody in the biz was like, "He's a songwriter; she's a songwriter." I was like, "Fuck that. I'm going to do aggressive, motivic development. I'm going to come up with chords that nobody uses."

I always felt our role as musicians or writers is to create our own thing, because that's all my jazz heroes did. You hear John Coltrane, and in five seconds, you know it's John Coltrane. Charlie Parker, same thing. Sonny Rollins. Bill Evans playing piano. Art Blakey on the drums. How do you do that? You learn from your heroes, but you try to push forward and do something that represents *your* voice. And that's what I've always tried to do—have our own thing.

ROGERS STEVENS: I like guitar solos. I don't like *dumb* guitar solos. To me, the way that it works is you have that top-line lead vocal that's happening throughout the song. And then it pauses and something else picks it up. Now, if properly done, the guitar solo is a great option. You can also go with a saxophone . . . or you can go with any number of things. Hell, if you're Jethro Tull, *you'll do a flute*. I don't think about it nearly as much as I used to because it was the only thing I could play. Barely.

PAGE HAMILTON: There was this "anti–guitar solo" thing—and I never subscribed to that. *Ever.* I love guitar solos. Because a guitar solo should be another little musical journey. It's part of the song—it's not so I can show that I practiced harmonic minor scales. And that's the problem I have with a lot of the shredder metal stuff—it seems like they're bringing their practice room to the stage or to the recording. And that, to me, was never the point. You learn this stuff to develop your ears and try to come up with new chord voicings and chord changes and a different vocabulary.

MATT SWEENEY: I remember J Mascis—who was really supportive of Chavez—was like, "How come you guys don't have guitar solos?" Even though Chavez *does* have guitar solos, we were trying to make them more different, I guess. But also, in hardcore there weren't any guitar solos. And when punk happened, it was like, "There aren't too many guitar solos." I don't think that was anything new. In the case of our band, we definitely were not interested in doing a "Sweet Child O' Mine"–style guitar solo. Even though I fuckin' love that shit. And then for that matter, by the late '90s, I was playing in a band called Endless Boogie—which is obviously nothing *but* guitar solos! But then again, I'm sure I could find total exceptions to that. Dinosaur Jr.—that's all they are, are guitar solos.

JOHN FRUSCIANTE'S AUDITION FOR THE MEAT PUPPETS

Meat Puppets bassist Cris Kirkwood contemplates what might have been.

We were set to go on tour with some friends of ours who are getting bigger and bigger—the Chili Peppers. And we're going to go do our first-ever tour of Australia with those guys. We fly all the way to Australia, and unbeknownst to us, in Japan [where the Chili Peppers were playing beforehand], their guitar player quits. Which led to John in a "post–leaving the Chilis interview" talking about the only band he would think about playing with at that point was the Meat Puppets. We were signed at the time to a major label, and they saw that and said, "Do you think he's serious?" So, we asked John.

He came out on the train. Which speaks of dope—not wanting to check in [at the airport] with a pocketful of gak. We picked him up at the train station—he was barefoot with his guitar . . . *without a case*. He was pretty obviously fucked up. We jammed, and it was pretty trippy. From the jam, I remember offering to let him use my tuner, and he said, "No. *I'll bend it in.*" Which is pretty bitchin'. He hung out for a while, and it was sweet. He continued to struggle [with drugs]. Had we not been so good at *not* succeeding, we could have figured out how to have him in the band—and gone multiplatinum again and again and again!

JOHN AGNELLO: J Mascis had his Fender guitars, and he was the first guy I knew who used the Electro-Harmonix Big Muff. That was one of his main pedals. And still to this day, when I was up at his house a year ago, in his living room is the "Big Muff Museum," which is a huge china closet filled with Big Muffs!

LOU BARLOW: [The Big Muff pedal] was important to J. And also Mudhoney, because they used it in a title [1988's *Superfuzz Big Muff*]. J was really unique because, to be brutally honest, I don't think anybody approached what J was doing with his pedals. A lot of people followed suit, but it was like your "noise pedal"—to create the illusion of dynamics. The way J used it was super-dynamic, and I never saw anybody play on that level.

MATT SWEENEY: I think it was actually because it was called a "Big Muff" people talked about it. I think it was just fun to say, "Big Muff."

JOHN AGNELLO: When you go see J live, he's got the wall of Marshalls behind him. But at home and even in our studio, there wasn't a ton of amps. Sometimes, it was even a small amp—but overdriven. And the way he plays—his fingering. I've watched him play for *so* long . . . he is amazing at the way he just touches and fingers the guitar. We had a thing one point in the studio where he was walking around playing guitar all the time while we were working—with a little Marshall amp on his belt. He plays *all the time*. He's a master at playing guitar.

In the analog of the '90s, with *Where You Been* and *Without a Sound*, when it was time for J to do the solos, a lot of times if he was in the mood, I would just start him from the beginning of the song and he would shred the whole length. Even "Start Choppin'," he would shred from the beginning when the band kicked in, and then when it was time to comp four tracks of guitar and put in the best stuff, then we would work on the solo and not use any of the other stuff.

He'd always be doing a different thing. He never learns the solo—*he just goes*. It's very improvised, but also feeling-wise, it's all there. If you listen to any of his solos, it's emotion, it's cool—but he's atypical from most of all the other guitar players I've worked with in my life. It's kind of freaky in a way—like a "grunge shred guy."

PAGE HAMILTON: After my first song, I didn't play open chords for twenty years. I got into the tuning thing because it got into my head one night, the drop-D tuning for "Repetition."

CHRIS HASKETT: Well, obviously, drop-D marked a dramatic change in what guitars sounded like. It's a cool sound—until *everybody* is using it. Also, though I have no science to back this up, it feels like playing the D octave strings makes chords ring differently than when you play the octave with two fingers. Even in the higher registers, they sound different—to me, anyway. But, as with everything, it's what you *do* with the tuning that matters. I think in that Seattle scene, Kim Thayil did the most interesting things by far with alternate tunings—going far beyond just dropped D.

LEE RANALDO (Sonic Youth guitarist): Well, I was dabbling in [alternate tunings] since I started to learn how to play guitar. When I was still a teenager learning to play acoustic guitar, I had an older cousin who showed me one particular open tuning that a lot of people like Crosby, Stills, Nash & Young and Joni Mitchell were using in the '60s. So, I was playing a lot of stuff in open tuning early on.

Then we [Ranaldo and Thurston Moore] both got to New York, and I guess we were aware that people like the Velvet Underground experimented with strange tunings on guitars, you know, all high-E strings or whatever. But when we got to New York, there were people like Glenn Branca and Rhys Chatham that were doing their own version of open tunings—very specific art tunings. We immediately fell in with them as well.

So, in a sense, it was in the air; it was something that was going around. But it was reinforced on a couple of different levels. For me, from old '60s folky stuff and then late-'70s New York art practice tunings. So, we fell into it pretty quickly.

You just have to use your ears, really. I mean, there's lots of published alternate tunings, some that are widely used, like this open-D tuning that I'm talking about earlier. But I'm just making them up. I'm not following anyone's prescribed method of what they should be. I'm just starting with my ears, twisting the strings a little bit and find something that sounds like something and then see if I can make some more out of it by threading the guitar or whatever.

JOHNNY TEMPLE: One of the things I've always loved about Sonic Youth is simply guitar tone. The richness of Sonic Youth's guitar sounds, combined with their really hallucinatory New York imagery, was really powerful. But they were sort of "guitar geniuses." Sonic Youth was pushing the guitar in interesting, new, experimental directions. Because their influence wasn't just punk rock—it was also John Cage and that New York experimental music. Sonic Youth was super-sophisticated in punk rock unsophisticated-looking trappings. With Sonic Youth, their guitar work was head and shoulders over most other bands.

MATT PINFIELD: Tom Morello is one of the most inventive guitarists. What he did on those Rage Against the Machine records was, he was a metal-loving rock fan; but he wasn't comfortable just playing guitar with things he already mastered. He was always trying to find ways to make the instrument do different things and sound different. He decided to try and challenge the audience *and* the instrument.

Billy Corgan defined an era, too—the way he used that "drenched" sound. He was inspired also by a lot of shoegaze music. Everything from Catherine Wheel to Deep Purple was an inspiration for Billy. He was very inventive for that period of time.

CHRIS HASKETT: I think part of Vernon Reid's genius is synthesis, fusion. When you hear [Living Colour's] "Cult of Personality," you get one of the greatest riffs in rock in the service of a perfectly crafted song which contains a solo that veers from fusion into free tonality

One of the things I've always loved about Sonic Youth is simply guitar tone. The richness of Sonic Youth's guitar sounds, combined with their really hallucinatory New York imagery, was really powerful.

JOHNNY TEMPLE

into metal and then back. It's not simply a hyphenated admixture like "funk metal" or "psychedelic rock." It's an actual amalgamation—all the elements produce something new.

Also, tonally, he's quite unmistakable. I can only think of a handful of guitar players that have succeeded in bending the arc of their guitar sound that far to complement their style. It's not a vintage Marshall and sweet SG. What comes out of the speaker cabinets is abrasive but with color and richness, and it lends a unique voice to his already-unique soloing. He also pulls off the magic trick of having a pedal board so large that it needs a zoning permit but somehow never becomes intrusive.

THE REVEREND HORTON HEAT: One of my favorite guitar players is Dexter Romweber from Flat Duo Jets. And he always just used one of those really cheap Sears Silvertone guitars. And man, it's cool. Flat Duo Jets was a two-piece band that really paved the way for the White Stripes. Even Jack White talks about Dexter Romweber and Flat Duo Jets.

MARY TIMONY: My number one favorite guitar player is Ash Bowie from Polvo. It's hard to describe how incredible Ash's guitar playing is. Some of it isn't even apparent with the Polvo recordings, because for whatever reason, the recording wasn't mixed right. He's a super-genius, but I don't know if anyone would know because the recordings are kind of obscured and it's hard to hear stuff. He had really amazing ideas and used all these alternate tunings—he had a million of them. His whole thing was using really cheap Japanese guitars, and he didn't like amps with tubes—it was only transistor amps. My other favorite is Justin Trosper from Unwound.

PAGE HAMILTON: I'll never forget Matt Sweeney from Chavez or David Sims from Jesus Lizard would say to me, "When I saw Helmet, I was like, '*Fuck! Goddammit! Assholes!*'" They were pissed that we had come up with this thing that was so different—the "minimalist riff thing." I credit Glenn [Branca] a lot because Glenn could play one chord for twenty minutes. But it was a very dense chord . . .

CHRIS HASKETT: I don't know if it was a return of riffs per se; there are always great riffs—[the Rolling Stones'] "Start Me Up," [Living Colour's] "Cult of Personality," [Bad Brains'] "Re-Ignition," pretty much all of Van Halen. But it's true that the post-*Nevermind* world saw a return to a focus on the guitar as the centerpiece of rock. And a good riff is pretty much the best use of an electric guitar. And, when the world was inundated in Richard Marx and Milli Vanilli, it was something that *had* to happen.

PAGE HAMILTON: I kept getting these rhythmic figures in my head. And you ride the subway all the time in New York, and there's this Steely Dan line on "Don't Take Me Alive" that says, "The mechanized hum of another world." And I always felt that New York had so much rhythm—whether it's traffic, trains. The sound of being underground, literally—the heat, the feel. And I always felt that *is* music. I was always trying to tap out time signatures on my leg.

If you think about it, it's just building tension with the rhythmic pattern. To my guitar students, I say, "The best metal riff ever was [Beethoven's] 'Symphony No. 5.'" And that's what we're doing—you're developing melodic fragments the way conversations are built. And that's how you build a song. There's songs like "Sinatra" where I had this one slow, dirge-y groove and have the tension build—expand, contract, expand, contract. And then finally, bust into a bridge where the chord changes feel so good.

CHRIS HASKETT: And interestingly, from a guitar point of view, you start seeing the rehabilitation of pawnshop guitars. All of a sudden, people are playing Mustangs, Jaguars, and Epiphones. All these $99 pawnshop guitars are suddenly cool again.

LEE RANALDO: Everybody in New York and elsewhere was playing used gear because it was all you could afford, and you could find good deals on really good guitars back then. We were playing a lot of cheapie pawnshop guitars in the early days. Maybe it was more of a "New York thing" in that people here were willing to take a guitar that wouldn't sound right played in a normal standard tuning and detune it or retune it to something where the tuning didn't matter as much as its effectiveness as a sound maker.

THE REVEREND HORTON HEAT: They could find different types of sounds and different types of emotions from using different guitars than just your normal Floyd Rose/Kramer thing.

LOU BARLOW: Vintage instruments were happening because there was always an undercurrent of like, a '60s revival. Sixties garage rock never really quite left, as far as being an influence. But J definitely did bring it back because it sounded better.

DAVID PAJO: In the '80s, nobody wanted Jaguars and Mustangs and stuff. Strats and Teles were always popular, but even in Slint, we put EMG pickups in there—'80s shredders pickups. Which, I think was cool, actually. Brian [McMahan] put EMGs in a fucking 1950s Tele . . . and a Kahler whammy bar! [*Laughs*] *Unbelievable.* And I remember buying my 1966 [Fender] Precision bass in the '80s for $300. It was the most beat-up, cheapest guitar. No one wanted it. And they said it had been played every day at a gospel church in the west end of Louisville.

It wasn't until I was touring with the Yeah Yeah Yeahs with that bass in 2009 that the guitar tech was like, "This is a really expensive guitar." And then *Bass Guitar* magazine took pictures of it and did a little article on it. I guess I was shocked because in my mind, I still thought that those Floyd Rose guitars were the expensive ones, and these were the shitty guitars. But almost immediately after *Nevermind* came out, all those guitars became expensive again.

MIKE JOHNSON: I never really thought of that, but it's true—the Charvels and Jacksons were out, and getting a Fender was cool again. Or what was old became new again.

Mike Watt at Roseland in New York City, August 3, 1995. “Most dudes, they go to the head [the bathroom] and as they’re pissing, they’re looking at the tile. Well, *we’re the grout*. We’re setting that tile up.”—Mike Watt *Steve Eichner/WireImage/Getty Images*

14 RHYTHM SECTION

"We're the grout"

Bass guitar and drums also played a prominent role in '90s alt-rock and spawned quite a few standout players when it came to each instrument.

FRED ARMISEN: I think it was the first time that it wasn't important to have a brand-new drum kit. In fact, it was almost like a badge of honor to have something that was a little weathered. And there was less of an emphasis on technical skill. But these were still great drummers. So, there was a new version of being a great drummer—which wasn't the same kind of music education. It's something that I wish drummers who are examining drumming could study it and re-create it. Because it seems easy, but to actually play like that is its own separate technique.

I always think of the drummer for Sonic Youth [Steve Shelley]—that, to me, sounds like what a lot of what drumming sounded like in the '90s. Also, Janet Weiss with Sleater-Kinney, Pavement, Fugazi. Like, each drum was very even. There was a democracy within the drum kit where it didn't have that sound where one drum was highlighted over all the others. There's a little bit of chaos to it . . . but a lot of spirit. And it wasn't hammy. It wasn't like, "*Look at me!*" But when I think of '90s drumming, it's really like shaking all the drums together.

DARREN JESSEE: Drumming . . . I think it's just the times. Most records now by bands, the drumming is kind of safe and kind of good for the structure of the song. And it implies a little excitement or tastefulness. But the drummers from that era, they did more than what people would want nowadays. And to be specific, look at Dave Grohl. In "Smells Like Teen Spirit," when Dave Grohl decided to do crashes—in stereo, with his right and left hand—on every downbeat, it was radical. It was really powerful. And it kind of shook people into something.

I did a ton of drum fills on the Ben Folds Five records—you don't hear a lot of that kind of "editorializing" on drums anymore. Drums are more sequence-y sounding to me—more placeholder-sounding these days. That is the times, and it's also how people listen to music. Drums used to be a part of the arranging more. And a live drumming performance was exciting to hear. It was kind of moody and part of what you liked. The younger generation right now, the attitude isn't in the drum parts and drum fills.

[Dave Grohl, Jimmy Chamberlin, and Matt Cameron] had a lot of attitude and played really exciting. I listen to a lot of music and tour and see bands, and I have noticed that it's very rare to see like a "star drummer" right now. Even my friends that play in arena bands, the drums are real controlled-feeling. A lot of the stuff that I was playing in the '90s was just *insane*. It was a different attitude.

MATT JOHNSON: I was listening to [Smashing Pumpkins'] Jimmy Chamberlin last night, and there are a couple of things going on with *Siamese Dream* where there's a lot of dynamics not only in the performance, but just take the way he's playing the snare drum. His snare drum is ringing, but it's not really ringing in a way that's disruptive. And it's quite an open sound. And the cymbals sounded like they were getting the shit kicked out of them. Very bottom-heavy in that way. Those mixes I really like—those were a big adjustment for a lot of top-heavy hair band mixes of the '80s that were real midrange-y without a lot of boom below. The sounds of what drummers were bringing and what the mixes were doing was real satisfying and real carnal.

And of course, there's Dave Grohl, who was hitting hard across the whole spectrum of the drums; but the condition of his body was one of being so astute and attentive and then also very emotional, driven, and inspired. But also, very relaxed. So, he was a combination of, like, a tennis player who is really relaxed with the dance of just following the ball. And the fact that that person was so relaxed, when the tennis ball would hit the racket, there was no waste of energy, and the tennis ball would go back at the opponent so fast or with such power. And I think of that with how Dave Grohl was hitting the drums with such power—but it was not a "gym rat kind of power." It wasn't stiff.

And then you've got Matt Cameron—another archetypal player of that time. Which was another set of strengths which would always serve the song and be really interesting with the parts. And using a unique library of types of grooves. Like, opening the hi-hat on the one. You find bands that do that—like Sunny Day Real Estate [drummer William Goldsmith].

There's songs off of *The Rising Tide*, where the drummer does that type of opening the hi-hat on the one with a lot of the beats. You'll hear Matt Cameron opening the hi-hat on the one, which, when you think about it, it's not very common. You take it for granted, like, "Oh, you open the hi-hat on one. Who cares?" It's like, "No. You're making a *style* out of this shit."

So, those three drummers for sure come up instantly—as if I were to rewind back to the '70s and I'm going to end up with John Bonham, Stewart Copeland, and Steve Gadd.

MATT PINFIELD: Two of the most important drummers from that era were Stephen Perkins and Matt Cameron, and those guys listened to all kinds of music—Buddy Rich and jazz guys. Also, all these guys loved Neil Peart. But the drumming and the rhythm section in Jane's Addiction was *such* a driving force. Perkins is not acknowledged enough for being one of the most important drummers in the '90s.

LES CLAYPOOL: If I were to compare [Primus's Tim "Herb" Alexander and Tool's Danny Carey, both of whom Claypool has played with], I would say Tim has more of that kind of Stewart Copeland/Bill Bruford feel to it. And they both have that Neil Peart thing going on. Danny, it's a little sparser; but I wouldn't consider him a sparse player. He leaves a little more space between the notes. And he's obviously a very heavy player. But they're both very melodic—which is very appealing.

IAN MacKAYE: The thing about [Fugazi's] Brendan [Canty] is he's probably a better guitar player than I am—that's for sure. He's so musical, and he never stops. His drumming, I think Brendan is one of the most responsive musical drummers. He's so effortless that I don't think people can't hear the drumming. It's a little bit to me like Ringo—people are like, "Oh, Ringo, he wasn't much of a drummer." Ringo was a *phenomenal* fucking drummer. And Charlie Watts. But they're not John Bonham—it's not like a centerpiece. If you actually sit down and listen, you understand just how nuanced and how specific their ideas are and how their ideas lift the song. They're not timekeepers—they're actually playing the songs. And I think Brendan is a master musician and a master drummer.

LES CLAYPOOL: With guys like Flea and Norwood [Fisher, from Fishbone] and me, all of a sudden, you're seeing the bass step forward more in not just the mix but also in the composition. *For good or ill.* [*Laughs*] But then again, it did hearken back to some of the '80s stuff because the bass was a lot more prevalent in stuff like Bow Wow Wow and Talking Heads. Because a lot of those bands were influenced by a lot of the same things that me, Norwood, and Flea were influenced by—which was old '60s and '70s soul and funk. And in those mixes, the bass was always very dominant.

Early Fishbone—I've never seen a greater live band than Fishbone back in the heyday. Norwood deserved a lot of that credit, too, because he really brought the bass out front for a lot of people of that era. I remember a friend of mine years ago saying, "You've got to see this band, the Red Hot Chili Peppers." I think I saw them at Ruthie's Inn—a legendary metal club. They played there and the Stone in San Francisco. It was them and Fishbone, and I went to those shows, and it absolutely blew my mind watching Flea. I was like, "He's doing all that shit that all these guys when I've been in bands before were telling me *not* to do. And he's doing it *all the time*." It was very encouraging to see.

JOHNNY TEMPLE: Les Claypool . . . it's like he deconstructed the bass guitar and rebuilt the instrument. Not *physically* deconstructed it, but in terms of what the bass can do—what the role of the bass is. In the sphere of rock 'n' roll music, he created his own bass genre. He's one of the few bass players who can play the bass as a lead instrument. The bass—sonically and tonally—is not really built to be a lead instrument.

But with Les's deconstruction of the instrument and then rebuilding it, he can play with his fingers, he can play with a pick, he can play chords. Les can strum the bass like no other. He can slap and pop, but Les Claypool decides what role it plays. And in whatever song, he's in full control. I'm also in total awe of people like Les Claypool on bass, where the instrument is like an extension of their body. You hear that more with guitar—it's very rare with bass. But with Les, he's so talented that it seems like his brain doesn't interfere as much with his body. His bass does what it wants to do—based on feeling, muscles, intuition.

David Sims from the Jesus Lizard was one of the most monster-crushing bass players. Joe Lally from Fugazi. There's a bass player named Erik Sanko who had a band called Skeleton Key of that era, and Erik was from more of a jazz background, and his best bass playing was *exquisite*. He had the best tone. Eric Avery's bass playing . . . I have certain songs I've written where the connection to Eric Avery's bass playing—even though we're not ripping off Jane's Addiction—the influence is right there on the surface. Even the chord changes.

LOU BARLOW: Bass got buried. It disappeared. As far as rock music, it got completely shoved to the back. I thought the '90s was a *terrible* time for an indie rock bass player. People wanted it to be invisible. Maybe some post-punk-ish math rock bands, the bass was there. And also the approach to the bass became much more "classic rock-y" and basic. Or there are people like Pearl Jam's Jeff Ament who are really agile bass players because they became primarily known for amazing live shows, and that's where the bass could speak. But as far as the records go, the '90s is a total wasteland for really unique bass playing—other than some bands that were bringing back dub style. Things got much better in the 2000s—*then* the bass started to make a comeback.

CRIS KIRKWOOD: [Mike Watt and Flea] are more like cohorts. Those two dudes, all of us are kind of the same person in a way. Well, Flea went on to become such a huge star. But those guys are friends of mine, and it was always these "little bass pals." Watt and I are so tight—Mike is such a fuckin' monster player. They're the guys that accepted me as a bass player, and there was something about that. Because these were guys that could really play their asses off as far as I was concerned.

I remember hearing Flea here in town one night. I saw them play at the Mason Jar, which was this bar here in town [Phoenix, Arizona], and Hillel [Slovak] was still in the band. And back then, Flea's tone was so incredible—it sounded like a synthesizer playing. Just a monster. And Mike's always been far out—from the first time I saw him, just instant kinship. He comes offstage, and he's bloodied himself. Bass-centric guys—not just laying back as strictly support, but an integral part of the entirety of what the band is all about. Just a couple of bass monsters.

MIKE WATT: There are some "macho sports" things about bass players that I can't stand. Because everything is vocabulary—when you're trying to put some dude down because he ain't doing what you're doing, *fuck you, ass*. At the end of the day, our job—I love the politics of bass—we look good making the other guys look good. It's aid and abet—whatever is gluing the shit together. We're kind of like mother-like. Most dudes, they go to the head [the bathroom] and as they're pissing, they're looking at the tile. Well, *we're the grout*. We're setting that tile up. But, man, you get these bass players by themselves, some of them get weird.

Fred Armisen at Cambridge, Massachusetts, May 23, 2019. "I think it was the first time that it wasn't important to have a brand-new drum kit. In fact, it was almost like a badge of honor to have something that was a little weathered."—Fred Armisen *John Atashian/Alamy*

Art Alexakis with Everclear at the Botanique in Brussels, Belgium, March 7, 1996. "I've seen friends of mine and people I've known in bands go through a bidding war, make money, but really get fucked by the whole process."—Art Alexakis *Gie Knaeps/Hulton Archive/Getty Images*

15 MAJOR LABELS AND INDIE LABELS

"The feeding frenzy was pretty crazy"

During the early to mid-'90s, it was growing increasingly difficult to keep track of all the indie bands that were suddenly scoring major label deals.

IAN MacKAYE: In the mid-to-late '80s, bands started to peel off of independent labels and started signing to majors. Specifically, I'm thinking of Hüsker Dü, Sonic Youth not much later than that, and a few others. And there were a couple of different things going on that created this development. I think people pointed fingers at the bands and said, "They're selling out." I don't think that was the case. I mean, maybe *some* of them were. But I think what was happening was that the independent labels were fucking up—they were not paying the artists, and they were not being nice to them.

And if you're facing the situation by choosing between being treated like a chump and having to fix your van or being treated like a chump and getting a tour bus, you might as well take the tour bus, right? So, I feel some of the larger independent labels were really fucking people over. They had adopted from the major label industry *the worst* aspects of the industry. They were not paying people. They were cheating them, and it was a hustle. So, I actually don't blame a lot of those bands for making that decision—even though I usually found the result of becoming an investment for a multinational corporation to not necessarily engender great creativity. By the early '90s, the conversation around bands wasn't about presentation or ideas; it was about contracts. And that was discouraging.

MATT SWEENEY: The same thing happened in the late '60s and early '70s, where major labels signed all the "druggie/cool bands" and you could go back and find all these really cool albums that were all these one-offs that got dropped by a major label. There was 100 percent precedent for what had happened in the '60s as to what was happening in the early '90s.

FRANK BLACK: And also the record companies, even though vinyl was dead and there was this whiff of the internet and the future and "What does that all look like?," they were still selling records by the truckload. The Pixies, the last couple of years of our first part of our career there before we broke up, we got involved in some distribution with a major label. It was Elektra Records in the United States. People perceived it then as "Oh, you 'graduated' from the indies to the majors." They had this whole "indie versus majors thing."

Butthole Surfers, May 1991. Left to right: King Coffey, Paul Leary, Jeff Pinkus, and Gibby Haynes. "We could have picked from among several different major labels that wanted to sign us." —Paul Leary *Clayton Call/Redferns/Getty Images*

So, the record companies—whether they were indie or major—were still kind of judging everything based on how many boxes of records were going out the door. So, of course your major artists were releasing records, and they were selling millions of copies around the world. People still sold *millions* of records. Hundreds of thousands of records. And so, a band like the Pixies, who were perceived as slowly going upward, moving from the indies to the majors—"Oh, we're playing a bigger hall this tour"—but it was still perceived as a kind of a failure if you put out a record and you sold two hundred thousand copies. They'd be like, "Eh . . . you're still in the game, *but you only sold two hundred thousand copies*." The numbers that people would kill for now.

MIKE JOHNSON: The feeding frenzy was pretty crazy. It was like *anybody* could get signed to a major after a bit. Even I put out a solo record on a major [1996's *Year of Mondays,* via TAG/Atlantic Records]—which I couldn't get signed to an indie before that. It seemed like the labels didn't know exactly what to go for, so they signed *everything* and just wade through it. I've met quite a few people over the years who were in bands that got signed to development deals and got buried because of it. They got a bunch of money but never got a record put out.

MIKE WATT: I'll tell ya, maybe because it was eleven years with SST, but I never had to make a demo. We didn't take up-front money, either. I think it was, you throw it against the wall and see what sticks. Somebody gave me a statistic that 90 percent of the signed acts lose money, but that 10 percent floated the boat. Maybe it was like Hollywood with *Easy Rider*. *Easy Rider* comes out, and then all these guys make their own movies for a little while. So, they waste all kinds of money with *Heaven's Gate*. [*Laughs*]

PAUL LEARY: One year in the late '80s, it was pointed out to us that we were the "top-grossing independent act on the road." Suddenly, we were in *Billboard* magazine as being a successful road act, and that got the major labels interested in us. We could have picked from among several different major labels that wanted to sign us. And we could have picked any producer we wanted because all the big producers threw their hat in the ring to produce us.

CHRIS HASKETT: All of a sudden, we get signed. The Melvins get signed to Atlantic—which is perfect. There was a T-shirt that you used to see around—it said, "I went to Seattle to score some heroin . . . and all I got was this lousy record contract." *It was absurd.*

IAN MacKAYE: The other thing that was happening was people who were "punks" or in the "underground music scene" in the early '80s, as they grew older, they had a connection to the music business and eventually made their way up into working for the major labels. And then they wound up bringing their friends along.

STEVE ALBINI: I wrote an essay that was kind of a cautionary tale about getting involved with a big record label capriciously . . . or without consideration. It's called "The Problem with Music." It was published in a magazine called *The Baffler*. And it's basically an articulation of all the things that can go wrong when a band is in cahoots with a big record label, and the big record label knows it has all the power. The intention of that was to be a warning to my peers that if you think you're grabbing for the brass ring, what you're actually grasping for is the end of your career.

PAGE HAMILTON: We had been touring and we did the Ugly American Overkill Tour in Europe—that was five AmRep bands on one tour bus doing a bunch of shows. We saw a huge change. All of a sudden, we were like . . . this *thing*. People were really getting excited about the band, and we were selling more merch than all the bands combined on the tour. We were like, "Something's going on here." We got home, and everybody and their mother was trying to sign us. Because I think by that point, Nirvana had already come out with *Nevermind*. We went from, "We want to give you guys $10,000 and your own van" to "Here's a million dollars" over the course of a couple of months.

LES CLAYPOOL: We decided to sign with Interscope, which was the smartest thing I think we ever did. Because there were a couple labels that were after us, so there was a bidding war. But part of the deal with Interscope was [label president] Tom Whalley came to our show to see a different band. And he saw us—not knowing anything about us—and saw how the crowd reacted, came backstage, and was like, "I want to sign you guys." Whereas the other labels wanted to sign us because we sold eighty thousand *Frizzle Frys* [Primus's indie-label debut studio album] or whatever. It wasn't based as much on initial reaction.

CRAIG WEDREN: It was really wild because there were A&R people at *every* show. And it did seem like every other day somebody was getting signed. And, coming from D.C., it meant something. And it meant something more to make the jump from, say, a Dischord to an Epic Records—which is what Shudder to Think did. And there was a lot of discomfort and dismay around it, locally. Not us specifically, just the "be true to your school" aspect of it. Which was never an issue for us because our goal was always to make our music and reach as many people as possible. As long as no one was dictating what we could, should, or ought to do, we were happy to play with anybody who could help us get our music out there.

KRISTIN HERSH: Those crazy old billionaires with the fake tans and hair plugs, and their personal assistants with narc-clean leather jackets and manicures . . . they were nuts. We'd let them take us out to dinner—because free food and because we liked watching trainwrecks. They'd name-drop old-fart bands and rock stars and get drunk in front of us. That's about it. Their faces would sort of . . . melt—the drunker they got. That was my impression of major labels. Super entertaining.

Fat Mike with NOFX at Pukkelpop Festival, Hasselt, Belgium, August 26, 1995. "I took one meeting [with a major label], and they made me feel bad about myself."—Fat Mike *Gie Knaeps/Hulton Archive/ Getty Images*

ART ALEXAKIS: All these bands that were struggling, that would show up to L.A. and play the Casbah to like 125 people . . . all of a sudden, you started seeing albums on major labels. It was like a glut of people signing bands. When I moved to Portland, I knew it was going to be my last band, because I was going to be thirty. At the time, that was *ancient*. And I had a new baby.

I started Everclear, and we weren't very good because my rhythm section wasn't very good. I got a chance to record an album for four hundred bucks in trade. I traded a couple of effects—a digital delay and a reverb. And that became our first album [1993's *World of Noise*]. We recorded every song we had. And I put a three-song demo in the mail to SXSW, and they actually called me and told me they'd put me on two showcases and can we show up in three weeks. I had no money—we were on welfare. So, we went and played—and that started it for us.

"NO THANK YOU" TO AHMET ERTEGUN AND MO OSTIN

Fugazi's Ian MacKaye meets two legendary music industry figures.

We were playing two nights at the Roseland in New York City [September 24 and 25, 1993]. I think it was the second night, and we had really thrown down—usually when we came offstage, we were pretty much a *puddle* because we were exhausted. We went down to the dressing room, and it's not uncommon as we go to the dressing room for us to meet friends and walk down. But this time, there was nobody else around—it was just us. We go down to our dressing room, and we were starting to strip off our clothes, and this man and woman walk in. I thought *maybe* it was somebody's grandfather, and the woman was a little bit younger. And this guy said, "Hi, my name is blah blah blah"—I couldn't understand the name. I'm like, "I'm sorry?" He goes, "*I'm Ahmet Ertegun from Atlantic.*"

The thing was, Jawbox had opened for us that night at the Roseland—and they're on Atlantic. So, I assumed that he had come down to see their new signing and maybe he'd stop in and say, "Hey, thanks for being cool. You made it easy for us." I said, "So, you're here to see Jawbox?" He's like, "Who? No. I came to see *you*. Your band is fantastic. I want you to be part of the Atlantic family." And I'm like, "Oh. No, we're good. We have our own label, and we're all squared away." He goes, "Well, then, I'll do a deal with you like I did with Mick." And what he was referring to was that Rolling Stones Records deal—where he did a deal with Mick Jagger and it was a label. So, I said, "Thank you. No. We're really happy with our arrangement." And then he left.

Ahmet did say to me that he had grown up in Washington, DC. He and his brother were part of the founding members of the label. And they were the sons of a Turkish ambassador—so, he grew up in Washington. He was saying, "Washington's my town!" I actually sent him a postcard—care of Atlantic—and said, "Thanks for coming down. Nice to see you. If you're ever in Washington, let me know—I'd love to hear more of your stories." He wrote back and said, "Would love to see you. The next time I'm there, I'll call you and take you to my favorite spot in funky Chinatown." But . . . never saw him again. It's been sort of expanded to where he was offering millions of dollars. In theory, yes. But he was basically saying, "Whatever you want, let's do it."

Another time, Mo Ostin was in town, and he wanted to meet me. He was starting DreamWorks Records, and we talked—he was telling me about Reprise and Jimi Hendrix and working with Frank Sinatra. Incredible stories. I remember I had toast and iced tea, and he was having breakfast—at a hotel restaurant. And he goes, "I'm starting this label. It's going to be the ultimate kind of anti-corporate label. I think you guys will be the perfect anti-corporate band to be the debut artist." And I said, "Thanks. But no." And then he said to me, "I told people I was going to talk to you, and they all said, 'You're going to talk to Ian, you're going to have a really nice time talking to him, you're going make your pitch, he's going to turn you down, and you're going to feel good about it.' And you know what? They're right!" Never saw him again, either.

MATT SWEENEY: At the time, there were some major labels looking at us, and Matador was looking at us. I was talking to a friend about it. I was like, "We're going to sign to Matador. We're not interested in major labels." And he's like, "Why? How much money are they offering?" I was like, "I really don't care. We trust Matador." And he's like, "Well, money is the only thing that's real. Matador can disappear tomorrow. *That money* is going to be there." Which is actually a very real way of looking at things. But I think that most of the bands around you weren't thinking about things like that. I know that we just wanted to be with people that we respected and not have to pay to play. We wanted to make good records and be around our friends and play shows with bands that we liked.

FAT MIKE: I took one meeting [with a major label], and they made me feel bad about myself. It was Hollywood Records. All the labels wanted to sign us. At dinner, I said, "NOFX, we don't really do promotion, and we sell out shows and we're selling lots of records. What can you do for us that Epitaph doesn't?" "We'll do this, this, and this." I'm like, "Well, we don't really need that. We're not making videos or doing interviews—we're just playing. We all have houses now; we're all stoked." And the guy said, "Well, if you want to play second fiddle to Rancid and the Offspring your whole career . . ." And I went, "Ah. Just like MTV! You're trying to make me feel bad about my career when *you're* the guy trying to sign *me*." I loved that! And I never took another meeting. And guess what? We put out our own records, and no one tells us what to do.

TRACY BONHAM: I can be honest now—that [*The Liverpool Sessions*] was a fake indie release. I was signed to Island Records, but I think the idea of coming out right with a major label release with all the money and backing behind it was considered not "alternative"—it was considered *uncool*. So, they subsidized a release by CherryDisc. And I remember sitting around the table with my manager and my manager's brother—who is [famed music manager] Doc McGhee—and we knew we were doing something that was more of a façade of where I came out and I had all this "history" of indie rock. And that's why we named it *The Liverpool Sessions*—that was my little poke and tongue-in-cheek joke as if I had been around forever. And I hadn't.

ART ALEXAKIS: We got signed in June of '94. It was building up to a bidding war. And I just said, "I've seen friends of mine and people I've known in bands go through a bidding war, make money, but really get fucked by the whole process." Because expectations were so high and so much money was put into it.

So I'm like, "Look. I want *this* much money. I want *these* many firm records. I want you to buy us a van. Tour support. I want half mechanicals going into it and three-quarter mechanicals on publishing when we hit *this* level. And once it goes to full mechanicals at one hundred thousand records, it stays there throughout the whole deal." And all the labels are like, "Wow . . . this kid knows his shit!"

We had like twenty-seven labels making offers. And then I send a fax out saying, "Oh, yeah, by the way—*I have total creative control over everything, and I produce my own albums*." And . . . POOF! Two-thirds of them went away, and seven or eight labels were left. I was like, "Okay. At least there's *some* left. That's cool." I went with Capitol because I loved their A&R guy [Perry Watts-Russell].

CHRIS HASKETT: Being on a major label . . . yes, all of a sudden you're getting to radio. But at the same time, they don't know what to do with you. So, that feeding frenzy on the one hand was kind of cool, but it worked better for the bands that were slightly already kind of commercial. So again, tons of bands get signed. But most of them are just not a good fit. *But who's going to say no to a bigger recording budget?*

FRED ARMISEN: I remember at the time it was an issue with bands who were bigger than us. I didn't care in that I just wanted our records to come out. It was a struggle trying to tour and play shows. We didn't sell enough records for it to ever be an issue. It didn't really matter. But at least we got records we could sell as merch on the road.

MIKE WATT: It was basically the distribution thing. One lame thing about the indie scene was the distribution. With the big labels, each label had their own system—you didn't have to worry about that. These distributors would have their own labels—you'd be competing against their labels! So, that was the hardest part. I remember coming in with the masters for the first fIREHOSE record on Columbia [1991's *Flyin' the Flannel*]. I came to Santa Monica there . . . and they sent me to the mail room—they didn't know I was a guy in the band!

I don't have any horror stories about a big label. Fourteen years I was on that label—more than SST. I didn't have to change anything. And my product manager, Peter Fletcher, wanted me to give talks to new bands. Because a lot of these new cats that got signed, they thought that was the E-ticket ride on the gravy train. Like it was all over, and things were just going to happen. Y'know, "My A&R man took me out to dinner." No, you took *yourself* out to dinner. These guys had no idea about things like that.

IAN MacKAYE: I think the most dramatic thing that I was privy to was the raiding of the underground music by the majors. Because when Nirvana popped, all the labels *immediately* swung into action and started signing anybody who could sell five thousand records. For real. I had two bands on Dischord [Jawbox and Shudder to Think] that got taken. And I'm not mad at them, either—just to be clear. I was really supportive. If that's what they wanted to do, I support them. But it was crazy. If you look back at the bands that were signed . . . most of them didn't do anything. The way I perceived it was bands were volunteering to be lottery tickets. And if you go to any 7-Eleven, where do you see most of the lottery tickets? *Torn up on the floor.*

16 MTV'S *120 MINUTES* AND *ALTERNATIVE NATION*

"The coolest fuckin' space you could be in"

Throughout the '90s, MTV was still the leading tastemaker when it came to introducing and breaking artists. And the station certainly played an enormous role in the popularity of alt-rock in the US, especially with their two specialty shows, *120 Minutes* and *Alternative Nation*.

BOB MOULD: MTV, in general—and Matt Pinfield and *120 Minutes*, specifically—did so much to elevate all of us that were making that kind of guitar-driven music in the early '90s. It was so important. There were other shows before it—a show back in the '80s, *The Cutting Edge*. I remember that because there was one episode, it was the first time the Smiths were on TV in America, I think. There was something with Morrissey talking. And that same episode, Hüsker Dü was on, as well. There was sort of a trampoline or foundation being set already before *120 Minutes*. But yeah, *120 Minutes* was the place that all of us wanted to be. It was the place where everyone found out about new music. It was the way to get there. No question about it.

JOHNETTE NAPOLITANO: I will never forget the first time we were on MTV. We were in Utah, and our road manager had us run out of gas—in the snow. I had to wait in the van while everybody went to get gas, and I was freezing my ass off. We got to the hotel, and on the TV pops "Still in Hollywood." I ran down the hall in my bra and underwear, knocking on everybody's door to tell everybody, "*We're on TV!*"

DAVE MARKEY: I came from the L.A. punk scene. We were very cynical toward MTV. I liked it early on because they were showing tons of Devo and not a lot of bands had music videos yet. It hadn't become the big platform for breaking artists like it did later in the '80s. Of course, it blew up a lot of mainstream

Kennedy, right, with Courtney Love at the MTV Video Music Awards in Los Angeles, California, September 2, 1993. "MTV was important in that alternative videos were much more groundbreaking than some of the pop videos because there was so much more artistry and experimentation." —Kennedy *Jeff Kravitz/FilmMagic/Getty Images* stuff that wasn't in my wheelhouse. In the '80s, we were kind of against it. The Dead Kennedys had the song "MTV Get Off the Air"—that was kind of our sentiment coming out of the punk scene. But obviously, things shifted rather quickly in the early '90s.

I had worked for years myself in a bubble as a kid down in Santa Monica, shooting these Super-8 films . . . and doing my own thing. But it was the perfect marriage when I got involved in the hardcore scene in L.A., by bringing my Super-8 camera out to these clubs—often in very dodgy neighborhoods in Los Angeles—shooting these live performances by these bands and putting it together in a film that isn't really a straight documentary, in a sense. *The Slog Movie* is interesting because if you look at it alongside *1991: The Year Punk Broke*, it's a similar film . . . just a decade earlier. With a lot less resources. And a lot of these bands that Kurt Cobain was certainly in tune with.

MIKE JOHNSON: I'm from Grants Pass, a little small town in Oregon. We got it before the big cities got it because we had it in the early '80s when I was in high school. They played bands like the Bongos—bands that you would never think would have their videos on TV.

GERALD CASALE: Their idealistic stated mission [early on] was, "We're a revolution. We're talking about sound and vision here. We're talking about groups that embrace visuals as an integrated part of their aesthetic from the beginning. So, regardless of Top 40 radio hits, we're showing interesting songs with videos fused to them." And we thought, "That's what *we've* been doing! You guys are great! Thanks for understanding!" And at the beginning, they needed our content because they didn't have any. We were one of the only bands that had a few things in the can at that point . . . and they *were* "in the can"—they were 16-millimeter films. So, they got transferred to video, and MTV was rotating them.

But within a year, MTV went from this artsy, fledgling concern in several cities to national broadcasting franchise, American Express money. And with a snap of the fingers, it was connected to the Parallel One FM Top 20 list. [Note: Parallel One Playlists was a section listed in the weekly trade publication *Radio & Records*, which listed the charts of FM stations throughout the US.] And that's what determined who got airplay—they didn't care how dumb the videos were.

ANGELO MOORE: MTV had a lot of rules, which kind of narrowed the alternative scope, too. So, you could depend on the underground stations to play the uncut, raw alternative music. And that's what I was digging. I remember we got banned from MTV! I had a marijuana zoot suit made out of hemp with glow-in-the-dark marijuana leaves and purple vertical stripes. And I was on *High Times* magazine with that outfit. I wanted to wear that on MTV, and MTV said, "You can't wear that." Nobody would even give a shit today.

FRED ARMISEN: I watched the hell out of it. And not just for the videos they would show—they had really good interviews. And the thrill of seeing videos from bands you wouldn't expect to see videos from. I loved *120 Minutes*.

CRAIG WEDREN: I used to go home after school in Cleveland to my grandma's house, which is where my first band used to rehearse. And I would watch MTV until it was time for rehearsal, and then I would watch MTV after rehearsal until I had to do my homework. And that habit really stuck—even after MTV started becoming a big drag in the hair metal era. But that would have been when *120 Minutes* started—and it was really cool and really exciting.

BILL GOULD: I think it was very important. It was important for us. I remember when *120 Minutes* played our video ["We Care a Lot"], we went up to our friend Anna's house, who worked at Slash Records. We brought some beers and got to watch our video on TV. And that was unheard of—two years before imagining a video of ours ever being on any TV anywhere was almost impossible. We were just this shitty, unknown band playing dive bars.

I mean, think about Butthole Surfers being on *120 Minutes*—that is *absolutely* influential on where the culture went from there. Totally. Actually, it's been said that Faith No More would have not even succeeded if they hadn't played the "Epic" video. It was the video that made our band where people "got it." I mean, we toured and toured for a few years before that and were hitting our heads against the wall, basically. But MTV actually facilitated a whole new crowd of people for us.

MATT PINFIELD: Of course I watched *120 Minutes* [before Pinfield was a host]. But here's the thing: Like other people, I would tape it. I was doing it on a very different level—I completely related to everything that was going on on *120*. Which is why I had the naivete and fearlessness when Dave Kendall left to say to the MTV people that I knew, "You need somebody like me, who bands will respect, and really knows this music"—because I was *that guy*. But never thinking that I would be hired as a host for *120 Minutes*, let alone be put on TV, because I was a short, bald, chubby guy.

But I was so enthusiastic about music, I was starting to make waves on radio, and people were saying about me at that time, "He's looking for reasons to play bands . . . not *not* to play them." And then I became friends with music directors and program directors around the country that were doing the same thing—they were on the crusade to break the new music. I felt *120 Minutes* was the greatest show. I loved it because it was all the music that, for me, was coming out that was exciting. It's not that I didn't love some of the rock and metal stuff, too—because I did. But I was living through that era, exposing bands in a regional way through WHTG-FM in Asbury Park, New Jersey. I loved *120 Minutes*, but I was always DJ'ing in nightclubs on Sunday night—so I could never watch it live.

Dave Kendall did a great job [as the host of *120 Minutes* from 1988 to 1992]. Dave Kendall needs to get credit where credit is due in a big way because Dave came up with the actual concept. And even though he wasn't the original host and they were trying other people, when he started, he would just be "behind the curtain" giving the top college radio albums of the week. And then eventually, he ended up being the host. It was programmed from the music department, but he was involved in it—like I was. I was actually in the programming department.

IAN MacKAYE: MTV made Nirvana. Not the other way around. MTV were kingmakers—if you got your video into rotation there. We don't have to look beyond McDonald's to know that advertising works. Advertising and convenience—the twin death knells of society. But those things work.

DAVE MARKEY: Stuff that was suppressed by MTV in the '80s was suddenly welcomed in. Kind of a changing of the guard. And Nirvana had everything to do with it—for good and bad. There wasn't much of a difference [between directing music videos in the early '90s and '80s]—even though all of a sudden, rather than being employed by an independent label, I was employed by Columbia/Sony, doing the fIREHOSE video on Super-8. I shot them and edited them in the same fashion that I was using in the mid-to-late '80s. Not much had changed as far as the production end of it.

AL JOURGENSEN: It made it corporate; it made it accessible. It's a double-edged sword—a lot more people know your music now because the people that are coming in from that expect you to play the game just like pop artists do.

MATT PINFIELD: But then Dave Kendall left. I filled in for *120 Minutes* first. Before Lewis Largent hosted the show, there were artists hosting, and they were trying to figure out what to do with the show. They brought me in, and in 1993 was my first show—with Depeche Mode, when *Songs of Faith and Devotion* came out. I'd never been in front of a camera before, except for my audition. And it's on YouTube; people can see it. Then they brought me up there and told me that they really liked the job I did and they would use me as a fill-in . . . but they were going to give the show to Lewis. Lewis was going to do it because he was VP of programming and had come from KROQ in Los Angeles as the music director. I was a little disappointed, to say the least.

KENNEDY: I was an intern at KROQ in Los Angeles, and I would pester the program director just about every day to put me on the air. It was an unpaid internship. So . . . he did. He gave me a two-night trial in the summer of 1991. And then in December of '91, he hired me to be a part-time DJ, and then I also got hired on *Kevin and Bean*'s morning radio show. And then in May of '92, Andy Schuon got poached by MTV for being a groundbreaking programmer, but also some of the ad campaigns and promotions that KROQ did were *so* funny. So, MTV heard about him, he went to MTV as a senior VP of programming, and they were getting a whole new slate of VJs at the end of that summer of '92. So, he asked me if I wanted to audition. I auditioned, I passed, and Judy McGrath gave me her golden stamp. I was hired that September.

120 Minutes was like the hardcore, way more serious, encyclopedic, muso show. And then *Alternative Nation* was like a twenty-year-old music fan screwing around doing interviews. But I kind of started doing "dayparts" on MTV—hosting random hours where they would plug the VJs in. I got there in early September, and it was October/November of '92 when they launched *Alternative Nation*—that was five nights a week at midnight.

Alternative Nation was for music fans who happened to like alternative music. Y'know, kids who were staying up late, who wanted to see the brand of music that they were really into. At first, it started with a lot of grunge: '92/'93—Pearl Jam, Soundgarden, Nirvana, and my favorite, Mudhoney. But then we also had Radiohead—Thom Yorke *hated* me. He took himself way too seriously—he probably still does to this day. So, I got to do interviews with bands that had never been on American TV before. And that was really fun.

No Doubt were *so* cute—they were like, excited kids. And the same with the Cranberries. I interviewed the Cranberries, and I believe it was Fergal and Dolores—and they were so quiet when we were on camera. They were whispering—like they didn't want to wake anyone up! But during commercials, they were way more jovial. And the same thing with Rivers Cuomo when I interviewed Weezer for the first time. I don't think Rivers had ever seen himself on TV, and he kept looking off camera at the monitor and was transfixed by his own image. My producer was getting really frustrated—he was like, "Get them to answer the question!" I was amused by it because they were so reluctant.

MATT PINFIELD: A position came about around the end of '94—they asked me if I wanted to be interviewed to be one of the music programming people at MTV. One of the ten people who picked the videos for the channel—and worked on *120 Minutes* and *Alternative Nation*. And at that point, *Headbangers Ball* was still on and *Yo! MTV Raps*. You'd get hired to have knowledge of all the different genres—which I did.

I got hired full-time in '95. Truth be told, I never expected to be on radio or TV again—I left the radio station, and it was bittersweet. And the next thing I know, one day they say to me, "You were pretty good that time you were on with Depeche Mode. We're going to put you on the air for three weeks and see how it goes."

I go on there with Oasis in '95, and Lauren Levine—she was the person who was in charge of the VJs—said, "*This needs to be your show every week.*" And the next thing I know, I'm on television every week. And I find out when they do research, there's a high rating because people like the "guy next door/neighbor/friend/music freak/fanatic personality." That was a major surprise to me as well—that I was one of the highest-rated VJs. So, they decided at that point, "We have to put him on more, because people really like what he's doing." That changed everything in my life.

GREEN DAY'S GO-TO VIDEO DIRECTOR

Mark Kohr describes his work with the massively popular East Bay pop-punk band.

We got a call saying, "We want Mark to do a video for this band . . . Green Day. They want the guy who did the Primus videos because they liked how weird they are." [*Laughs*] So, I went and met with them in Oakland at the offices of Jeff Saltzman [the band's then co-manager]. With "Longview," I met with the band, and I didn't know what to expect. I had that meeting, and they were *really* young looking. And real joke-y—they had a real sense of humor about themselves. And Billie [Joe Armstrong] had dreads, almost—he cut his hair by the video, but they were sort of short dreads. Billie said, "We thought it would be funny if it's us sitting on the couch watching TV." Instead of the band [on the couch] it was Billie, and I felt like, "These guys also need to have a performance." I wanted to have a new kind of light for them, because grunge had a look, very "light and shadow." So, I did a total front-light and developed this story, which is about feeling bored at home and the frustration that comes with that.

"Basket Case," that was an homage to *One Flew Over the Cuckoo's Nest*. And what was going on was Nirvana was doing all that amazing work with Anton Corbijn and Kevin Kerslake. And Ted Turner was colorizing old black-and-white movies—and Anton used it on a Nirvana video ["Heart-Shaped Box"]. And I was like, "I really want to use that technique for a Green Day video." We took those ideas from *One Flew Over the Cuckoo's Nest* and put a performance in there—while colorizing it. What's wild is Mike [Dirnt], his mom had some sort of neurological issues that put her in that place where we shot [Agnews Developmental Center in Santa Clara County, California].

"When I Come Around" happened when I was told by the manager, "They want to do a video for 'When I Come Around.' And the band was talking about making it about voyeurism. I think it would be really cool if we have an evil kid looking through the window at a girl at night." And I said to myself, "Don't you get it? I'm making 'children's educational television.'" There's a sequence in *2001: A Space Odyssey* where David Bowman, the astronaut, goes through a cosmic stargate in the pod, lands in the French hotel room, looks out the window, and sees himself standing outside the pod [and then cuts to various shots of Bowman]. That sequence as a viewer, you're all the one character; but as that one character, you're going from one version of yourself to another. And then I remembered a line from the movie *Wings of Desire* from Wim Wenders: "The beautiful stranger." I wanted to make it about that we're all looking with the same eyes.

At a certain point, I said, "You guys shouldn't do all your videos with me. Try to stir it up a bit and see what happens." So, they went off and did videos [with other directors]. It was a little lull in Green Day's fame, and I got word, "They want to do a video for 'Time of Your Life.' But you are writing against three other directors." So, I wrote an idea and submitted that, and I got word, "They don't like any of the ideas—from you or any of the other directors. But they want you to go and meet with them in New York and come up with an idea."

I went to New York and Billie said, "I was thinking that we kind of make it like a Pogues video with ordinary people . . . but kind of like they're drunk." And I was like, "Sounds good. That's what I'll do." In other cases, I would research it; but I didn't look up a Pogues video—I didn't know what they were like. I imagined, "Ordinary people. But it's beautiful, and it's like they're drunk." But I didn't want to do the drunk part because the song is too beautiful. I was like, "Okay. I want to make it really about Satori—about awakening. Where you have this moment where everything is really clear and you feel aware."

The song—massive impact all over with a whole generation of people. Being a part of making the video, I'm so happy I was able to make it the way that I did and it had the impact that it did. I've told my wife, "I can't believe *I'm the guy* that directed 'Time of Your Life.'" [*Laughs*]

The VJ thing is different from the music department thing, obviously. Me and Lewis Largent were the only people that crossed over, that both programmed the station and the videos. Everybody else that did on-air were *just* on-air.

KENNEDY: J Mascis was very difficult to interview. It turned out to be kind of funny at the end, but it was hysterically painful. The Verve Pipe, also very painful—and I didn't feel like they were big enough to be kind of jerks. That was the thing that kind of drove me crazy—when bands acted "too cool for school." I actually learned a lot from that, because if someone is putting you on camera or putting a microphone in front of your face, they want to hear your story. It means that what you do for art has moved people, so if you agree to sit down for the interview, you should talk. But I also understand people didn't want to be seen as uncool.

Henry Rollins was definitely my favorite interview, because I could get him to laugh. Everyone was *so* scared of him. And it's like from the first time I met him when I was a DJ at KROQ backstage at a music festival in Arizona, I did everything I could to crack his exterior. Which wasn't hard, because he has an amazing sense of humor. He would come on, and getting him to laugh was so much fun.

CHRIS HASKETT: I hated making videos. I'd always say, "It was akin to making pornography"—which is you take something you love doing, pretend to do it on film, and then look like you're enjoying it. Making a video was like giving a cat a bath. But you had to have one—it's just what was needed by then.

FERGAL LAWLER: Dolores didn't mind doing videos because she was the singer and the one who wrote the lyrics, so she had a better picture of what she wanted and talked to the directors. But the rest of us found it a chore because you're sitting around usually in the cold all day. And then toward the end of the day, it's like, "Okay. You're on!" And you do your performance for an hour or two . . . and that's it.

MATT JOHNSON: I do remember making a video [with Jeff Buckley], and I was so embarrassed to be in front of a camera. I think what happened was my brain was scrolling through a metaphorical Rolodex of different archetypes that would be in some music video because I grew up on MTV. So, Flock of Seagulls videos . . . Iron Maiden videos . . . Tony Basil videos . . . Pat Benatar videos . . . the Go-Go's videos . . . Loverboy videos! I'm like, "Oh, my God. There are so many ways that I do not want to be in a video." I was very shy.

And I think Jeff probably did a wonderful job because I think they captured really great footage of him singing, and he was very expressive. And I was glad that Jeff was there to mop up all the attention. And I was glad that [bassist] Mick [Grøndahl] was there, too—because Mick is very handsome and tall. So, I was definitely in my head during the making of those videos, feeling very shy and embarrassed. I definitely was not prepared mentally for being on camera. And then as I got older, I was like, "Eh, this shit's no big deal. Don't worry about it." But I think I was taking everything *so* seriously.

IAN MacKAYE: We were *never* going to do a video. I had a rap about MTV. People used to say, "You guys should definitely do a video because you would bring something good to the station." And I'd say, "Here's something to think about. You have two fifty-gallon drums. One of them is spotless. Stainless steel. Clean. The other one is brimming with shit. You can take a spoon of shit and throw it into the clean one, and you'll see it. You can't throw a spoonful of 'clean' into a barrel of shit." No matter what you do, when you get into these larger things, don't fool yourself into thinking that somehow, this will bring some legitimacy to the proceedings. Now, I'm not saying people shouldn't do it. Just don't operate under this pretense—the reality is you always become part of the machine.

When I see videos, I see advertisements. And frankly, there are some songs that when I think of the song, I just see the images that were in the video. And that's not what music is about for us. Music is about the pictures you create in your own mind listening to music. So, I don't want you to listen to "Waiting Room" and see someone smashing a mirror in slow motion or throwing cake at each other. *Fuck that.* That seems absurd. It's just advertisements. And we're *a band*—we made music. That's one of the reasons we didn't make T-shirts, either. Often, people think, "Oh, you're making us feel bad about what we're doing." That's not the idea. The idea is that we are a band and we make music, and if other people want to do something, that's their business. But this is what *we* do.

FAT MIKE: NOFX made our first video in 1989 ["S&M Airlines"] and Gore Verbinski did it—he later did *a little thing* called *Pirates of the Caribbean*. We sent it to *120 Minutes*, and they wouldn't play it. They said, "Not interested." And then two years later, we made a video called "Stick It in My Eye"—they turned it down. Then we made the "Bob" video, sent it to *120 Minutes*—they turned it down. We were on Epitaph and they played Bad Religion one or two times, but they weren't interested in NOFX.

And then we made a video for "Leave It Alone" in 1994, and that's when punk broke. All these majors were coming after us, and I was super-stressed. I just decided and convinced my band, "*Fuck this shit.*" MTV wanted the "Leave It Alone" video because Green Day and the Offspring just broke. So . . . we canned that video. And MTV were like, "Why?" "Well, because we sent you three videos over the past three years and you never played one of them once on *120 Minutes*. You're supposed to be alternative music on *120 Minutes*, and all you're really playing is 'college rock.'"

So, NOFX is playing a small festival in L.A., and at the time I had Fat Wreck Chords, and No Use for a Name were on tour with the Offspring, and they were doing very well. They had a video called "Soulmate." And I talked to the program director at *120 Minutes*—it's not Matt Pinfield—and he's like, "So, why won't you give us the 'Leave It Alone' video?" I said, "Dude, I don't want to be on this big 'punk wave.' Our career is going very well, and I want to keep it like that." In fact, we didn't do any interviews for eight years. We did *nothing*. Because I didn't like how it was going. I thought we'd get big and then dropped.

So, the guy from MTV said, "Y'know, we've played the No Use for a Name video." I go, "I know. Thanks." He's like, "Well, if you don't give us the NOFX video, I don't think No Use for a Name will be played on MTV anymore." And I was like, "You're trying to threaten me with taking my Fat Wreck Chords bands off?" He's like, "No, I'm not. I just don't see them lasting." And they never played No Use for a Name again. It made my case—"I *thought* you guys were assholes. And now, I *know* you're assholes!"

FRANK BLACK: To give you an example of how people still threw money at the situation, the Pixies were maybe considered a struggling act by our major record players around the time 1990–1991. We made *Bossanova* and *Trompe le Monde*. I remember on *Trompe le Monde*, they hooked us up with a with a popular filmmaker who was getting a lot of action over there on MTV—a guy called David Wild.

And filmmaking and the production value of videomaking at that time was still such that people were pretty convinced that if you wanted to have any kind of fighting chance promoting your records via video, that you had to spend another $100,000, $200,000, $300,000. They had no problem with it! They would just fucking sign the check—"Here's $200,000. You need to make a video to do this properly. If you're going to be taken seriously, you've got to spend $200,000 *minimum* on a video." And we're like, "$200,000? *Jesus Christ.* That's almost as much as we spent on the record—to make one little fucking clip!"

ART ALEXAKIS: Our first album [1993's *World of Noise*] had sold one hundred thousand records—just from us touring and touring and touring. That's an album that was recorded for four hundred bucks. By the time our first major label album came out, *Sparkle and Fade*, in May of '95, our first single was a song called "Heroin Girl"—that only got played in fifteen markets because of the word "heroin." People wouldn't play it. The markets where it got played, we were top ten/top five. And in a few cities, we were number one. It was *really* difficult.

When we made the video for "Santa Monica" and they went to go get adds, "Santa Monica" had a hard time. It got into the top twenty, but just barely. It started getting played on MTV on *120 Minutes* and *Alternative Nation* in the fall of '95. And it started getting played at night—what they call "dayparting," where they would play it at night on radio. And it *slowly* crept up. We were touring constantly and a lot of word of mouth.

There is a two-week period where the industry shuts down, about three days before Christmas and up to the first week of January. You can't find out how your record's selling, what SoundScan is. But I remember going into that break, we were selling about six to seven thousand records a week, which is really good back then for an indie band. And then it went into blackout, but we found out that MTV had added us into Buzz Bin—that's when they don't daypart your record; they play you a minimum of ten times in a twenty-four-hour period. We found out on January 2nd or 3rd that our record had gone from six thousand records a week to *thirty-six thousand* records a week. That's all due to MTV.

MATT PINFIELD: MTV had that thing called Buzz Bin . . . or many times, the videos were referred to as a "buzz clip." Now, when we put those songs in that category—which meant they would get played a lot more and featured and focused—eight times out of ten, those bands or artists would literally go from point A to point B. And almost always go half a million to a million records. Sometimes the record labels would be disappointed if the record *only* sold three hundred thousand when you got a buzz clip.

ROGERS STEVENS: At the time, the "No Rain" video was on *so* much. It was a weird feeling that you would turn the TV on and it would be on and being talked about. That moment was very surreal in a way.

The video . . . I think simple ideas translate the furthest. If you effectively execute a simple idea, it's powerful. And that's what that video is to me. Uncomplicated.

The right way to do it is say, "*Here's what we're going to do.*" And that was really what happened with "No Rain." We said, "We want to use *this image*." And once we gave that direction, at least it was directly involved—and it worked. [The "bee girl" character] shouldn't have been used again in another video ["Tones of Home"]—it was not a mascot. It was a one-off idea.

FERGAL LAWLER: [Director] Sam Bayer said, "I really want to go and get some footage in Belfast" [for the Cranberries' "Zombie" video]. So, he headed off to Belfast with a couple of crew guys and had no plan or anything—just took shots of graffiti, soldiers, and kids playing. Got a load of footage, came back to Dublin, and then did our performance bit. And then for the other part of the "Zombie" video, Dolores flew to L.A. and did the whole "covered in gold paint thing."

ART ALEXAKIS: The director had this idea of me swimming in this machine [for Everclear's "Santa Monica" video]. He put me in this swimming machine that looked kind of like a Houdini water-torture machine. He put it up on this high hill overlooking the beach, and they filled it up with water from a water tank—which was 60 degrees. They put me in a suit and I'm swimming in it, and there's no way to stop swimming—they didn't make it so that I could rest! I'm in 60-degree water . . . I got hypothermia *really* bad. I went back to the hotel and a doctor had to give me saline. I was shaking all night. In the morning, we went to Burbank and it was 110 degrees inside this house, and we filmed that stuff there.

PAUL LEARY: The "Pepper" video was a lot of fun. [Butthole Surfers] went out to Los Angeles, and they rented out a soundstage that had been used in the filming of *The Wizard of Oz*, so I was pretty freaked out being in this old building. They had a little trailer for us to hang out. And I'm hanging out on the porch of a trailer, smoking a cigar, and this limo pulls up. And the window rolls down . . . *and it's Erik Estrada*. He goes, "You like cigars?" And the guy pulls out three of the nicest Cuban cigars I've ever seen in my life and handed them to me.

So, I'm pretty endeared to Erik Estrada—he was a lot of fun to hang out with on the set. He stood around telling jokes. We had a scene where he was supposed to eat cream corn from a can. And in between takes, he was still eating cream corn from that can. I think they wanted Don Knotts originally, but Don Knotts wanted too much money, so we got Erik Estrada. *And Erik Estrada was perfect.*

CRAIG WEDREN: *Beavis and Butthead* was a generational/cultural thing. I have no idea of what it did or didn't do for bands. We certainly in Shudder to Think appreciated their coverage of the "Hit Liquor" video—which still cracks me up to this day. We all took their "no comment silence reaction" as a very high compliment. But I was watching *Beavis and Butthead* more for the cartoon and less for the music. I love *Beavis and Butthead*.

DANA COLLEY: It's exposure. These guys [Beavis and Butthead] would just insult everything they saw. So, if you go through it with a bruise or a minor scrape, then you were successful. It was good for the band—either way. I think they said something like Mark [Sandman] reminded them of a "hungover Jon Stewart."

KEVIN MARTIN: If you got on *Beavis and Butthead*, you made it—whether or not they liked you. We were pleasantly surprised that they actually included [Candlebox] in that world. I've never met Mike Judge, but I was a huge fan of that show, and I love everything he's done. Being such an influential cartoon—much like if you're on *Family Guy* now or *The Simpsons*—you thought to yourself, "Okay. We've made it." It's like when you see your cassette tape at a truck stop.

PAUL Q. KOLDERIE: *Unplugged* first started with a friend of mine, Jules Shear, who came up with the idea of just taking some people who were famous for doing electric music and putting them in a different context.

MATT PINFIELD: Why it worked in an "*Unplugged* atmosphere" [for such alt-rockers as Nirvana, Pearl Jam, Alice in Chains, and Stone Temple Pilots] was because . . . at the root of it all, the songs were all so well constructed. They could work in many different genres. When you strip a great song down, it's still a great song. And there was so much passion in those songs and performances because it was artists being honest.

SPEECH: For us, personally, *Unplugged* was another great vehicle to introduce people to [Arrested Development]. I'm the producer of this group, so I sampled a lot of live instrumentation stuff in a way that emphasized the liveness of the groove that I was sampling. So, instead of it sounding more machine-like, I was purposely trying to go with a live sound and a live feel. And we had live instruments on the album as well.

So, *Unplugged* for us was a great opportunity to expand what hip-hop is to people and show them more of what it can be, and what it is. Before us [on *Unplugged*] was LL Cool J and A Tribe Called Quest. Ours was a literal album [1993's *Unplugged*]—I don't think theirs became albums. And it sold very well—it went gold. It was a very big part of our trajectory as a group.

KENNEDY: MTV was important in that alternative videos were much more groundbreaking than some of the pop videos because there was so much more artistry and experimentation. And some of the up-and-coming video directors at the time were able to work with these artists, and a lot of them didn't want to be on camera. You think about Tool, and even Pearl Jam, were really hesitant to be a part of their videos. Spike Jonze . . . I was talking to my boyfriend the other day about [the Beastie Boys'] "Sabotage" and how funny and groundbreaking that video was. Spike was really a skateboard photographer and videographer and had come up through that culture and used that imagery so beautifully with different bands and expanded what could be done on a visual medium with incredible songs and artists.

MARK KOHR: It became this thing where in the '90s, David Fincher brought cinema to music videos. Mark Romanek brought fashion and art photography to music videos. Spike Jonze brought comedy to music videos. I don't know what *I* brought, other than maybe a sincerity or heart, to music videos.

EDDIE "KING" ROESER: Honestly, you look at any video from that era, and you sort of scratch your head. It's like, "*What were any of us thinking?*" Even as cool as the "Sister Havana" video is, videos in general . . . I find them quite painful to watch.

ROGERS STEVENS: The video for [Blind Melon's] "Change" was ridiculous. That's a good example of "*What the fuck?!*" Now, Sam Bayer's a great guy and obviously hit a home run for us [with the "No Rain" video]. So, they're like, "Well, let's use him again. Third time's a charm." That was all done on a soundstage, and we were in our "dark stage"—we were burnt the fuck out. We should have made that video like . . . a year before. And much simpler.

But you've been having a lot of success, and people start to think that every one of their ideas is good. Sam's like, "Let's paint Shannon gold." And then there's a guy with a pig. I don't know what *any* of that meant. I mean, think of the message of the song. It's not represented in that video. *It's just dumb.* We would have been much better off just showing the band playing it live—that would have been timeless. I look at them, and I'm embarrassed. I don't want to see them.

BILL GOULD: We did [Faith No More's] "A Small Victory" in 1992, that video. And that was still "peak MTV." And that video cost *a lot* of money. There were big budgets for that. So, that was still going strong.

Gerald Casale with Devo at Kentish Town Forum in London, May 6, 2009. "Baby pictures for the record company."—Gerald Casale *WENN Rights/Alamy*

MIKE WATT: That's when bands are spending more on the video than on *the record*. Think about that—the commercial is bigger than the thing that you're selling. I guess movies are like that, right? They spend a boatload of money on movies, but then, the promo. So, they graduated to that point.

DAVE MARKEY: The Gumball videos [that Markey directed] were modest budgets—I think the first one, "Accelerator," was twenty grand or under. We're not talking fifty to a hundred thousand for the other videos I did in the mid part of the '90s. I think the major labels themselves weren't that used to working with someone like me and the way that I work.

MARK KOHR: Video budgets from '94 to '96, all the new bands I directed were like, a hundred and twenty-five grand. And then quickly, it popped up to two hundred and twenty-five grand. And then they got pretty damn big—I was working with a lot of budgets that were anywhere from two hundred fifty thousand up to four hundred thousand dollars.

IAN MacKAYE: It broke my heart seeing all these young bands spend twice their recording budget making a video that would never get shown—because of the gatekeepers.

ART ALEXAKIS: The "Santa Monica" video wasn't a very big budget at all. Because bands were spending a hundred and fifty thousand to two hundred thousand dollars or more on videos. Originally, Capitol said sixty thousand, and I got them up to eighty-five thousand. There were two shoots: One was up in Malibu and one day in Burbank on a set, at the Warner Bros. set.

KENNEDY: Spike Jonze and I were hanging out one night, and we were going through Times Square singing songs, pretending we were in an impromptu musical, and singing and dancing around. And that was part of the inspiration for [Björk's] "It's Oh So Quiet" and the Fatboy Slim video that he did ["Weapon of Choice," starring a dancing Christopher Walken], which was awesome. You never know where inspiration is going to come from.

And Spike Jonze told me his creative process—which inspires me to this day, and anyone who writes or creates I would suggest this—he says he gets a yellow pad and he listens to the music and he writes down every thought that comes into his head, and he doesn't edit himself at all. And I do that if I'm writing a monologue or I'm writing a story for *The Daily Mail*. Because when that creative vein is completely open, you get these *insane* ideas—and some of them are very usable.

Again, it's like, Beastie Boys: "Sabotage." Great song, incredible, iconic video. No one will ever forget that video as long as they live. I think Spike Jonze is an absolute genius, and he did as much visually as all the bands he tried to honor with great ideas, as they did musically.

"IS THIS ABOUT COURTNEY LOVE?"

Gerald Casale offers memories of working with Foo Fighters, Soundgarden, and Silverchair.

Dave Grohl and company had decided that they could trust me to direct ["I'll Stick Around"] when they had been anti-video and bucking the record company. And then obviously, they acquiesced and decided, "Okay, we like Devo and we like what Gerald Casale did with Devo videos. He's not going to embarrass us." So, they accepted me based on my treatment.

They showed up four hours late to the soundstage, and the shot list was very architecturally laid out to get the shots we needed to composite with the CGI 3D "virus" that I was putting in there—modeled after microscope enlargements of the AIDS virus. But I got half the shots I needed, so I couldn't have all these edits that I wanted and all the cool things happening with the angles and the virus. And when they did show up, Dave suddenly had ideas he never talked about—eating the chess pieces. Which, that was stop-action—and that took up an extra hour.

And it was *very* low budget. I think they were spending their own money at that point, and the whole thing was sixty grand, which is nothing—especially with CGI composited with live action. We had talked about what the song was about, and I asked him, "Is this about Courtney Love?" And he goes, "Well . . . *think what you want*." I assume it was. And I agreed with his sentiments.

Soundgarden's "Blow Up the Outside World" was a strange experience, because each of those guys are great; but they all had their own dressing room. They clearly weren't talking much with each other. They each had their own "person" with them. And even though that was a huge budget and they signed off on it with a complete two-and-half-day shoot, I was told, "Don't *ever* have the band come out unless you're totally ready to roll camera. Use whatever stand-ins or crew you need and do *not* let them come out here and wait more than one minute for the cameras to roll." And I went, "Jesus. *Okay.*"

They were all very nice and polite, but they would all come out of their dressing rooms, assemble for the shots, and then . . . back. There were a lot of single shots, and the most single shots were of Chris Cornell because he's singing the song and he's involved in the B-roll of him being bound in a chair like Alex from *A Clockwork Orange*. Once he was alone, he relaxed and opened up. He was very thoughtful, a very smart guy. But very down. They broke up right after that.

I like those guys [in Silverchair], but I could see what was going on then, because [singer/guitarist] Daniel Johns, that poor guy—the manager had *total control* over this band. It was almost like treating him like a boy band—overmanaging them, telling them what to do at every moment. The guy came to me—he was overbearing and obnoxious—and said, "Just so you know, this video will have to be 50 percent close-ups on Daniel no matter what idea they signed off on is. *I don't care.* " So, that was "Freak."

I had a really great edit that told the story of how they're playing in this controlled environment and they're sweating, and the sweat is going through the open grating on the floor, and there are maniacal people collecting the sweat and turning it into a serum to take this old woman and make her young. It's like *Attack of the Giant Leeches*. It was such a fantastic edit . . . I had to cut out half of it to show close-ups of Daniel. So, you don't really know what's going on in the one that was broadcast.

And then when we got to "Cemetery," that was like their dirge, their "Blow Up the Outside World." By that time, enough time had passed that Daniel seemed very disturbed and very depressed. He seemed like he needed medication. And shortly after that is where you find out through the grapevine that he kind of had a breakdown. And I don't find that surprising, given how they were being overmanaged and manipulated.

MARK KOHR: At that time, the standard fee [for making music videos] was 10 percent of the budget went to the director and 15 percent went to the production company. At the time, it was a sizable amount. When I was making videos for $125,000, I was making twelve grand a pop. If I had a penny for every time Green Day was watched on YouTube and television . . . that would have been nice.

GERALD CASALE: Then MTV was turning their back on music videos being their bread and butter. It was this burgeoning reality-show programming [starting with the popular *The Real World* series in 1992]—and anything *but* music videos in primetime. You had to see music videos early in the morning or late at night. And less were being programmed, so it was tougher for a band to get on MTV. And they were dictating to directors what they wanted to see—like a machine. "Baby pictures for the record company." The art of it was gone.

MIKE WATT: And notice that the video thing is gone now. Maybe YouTube, right? Why did that disappear? I guess when the big labels went under, they couldn't afford to make expensive videos—or MTV decided that they weren't going to be some promotion arm.

DARREN JESSEE: I would say YouTube is MTV now—and it's all free. So, another huge example of how everything has changed.

GERALD CASALE: Mercifully, there's some kind of balance in the cosmos, because once record companies quit being who they were and they weren't giving bands advances anymore—they were just signing somebody and doing a three-sixty deal and hoping to make money off them from their merchandise and live gigs, and a piece of publishing—they weren't spending hundreds of thousands of dollars on videos anymore. So luckily, the new technology comes along that puts more power into the hands of do-it-yourself people—less expensive than ever to have the means to create something that's decent looking and get your idea out there.

KENNEDY: I'll never forget, one of the first weekends I was in New York, Lewis [Largent] took me out shopping to try and figure out what my taste was, to buy some stuff that I could wear on camera—so I didn't look like a hillbilly, which I thought was a great look. But I did my first night wearing a fringed, tan suede jacket—without ironing. So, he took me out and was like, "You're not going to be here very long. You don't know how long this job is going to last. Take advantage of every single moment." And he meant, "Take advantage of every moment and create relationships with outside networks so you can have a job."

I internalized it as, "Take advantage of every single moment and every show and every person and every band that came through." I wish I could go in a time machine to my twelve-year-old self and say, "*You are not going to believe what will happen to you and the people that you will see on a day-to-day basis.*" [Note: Largent would pass away on February 20, 2023, at the age of fifty-eight.]

MATT PINFIELD: *120 Minutes* changed a lot of people's lives. My girlfriend—who worked with Lady Gaga and so many other people in video and TV production—said, "I know a lot of people who are more famous than you are. But I've never seen anybody stopped so much to be told that *120 Minutes* changed their lives and the way [they] looked at music." And that's an incredibly high compliment and something to be proud of. I'm grateful to have been a part of that crew—with Dave Kendall and Lewis Largent, and the incredible people behind the scenes that programmed the show with us. It was an exciting time to be in college radio, to be in commercial alternative radio, and to be on MTV.

DANNY SABER: When Matt Pinfield is introducing your video on *120 Minutes* . . . you know you made it, in a way. There was a time where that was the coolest fuckin' space you could be in. Because Black Grape wasn't getting played on MTV in the US during the day . . . but we were on *120 Minutes*. And *that's* where you wanted to be.

Matt Pinfield in New York City, January 19, 2010. "When Matt Pinfield is introducing your video on *120 Minutes* . . . you know you made it, in a way."—Danny Saber *Steve Mack/Alamy*

Angelo Moore with Fishbone at Limelight, New York City, July 13, 1993. "From the TV, man, they have it looking like it's a big space. *But it's a little studio.*" —Angelo Moore *Steve Eichner/WireImage/Getty Images*

17 OTHER WAYS OF SPREADING THE WORD

"People actually used to have to pay for shit"

Sure, MTV played a large part in breaking alt-rock artists. But there were other ways you could connect to the masses in the '90s, as well.

SEVEN-INCH SINGLES

MARY TIMONY: Everyone had a seven-inch, and everyone would give you their seven-inch. I still have boxes and boxes full of seven-inch singles from the early '90s. It was like a calling card for a band. People sometimes didn't even make full-length records—they'd just make seven-inches. Maybe it was easier to record two songs. You'd give it out to your friends for free.

LOU BARLOW: I *inhaled* records. Particularly seven-inches, because that's always been my favorite way of consuming music—singles. I love that immediacy. And I love how singles are always a surprise—you can buy them based on the cover. It was relatively low-risk at that time.

STICKERS

FRED ARMISEN: My memory of it is there were *a lot* of stickers. You'd go backstage, and a band would have their sticker up somewhere. I don't think they do that as much anymore. Stickers were like a real language of representing bands that you liked. It sort of made your personality: "Which stickers do I put on my car?" That says a lot about you.

But also for bands themselves, it was like their "Morse code" for each other. There were bands that don't get discussed as much, but you saw their stickers *everywhere*. It was really important. Bands didn't have websites back then . . . but they had stickers. I think in the '70s it was posters—it was an actual product, to get like a Boston or Styx poster. And then somewhere in the '90s, it became stickers.

LIVE SHOWS

MIKI BERENYI: A lot of that alternative music was also a lot about live. There was a circuit. Bands played, they met each other, they socialized—there was more than just sitting in a bedroom writing music and putting it on a platform and then doing nothing with it except for waiting for people to hear it. To me, that seems incredibly passive.

JOHNNY TEMPLE: For a lot of bands back in the '90s, if you put on a good show, you could tour and tour again. And that's how you built your audience. That was pretty exciting—to be able to come back to a place and realize you played such a great show last time that now there's more people.

The great live bands were going back to the evangelical mindset—I think of Fugazi and the Jesus Lizard as being two of the very best. It was total sensory overload and so visceral. There were a lot of bands that were really trying to rip your head off—not necessarily trying to blast you with high volume, but really trying to provoke visceral reactions out of people. The bands that I was drawn to had live shows that turned your stomach or provoked goosebumps—physical bodily reactions.

IAN MacKAYE: We would often tour with the songs before they were on records. There was this sort of peculiar thing where people would say, "Are you touring behind this record?" And that's an industry thing. We looked at it completely the other way around. People say you tour to support records, but our position is you put out records to support the show. Fugazi had a mantra: "The record is the menu, the show is the meal." This whole idea that human beings are supposed to load themselves into a van and then drive hours and hours, lug the gear in, set it up, play the show, break this gear down, pack it up, drive, and do it over and over again—all in service of selling plastic? *Fuck that.*

LORI BARBERO: Live, [Babes in Toyland singer/guitarist] Kat [Bjelland] would make a setlist and I wouldn't know what song it was. So, Kat would always have to play the first two or three notes . . . and then I'd know what song it was.

DARREN JESSEE: You could go do a show and play things any way you want. It was an experience to be shared with the audience *that night*. And the same thing with photos—we would take photos, but you would never see them. Now, every photo is on the internet, and every live thing ends up on YouTube. Everything is on the grid now and a little safer—because everyone is so hyper aware now that there's going to be a visibility on the internet to everything. The '90s were a great era because I didn't have a mobile phone, I didn't have a website—*we were out playing shows*. And every time we went onstage, we had a great show; and that was all it was about. It was just having a thrilling musical experience in *that moment*.

TV APPEARANCES

ANGELO MOORE: The producer we were with [when Fishbone was the musical guest on *Saturday Night Live* on March 23, 1991], David Kahne, was like, "Alright, you guys . . . you've finally made it. You're famous!" The studio was such a little studio. From the TV, man, they have it looking like it's a big space. *But it's a little studio.* The crowd really isn't that far from the stage that you're performing on. The cameras make it look a lot bigger than it is. I would hear people tell me, "I saw you on *Saturday Night Live*." So, when you put two and two together, they put you on national television, they see you, then you come to their town and they see you.

ROGERS STEVENS: When [Blind Melon] did *The Jon Stewart Show*, I think he had just gotten the show. And it didn't last long. He was very young. He wasn't the same guy—he hadn't developed *The Daily Show* act. He was trying *everything*. They had some funny people on there, though. But we were in and out. That stuff didn't really matter to us that much. You'd be on tour, you'd be in New York, and they'd say, "Hey. We're going to go to the studio in the afternoon and do this, and then you're going to go straight to sound check, and then the show."

The big ones, of course, we knew about—like *Saturday Night Live* and *Late Show with David Letterman*. By the time we played on *Saturday Night Live* [on January 8, 1994], we were burnt out and weren't necessarily at our most energetic, best performance. I mean, we played okay, but at that point, we were thumbing our nose at the whole fucking thing. Which is dumb—if you're going to do something like that, you've got to come in with your A game.

It was cold—always freezing [at the *Letterman* taping]. Which made me miserable. And I remember on all those studio shows just how close the set is. It looks like a big set that is wide, but when you're in it, it feels like you're in somebody's bedroom. It's an illusion.

Sebadoh, 1995. Left to right: Bob Fay, Jason Loewenstein, and Lou Barlow. "I inhaled records. Particularly seven-inches, because that's always been my favorite way of consuming music—singles."—Lou Barlow *Andy Willsher/Redferns/Getty Images*

DANA COLLEY: Jon Stewart was great. He had [Morphine] on—on the same week that show was being canceled. I think we were on the same show with Ted Nugent—some wildlife guy came on with a big bird, and the bird got loose in the studio, just as we were going to play our song and flew into the audience and pecked somebody . . . who had to be removed and went to the hospital! But Jon was amazing—he and Mark [Sandman] really hit it off. He said Mark reminded him of his older brother.

We were on *Late Night with Conan O'Brien* a couple of times, and we really noticed a difference. We were touring south and we stopped in New York, did the show, and then kept traveling down. I think by the time we got down to Atlanta, we noticed a big difference in our turnout. And a lot of it was because of that exposure. It was the only game in town really, when you think about it. There weren't a lot of outlets other than MTV and *Conan*.

JONN PENNEY: I actually remember having a conversation—it's hard to believe you would have it—about whether or not [Ned's Atomic Dustbin] would go on *Top of the Pops*. It's kind of a similar conversation to would we really sign to Sony Music—a major label. "Isn't that really uncool? Isn't that like going with the mainstream?" And what swung it for me was I read an interview with Robert Smith from the Cure, and it turned out they had the very same conversation.

There were late-night programs [in England] like *The Tube*—that were very much niche. And they grew through the new wave era, and people were certainly looking out for wanting to see these kind of bands on their TVs. But yes, it was kind of like living in that late-night area, where it's a niche audience. Whereas *Top of the Pops*, it was like your stepmother, grandma, or your mates at school that you don't know that well, they'd say, "Are you in a band?" "Yeah, yeah, yeah." "When are you going to be on *Top of the Pops*?"

RECORD STORES

JOHNNY TEMPLE: Record stores used to make the music business go 'round. And the people that worked in record stores were music fanatics/music lovers . . . almost *evangelical*. It wasn't just the record stores that had the records—it was the people who would work in the record stores that would champion music and bands, not because they were being paid promotional money. A lot of record stores were this haven away from this corporate mindset that has infiltrated so much of our culture.

MARY TIMONY: I did go to Tower Records to buy stuff, but I liked smaller record stores more, probably. Later in the '90s, there was this record store called Other Music that opened up in Newark and also in Boston. There was a store called In Your Ear I really liked in Boston. Tower Records I knew I could find something there if I wanted to find something, but I don't think I ever bought stuff randomly there as much . . . also, Newbury Comics I liked a lot.

MATT PINFIELD: Tower Records was a really important record chain. That was the high point of selling CDs and cassettes—CDs and cassettes were *so* important then. In the '90s, they definitely had a lot more locations before everything went belly up. The Tower in New York City was amazing. I used to go there, and there were people working there that cared about music. Record stores in general at that time, it was a big part of everybody's life.

SOUNDTRACKS

CHRIS HASKETT: Part of the adjunct to being on a major label was the major labels would get music onto soundtracks and TV shows.

JOHN AGNELLO: For me, the *Singles* soundtrack started it all—that had the Screaming Trees song on it, "Nearly Lost You." That song got placed on the record after our record, *Sweet Oblivion*, was recorded [which Agnello engineered]. They just put it in the movie, and it was great. But after that record is when I started getting calls from J [Mascis] from Dinosaur Jr., going, "We've got to do a song for *Judgment Night* with Del the Funky Homosapien in L.A." and all that. But it was great—because people bought those records.

PAGE HAMILTON: I think I'm the first quote in a *Rolling Stone* article about the *Judgment Night* soundtrack [which featured collaborations between rock and hip-hop acts]. They were like, "This combination of rock and rap . . . this could be something." And I'm like, "Ahhh, I don't think so, man. This is a one-off kind of thing. *Some* of it works." [*Laughs*]

CHRIS HASKETT: What appearing on *The Crow* soundtrack meant to us was I think we bought Alan Vega a house. [Note: Vega co-wrote the song "Ghostrider" with his Suicide bandmate, Martin Rev, which Rollins Band covered on the soundtrack.] But soundtracks were very important because they started cramming more and more songs into movies. You can legitimately put a song on a soundtrack if . . . I think in *The Crow*, our version of "Ghostrider" is playing on a radio for like, ten seconds or less in one scene. But when I get my BMI checks, they're from *The Crow*. It's *still* paying now.

PAGE HAMILTON: [Helmet] got asked to be in *The Crow*, and we declined. We had a tour thing going and it conflicted, so they used My Life with the Thrill Kill Kult. And that's the scene where Brandon Lee was accidentally shot and killed. We were working on *Betty* already, and Butch Vig came to town. I always wanted to work with Butch since Killdozer. When we got asked to do it, it was just about money, basically. I mean, "You'll pay us to put a song in a movie? Fuck yeah, we'll do that!" And the same way with [our cameo in] *The Jerky Boys*—they're like, "Ozzy Osbourne is going to be your manager . . ." And I'm like, "In! Done! Good!"

TRIBUTE ALBUMS

COREY GLOVER: For the artists [who appeared on tribute albums], these are the influential people of their lives. These are the records and the songs they heard on the radio—that put them in the mindset to do a certain kind of music. And to think that Jimi Hendrix, Neil Young, Parliament, or any of those people were outliers in that they were sort of bucking the system. They're heroes.

JOHN AGNELLO: Tribute records were great—that was so much fun. Dinosaur Jr. did a great job of "Goin' Blind" [for the 1994 tribute album, *Kiss My Ass: Classic Kiss Regrooved*]. I think Gene Simmons called J—while we were in the studio—and we played it back, through the phone!

PAUL Q. KOLDERIE: Tribute records became more a strategy after the record business started dying—the idea that instead of trying to get people to buy one record of twelve songs by one band, you'd give people twelve songs by twelve *different* famous bands and hope there were enough people who liked enough of those bands that they would buy the record. Obviously, you can't do it now because no one would care . . . I think people put out "tribute songs" or songs for causes. It was like everything else—good idea at first, then overused eventually. Overrun with mediocre competition.

REMIXES

MOBY: I've done remixes for everybody from Freddie Mercury and Michael Jackson to the Beastie Boys and Daft Punk to Smashing Pumpkins, Metallica, and Soundgarden. And the funniest story from my perspective was I did the Soundgarden remix [for the song "Dusty"] because I loved Soundgarden. And I was on tour with Soundgarden, and I remember I was on a boat with Chris Cornell from Sweden or Denmark to Finland. We were talking—he was the sweetest, most wonderful man—and he goes, "Oh, I really love that version you did of our song. What are you going to do with it?" Because he didn't understand "remix culture." And I had to explain to him, "You own it." And he was like, "But *you* made it." And I was like, "No. Your record company paid me to do this, so, *it's yours*."

It started in the early '80s when you had organizations like Rock Pool, which delivered records to DJs. And someone at Warner Bros. would send a rock record to a DJ, and the DJ would be like, "Well, this is nice . . . but I can't play it." Then, that DJ would go into the studio and do a remix. At that point, it was one-inch tape or half-inch tape and razor blades, and they would craft something that was the "dance-mix version." And it became incredibly successful. Bands like Depeche Mode, they would have the "radio version" that a DJ could never play; but then they'd have the "dance version," which became bigger than the original.

I think of Fatboy Slim [aka Norman Cook] when he did his remix of Cornershop's "Brimful of Asha." I don't know even if anyone's heard the original, but his remix became a number one song in the UK. Or when Andrew Weatherall did the remix of Primal Scream's "Loaded" [which was actually a remix of an earlier song, "I'm Losing More Than I'll Ever Have"]—I don't think I've ever heard the original, whereas his remix became an iconic song that got played a million times.

DANNY SABER: People actually used to have to *pay* for shit. So, if you're going to package a CD single and it's a song that's already on a record, you've got to give them some incentive to buy the thing. And, like, U2—imagine all the people that did remixes for U2 over their career. A few years back they packaged a collection of all their favorite remixes, and I had two on there, which was pretty cool. But there was added value. There was sort of a defined "brief": "Here's what they're asking for." It sort of ran the gamut from making it sparkle a little for radio or taking the vocal and making a whole new song.

MAGAZINES

MATT SWEENEY: Lots of young band people could work in the mail room at *CMJ*—which I did. College radio played records that weren't played on mainstream radio, and *CMJ*—which was called *College Music Journal*—the college radio stations would send in their playlists of records, and they would report those to *CMJ*, and then *CMJ* would compile them. And that would be a consensus of what was going on in the underground. Things like *Pitchfork* and South by Southwest do what *CMJ* did—it's just it was way more specialized back then. But it was enough that people were making big money off of it.

The *CMJ* Music Marathon I think was seen as a little more music-oriented, and New Music Seminar was maybe a little more glitzy. But they would happen at the same time. The *CMJ* Music Marathon was SXSW but in New York—except not as toxic and not as steroid-ed. It would happen over a four-day weekend, and all the downtown clubs would be taken over. It was exactly like SXSW, but there was less desperation. More people weren't trying to make their careers—they were trying to do drugs, get laid, and make a record.

TANYA DONELLY: I feel like *CMJ* was the informational center for a while, where you would find out what music scenes were cropping up and where and how to connect with that as a traveling musician. *SPIN* was the more sort of "mainstream indie publication." And they also focused on actually continuing [the] indie scene under the mainstream. I feel like they were more comprehensive. And *Rolling Stone* at the time had already shifted toward a different vibe. *Rolling Stone* was like "my parents'" magazine when I was a kid. But by the time I was a working musician, it had already shifted.

MATT SWEENEY: Being on the cover of *Rolling Stone* was a big fucking deal. And *SPIN*. These sort of consensus-based aspirational magazines about people being famous. It was slightly weird because it was at odds with a lot of the indie rock bands. I wasn't interested in being famous—I just wanted it to be cool. That's why Kurt Cobain wearing a shirt that said "CORPORATE MAGAZINES STILL SUCK" [on the cover of the April 16, 1992, issue of *Rolling Stone*] . . . but, of course, *he's excited* about being on the cover of a corporate magazine.

DARREN JESSEE: You had writers like . . . David Fricke comes to mind, writing for big magazines like *Rolling Stone*. Since there was no internet presence, people would buy magazines to keep up with stuff. So, there was a thoughtful conversation about things.

JASON PETTIGREW: *Alternative Press* was basically a bunch of misfits who hated MTV and FM radio/playlists/Clear Channel—that whole commodification of everything. And everybody liked a lot of different stuff. If you look at twelve months of any year of *Alternative Press* from the '90s, it was sonically diverse. We were fans first and professional journalists later. The most disappointing thing about *Alternative Press* is that I think that everybody loves music the way I do. And there wasn't an internet, so you bought a lot of things—British weeklies, fanzines. You heard about regional scenes. What was a magazine without a "scene report"?

MATT PINFIELD: We also got a lot of information from the British magazines, like the *NME*, *Melody Maker*, *Sounds*, and *Q*.

MIKE EDWARDS: The three main music papers [in the UK] when Jesus Jones came out were the *NME*, *Melody Maker*, and *Sounds*. *Sounds* was kind of the "runt of the litter"—it had kind of dug itself into more of a heavy metal hole. And then there was a strange period where *Melody Maker* and the *NME*, in order to set each other apart, they became quite antagonistic. Which was a problem for bands. Because as soon as you became championed by one of those music papers, the other music paper would dislike you. Which is fine for the music papers. But for bands, it was terrible—because you wanted both papers to champion you and you wanted the people to find out about you.

We initially had good reviews in *Melody Maker* and a little in the *NME*. But then like many British bands, we kind of fell out of favor. I attribute a lot of the lack of success of our third album, *Perverse*, to the hatred that the editor of the *NME* had. It was reported to me that he had said the *NME*'s sponsorship of the Glastonbury Music Festival in '93 or '94 was dependent on Jesus Jones *not* appearing. Whether it's true or not, it's very believable; and it does illustrate how influential the music papers were on the alternative music scene in the early '90s.

JONN PENNEY: *Kerrang!* was just a realm of hair metal before the likes of Pearl Jam, Nirvana, and Soundgarden. From not being a metal fan and observing from the outside, bands like Metallica were still viewed as cool. But even [Ned's Atomic Dustbin] ended up doing interviews for metal magazines—the more "muso" ones. So, we'd get asked about having two bass players and what the gear was.

JASON PETTIGREW: We wanted to have in America the type of thing that Great Britian had with stuff like *NME*, *Melody Maker*, and *Sounds*.

RADIO

MATT PINFIELD: People used to tape my radio shows, and I was going through some cassettes of my shows from the early '90s—and, holy shit, it's one great song after another.

KENNEDY: There was a little bit of lag between MTV and alternative radio. When I was working at KROQ in Los Angeles before MTV, KROQ actually broke a lot of bands and a lot of songs. Which then, those artists kind of made their way through some of the commercial alternative radio stations and then made videos that made some of the people superstars—like Sinéad O'Connor and Seal.

VADEN TODD LEWIS: Alternative radio was where it was at. To keep our label on their toes, [Toadies] would always check the radio stations when we rolled into town that we were supposed to be on and go to the local record stores to make sure that our record was in stock. Like "policing our label," I guess. And listening to these [commercial rock] radio stations at the time in '95 was such a weird experience, because it would be Bachman Turner Overdrive, ELO, Toadies, Foghat. It was just weird. Because everything was changing, and they didn't know where to put this stuff.

MATT PINFIELD: In the '90s, you could hear Stereo MC's "Connected"—which could be considered a British hip-hop record—on the same station you'd hear Alice in Chains' "Man in the Box."

MIKE EDWARDS: I was always mortified that John Peel didn't like [Jesus Jones]. I think he played us once because his audience insisted he do so—in his Christmas Top 10 of 1989 or whatever it was. But there were other people who championed us, who had a very similar kind of influencer-like role—people like Andy Kershaw. But that was the only way that you got out to people—was being played on those kind of radio shows. Typically, shows that didn't start until nine or ten at night.

FAT MIKE: I'm kind of a punk rock elitist, and I don't like most music. I've never listened to the radio my whole life.

FESTIVALS

DANA COLLEY: European festivals still remain the high mark of music production, hospitality, and organization. I think what Europe has that the States don't is that they have a state-subsidized budget for entertainment, for culture. So, a lot of the venues are subsidized by the state—which gives them a lot more freedom in terms of having to make their nut and also paying bands. It's a healthier culture in general for music, and because it's something that they value and built into their social structures. So, big festivals were really well organized.

For [Morphine], going to Pinkpop was pretty amazing. It still has resonance to this day. It was in Landgraaf, Holland, way down south, and we were on at eleven o'clock in the morning. They had multicameras onstage; it was a live broadcast throughout the country. So, you can't underplay what kind of exposure that would bring. Not only the people who were there at the actual festival itself, but the *entire nation* was watching and tuning in. So, that really helped to once again give us the kind of exposure that opened up doors and opened up other opportunities for us. The same with Glastonbury.

ANGELO MOORE: It's a lot of people, a lot of space, a lot of stages. And everybody is out there. The only difference is you've got the language barrier—people speak a different language over in Europe. It's not just English—you've got French, Dutch, German, a lot of different languages.

ROGERS STEVENS: You could go over there in the summer every year and there would be this incredible culture over there. And they were different—the metal festivals were as you would imagine. But Glastonbury and Reading are the big ones that I remember. And then there are a couple that are in Germany or something, that I remember thinking, "This is fucking *huge*. Insane."

MIKE EDWARDS: They were huge. Particularly Reading—which is an alternative one. Glastonbury had a little more mainstream stuff going on, but it was a bigger festival. It was a dream come true if you appeared at any of those. Every band wanted to do it.

JONN PENNEY: The Reading Festival, all of a sudden, was *all* grunge—and before alt-rock, it had been metal. So, it was metal, alt-rock, and then it became massively grunge.

CHRIS HASKETT: Lollapalooza [compared to the other aforementioned festivals] was really relaxed because it was also really consistent and known. Every day, you knew the crew, you knew the gear. All those sheds are the same—you play Pine Knob, Great Woods, Irvine Meadows, you know what you're getting. They're cookie-cutter. Woodstock '94 [held from August 12–14, 1994, in Saugerties, New York, with an estimated crowd of 350,000] was something else entirely. Playing in front of a big crowd wasn't really the issue. The issue was more it was going to be broadcast live and there's no real sound check. Those kinds of festivals tend to be more stress because there is no routine. On Lollapalooza, there *was* a routine—the Butthole Surfers' gear goes here, Living Colour's gear goes there, Rollins Band would come offstage and their stuff goes there. Whereas Woodstock, Roskilde, Reading, or any of those, it's a lot more that can go wrong.

CHAD TAYLOR: Woodstock '94 was amazing and, of course, intimidating. [Live] played "Iris" as our opening song, and I can remember barely being able to hold the chord as my hands were shaking.

FERGAL LAWLER: Woodstock '94 was great. I remember walking on the stage and going, "Holy shit. *I've never seen so many people in my life.*" It was mind-blowing. I still look back with fond memories.

ROGERS STEVENS: People seem to think Woodstock '94 was more important than [Blind Melon] thought it was at the time. Because we thought we did a bad show—or at least *I* did. I thought the band wasn't great, but Shannon was off the hook. And especially I thought there were bands that overshadowed everybody that weekend. Like Green Day—that made them stars. It was, like, instant how big that band got after that show. And talk about rising to the moment—that showed who they are, basically. And as far I can tell, they *still* are.

CHRIS HASKETT: We had to stop while they moved everything back and they got the squeegees out [when a rainstorm broke out during the Rollins Band's set at Woodstock]. But it was kind of apt—all of a sudden, the fury of the heavens coming down in the middle of the Rollins Band's set. But it was like, "This isn't going to stop us." So, it added to the experience.

LES CLAYPOOL: I don't really get nervous before I go onstage. I might get anxious—like I just want to go. That one I was nervous for. Not because of all the people, but because Primus hadn't played together in *months*. I was actually on tour with Sausage at that time. I drove in on the tour bus, and [Primus bandmates] Ler and Herb flew in in a helicopter. I spent the afternoon with my six-string bass trying to relearn these songs—or polish up these songs.

Sometimes, you can be in the middle of a tour and be as well rehearsed as you can possibly be, but you're not having a good night and things fall apart. But this was one of those shows where, whatever metaphor you want to use, all the planets aligned, all the mojo was there—it was one of the best shows we ever played. We came out, and we were on fire. It was incredible.

And then of course, as soon as I said, "My name is mud," I see this *sea* of clumps coming my way. Ler runs and Herb runs. And then I got on the mic and said, "*People that throw things up onstage at artists have small and insignificant genitalia.*" And it all stopped—I couldn't believe it! To this day, I still have splatters of mud in those bass amplifier cabinets.

MIKE EDWARDS: It was a rite of passage—being played on John Peel or Andy Kershaw, getting an interview in the *Melody Maker* or the *NME*, appearing at three in the afternoon at the Reading Festival or Glastonbury Festival. Those things were important in terms of our career but also in terms of your morale—because if you get a good slot at the Glastonbury Festival, then, "Yeah! We're *really* on our way."

18 LOLLAPALOOZA 1992–1995

"It was the best party on wheels"

Lollapalooza continued to attract the masses and earn mucho dinero as a traveling roadshow—even after its inaugural year.

AL JOURGENSEN: I was on the second Lollapalooza with Soundgarden and Pearl Jam. And Chris and Eddie and I would talk about stuff like this and go, "Yeah, but in the long run . . ." We felt that we were being bought out and being used as pawns. We tried to keep some integrity. I'll never forget—at one point, I *declined* to be on Lollapalooza. There was only one of them as a template, and I wasn't sure about this. I thought, "This is some sort of corporate sellout thing."

And not only that, but they had us scheduled to play midafternoon or something like that . . . so then I canceled. And then I get a call from not only them but members from Soundgarden and Pearl Jam. I told them, "Look, Ministry is not a 'picnic band.' We don't play during the day—that's not our thing. So, I'd rather play in a dingy club in the dark, where we can have our visuals and all this other stuff to affect the climate and the mood that Ministry wants to portend."

They offered up their slots to me—so it was the Chili Peppers [as headliner] and then Ministry. Which, there was *no way* that we should have been up that high in the slot. But Chris and Eddie decided, "It's worth it for the integrity of the show." They didn't mind playing during the day, whereas I did. So, it was a real camaraderie between us—to try and not make it so corporate. But now, that's out the door. Right now, everything is just a giant Coachella—no matter what you do.

Lori Barbero (behind the drum kit) and Kat Bjelland of Babes in Toyland at Lollapalooza, Waterloo Village, Stanhope, New Jersey, July 13, 1993. "Everyone became friends—meeting new people and seeing new places."—Lori Barbero
Steve Eichner/ WireImage/ Getty Images

MIKI BERENYI: That Lollapalooza tour [in 1992], I was a bit terrified. But the audiences did come and listen to you. They didn't throw bottles of piss at you. They were quite open to listening to different kinds of music. I think that changed. Even when we toured with the Flaming Lips and Babes in Toyland supporting us, I always liked having support bands that sounded completely different. I thought that was the point. Y'know, you don't want to go to a gig where two bands sound exactly the same.

But what I didn't like about that transition was it became mainstream. The mainstream came in, the mainstream was funding it, and they were trying to appeal to mainstream people. And those are people who have never been particularly curious about music. I get it. I don't have a problem with it—go and listen to whatever the fuck you want to. But what annoyed me was, now the alternative scene was being destroyed—because it was being monetized. And that meant ripping the heart out of it. It's not like the masses are going to change and become more musical to fit what you're marketing. No, you've got to make bands who are blander and more mainstream to fit in with the demand of what that listening audience is. And to me, that was the beginning of the end.

LES CLAYPOOL: We originally weren't supposed to headline [in 1993]. I think it was going to be Alice in Chains, and Alice in Chains didn't want to close. So, they were like, "Do you want to headline it?" And we were like, "Yeah, let's do it! What the hell?" Like idiots, here's the biggest show that we had done on our own not as an opener or support, and we decided to hire a good friend of [guitarist] Larry LaLonde's to do the lights for that show—just because he'd gone to two hundred Grateful Dead shows. He didn't know how to

Arrested Development at Lollapalooza, Waterloo Village, Stanhope, New Jersey, July 13, 1993. Left to right: Nadirah Shakoor, Speech (with arm up), Baba Oje (in background), Foley, Headliner, and Aerle Taree. "We felt like we were, in a sense, converting a lot of people to what we were doing. It felt powerful."—Speech *Steve Eichner/WireImage/Getty Images*

THE MYSTERIOUS OLDER MEMBER OF ARRESTED DEVELOPMENT

Speech explains the role of Baba Oje.

Baba Oje's role was primarily symbolic. I saw this generational gap becoming sort of baked into American pop culture or young culture. And I never agreed with it. I went to Jamaica when I was younger, and I went to a party. At the time, I was in high school, and all of these beautiful, young, vibrant college and high school–age kids were partying to groups that were in their forties and fifties. And I was like, "Wow. We don't do this a lot in the States anymore. I really feel like the gap between elders and youth is unnecessary and uncool. There's so much that we could be getting from each other." And so, I purposely was wanting to add an elder into our group.

There was a guy named OJ Johnson who used to hang with the college students at this university I was in at the time, UWM [University of Wisconsin–Milwaukee], and he was really cool with all of us. He was fifty-seven at the time, but he had no issues just hanging out with all of us young people—who were nineteen, twenty, twenty-one. So, I asked him to be in our hip-hop group. At first, he was like, "Are you crazy? *Hell no!* I don't want to be in a hip-hop group." And then he realized I was serious and that he knew my mom and dad. It turned out he researched me and said, "Oh, you're Robert and Patricia's son." He was the best man at their wedding! I had no clue about any of that history.

He was like, "I don't want to discourage this young guy . . . so let me say yes." And it's not going to mean anything anyway, he was feeling—because the group's not going to go anywhere. We're living in Milwaukee, Wisconsin. No hip-hop was breaking out of Milwaukee any time soon. He didn't feel too worried about it ever doing anything. And then, of course, *it did*. It changed his whole life. He became world renowned—as we as a group did. He's Baba Oje—the oldest person in hip-hop history at the time. [Note: Oje would pass away in 2018 at the age of eighty-six.]

do lights . . . but we hired him because he was a good friend. But that was kind of the way we did things—we were always trying to "homegrow" everything.

SPEECH: First of all, it was absolutely exciting for me. It was an emotional high every day. Lollapalooza now is different—it's in one city [Chicago]. But we toured throughout the nation—twenty thousand or more people per show. We're on with some of the biggest legends in music at the time. The fact that we're a hip-hop group performing for this huge, white crowd of rock fans. We were the only hip-hop group on the entire tour. So, we knew we were reaching new people that maybe wouldn't have given us a shot. That was incredible.

We were performing to twenty thousand people, which, prior to Lollapalooza, had never happened for us. The biggest we had done prior to Lollapalooza was with En Vogue, and that was probably five thousand people. And with En Vogue, we went on so early in the lineup that there wasn't a packed crowd a lot of nights. With Lollapalooza, we were right in the middle of the afternoon, and it was packed every day. And everyone was very curious about this group Arrested Development, so we got a chance to have a conversation with millions of people during that tour. We felt like we were, in a sense, converting a lot of people to what we were doing. It felt powerful. And not to mention, we made a lot of great friends.

LORI BARBERO: It was the best party on wheels. Everyone became friends—meeting new people and seeing new places. It was really a wonderful experience. For me, it's one of the highlights in my life.

JENNIFER HERREMA: Lollapalooza was a really fun tour. But that seemed like there's all these people onstage with all this huge, expensive gear. It seemed like a totally different echelon of money and backing and something that was not part of our world. But I appreciated it just the same.

LOU BARLOW: It was weird, but it was awesome. Sebadoh did the side stage [in 1993], and we went right through the Southwest in the middle of the summer—played in the blazing sun, at like 110, 120 degrees in the middle of the afternoon on this raceway. But the shows were cool because the kids that came to the side stage came there for us. Kim Gordon and Thurston Moore were also doing our side stage, and Tsunami. And then I had a little bit of communication with J. [Note: By this point, Barlow had left Dinosaur Jr., who were on the main stage that year.] It was kind of cool to be in the realm with them. The main stage was so far away . . . the closest I got to the main stage was when Rage Against the Machine played. I mean, talk about a complete '90s blowout act—Rage Against the Machine were *incredible*. And we got paid a thousand dollars in cash a day!

SPEECH: Rage Against the Machine came out butt naked onstage [on July 18, 1993, in Philadelphia]! So, they were making other statements. Y'know, the Red Hot Chili Peppers came out with socks on their, *y'know*. But Rage came out butt naked. The statement forced you to listen.

LES CLAYPOOL: I first saw and met Tool on Lollapalooza '93. And here's [Tool singer] Maynard [James Keenan] running around—he had this weird mohawk and was always hunched over. He looked like a gargoyle or something. And he was always working out backstage. And for some reason, he had turkeys at his house.

JENNIFER HERREMA: Tool was on our second stage. I remember there was a "graduation party" for Tool . . . I thought everything was kind of absurd. It's kind of like Smashing Pumpkins being on Caroline Records, and all of a sudden you're "graduating."

LES CLAYPOOL: I think 1993 was the first time that people kind of "threw rocks" at Lollapalooza—because we were headlining. People thought it wasn't that strong of a bill. But because Tool and Rage Against the Machine were flip-flopping opening the main stage or closing the second stage—they both obviously became huge. In hindsight, the tour was a pretty spectacular lineup.

JIMMY FLEMION: We opened Lollapalooza 1994. We were the very first act to play at noon in 117 degrees in Sam Boyd Stadium in Las Vegas, Nevada. And then we had the makeup on and the costumes, so it was *super* hot. We opened with "Fuck Off," I believe. And there was Billy [Corgan] joining us onstage for a few of the performances, which was nice. And that was the thing, Billy and Kurt were the two who said, "We want the Frogs to play Lollapalooza"—they were going to be the top two bills of the whole event. [Note: Originally, Nirvana was going to be part of Lollapalooza that year but dropped off shortly before Cobain's death, resulting in the Smashing Pumpkins being appointed as headliner.]

MARY TIMONY: We were on the side stage [in 1995], we played with Built to Spill, Moby, Superchunk. I remember Courtney Love could barely stand up because she was on so many drugs, and they had to cart her to stage. I remember Allen Ginsberg hanging out backstage, Pavement getting pelted by mud, and playing in Pittsburgh and these two kids stood in front of the stage and gave me the finger the entire set.

MOBY: I got *so* lucky because I was offered to play on the second stage [in 1995], and at first I was a little bummed out. I was like, "Gosh, it would be nice to be big enough that I could play on the main stage." But we were mainly playing sheds—amphitheaters. And what happened—which was surprisingly wonderful, selfishly for me—is the main stage during the day, no one wanted to be there because there were all these empty seats. If you're at the main stage watching Beck, Pavement, or even the Bosstones, it was a hundred people in seats that held twenty thousand people. So, the bands were *miserable*. I remember Beck and Pavement being like, "What are we doing? This is *so* depressing. We thought this was going to be super glamorous." But they're playing at 3 p.m., essentially in an empty amphitheater.

But what happened was the second stage where I was playing, there were no seats. So *that's* where all the kids went. Eventually, all the main stage bands started coming over to try

THE BAND THAT INSPIRED RAGE AGAINST THE MACHINE?

Rudeboy Remington states his case.

I came to the DNA Lounge [in San Francisco, a show that Urban Dance Squad headlined on September 29, 1990] real early with the crew. Go into the venue, and then the opening band comes in—a band called Lock Up. They set up their things, and the drummer wanted to say hi to them, and they kind of gave him the cold shoulder. So, he went back and he was taping his hands, and I said, "So, how's the other band?" He said, "Oh, they're assholes." I said, "Really? Let's fuck them up!" He said, "No, no. Don't do anything . . . tonight, *we play them to the ground*."

So, we had the same dressing room as Lock Up. They started their show, I checked—they knew how to play . . . but it was like typical meat and potatoes "American rock music." We figured, "*We're going to destroy you.*" And we did. So, come back in the dressing room, and these guys were awfully quiet. But one guy came to us, and he said, "Oh, man, I loved your show." That was one of the guitar players. Two years later, I see him on Pinkpop and I figured, "This guy is from Lock Up!" So, he [Tom Morello] obviously saw us, and whatever he is doing is no problem, because he might get inspired or something. But the fact is he wasn't [yet] in Rage Against the Machine—*he was in Lock Up*.

and play on the second stage. Like, Thurston Moore was doing that, and Beck was doing it. All of the energy—until the sun went down—was happening at this second stage. For me, it was transformational because all of a sudden, you realized that electronic music played with a band and guitars excited the audience just as much, if not more, than traditional rock. You'd be playing to Nirvana fans . . . and on the second stage there'd be five thousand people going crazy—seeing mosh pits to electronic music. It was a really special moment. And also, the lineup of that '95 Lollapalooza still stands as so eclectic and special.

BILL GOULD: I think there were two things [concerning why Faith No More was never on a Lollapalooza bill in the '90s]. I don't know if Perry Farrell was ever a big fan of Faith No More—that was one thing. That's what I've been told—I've never actually personally met him. Another thing is I learned later—like fifteen years later—that when we did our Guns N' Roses/Metallica tour [in 1992], that we had actually been offered to play Lollapalooza as well. And our management chose the Guns N' Roses/Metallica tour. Which I never knew about. And if you think about it, I can understand why they made that decision. But if you're looking at it for the band and where the band probably would have fit in better, I think it probably would have been Lollapalooza over the "mega-tour."

MIKI BERENYI: I think what Lollapalooza did was that camaraderie where all the crew for the different bands were working together and people were going onstage and they were spending nine weeks traveling around and getting to know each other—that was actually a really great experience. And no one was arriving in a fucking helicopter. Everyone was on their tour bus, and people were getting lifts with each other and hanging out. It genuinely had a sense of community to it for such an ambitious stage show with however many bands, plus second stages. The idea of having all that working together actually makes it an infinitely better experience for the bands involved. Which I would assume translates to the audience as well. I don't know if by year four or five that changed, because I did hear that, "Oh, it suddenly got a bit 'main band in this enclosure and more high security.' We were in a very early period of it, and it was genuinely great fun. I mean, it nearly fucking destroyed me." [*Laughs*]

19 SECOND WAVERS

"People trying to get rich and famous have a lot in common"

It seemed like post-1991, the amount of new alt-rock artists truly putting their own unique spin on things became increasingly rare with each passing year—as a more "familiar" sound was detected among most newcomers.

DAVE MARKEY: There was a lot of stuff that got signed that seemed to me to be bands that would have ended up being hair metal bands . . . but they were jumping on the "grunge/alt bandwagon" in a sense. It was a mixed bag.

RUDEBOY REMINGTON: As soon as Nirvana became higher than everybody else, that's where the problem started. Because record companies suddenly realized there was a lot of money involved.

KRISTIN HERSH: Once the superficial aspects of what was eventually called grunge were identified and simplified in the '90s, I found it all to be diluted enough to seem comparatively same-y. People trying to get rich and famous have a lot in common, in other words. [*Laughs*] And that desperation is boring compared to the visionary quality of the energetic, more Zeitgeist-ian singularity of a true scene.

Stone Temple Pilots at MTV Movie Awards, Burbank, California, June 8, 1993. Left to right: Scott Weiland, Robert DeLeo, Dean DeLeo, and Eric Kretz. "We're not going to put Stone Temple Pilots on the cover. We're not going to put Our Lady Peace on the cover."—Jason Pettigrew *Jeff Kravitz/FilmMagic/Getty Images*

JENNIFER HERREMA: Anything that was put together and created and nurtured by Hollywood is definitely going to have synthetic elements. Part of it is not organic. There are so many bands like that, whether it be Hole or whatever. I can't even speak of the music—it was just bullshit as far as I was concerned—when people come from different states. Y'know, Axl Rose came from Indiana—people come and congregate and look for a deal. It never occurred to me that there was ever a deal to be had. We really got lucky, and I'm grateful. But it seems like there's a lot more that goes into things that I've never been privy to or understood.

JASON PETTIGREW: Once it got to the "exploitation machine," all the stuff that didn't sound like Journey, Styx, or Foreigner was now called "alternative." And there was stuff that *Alternative Press* simply would *not* cover. We're not going to put Stone Temple Pilots on the cover. We're not going to put Our Lady Peace on the cover.

MIKE WATT: This is 120 years ago—there was an artist in France, and his big shtick was he was a "fartist." He whipped up this whole act about farting—singing the songs. He came to the US to do it . . . and found out there was a guy ripping him off! He had to sue him. So, humans, they're fucked up—there's always someone trying to find the easy way to win the lotto . . . so you can squander it all. [*Laughs*] I always look at SST, the three trios—Hüsker Dü, Meat Puppets, and the Minutemen—all just using bass, guitar, and drums. And each sounded *way* different. Also, Greg [Ginn] not signing a bunch of bands that sounded like Black Flag.

Clones, I don't see how anybody digs that shit. I remember the guy who sang like Ed Vedder—and they probably sold as much records because he copied his voice sound. He could probably sing like anybody; he was really good—Scott [Weiland]. He was a sweet guy. The last fIREHOSE tour was the Butthole Surfers and Stone Temple Pilots, and Gibby

Candlebox at Lowlands Festival, Biddinghuizen, Netherlands, August 23, 1994. Left to right: Peter Klett, Bardi Martin, Kevin Martin, and Scott Mercado. "Candlebox never really became a Stone Temple Pilots, where everybody knew who Robert, Dean, Eric, and Scott were."—Kevin Martin *Niels Van Iperen/Hulton Archive/Getty Images*

Haynes giving them *so much* shit. Gibby printed up a shirt that said, "Met at a Black Flag show," and it showed these guys in puffy shirts and shit, like New Romantics. Talk about low-hanging fruit. And then the guy turns into this whole drug thing. He was a really sweet kid—it was really terrible what happened. But I think he was just wanting to get in with the people.

And he found his voice—he found his thing. And the [DeLeo] brothers—especially the bass man—could write some songs. I liked those guys a lot. It's like, you want to get in there and you want to belong, but I don't think that it's always really self-conscious, "It's going to be Halloween 365, 24/7—I'm going to wear these other guys' clothes." It's hard to know motivations like that.

ROBERT DeLEO: I think that whole label [grunge] was a sales pitch. It was the way for record companies to put a name on something they could sell. That's how I look at it. I don't think any of us in STP enjoyed being characterized as a "grunge band." It's funny, because you get signed to a label and you're kind of constantly fighting against what they're trying to promote you as. It's an interesting position to be in—and it's not always a fulfilling one and a happy one. I think by when the second record came out, [1994's] *Purple*, we showed where we were musically going. Even on the first record, I don't know if it was "grunge."

PAUL LEARY: It almost blew up after the first couple of shows [on the aforementioned Butthole Surfers/fIREHOSE/Stone Temple Pilots 1993 tour]. Because Gibby was rude to Stone Temple Pilots and would say things about them from the stage that would upset Scott Weiland, who at one point tried to rush the stage to fight Gibby—and he had to be held back. And then they discovered a mutual interest in drugs. And all of a sudden they were best friends! And Gibby wasn't riding on our bus anymore—he was riding on the Stone Temple Pilots' bus. I remember hanging out with Dean DeLeo—who is hysterical. If I'd have gone to high school with him, he'd have been my best friend.

PAGE HAMILTON: When Stone Temple Pilots, Pearl Jam, and Alice in Chains started to come out, I didn't feel like they were part of "our scene." They just seemed to be huge from day one. I saw Soundgarden open for Mudhoney at Maxwell's in New Jersey. So, Nirvana and Soundgarden felt like they were part of our "indie rock scene." And the other bands came after that. I'm not saying that one way or another that doesn't make them cool. I never group those bands in with our little indie scene.

CRIS KIRKWOOD: Here's what people didn't get: Scott was from San Diego; Eddie was from San Diego. Eddie was imitating Scott—it's not the other way around!

MOBY: When I first heard [Stone Temple Pilots], I thought they were Pearl Jam. So, I fully understood when people dismissed them as being "Eddie Vedder wannabes." That early stuff definitely sounds that way. But I remember driving on the 10 from L.A. to San Diego and hearing some of the later stuff—it had this glam quality to it, and it *really* stood out. A lot of those early-'90s grunge bands, they didn't evolve or they died or they disappeared into obscurity. Whereas Stone Temple Pilots evolved in a really interesting way.

BOB MOULD: I remember going to see Stone Temple Pilots in 2000 or something with a friend. And after like, the thirteenth song, I looked at my friend like, "These are all Stone Temple Pilots songs?" I had heard all of these songs forever, but I didn't know who they were.

MATT PINFIELD: I thought it was unfair that Stone Temple Pilots got criticized. Because, granted, when "Plush" blew up, there was a feel similar to Pearl Jam's. But the rest of the record, *Core*, did not sound like really anybody else. And I thought they were a special band from the beginning. But that second album, *Purple*—that cemented any questions anybody had about whether they had staying power. I love that record. *Tiny Music* was an album that also was incredible—it went in a different direction completely. Stone Temple Pilots are definitely one of the most important bands of the '90s—I don't care what anybody says.

ROBERT DeLEO: I always go back to someone like the Police. Look at the first Police record to the fourth Police record. Or U2. U2 is a perfect example of a band who really was moving forward musically and not concerned about certain boxes they were put into. Look where U2 has gone musically—they've grown and grown. By the time we hit *Shangri-La Dee Da* [STP's fifth album], I think, musically, that's where I wanted to see the band be—making that kind of music. It's a highly under-the-radar record. And musically, it's the most satisfying for me—to listen to that record.

CRIS KIRKWOOD: Stone Temple Pilots are fucking good. If anything, they're a *Led Zeppelin* rip-off. And the only thing that Pearl Jam managed to do was have a cool name and have people like their singer or whatever the fuck it is that makes people like anything. None of the rock 'n' roll that got made holds a candle to rock of the '70s in a lot of ways. The DeLeos are Jersey guys and knew their rock 'n' roll. I don't know, people all have their opinions . . . and they can all go choke. Here's my only quote that I've ever come up with that I think is worth a shit: "The only thing that I can stand about other people is the fact that they'll all die."

PAUL LEARY: We were touring with Stone Temple Pilots, and they were recording an album [*Purple*]. And I think they were trying to get recording done during the tour. They would go into studios on the road. And we were passing through Minneapolis, so they booked a day at Paisley Park. So, I went to Paisley Park to play a guitar solo on a song ["Lounge Fly"], and I showed up at the time they wanted me to be there . . . and ended up having to wait like two hours in a little room. I was just smoking pot and getting drunk, so I was pretty blitzed by the time they got me in the room. I don't even remember playing. They told me not to look at Prince [who owned the studio]. But I did. *And nothing bad happened.*

MIKE EDWARDS: There's always that kind of thing of the floodgates opening and the first bands come through—the interesting ones. And then after that, it's just more of the same. There is that swing of the pendulum. It doesn't matter what art world you're dealing with or whether it is music or fashion—there's always a reaction against what came before. When you were in the '90s, the worst decade that ever was was the '80s. When you were in the '80s, the worst decade that ever was was the '70s, and so on.

ROGER JOSEPH MANNING JR.: You're always going to have artists who are quite talented in their own right, but their skill set may be better at copying or running with a trend than having a highly original statement. If I look back at my favorite groups of the '60s—both the British Invasion and what was happening in America—the groups that I love, a lot of them were just trying to go for some B-level Beatles. Or B-level Kinks. But in the process wrote some *amazing* songs.

MATT PINFIELD: One of the underlying things in the '90s was the indie rock/punk rock snobbery. There was some "punk rock guilt" that I'm sure Kurt Cobain felt, which he shouldn't have because he was incredible at what he did. Which doesn't mean fuck-all now. Because people love those records and they are a big part of their lives. In retrospect, I think bands like Bush and Stone Temple Pilots are completely loved.

VADEN TODD LEWIS: Other people's perception of me, I just can't give it any thought. It is weird to me that we get called "grunge." I didn't think of myself as grunge. But looking back at the photos, "Oh, yeah, we had plaid in the look." So, I get it.

GERALD CASALE: To me, they [songs by subsequent more "mature-sounding" bands like Counting Crows and Matchbox Twenty] were being called "alt-rock songs," but they were really modern kind of pop songs to me—featuring an emotive singer. So, it was slick. And the mixes were very professional.

ROGER JOSEPH MANNING JR.: At that point, it's kind of "in the air"—certain songwriting styles, chord progressions. Singing styles—everybody makes fun of what has now become to be known as "yarl." It was a kind of sound, it was a trend, it was a way to say, "We like lead rock singing, but we're not going to try to be Freddie Mercury or Robert Plant. That has nothing to do with us."

KEVIN MARTIN: Candlebox never really became a Stone Temple Pilots, where everybody knew who Robert, Dean, Eric, and Scott were. So, we were kind of the "faceless rock band from Seattle." And we were fine with it. It did well for us, and here I am thirty years later making music and still touring and playing on an album that changed millions of peoples' lives [1993's self-titled debut].

ART ALEXAKIS: On *MTV News*, I remember they asked Dave Grohl, "A lot of people think Everclear sounds like Nirvana." And he said, "I don't think they sound at all like Nirvana . . . but I think *Bush* sounds like Nirvana." [*Laughs*] It was kind of a burn. But there were bands that came out, and we had been around for a while at the local level and the indie level. And Bush's record [1994's *Sixteen Stone*] broke about a year before ours did. And Candlebox . . . I don't know where Candlebox fits in. They were a band in Seattle, but they didn't sound like anything else in Seattle. They almost sounded like an old-school metal band—a pop-metal band.

Unfortunately, during the period, a lot of bands were signed for one song. They were signed for the song that became their "big hit song." And that is kind of a career killer. When we were signed to Capitol, we didn't have "Santa Monica." I didn't write that until a month or two after we signed, when I was up in Portland in my basement, working out songs at night and then the next day, Craig [Montoya] and Greg [Eklund] would come over and we'd work on the songs.

But that was hard for a lot of the bands at that time because they'd get all blown up, and then once the single would come out, the label would just cut their losses and then move on.

THE REVEREND HORTON HEAT: I don't really want to pinpoint Nickelback . . . I just did, I guess! But hey, [Horton Heat bassist] Jimbo [Wallace] loves Nickelback.

CHRIS HASKETT: Where we were a big band in 1990 on the indie circuit, by 1992, we're pretty much the same size. But Alice in Chains—massive. Stone Temple Pilots—massive. It felt like us and the Melvins were stuck in second—because what we are doing is less "consumer-friendly." But at the same time, look at what's going on elsewhere—you've got Morphine, Fugazi, all these other bands that are still doing this incredible indie shit. And *really* original. Who are big but are staying big in an "indie way."

It sort of raised the water level for everybody. Local H—that would be a good example, right? I don't think in the pre-Nirvana world they would have been playing where they were on the festivals in the post-Nirvana world. It's not a criticism of them—suddenly, there was more attention being paid.

GERALD CASALE: I thought it was nakedly commercialized grunge because there was kind of a "pop chord progression" and a mix that was more friendly for radio. But you can't begrudge somebody of that—not everybody can be Nine Inch Nails. There are a lot of bands that their credo or mission is to be commercial. And they're trying to be commercial—they're not hiding it.

THE REVEREND HORTON HEAT: That's one of the catch-22s of music—it's cool when you're the only kid on the block that likes Nirvana. Then all of a sudden, it's not that cool when everyone on the block is wearing a Nirvana T-shirt. There's always going to be a decline once things lose their "coolness factor." As long as people are trying to be artistic and creative, even if it's derivative of some other band . . . there's a lot of people who love Pearl Jam. That band I never really got, but it's okay—those songs bring back memories.

MIKE WATT: Humans always gravitate to these things that inspire individualistic moves that gives the geo to other people to be creative . . . but then at the other time, they'll get into this "herd mentality." Remember hardcore? "Anarchy" was the slogan—and then it was one same outfit.

CRIS KIRKWOOD: But that happens—people make art and then people have their opinions about it. And you've got to be careful if you're sensitive . . . because it can hurt your feelings.

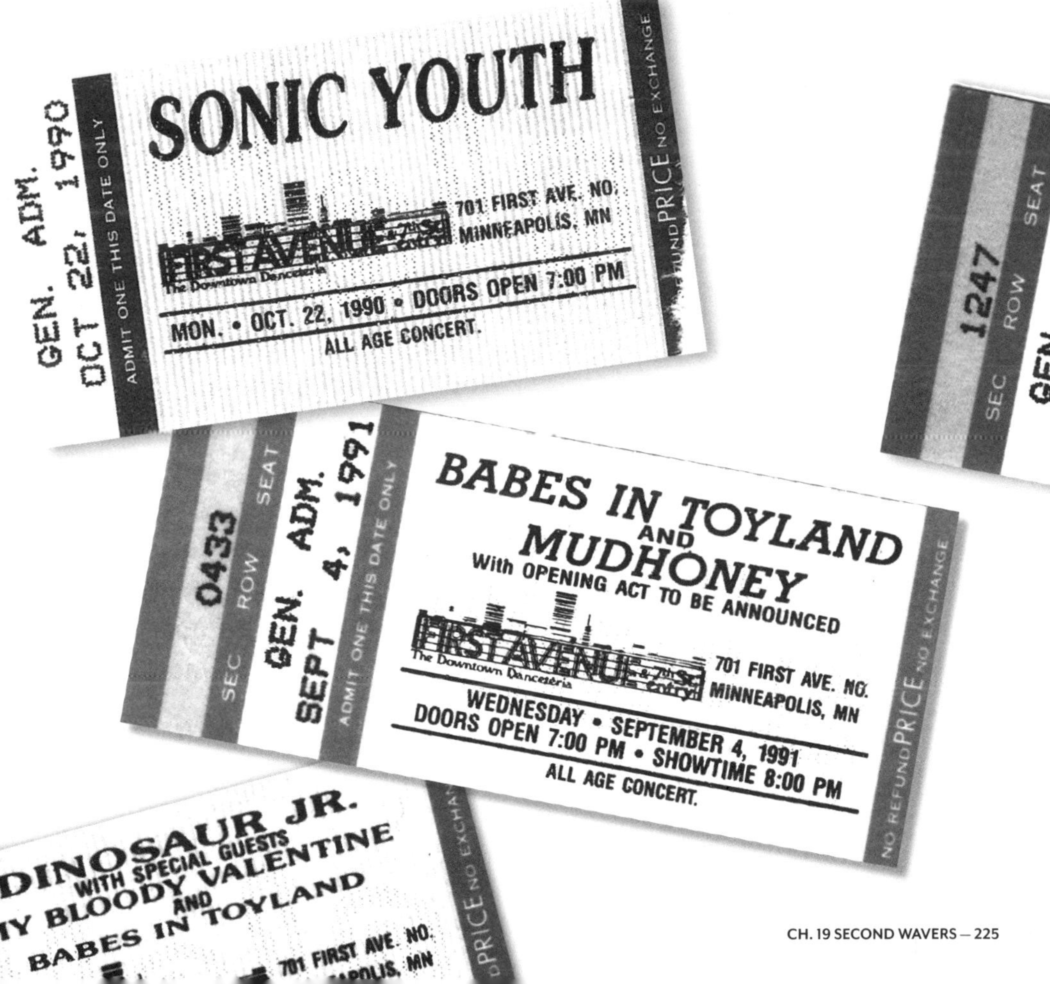

Al Jourgensen with Ministry at Big Day Out, Milton Keynes Bowl, England, July 10, 1999. "By the '90s, all I cared about was if my dealer was on time. I lived on DST—'dealer's standard time,' man."—Al Jourgensen *PA Images/Alamy*

20 DRUGS AND ADDICTION

"I didn't have time to listen to music—'I've got to meet my dealer!'"

Drug addiction—and particularly, heroin—proved detrimental to some of alt-rock's top artists of the era. But was it any more widespread than it was in other musical movements before or since?

AL JOURGENSEN: By the '90s, all I cared about was if my dealer was on time. I lived on DST—"dealer's standard time," man. I didn't have time to listen to music—"*I've got to meet my dealer!*"

EDDIE "KING" ROESER: There was a lot of substance abuse going on. It was endemic for whatever reason. I wasn't really aware of how common it was—even in my own band—until it was too late. It was sort of like a marriage, in that the people who are interested in underground rock are really into drugs.

PAUL LEARY: I know it affected our kind of music—people were dropping like flies. I'm pretty amazed that we survived.

MIKE JOHNSON: The heroin thing was shocking—how prevalent it was and how deeply so many people got into it and died. There are a lot of corpses—*it was just awful*. I don't know about how much it affected the music or anything. But it sure was around . . . and everything else—I had a horrible drinking problem at the time. So, I pass no judgment on people who do what they do. It's interesting to me, like, "Why was heroin around?" I don't know why people got into it.

KEVIN MARTIN: Well . . . Jimmy Chamberlin and Jonathan Melvoin—Jonathan died and Jimmy survived [on July 12, 1996, just before Smashing Pumpkins was to play two shows at Madison Square Garden]. I think heroin was certainly a part of some musicians from that era's makeup—Mark Lanegan, Layne Staley, Kurt Cobain, Andy Wood, and Scott Weiland. It was certainly prominent in that arena of music.

Meat Puppets, New York City, 1993. Left to right: Cris Kirkwood, Curt Kirkwood, and Derrick Bostrom. "*We partied like fuckin' fiends*."—Cris Kirkwood *Bob Berg/Getty Images*

And it might have to do with the depressive notion of what Seattle brought to the table or the availability of it. I had several friends in high school who wound up becoming junkies that now are clean and sober—and have been for thirty-plus years. It seemed like in Seattle it was so available and easy to get your hands on—even much more than cocaine and marijuana, which I think is odd. It was mainly coming in from the harbor up there.

I think every generation has its "drug of choice." Crystal meth was certainly something that was in the late '90s that a lot of people were experimenting with. And in the early 2000s, it seemed like everyone was smoking tons of weed. I don't know really what that hold was that [heroin] had on the Seattle music scene, but a lot of the musicians that we toured with or we would do shows with had their experience with it. So, it did seem that was the drug of choice for that generation of rock bands.

LOU BARLOW: I loved pot. It was illegal, so I was really loathed to actually find it and score weed. I never actually scored my own weed—I found people to score it for me. One being Bob Fay, the drummer of Sebadoh! Weed was wonderful—what's not to love? You're in your early twenties, you don't have kids . . . weed and music are a wonderful combination.

MOBY: MDMA [aka ecstasy] had not been a Class A narcotic. It was prescribed in the '80s—it was a therapy drug. And then some British DJ in Ibiza realized that if you take ecstasy and dance to electronic music, it's a pretty solid combination. And then the entire nation of England—and then Europe—discovered it and electronic music exploded. It became sort of—kind of a strange expression for a vegan to use—a chicken and the egg scenario, where the ecstasy influenced the music and the music influenced the ecstasy. And the end result was, suddenly out of nowhere, there are fifty thousand people out of their minds on ecstasy hugging each other, dancing in a field.

CRIS KIRKWOOD: *We partied like fuckin' fiends.* My drug addiction happened . . . I mean, I knew better. We were libertines and had done everything—and lots of it. And I absolutely knew that certain drugs will get ahold of you if you allow them to—any of the narcotics, booze. Anything to excess. Suddenly, the circumstances hit me the right way—to where I wanted to self-medicate. And mostly what happened is my and Curt's mom got sick and was dying [from cancer], and I moved in with her to take care of her. She had an awful death. And it's no excuse—I knew better still, and yet, I consciously went, "I don't care. I cannot handle this." And then suddenly, I was fucked up.

You look at some of the people that it's gotten—Prince, Tom Petty. People that have been around it and are exceedingly successful and have every reason to keep living. And they still manage to get ahold of them, and it's a goddamn shame. It's the arts—why did van Gogh need to shoot himself? Why did Cobain need to shoot himself? Why do people do the things that they do?

HOW A TUNE FROM *JERRY MAGUIRE* INSPIRED AN EVERCLEAR CLASSIC

Art Alexakis recalls being down and depressed in NYC.

A lot of pressure [while working on the follow-up to *Sparkle and Fade*, which would be titled *So Much for the Afterglow*]. I tried to deny the pressure, because I was like, "Fuck you. I'm not going to play into that. I'm just going to make the record I'm going to make. And I'm going to be above all that." Where, in reality, I wasn't. So, late '96 we went in the studio in L.A.—big-ass studio—to record songs for what the working title was *Pure White Evil*. We recorded about fifteen songs and then went back to Portland and did some overdubs up there. And I recorded another song I'd written, called "I Will Buy You a New Life."

"Father of Mine," "I Will Buy You a New Life," and "Everything to Everyone" were on that original record. But a lot of the songs were different. Then in January, we went to New York to mix it . . . and I knew it wasn't great, but everyone that was around me was saying it was great. And then when it was finally mixed, done, and put together, I played it for my A&R guy, Perry [Watts-Russell], who never had a problem being brutally honest with me. After he listened to it, he's like, "Well, it's not bad. There's some really cool songs and really cool stuff going on. Arthur . . . *it's not great*. It's not the best record you could make, and it's not going to do for you what you want it to. You've got a better record in you. A lot of the songs are great. I don't think you need to start from scratch, but you need to rethink a lot of it, and you definitely need to remix it."

I just went into a depression. I stayed in New York, and my wife flew back to Portland. I just stayed in my hotel, walked around every day, and saw a movie called *Jerry Maguire*. There was a song in it: "Secret Garden" [by Bruce Springsteen]. And I was just in a place where the lyrics and the music and just where it was in the movie hit me. I saw that movie, like, five or six times. And over a period of two weeks of walking around New York listening to the songs on my Walkman, I got two notebooks and started writing notes of what to do to make those songs better and what songs to get rid of. And then in another notebook, I was writing new songs.

When I finally had the songs that I knew that I wanted to go on the record, I called everybody up and said, "Do this, this, and this. I need to book this studio. And Perry, you've been trying to get me to get Andy Wallace to mix this . . . fuckin' go get him." He got Andy Wallace to mix it in a studio in L.A., recorded some new songs—one of them being "So Much for the Afterglow." And another being "Song from an American Movie"—we recorded that, but it didn't come out until the next record.

We remixed it with Andy Wallace, and a friend of mine, Lars Fox, had been wanting to get into Pro Tools. I bought him a system, and he came down to L.A. to work on some stuff. We had done this instrumental jam in the studio, and it became "El Distorto de Melodica." When that album later the next year sold two million records . . . that was the only song that we got nominated for a Grammy for! That's the only one we've *ever* been nominated for.

Self-destructiveness was all around, and it was an odd thing. It was never my bag—mine was pushing it out to the very edges and seeing what was out there. But not in terms of hurting myself. And then it became that . . . it had to do with reaching a certain age. I was well into my thirties by the time I let myself get fucked up. I wasn't as tough as I was when I was younger—a little more emotionally unstable. Circumstances just lined up to where I suddenly found myself not taking the kind of care that I'd always taken.

ROGERS STEVENS: Look at the opioid epidemic—*drugs affect humans*. Now, if you become successful and you have the means to indulge in your vices, that doesn't help. And it is a profession—if you can call it that—that is remarkably forgiving for that stuff. Debauchery and whatnot.

EVAN DANDO: They have their place, and very few people—I'm one of them—can determine where they belong and where they don't belong. My aim is to be sober because that's the new high for me. Ever since I was ten, I wanted to be a drug addict—I swear to God. It's like, when I was eleven or twelve I read all these books, like Carlos Castaneda and William S. Burroughs. And I was like, "*I want to be a junkie.*" That's what seemed interesting to me—because it was illegal. That's why. That's the problem with the drug war: It makes it more attractive to everybody . . . and way more expensive.

AL JOURGENSEN: I can't speak for other styles of music and whether drugs affected them. For us . . . look, man, society changes. And at that point, it's like in the '70s when Studio 54 and cocaine were going. And you had disco and that took off—because it's a societal shift. And in the '90s, the societal shift was a bunch of people trying heroin—heroin escaped the ghetto and went out to the suburbs. And that was all our kids. Also, white kids started going into neighborhoods to get crack and heroin and all that—and it was a societal shift. Of course, it influenced music. And once again, it's a double-edged sword—probably why we had so many deaths, ODs, and this and that. And people dying younger than they should because of the shit we were doing in the '90s. You kind of are a product of your times. And those were the times.

JOHN AGNELLO: I didn't start at the Record Plant until '79. I became an assistant in 1982 and assisted on an Aerosmith record, *Rock in a Hard Place*. It was about two or three months of overdubs, and I'm running the tape machine. But they're showing up eight hours late, and at two in the morning, if I have to go pee, I open the bathroom door and there's six people freebasing in there. It was totally chaotic—a lot of cocaine and a lot of heroin.

I won't say *everybody* did it—the Cyndi Lauper record [1983's *She's So Unusual*, on which Agnello was an assistant engineer] was very clean. There were certain records that at the end of the mixing on the last night, you'd spell the band's name out in cocaine on a mirror. But the Aerosmith one was pretty nuts—I opened the door to the cassette dub room, and I look down, and there's Steven Tyler and Rick James freebasing.

The '90s, we talk about Mark Lanegan and the heroin or whatever, but then you have a guy like J Mascis, who maybe sips scotch at the end of the night—and that was it. Never any drugs. You never woke up with a hangover on a Dinosaur Jr. record and then went back to work. And also with Redd Kross, Steven and Jeff McDonald were in AA, so they didn't drink at all—they binged on candy the whole time!

LORI BARBERO: Billie Holiday—she's not rock 'n' roll, but I think every musician has done drugs since the get-go. It doesn't even mean that it has to be hard drugs—alcohol is a drug. That's why they say, "Sex, drugs, and rock 'n' roll." Nothing could be more true. It all goes hand in hand from my observation of living it/being in it. Some people are addicts, and some people can do it casually—drinking, heroin, meth, speed, cocaine.

It all has to do with chemistry, too. Artists are different people—they think differently and act differently, so there may be a different chemical. If you read anybody's autobiography, they struggled with one thing or the other. And I also know somebody who they tried to get them in treatment or even just therapy, and they said, "I can't," because they thought if they weren't mentally unstable, they wouldn't write good music anymore.

ART ALEXAKIS: Substances have always been a part of musicians, and it still is. They're just using pills—oxycodone and fentanyl. But there was a lot of dope going around in the Northwest and Portland. I remember when black tar Mexican heroin came there right as I was moving there—as opposed to the old Mexican brown. At that point, I was two years going on three years sober. But I was still an addict . . . I'm *still* an addict. I'm still fascinated by it. I know what that buzz means. It really got a lot of attention because of Kurt. I've been in recovery for thirty-four years—going on thirty-five. I'm a sober-life coach, and I work with a lot of people in and out of the program. And a lot of them are creative. But I don't think that it's unique to the '90s.

THE REVEREND HORTON HEAT: I've got a list of musician people that I knew personally who OD'd and died of heroin. It's a long list—it's almost, like, thirty people. And I really think that is why Nirvana is not around now. And the reason why a lot of bands are around is because they quit doing it. Nothing is a good excuse for it, but what happens is to be on the road that much, it's a weird way to live. That's why a lot of them get into it.

Because you're at such peaks—you're at such a high during your show, and then you wind down from that and drink and smoke a joint. Then a few hours later, you're in a hotel room just by yourself. Or you're on the road at a truck stop, buying a roller dog and nobody cares who you are then. The majority of the time you're alive is not the time you're onstage and everybody loves you. The rest of the time, you're basically just a glorified truck driver or a guy by himself in a hotel room. So, that's why a lot of these people get into drugs—because of the way a musician's lifestyle is. It's a lot harder job than people think it is.

GERALD CASALE: Drugs fuel creative people—that's just a fact. It should stop being looked at as a criminal thing or a bad thing—*it's a fact of life*. Clearly, if you're a creative person, what are you doing? You think that you've got something to say that people should listen to. Which is already an outrageous position to take, right? "Why should I get onstage and put this in front of you?" Well, because something is driving you to do it. So, it doesn't matter if it's a bottle of bourbon or cheap wine or coke or hash or heroin—everybody's always done it. And they always will.

JENNIFER HERREMA: "The Spectre," "Blood Flowers," there were a few songs about [drug use]. We tried to stay away from talking about that, because nothing good could come from it. You can have a great time, you can get high, and it was a great day, great week, great month, great year . . . but eventually, it's not so great.

EVAN DANDO: If anyone looks too hard at drugs, they're going to see that they're no good for you and all that shit is up in your brain anyway. And if you're smart, you don't start. But I can understand kids wanting to get high because they're all in the same moment together and they're making music. It's what we did—for a lot of our records, we were on drugs.

Jennifer Herrema with Royal Trux at the Reading Festival, England, August 30, 1998. "You can have a great time, you can get high, and it was a great day, great week, great month, great year . . . but eventually, it's not so great."—Jennifer Herrema *Rob Watkins/Alamy*

DID ROYAL TRUX BLOW AN ENTIRE ADVANCE ON DRUGS?

Vocalist Jennifer Herrema comes clean.

It was '90. It was probably five grand. Gerard Cosloy came to San Francisco to meet with us, and he wanted to put the record out on Matador. It might not have even been five thousand . . . it may have been two thousand. But when you're a junkie and live in San Francisco, that was *big* money. We didn't spend all of it, but we did use some of it on . . . we were recording at Greg Freeman's warehouse [Lowdown Studios]. He had some old equipment. He was incredibly tolerant and patient and was the perfect guy for *Twin Infinitives*, because it felt like it took three years, but it probably only took maybe nine months. Whenever we would have some cash, we would go in and continue on. So, when we got that cash, we'd put some money toward the studio time, and then being strung out, yeah, we spent [it on drugs]. Nobody was ever mad about it. But it *is* true.

I was trying my hardest to fuck things up—that's the funny thing. I would try anything I could—I wanted to really have "the adventure." And what happens? You lose your fucking voice when you stay up when you're touring, and it sucks for the people that came. And you feel really bad. I fell right off the stage one night and fell eight feet into the pit—nobody there—and I landed on my guitar. The guitar was bent, but it saved me—I didn't get hurt at all.

ROBERT DeLEO: I think that goes back to childhood. I'm not a psychologist, but I think everyone's got their own issues. I can't even explain what it's like being in . . . a band that has had success. It's not really normal.

You have to remember who you are. That's a constant reminder along the way—it has been to me. That's really a Native American way of looking at things: Remember who you are. And that goes back to before any of that happened, meaning signing a record contract and making money, joining the circus and doing whatever the hell you want to do.

I think you have to remember who you are. Some people don't, and they can get consumed by it. In the end, it kind of compounds and there's no stopping it. It's a blueprint of people in entertainment. You can watch it and see it. That—like addiction—turns into the same thing. You either die or you go to jail.

MATT JOHNSON: I wish in the case of Jimi Hendrix there would have been a little bit more moderation going on. But I guess there's the whole argument for total abandon. And then, how does that argument for total abandon feed into the art that's being made? If you have to exercise total abandon to make great art, then I guess everyone is just going to end up in the 27 Club and humanity is in for a real shit show for the rest of eternity. I can't believe that. People have to be able to moderate and respect their own talent—without somehow losing it into some state of navel-gazing and self-deception in that process of moderation.

JENNIFER HERREMA: '93 was when we got clean again, and it stuck with [Royal Trux bandmate Neil Hagerty], but I went back maybe four years later—but then I brought myself back again. Once he got clean, he's been clean. The last time I did it was when everything fell apart toward the end of the '90s—my dad was dying, and I couldn't handle anything at that time. I just knew something had to change—and that's when I walked away from everything. And I've been clean since then.

AL JOURGENSEN: You bottom out. I've never relapsed. Let's see, 2001 . . . so, twenty-two, twenty-three years. No coke, no heroin, no pills. You just bottom out, and you have to decide, "Look, do I want to fuckin' die today or not? Because if not, then shut the fuck up and do something about it." Literally, it has to be that. Y'know, they put me in interventions and rehabs and this and that, and it doesn't work unless you finally just say . . . my late/great best friend and guitar player, Mike Scaccia, said, "Just do it until you make yourself sick, man. Until you're ready to puke. Keep doing it until you gross yourself out." And at one point, I just said, "*I'm grossed out.*"

CRIS KIRKWOOD: When I finally got out of prison [in 2005], who should be coming to town but the Chili Peppers. I go to see Flea, and we went out to dinner the night before the gig, and I'm like, "I'm feeling better now. But boy, I *really* fucked myself up." And I'm showing him my scars [on his arms from intravenous drug use], and he's like, "Yeah . . . *wait 'til you see John*." [Guitarist John] Frusciante was back in the band at that point. And then the next night at the gig, yes, John was more scarred than I am. It's a question of, "Well, that's *multiple* hit songs worth of scarring, as opposed to me being in a band that had *a* hit song . . . that I didn't write."

ROBERT DeLEO: People think drugs enhance what you're doing. But take it from me, ultimately it *really* gets in the way.

21 COBAIN'S DEATH

"It seemed like he felt guilty for his position"

Much has been said and written about Kurt Cobain's death over the years. But looking back, did it alter the course of alt-rock?

FRED ARMISEN: Everything about him was like a big shift—as a major rock star, to have that kind of creativity and brilliance.

DAVE MARKEY: So much changed by the end of '91. It was a completely different world. A world that maybe I don't think someone like an artist like Cobain could quite understand. Sadly, enough that he couldn't get it together and just render all of that. After *In Utero*, I thought, "Okay. He's going to be good. He's going to pick up the ball and run." But sadly, that didn't happen.

KENNEDY: These alternative stars were reluctant but very excited to play stadiums and festivals and things like that. It was a double-edged sword for them, because they didn't want to be seen as "sellouts." Their relationship with their hardcore fans was so, so important. It's foreign in today's celebrity climate—people just want to be famous, and people make millions of dollars just being famous. Whereas in the '90s, that was kind of frowned upon.

LES CLAYPOOL: They came out with *In Utero*, which I thought was absolutely brilliant. And they made a video ["Heart-Shaped Box"] with—literally—embryos hanging from trees. And there was *no way in hell* a band like Primus would ever be able to make a video like that and get it on MTV. But because they were in such a position of power, they were able to do something like that. They weren't afraid to push the buttons.

CRIS KIRKWOOD: I often wonder about people like Cobain. Imagine the life of the Beatles—being some guy who can go anywhere, and suddenly, you become somebody who girls are peeing their pants over and you can't walk out the door. And what that would do to you. Look what that did to *him*.

Kurt Cobain taping MTV's *Live and Loud* in Seattle, Washington, December 13, 1993. "It was a completely different world. A world that maybe I don't think someone like an artist like Cobain could quite understand." —Dave Markey *KMazur/WireImage/Getty Images*

MIKE WATT: I met him several times—he'd come to my gigs. A beautiful guy. But the last time [when Nirvana headlined the Los Angeles Forum, on December 30, 1993] was very strange. It was very scary, in a way—he wanted to talk to me about guns. First, he comes up to me and says, "Good to see you, Mike." I said, "Good to see you too, Kurt." He says, "No. It's *really* good to see you." Krist went and got some scissors and cut the bottoms of my pants off or some shit. [*Laughs*]

But then it's just me and Kurt, and he starts telling me about policemen came to his pad and took his guns away. He said, "They shouldn't be able to do that, should they, Mike?" It was a weird subject because we never talked about guns like that. And a few months later was the horrible thing. I remember him showing me the Germs burn on his hand. And them getting Pat Smear in the band was incredible. But that's where my guess is where he was looking—not really at being "the new Cars." Nothing against the Cars or anything, but he liked looking at the Germs.

PAUL LEARY: We liked hanging out with Kurt—he was a real nice guy. But Courtney was on tour with them as well, and she was not so pleasant to be around. And she certainly did *not* like Kurt hanging out with the Butthole Surfers. If she ever caught him hanging out with us, she would grab him by the earlobe and drag him out of the room.

DAVE MARKEY: It was at the Los Angeles Forum. I brought a video camera . . . actually, it wasn't even my video camera—it was Thurston Moore's camera, who had gotten the camera in [the venue]. I remember I was like, "*I've got to film Nirvana's set.*" I remember their manager, John Silva, kind of scowling at me. But they didn't shut me down.

MIKE WATT: I'm at the front and I see Pat having the time of his life, and I'm thinking about seeing him with the Germs. Then I'm looking over, and I see Kurt. And he's like, "*I do not want to fucking be here.*"

JIMMY FLEMION: We'd heard from Pat Smear that when Kurt overdosed in Rome [on March 4, 1994], the first thing he asked for was his Frogs tapes and a strawberry shake—when he came out of the coma.

PAUL LEARY: I was in the middle of recording Daniel Johnston [on April 8, 1994]. I went to his parents' house in Waller, Texas, and set up a studio in the garage and was recording Daniel. And at the end of the day, Mrs. Johnston had made us some tacos for dinner, and they were sitting around watching the nightly news on TV. Daniel and I were standing there talking, and all of a sudden the story came out that Kurt Cobain had died. It was very much a shock. And Daniel's parents were like, "Who is that?" And Daniel was like, "That's the fellow who wore my T-shirt!"

Kurt Cobain taping *MTV Unplugged* in New York City, November 18, 1993. "Nothing would ever be the same." —Kennedy *Frank Micelotta Archive/Hulton Archive/Getty Images*

DAVE MARKEY: It seemed like he felt guilty for his position, in a sense. Or he couldn't render it with his own "punk worldviews."

MIKE WATT: I think he was feeling used by a lot of things—not people in particular, but just the situation. You know that Germs song, "We Must Bleed"? Y'know, "*I want out now.*"

GERALD CASALE: It didn't surprise me. Once you combine heroin with serious mental depression, it's definitely a prescription you can predict where it's going to end up.

BILL GOULD: From what I can remember, my feeling was when Kurt died, Nirvana had already peaked. And they were not doing the business live like they had been doing up to that point. I think their star was starting to fade—and I think his death brought that momentum back. If he hadn't have died . . . I wonder if something would have happened—some other thing would have replaced what had been going on there.

MIKE WATT: Him dying . . . you see Krist talking about it, "*He shouldn't have done that.*" But I'm not close enough to judge like that. I was just very sad for him. Because he was such a "music cat." He could have got into mariachi and been good at it.

MIKE JOHNSON: Of all the bands that were huge, he was obviously the most authentic. He was real, and there was no pretense to what he was doing. It seemed *completely* authentic. And not that the other ones weren't, but there was something so visceral and direct about what he was doing—and it connected so much with such a wide array of people.

Him passing couldn't help but leave a void that nobody could possibly . . . I know that's what he reacted to—I know that he was not in it to be anybody's voice of a generation and all that bullshit. But he was the one that we looked at and thought, "This is 'the guy' of that scene." Although he didn't want to be the king of the scene. It's just speculation to say that really affected the way trends went, but to me things didn't get better.

PAUL LEARY: I don't think his death changed anything. I think grunge was never destined to have long legs and go on forever. I think things would have changed regardless after Kurt's death. To tell you the truth, I was not a "grunge fan." I remember when we came out with "Pepper" and Capitol Records wanted to promote us, they came up with a big press release, and they wanted to call us "the godfathers of grunge." And that upset me terribly. I told him if they called us the godfathers of grunge, I was quitting and retiring from music. I got them to drop that.

FRED ARMISEN: Someone's death affecting the trajectory of music . . . I don't think it works that way.

CHRIS HASKETT: I think Nirvana would have had a couple more great records in them. But at the same time, we got the Foo Fighters out of it.

JENNIFER HERREMA: Dinosaur Jr., Sonic Youth—people just kept going. They'd been there before Kurt, and they were there after Kurt.

PAUL Q. KOLDERIE: It turned into this "grunge thing" and ultimately devolved into Limp Bizkit, Korn, and Slipknot. I mean, Kurt was a pessimist—I'm not sure that he might not have just given up trying to save rock music. That's a lot to take on your shoulders. He was a more fragile person than, say, Dave Grohl has turned out to be.

CRAIG WEDREN: I was listening to *Bleach* yesterday, and I was thinking about his voice and the way one's voice changes with age. And thinking, "Where would he have gone with his songwriting and with his voice?" It's very hard to imagine. When somebody dies young, and when they're that beautiful and talented, it does something. In a way, it kind of codifies the moment—Janis Joplin, Jim Morrison, Jimi Hendrix. In a way, it freezes it historically in time so that it can't ever decay. Which probably has more staying power and longevity than if somebody continues. I don't know—maybe his dying helped the historical mythology of alt-rock or punk rock . . . but I don't really like to aggrandize suicide, drug addiction, or premature death. I think that's actually really sad and an old story.

CHAD TAYLOR: It would be a mistake to write anything about '90s music without acknowledging the underlying mental health crisis most of us musicians are facing. This includes myself and, to varying degrees, my band. It is interwoven with the journey of our music and our relationship with each other.

MATT PINFIELD: A lot of people were channeling their pain and things that they felt through the music itself. It was almost a cathartic, therapeutic experience in a way to deal with things. And that's in a way why we've lost so many great people from that decade. Some have found their way; others either succumbed to the sadness of depression, drug addiction, and other things—because you have to relive those things that you're writing and singing about every night.

EDDIE "KING" ROESER: The time from when we got signed and put out a major label record and to the point Kurt shot himself it was like a blink of an eye. And the thing was over. The *fun* was over. It was like, "Here's a band that has everything you could ever imagine good happening from the second you want to go onstage and play." And that was such a tragic thing for everybody that we were involved with. It was like, "Well, this really *isn't* all that great."

KENNEDY: Kurt Cobain's death . . . it was like the light going on at the end of the night and you saw all these people for who they were in a starkly lit room . . . *and it was shocking*. And nothing would ever be the same. And I don't know if that directly led to a decline in music, but it created a sadness—and took some of the urgency away. It's like, any time you have layers trying to replicate something that is so authentic and special, it's really just an impression of it. *It's never quite the same thing.*

22 DECLINE?

"There was great stuff that was happening in the underground, but I don't think anybody wanted to hear it."

The alt-rock landscape certainly looked—or rather, *sounded*—quite different when comparing the early '90s to the middle and latter parts of the decade . . .

CRAIG WEDREN: Whoever got huge around then [during the early '90s], on one hand it's great because there were opportunities for bands like Shudder to Think to reach a much larger, more mainstream audience without having to "mainstream" our sound. But that was when the wave crested and broke—not when it started. But you don't know that until afterward. And then once you see it, you're like, "Oh, of course. *That's the end, not the beginning.*"

STEVE ALBINI: Everything is cyclical, and there were—*and are still*—underground bands or independent bands. But the stylistic aspects of it change over time. And you saw as times change different stylistic elements becoming more popular than sort of the elaborated garage band aesthetic that was in the '90s.

LES CLAYPOOL: All of a sudden, "alternative" was encompassing a lot of different things. And it became the term for pop music. So, it already defeated its own definition.

FERGAL LAWLER: Alternative music was flavor of the month for those few years, and then something else takes over, and then alternative music goes back underground. And then rap became mainstream—which was an underground thing. And then gangsta rap is massive, and it goes down again, and then something else takes over.

MATT PINFIELD: There was still a lot of other things to come. Look, there are people that will say Nirvana's explosion was *the end* of alternative rock. I disagree with all of that, because although that was an amazing golden age, and yes, there was an explosion of commercial alternative stations once the Seattle

Fred Durst of Limp Bizkit, Woodstock Festival, Rome, New York, July 24, 1999. "Almost overnight, every modern-rock station in the United States stopped playing the Wallflowers and started playing Korn and Limp Bizkit." —Moby *Frank Micelotta Archive/Hulton Archive/ Getty Images* thing took place, there were a lot of people who liked the older alternative stuff that felt, "The Seattle thing is not alternative." Some loved it, some didn't. I certainly did.

But then you go on through the early 2000s, and you had the whole Strokes/White Stripes/Hives/Killers thing that was happening. For me, when people say that when Kurt Cobain died that was the decline, I'm like, "But Oasis hadn't put out a record yet." So, the golden age? The *real* golden age for some people was the pre-Nirvana explosion. But then, there were the people that were introduced and found out more and realized there was a whole other world of music out there because of the Nirvana explosion—which is also something that needs to be credited.

JASON PETTIGREW: *Alternative Press* was the first national magazine to slap Jane's Addiction on the cover. And now, if you wanted to talk, we had to get in line behind everybody else for a Porno for Pyros cover. *SPIN* got the exclusive and then *Ray Gun*, and they both even had *the same* cover text: "Perry Farrell's New Addiction"! Now it turned into the publicists and the managers of all the bands are like, "We want to be in the mag with the biggest distribution. Yeah, *Alternative Press*, sixty thousand copies is nice . . . but *Rolling Stone* has *a million* subscribers." And there was the "cold war" between *SPIN* and *Rolling Stone*. And we were like, "I guess we're just going to have to decide we're going to be a farm team." Because Nine Inch Nails and Marilyn Manson took off and we knew we wouldn't be getting the first covers of things anymore.

ROGER JOSEPH MANNING JR.: In a lot of ways, what was happening was, it was almost like *another* movement. Grunge was certainly coming to a close and what I would consider one of the eras of college rock. So, if you're looking at the Pixies, a lot of that is starting to fade out, and you're getting more post–Green Day, whatever this version of "now" punk rock is. But it's kind of "jock," and there's even some elements of rap coming into it. And I'm not saying that any of this is bad, but it was a different color. And it's less intellectual—it's more dumbed-down/every guy.

I was having fun—personally speaking—with the moody stuff that is happening. I thought Trent Reznor and Marilyn Manson were doing some of their best stuff at the time. Like this really great theater . . . goth was coming into its forefront. Dandy Warhols, the Verve—great groups, but it was very moody. So, you're also getting this thing where alternative rock starts becoming, "Oh. The computer and samples are a very fresh tool." Of course, my boss [Note: Manning has been a longtime member of Beck's backing band] was really showing how it was all done with *Mellow Gold* and *Odelay*.

But at the same time, I think one of the best things happening in the whole world was Supergrass. To this day, the songs are *so* fantastically strong. The same with Blur. Blur and Supergrass were making me sad that Jellyfish had disbanded [in 1994]. Because it was this great, new offering of classicism of pop rock—from the '60s, '70s, and '80s—and now here's this '90s statement. Bands like Oasis, Blur, Jellyfish, and Supergrass didn't necessarily come up with fresh, new sounds—to me, we were making our own statements in a tradition of pop rock that had everything to do with the Kinks to Wings to Cheap Trick. We were carrying that forward.

The '90s, there was still people experimenting, wanting to have their own sound. I mean, the Chemical Brothers—what a fresh and exciting sound. And Prodigy. It was *super* original—it was like all this state-of-the-art technology happening with do-it-yourself samplers and all this technology becoming way more affordable. But still, a lot of punk rock ethos happening. And a lot of instrumental music coming back and having success. Who saw *that* coming? We came from an era with grunge where you've got to have the frontman out front. And then within two or three years, you've got two guys behind a wall of keyboards and DJ equipment, who we can't even identify what they look like.

MIKE EDWARDS: Britpop was a reaction to grunge. It was also a reaction to the bands that came immediately before. So much of fashion in the whole of art is about swings of the pendulum—you go from flared trousers to skinny trousers in the course of six months. And that's the same with Britpop. For me, I found that in my entire life to be one of the most *depressing* periods in rock music—in that we made all these really fascinating leaps forward. We'd made this progression into making new types of sounds, and we were following in the "exploratory footsteps" of people who came a generation before us—people like the Beatles or the Stones. And Britpop basically started with that . . . and then finished with it. And took it nowhere further.

JONN PENNEY: It was a lesser case of Britpop forcing its way into the mainstream and maybe a bit more of a case of grunge running its course a bit. But they did coexist for a while.

MIKE EDWARDS: You listen to these bands and think, "I know which song was influencing you here. That sounds *exactly* like that." You had all these bands that would release singles, and they got sued by the people that made the songs twenty, thirty years earlier! That's really depressing when that happens. That's *so* unambitious. Britpop was really the nadir for me.

MIKI BERENYI: For me, it becomes very personal; it becomes about our albums. So, we were a new band on Warner Bros.—they put us on tour with Ride. Great. We get Lollapalooza; everything's fucking amazing. We put out *Split*, which doesn't do well in Britain but still does okay in America. So, we're still touring. And then we put out *Lovelife*. But the problem is that *Lovelife*, it now becomes like a Britpop record, and there's been a whole sweeping change at Warner Bros. Most of the people who were our A&R people and the people who were supporting us early on, they're all gone. And there's a whole new crew, and none of these people give a flying fuck about Lush—especially not with this album because they don't see how they're going to sell it.

My kind of view of how that world changed is very much filtered through each individual album and an experience of arriving in the country and, "Oh, there's no interviews." Or now we're being made to do these weird radio station festival gigs, where what looks to me like a sea of people who don't give a shit about music—they just want to be jocks and they want some background music to their acting like dicks. But it is the intolerance of, "Okay, there are two girls coming out onstage, and one of them's got a twelve-string. We're going to start throwing shit immediately." It's Woodstock '99 or whatever that kind of disaster program is.

CHAD TAYLOR: Woodstock '99 was terrible. The energy was full-blown masculine stupidity. It reminded me why I thought '80s hair metal pop was so wrong. I wish we had not played.

JASON PETTIGREW: You had the death of grunge, and it was replaced by nu metal. Nu metal was too "hard rock" and "hip-hop," and when you mix those two things together . . . I mean, why not? Because it's both "*party music, maaan*." But at the same time, while you consider heavy metal and hip-hop "party music," they're also bold declarations of intent—which is basically "Fuck the man." Thanks for everything, Zack de la Rocha!

But then it turned into the lowest common denominator—that's how you wound up with Woodstock '99. Definitely *Lord of the Flies*, for sure. You didn't have the genuine sincerity of a wounded Kurt Cobain. Half of it would be like, "Woe is me . . . and now you're going to die, bitch." All the worst parts of toxic masculinity replaced everything. And then, once again, all those bands started to sound the same.

And of course, being in the situation where you're running a magazine, you need these people to sell issues. But the problem is there weren't enough people that were buying *Alternative Press* that you could put *any* band on the cover and still survive. But you put these [nu metal] guys on the cover—and you're assuming that their fans actually know how to read. And the second thing is all of your base is like, "Really, *Alternative Press*? Goodbye." So, we were ultimately trapped and didn't recover until we embraced our "inner Warped Tour."

LES CLAYPOOL: To me, as Lollapalooza started to lose its glimmer—I think that was a big turning point.

GERALD CASALE: Lollapalooza had morphed from its idealistic beginnings into a real corporate enterprise [by the time Devo played some Lolla shows in 1996]. And there was a hierarchy, of course. And there was the fact that some of these genres weren't mixing. A lot of the crowd hated Devo. Like, "What the fuck are *you guys* doing here?" But then a lot of kids hadn't seen Devo and had heard about Devo, and when they saw us, they were converted.

So, it was interesting to put yourself out of your comfort zone in this situation where a lot of the crowd is against you—which took us back to our roots, when crowds would threaten us and throw things at us. It didn't get *that* bad, but there was booing, and you could see people walking away. Metallica was the headliner, Soundgarden was before them, and we played just before Soundgarden. So, it was like, "Okay, kids, here's 'retro Devo' . . . *before you get into your grunge*."

JASON PETTIGREW: I left before Metallica came on. My ex-wife and I were like, "Oh . . . *hell no*." There were other stages that still had cool stuff—like Moonshake and Girls Against Boys. But I think the novelty wore off. There was great stuff that was happening in the underground, but I don't think anybody wanted to hear it.

EDDIE "KING" ROESER: It's been a long time since Lollapalooza was this "big thing." It still exists, but when Lollapalooza came to town, *everybody* knew who the bands were. Now you look, and there's fifty or a hundred bands, and I don't know who any of them are. And I don't think anybody else does, either.

FAT MIKE: I didn't see [the punk-pop explosion] coming. But I just thought, "Finally! People see how good punk rock is."

CHRIS HASKETT: All those [pop-punk] bands that sounded like Stiff Little Fingers but aren't, that would have happened anyway. But there's a lot of others. I wouldn't put Weezer in that category—I see Weezer almost more with Wilco.

MIKE WATT: It seemed like they had picked up what the Buzzcocks were doing in England in the late '70s. I think the guy [Green Day's Billie Joe Armstrong] kind of sang with an English accent, right? But y'know, John Fogerty—very "northwest bayou." [*Laughs*] Music is about transcending reality sometimes. So, authenticity? I don't know about making that too much of an issue. Some things, when they say "perfect storm"—they just come together. People win the lotto . . . and Vincent van Gogh sells *one painting*.

BILL GOULD: I didn't find [pop-punk] offensive—if someone was playing it on the radio, it wouldn't bother me. It didn't agitate me as much as some other stuff did. But I didn't listen to it, either—I didn't have any of their records.

FAT MIKE: People say they're sellouts—the Offspring. None of those bands were selling out. *The world discovered how good punk rock is.* It was so joyous. Because punk bands, we're all family—we all grew up together. We're very inclusive.

MIKE WATT: I remember playing with these avant-garde guys from Italy and doing interviews, "Hey, where did you come from?" And they were all embarrassed to say, "I was into Green Day and Blink-182." Because that's when they were born! They say freedom of choice and stuff, but you can only choose what's there, what you know of, and what the situation presents to you.

It's like, me and [Minutemen bandmate] D. Boon could have got into that club thing—the Stooges were playing up at the Whisky a Go Go in the early '70s. We just thought all gigs were "arena rock." Our first gig was T. Rex in '73, which was pretty good; but it was the Long Beach Auditorium. We didn't know. So, how do you choose? And then when you've got something like Viacom putting it on cable TV, there was a big audience.

CRAIG WEDREN: I was frankly really relieved when pop came in the picture. Not pop-punk. I was like, "We already have the Ramones and the Descendents. What more do we need?" But it was literally like . . . *Backstreet Boys*. I was like, "Thank God. I don't need Nickelback. I much prefer Backstreet Boys." The sort of dulling of what had been exciting a few years before with mainstream alternative in the late '90s was just a bummer—the sub–Pearl Jams, the sub-Nirvanas.

BILL GOULD: Anybody that brought some obscure influences and got into the mainstream . . . Nirvana would bring in influences that maybe hadn't been acknowledged in a mainstream way before. And I think what came during the end of the '90s was these people who discovered those things, it became this sort of "hipster thing," where then somebody had more obscure records and things started breaking up and getting into these little factions. And San Francisco became an unbearable place of hipsters. I absolutely *hated* these vinyl-collecting, really pretentious assholes. And that was an offshoot of bringing left field stuff into the mainstream—that you could never be "left field enough." That's what I saw toward the end of the '90s.

FRANK BLACK: So, there was an atmosphere of the record companies, and everybody still had a lot of money in the coffers. They were throwing money at situations because they were trying to hold on to this sort of changing [business model]. "We're not selling any more vinyl records—that is dead and over with. People are only buying CDs." Streaming hadn't started yet, but people knew you could go on the internet and people could get bootlegs. Everyone was worried about the bootleggers and the MP3s.

KRISTIN HERSH: Payola meant that success was a bought and paid for thing in the US then. Audiences didn't vote a band into popularity—the labels bought radio, press, and shelf space in record stores; and people assumed that bandwagon marketing meant that other people were listening. Music without promotion was buried. Warner Bros. told us they were burying our record, [Throwing Muses'] *University*, so that the band they'd put promotional money behind would succeed.

DJs called saying that our label took our single off the radio; record stores told us they'd ordered the record but didn't receive it, et cetera. We drove to the warehouses and physically brought our records to stores that had ordered it, and some brave radio stations played our song even though they'd lose payola money. The record companies controlled almost

All of a sudden, 'alternative' was encompassing a lot of different things. And it became the term for pop music. So, it already defeated its own definition.

LES CLAYPOOL

everything, but we had loyal followers, and we were willing to be poor so we're still working today—whereas those whose success was bought have mostly disappeared.

PAUL Q. KOLDERIE: "Payola" is a '50s word that literally described cash bribes. The way that they worked it out was there were all these "favors" that you did . . . there was a lot of ways that they could move payola through the system in at least a quasi-legal way. But it was definitely expensive to mount a full-scale radio campaign at the end of the '90s because the labels were making so much money off CDs and off alternative rock. Think of how much money Geffen made off of Nirvana, y'know? The money was there. So, labels were like, "We have to spend half a million dollars to get this song going. But if it makes the record take off and we sell ten million copies, then it's worth it." So, once people are willing to do that, it becomes a bidding war for who will pay the most and who will give you the most favors.

EDDIE "KING" ROESER: We had a pretty good relationship with the label, and a couple of bands came along that were unexpected hits and became really big. Which is Weezer—who are very straight shooters. Great band, but nobody expected them to have this massive hit. And the Counting Crows was another thorn in our side—they were sort of not part of that dark . . . not that we were trying to be, but the timing of it was kind of unfortunate for my band.

COREY GLOVER: There's a point where you didn't see yourself in the landscape. Or people didn't want to see you in the landscape—they wanted to move on to something else. *Really quickly.* And you had to think about "Well . . . why am I here? If you don't want to see me, why am I here?"

MATT JOHNSON: [Jeff Buckley's death on May 29, 1997] was incalculable—because of what he would have done. I do think that if one were to try to construct possible inspiring trajectories from Jeff's life, a lot of times I think about how Radiohead came about a little bit later and was closer to an alternative band and then they evolved into something that is totally relevant today—to a completely new generation.

I was recently watching a certain artist of the '80s play and sing a song that goes back to the early '80s on an acoustic guitar, solo. And the voice sounded good, the song sounded not very good, the guitar playing was fucking terrible. And I'm going, "Wow. The level of talent Jeff already had before he even got a record deal—with singing, songwriting, and guitar playing . . ." And having the ability to interact with and work an audience—not in a cynical or showbiz kind of way but in a really *authentic* way—all that stuff was super-high-level with Jeff.

TANYA DONELLY: I think if we could have flipped the trajectory and started with *King*-level success—which, that album sold really well, which I think it's funny when people say, "Their *unsuccessful* second album." If we had started with that level and then moved on, I think we would have at least made one or two more albums. But [Belly's split in 1996] was a combination of things—getting thrown into the deep end too fast and not navigating that maturely. We all come from very working-class families, and the work ethic is strong in all of our families. There was no "No" in our vocabulary at the time. We would just say "Yes" to every festival, every show, every special event.

VADEN TODD LEWIS: The reason it took so long [for Toadies to follow up *Rubberneck*] was I had just gotten out of the habit of writing. So, it took a long time. Once I had the songs together, they were looking for another "Possum Kingdom," "Tyler," or "Away." Nobody would tell me that straight out, but I knew that's what was going on. So, I wanted to write a little bit of a different kind of record. I wanted to go somewhere else. That caused a lot of friction with the label, and we kept getting pushed back. At one point, we got approval based on my demos, went in and did a whole session, and in between getting it recorded and mixed, the approval got pulled. Had to start all over again from scratch. So, that's a ton of money, effort, and frustration.

COREY GLOVER: We were exhausted [which led to Living Colour's split in 1995]. We had been hitting it really hard, and quite frankly, there was a ceiling to it all that we were hitting our head on—constantly. Because, truth be told, we weren't alternative enough for the audiences of Lollapalooza. We were a "pop band with an edge" to some people—which is bullshit. But I don't think we were given a real chance to show people that there was much more going on than that one song that they knew ["Cult of Personality"].

EDDIE "KING" ROESER: By that time [1997], there had been enough creative differences that we were our own demise—where we decided to stop recording before there were real worse divisions happening. We sort of agreed mutually to not do any more records for Geffen—or we put it on hold. Which, I think in hindsight, we could have been a bit more patient and took a year off or something.

PAUL Q. KOLDERIE: Even the Pixies—who had so much going for them—they had squabbles. And they made the mistake of going out on the road opening for U2, which was supposed to be a plumb job, because U2 chose them. But the problem is you're an *opening act*, you get thirty minutes, you get kind of treated like shit, and all of a sudden, they weren't stars anymore—they were like the "extra little sideshow attraction." And that tour broke them up [in 1993].

VINNIE DOMBROSKI: Alice in Chains was not really active at all anymore. Soundgarden had taken a break. Smashing Pumpkins would soon take a break. There was this weird time and a weird vacuum that was going on. I think it was a time where a lot of the alternative bands tapped out for a minute.

LOU BARLOW: '96, '97 . . . Pavement seemed to run out of steam, Sebadoh was floundering, Sonic Youth was kind of dipping. But at that same moment, the beginnings of all this insane shit from the Pacific Northwest started to happen—Modest Mouse.

BOB MOULD: I think [Sugar's] last show was in Sendai, Japan, in January of '95. And then I retreated quietly, knowing that that project was done. I kept writing music. Recorded an album—some of it at home, some of it in a small studio in Austin—and that became the eponymous album that a lot of us call *Hubcap*.

I did not intend to tour on that record. The ask from Pete Townshend to open a couple shows of his in New York in the spring of '96 got me thinking about getting out and working again, and went out and did a lot of solo touring. And then '98 was *The Last Dog and Pony Show*, and by the time I got there, I was starting to get restless for something new in my own

Page Hamilton with Helmet, New York City, September 1995. "I had heard that we influenced [the Deftones], and the song the kid wanted to learn is called 'Engine No. 9' . . . *and it was a Helmet riff!*"—Page Hamilton *Bob Berg/Hulton Archive/Getty Images*

life. Not my professional life, but my personal life. I had moved back to New York City and was integrating with the LGBTQ community more than I ever had. So I was enriching my life in that direction, and thought, "Maybe this would be a good time to stop being only the rock guy who's on the road in a van for his whole life."

And so that notion of stepping away from rock touring with that record, that was 100 percent in earnest, that I just felt like, "I'm gonna take a break here, and I'm gonna build this other life that I never really took the time to build." I think that's it in a nutshell. There's the pro wrestling stuff in the fall of '99 through spring of 2000—that sort of ran parallel to my gay life in New York, my interest in electronic music. A lot of things were shifting. To go write pro wrestling scripts and start writing electronic music, that eventually led me to DJing for most of the aughts. I knew I wanted to change, I didn't know what form it would exactly take, but it all came together pretty well. Naturally, I think.

CRIS KIRKWOOD: In a perfect world, had we been called something other than "Meat Puppets"—take away the ugly word "Meat" and Curt's as good as anybody. As far as the art is concerned, I think it speaks for itself. As far as our commercial successes? Blame it on me not being that appealing and pretty fuckin' creepy . . . and so is [drummer] Derrick [Bostrom] . . . and so is the word "Meat." We should have played country-western, we should have called the band "Kirkwood," and we should have been sold on my and Curt's good looks as young men.

MOBY: There was that moment in '95–'96 where alternative music was unbelievably gentle. It was Jewel, the Wallflowers, and Hootie and the Blowfish. Really nice music . . . but *incredibly* gentle. And then, at some point—I don't know if it was KROQ or Live 105, or one of those stations—they started playing Metallica. And then they were playing Korn. And then they were playing Limp Bizkit. And all of a sudden, their numbers went through the roof.

As a result, almost overnight, every modern-rock station in the United States stopped playing the Wallflowers and started playing Korn and Limp Bizkit. Which, Korn and Limp Bizkit are very exciting. I understood why it happened. But it seemed like the alternative ethos of R.E.M. and Nirvana and this introspective approach to lyrics and music kind of got thrown out the window—for bombast. And again, I like that music. But it was hard to draw a throughline from a delicate Echo and the Bunnymen song to Kid Rock.

MATT JOHNSON: There were bands that I think of as sort of "mashup bands." Like, "You got your peanut butter in my chocolate" or "You got your chocolate in my peanut butter." "Why don't we mix hip-hop with metal?" Some of that nu metal stuff comes from that.

PAGE HAMILTON: I just taught a student a Deftones song the other day—and I'm not super-familiar with Deftones. And I had heard that we influenced them, and the song the kid wanted to learn is called "Engine No. 9" . . . *and it was a Helmet riff!* [*Laughs*]

LES CLAYPOOL: In the late '90s, I kind of got discouraged with the whole scene. And luckily, that's when I fell in with the whole Oysterhead thing and started getting more into improvisational music. The late '90s seemed more image-oriented than music-oriented.

COREY GLOVER: It was a *difference*. It wasn't a *decline*—it just changed. That was the alternative to the alternative. And that's when you heard the rapcore stuff and Limp Bizkit came along. It was sort of an alternative to the idea of what this alternative thing was. It was not a rejection of it—but an incorporation of other things.

GERALD CASALE: And then in the big picture, rock didn't matter at all—because rock ate itself and stopped being vital. It stopped being something people wanted to hear. Hip-hop took over.

POE: There was a program director up in Portland who had been a very big supporter of *Hello*, and I'd done a ton of radio festival shows up there and really liked them. There was kind of a weird brewing discomfort that I couldn't really put my finger on what was happening—Atlantic would make decisions, and then the decisions would change. The chain of command was weird. And I had new management. I got wind of the fact that the alternative stations that supported me in the past were not going to play women anymore. Like, *outright*. So, I called my friend in Portland, and I said, "Will you play my single?" And he said, "I can't. I can't play women." Which is crazy, right? And my friend in Dallas—same thing.

ANGELO MOORE: I remember when Napster came onto the scene, I thought to myself, "Wow. That's really fucked up, man. These guys think it's okay to just steal music from other people." And I guess they thought that Metallica had so much money that they didn't need it. But in actuality, *it's stealing music*. So now, the artists had to find another way to make money.

GERALD CASALE: The Napster model took over, and nobody thought that you should have to pay money for music—and the record companies were tanking. And what they became were pseudo-advertising companies. I've often said that record companies should be hiring really cool, young admen that came up through advertising agencies through the main arm of the record company—because that's what it's about. That's the only advantage that they can give you. They're not going to radio and paying independent programmers with cocaine and prostitutes anymore—that doesn't work.

DARREN JESSEE: The price of a CD got *really* expensive. So, Napster came around and was a natural reaction to music being so expensive. And something in there changed everything. A band like Radiohead got real "spacious" . . . like, "Creep" was a huge hit—a really focused kind of thing. And their music became more expansive and more textural. Everyone got a little heady and textural. And even Ben Folds Five's album, [1999's]

The Unauthorized Biography of Reinhold Messner, it was a moody, more textural, orchestral thing. I think everyone was beginning to move away from just being loud and over the top.

CRIS KIRKWOOD: At a point, the record companies or whoever decided, "Let's stop even bothering trying out bands. Let's just start a TV show [*American Idol*] and ask America who they like." And it worked. You go, "Do you like *them* or *them* or *them*?" And stars are born—rather than, "Let's sign some acts, put them out there, the ones that don't work are our tax write-offs, and the ones that do become stars."

RUDEBOY REMINGTON: All these record companies, they felt they had to sign people on a video—not even on a record. There was no career planning anymore. Career planning in the sense that you believe in a band, you build them up—maybe not with the first record but the second or the third . . . bingo. Out the window. You even only got signed by one video. If that didn't hit, you were gone.

MARK KOHR: MTV was almost gone—they didn't show videos. Television was fading. And Netflix and streaming hadn't developed yet. Everything *crashed*.

LES CLAYPOOL: But then there was all this cool stuff going on in Britain—Radiohead and Blur and stuff like that.

FERGAL LAWLER: There were plenty of great alternative bands that still lasted late into the '90s, early 2000s. And even a band like the Arctic Monkeys that came out in the 2000s—I would consider them an "alternative act." And they kind of grew from all that music in the '90s.

MIKE WATT: Man, I really thought when the internet came and websites, that would be everybody's personal fanzine. But no—they all gravitate to the corporate ones.

MARY TIMONY: After the internet came around, people were exposed to more music all the time. I think in the '90s, people were still conscious of this timeline of rock music—we were still trying to do stuff that hadn't been done before.

POE: The industry pre-2000 was still kind of run by a bunch of old hippies. Who, quite frankly, made a lot of record deals over piles of drugs, in a transcendent mood of art and music. It wasn't accountants that were making creative decisions. That was another thing that was important to the '90s—a lot of them made their names as twenty-year-old managers in the '60s, and now they were fifty-five, running [major labels]. They would never step on the toes of the artists' creativity. It was always about, "What can I do, and how can I help?" It was never about, "Here are the numbers" and "You've got to get better numbers next time." When that big AOL merger came down in 2000, *that's* where the culture began to change dramatically—and it was only about the bottom line.

A SUBLIME STORY

Butthole Surfer Paul Leary offers memories of his time producing Sublime.

[Sublime] are super-lovable guys. It was for the most part pretty fun working with them because they were so fucking talented. You just had to have everything set up, and you had to hit record and let them do their thing. But it was a circus. *Every day something would happen.* We were working at Willie Nelson's studio [Pedernales Studio, in Austin, Texas] out in the Hill Country, and Willie had a lot of memorabilia on the walls. And one of the things was a poster from one of his Fourth of July Picnics that had Willie Nelson portrayed as Uncle Sam. And [singer/guitarist] Bradley [Nowell] grabbed a Sharpie and drew a Hitler moustache on Willie's face!

I almost lost it. At that point, my nerves were pretty frayed, and I almost ended the session right there. And Miguel—who was their soundman, road manager, and confidant—went to the store and bought some colored pencils and whiteout, and he worked for *hours* on that poster. And when he was done, you couldn't really tell it had ever been defaced.

They brought all their dogs to the studio. And I told them, "Look, the studio doesn't want dogs." And of course, they brought all their dogs. And the dogs chewed up the door to the studio and they got kicked out of about three condominiums they had rented to stay at. They were lovable, fun guys; but when they were around, things would get broken—that's just the way it was.

They tended to do everything mostly live. Some of their songs weren't worked out so good, so they'd play songs and they'd go on for eight minutes. Willie Nelson's studio had a golf course on the studio property, so after they recorded these songs, I sent them off to play golf; and when they'd come back, those eight-minute songs would suddenly be three-minute songs.

[Nowell's passing on May 25, 1996, from a drug overdose] did not come as a surprise, unfortunately. I was having a lot of thoughts about, "Is this really even the right thing to do? He's in bad shape. He's doing heroin. I don't want to be exploiting a guy like this on heroin." I had enough, and I said, "I'm sorry. You're going home. I'm not going to watch you die here in the studio. I'm not going to send you home in a bag." He got really angry and fired me and fired his manager.

They went to their condo and the next morning I drove over there—and Bradley and I made amends. He told me he understood why I was doing what I was doing. He had track marks all up and down his arms. I felt like that would be the last time I'd ever see him. It really made me sad. And then sure enough, I think the Butthole Surfers were in Europe playing a festival in Belgium, and I was at a hotel, and I got a call from my wife at the time, and she told me.

Universal Music put it on the shelf and said, "It's not going to come out." I think Miguel took a cassette of it to a strip club in Los Angeles, and he hooked up with the programming director for KROQ. He talked the programming director into going into his limousine with a couple of strippers and played the album for him. And the guy was like, "That's a hit! I'm going to play that on the radio." He took the tape and played it on KROQ the next day, and *wham*—it took off. So, Universal Music changed their mind and decided to put the record out. [Note: Released on July 30, 1996, *Sublime* went on to sell five million copies in the US alone and spawned such massive alt-rock hits as "What I Got," "Santeria," and "Wrong Way."]

JASON PETTIGREW: The invention of the iPod democratized what you listen to. Because there's no more "guilty pleasures"—there's just everything that I like, and it's on here. So yes, I have black Norwegian death metal and a Taylor Swift song right after that—because it's a really cool song.

MATT SWEENEY: It's about luck and timing, and whether the person is a dick or not. *So much fucking luck.* But also, how do the musicians handle themselves? And there's also a great degree of luck with that, too! It's like, "Who are those people who made it who still have careers?" They're really smart, they have their shit together, they're really tough . . . and they're really fuckin' lucky.

MIKE EDWARDS: There are things within your control—not punching out your cowriter or sleeping with his wife—those things help bands stay together, at least. But I think creativity is a very finely balanced thing. It blows away in the wind quite easily.

DANA COLLEY: Nothing lasts forever, essentially. Things have to change. You could point to a lot of things—the advent of smartphones. Whereas I think there was a real desire to go out and see music in the '90s and to be in the room. Because that was really the only way you were going to understand. You might hear a song by a band on the radio and you think, "I like that. I'd like to see them when they come to town." You couldn't necessarily at that time Google the band and see what they looked like or see other concerts someone had recorded. There was no real way to fully immerse yourself in the music without actually showing up and being there in the room. Which was *an event*—a social event, a cultural event—that you were taking part of, along with hundreds of other people.

And, unfortunately, what you're looking at on a phone is so depleted from the actual live experience. You can be watching Stevie Ray Vaughan on your phone and think, "Oh, my God, this is an amazing performance. He's an amazing guitar player." But then there's the twelve-year-old who has just caught Stevie Ray Vaughan on your next TikTok feed, and he's doing the same thing. The brilliance gets watered down to such a degree that it's no longer uplifting in a way that it was if you were standing in that room for the first time and had no idea what you were going to see, and Stevie Ray Vaughan walks on . . . *and just shreds your face off*. It's a whole other experience. It's getting muted by the concentration of information.

PAUL Q. KOLDERIE: Right now, I can't get my head around who's paying who to do what on Facebook or TikTok. How is that working? You *know* that there is all this dark money flying around.

KENNEDY: Now, they just want to futz around on their iPhone and try and make something. Because everyone thinks they're brilliant now, so no one tries hard enough. Everyone's been told how special they are—"You're so special, you're so amazing." And it's like, "No, you're not. *You're very ordinary.*"

MATT SWEENEY: There's only so much enthusiasm one can have, and there's only so much joy you get out of the rock experience. After thirty-five, that's really pushing it. I mean, Chavez was even about the feeling of losing enthusiasm for intense rock. For me, it was like, "This is the last live band I'm ever going to do." And certainly, at the time, older people say, "*This* sounds like *that*."

CRAIG WEDREN: I think that's just what happens—with or without Kurt Cobain. Things ripen and then rot. Is there any exception to that trajectory with any movement or style that starts in the underground, gradually claws its way to the surface, spends a day in the sun, and then starts to mutate or wither or get knocked out by something else?

PAUL Q. KOLDERIE: The story of alternative rock is the story of any genre—it comes up, it's fresh . . . then it gets co-opted. *Elvis Presley*, y'know? For a minute there, he was the rockingest thing going. But look where Elvis ended up. Dying on the toilet bowl because he hadn't taken a shit in a month.

LOU BARLOW: The 2000s, that's *really* when indie rock took over. The '90s were kind of the lead-up to it, but especially when the record labels crashed and everybody stopped buying records. And then there were these amazing things that happened, where bands like Neutral Milk Hotel started to rise up. Merge Records started to put out number one records. Spoon, Arcade Fire, the Strokes. And people were much more open to mixing influences, too—bands like Grizzly Bear and Animal Collective.

FRED ARMISEN: It keeps on going. There were still bands coming out. Even though it's a different decade, I still hear bands that I connected to that time. There were great records coming out all the way through. I don't remember there was a time where there was a decline in quality records. My whole life, there's *always* a new record that I love.

IAN MacKAYE: I had this sort of vision that the major labels are always flying their planes and they're looking down for fertile ground—something where they can raise their crop of cash. And punk rock was in this little valley they kept flying over—they didn't notice it. And then one day . . . they noticed it. So, they go down and start buying up the "farms." Every band is a farm, and they buy them up one after the other. But the thing is, *they're not there for the long haul*. They come in to rape the ground. They're going to get as much crop out of that ground as possible. And then they're going to get back in their planes and fly on. And that's exactly what the fuck happened.

Henry Rollins with the Rollins Band, Lollapalooza, Irvine, California, July 21, 1991. "I think people always will want something a little more authentic."
—Mike Johnson *MediaPunch/Alamy*

23 COULD IT HAPPEN AGAIN?

"It won't sound like it did in the '90s"

Given the state of music and media at the time of this book's release, the unique circumstances of the '90s, and everything that's happened in the intervening decades, could history ever repeat itself and give us another alt-rock revolution?

MIKE WATT: Yes . . . but I'd like to see it a little bit more like the late '70s. [*Laughs*]

AL JOURGENSEN: Of course. It's cyclical. Everything's cyclical. There is nothing new. Everything keeps coming back around. History is cyclical. Y'know, in the 1930s, right-wing populism. And here we are in the 2020s with right-wing populism springing up all over the world. This isn't new. And yes, there will be a point in time where rap will be out of favor . . . and then rap will come back. Jazz will come back. It all comes back.

BILL GOULD: I realize that so much of what we thought was spontaneous and natural culture really had to do with something being bankrolled. There was an industry that made money selling records. And with the money that they made—

and they made a lot—they could feed the culture with some of that and have a fertile ground that could possibly grow some random, interesting things. That is completely out now.

Backstage to me is a perfect example—it became such a boring experience. If you look back at 1989–1990, backstages were really fun—you'd get all kinds of random people back there. It was a scene. It was a vibe. You look at 2000 and then you look at 2010 and you look at 2022, it is *completely* a dead zone. There is no energy there. There's no cultural energy there. So, can that happen now? We're talking how a mainstream thinks about things. It would take a lot of resources to do it. I would like to see it happen. But I don't know if it could or not.

FRANK BLACK: I don't think anything like that could be re-created right now [from a business standpoint]. Because you did have that infusion of cash. It was the last gasp of that—of all that cash flowing into even the indie bands' pockets. You don't have that now. Which I think is probably better for the art. But there's nothing wrong with spending a lot of money on a record. You might come out with a bad record . . . but you might come out with a really great record, too. Some people crawl down the rabbit hole, and they spend three years working on a record and a gazillion dollars, and lo and behold, they do come up with some magical thing that saves the day.

I guess what I'm trying to say is, I don't think that could be replicated now. The whole dynamic of how things are patronized and how things are paid for and how people are making their money out of all of this has all shifted. And money *does* change things. Money does affect things—for bad and for good. I would say we're in a different world financially and contractually than we were thirty years ago. For all artists—whether they're seasoned artists or whether they're brand-new people—it's all different now. The way contracts are done, the expectations, where people are making their money.

It's still showbiz—we're still hawking something here. But a lot of the dynamics had shifted in big ways. So, I think that was the last moment that the old record company system, the way that things worked. That was the last time—early '90s. After that, it all shifted. A lot of people think of it in terms of falling apart. Certainly, the record companies would think about it that way: "Now we don't sell records. People can just go on the internet and hear music for free." From the artists' point of view, "Oh, I don't make money anymore. I don't sell so many records." It's all different. But I don't really have a negative take on that. I just think that's showbiz—that's just the way that it is.

I think for a while in the '80s and the '90s, a lot of artists were kind of in a housing bubble. It was a little bit artificial. There was something about all of that, that was artificially held together. And I think that digital and the internet came along and popped that, the bubble burst, and it was over. So, while some people think, "Boo-hoo, it's over," I think, "No, it's more honest. It was eventually going to happen one way or the other." The bubble was going to get popped, and there's nothing you can do about that. We were living in a kind of artificial era of abundance.

MIKE JOHNSON: I would assume so. I always think that something will come around that will be popular and at the same time coming out of an authentic, grassroots type of thing. Although it felt like fifty/fifty to me at the time—there were a lot of phonies and a lot of genuine fans that came out of the DIY punk scene, like Nirvana, Dinosaur Jr., and Screaming Trees. But I think it always comes around. I think people always will want something a little more authentic—if that was the case.

STEVE ALBINI: There is music still underway that is in all of its aspects behaving very similarly. It's sort of like asking if psychedelic music will ever come back. I mean, there's *still* psychedelic music being played, and there has been psychedelic music played since the '60s. Is it likely ever to become a mass movement? I don't know. There's always something that's very popular, and I don't concern myself with popularity that much.

ANGELO MOORE: History repeats itself. But every time it repeats itself, it repeats itself a little differently than the last time. When it makes another revolution around the sun, it comes back around with something just a little bit different on it.

Green Day at Paradise Lounge, San Francisco, California, February 16, 1994. Left to right: Billie Joe Armstrong, Tre Cool, and Mike Dirnt. "I think for a while in the '80s and the '90s, a lot of artists were kind of in a housing bubble."—Frank Black *Anthony Pidgeon/Redferns/ Getty Images*

DAVID PAJO: Because of the internet and the lack of mystery that the internet provides, I don't think that it could happen the way it happened back then. Only because you *really* had to dig and find. An algorithm wouldn't introduce you to a band—you had to search it out yourself. And word of mouth. And that creates a different kind of energy than looking up the band on Wikipedia and finding out exactly when they started, who the band members are, what their approach is.

If all you have is one photo on an album and you know nothing else about the band, you end up staring at the photo for a long time and inventing what you think they're like. I think that kind of personal interpretation is what's lacking—because of the inundation of all the information. If I go to see a band and there's a local opening band, and you're like, "Whoa! Who are these guys? This is great!" That's exactly like the '90s—you walk into something that you weren't expecting.

FERGAL LAWLER: It's like, "You've got to give it a chance to *breathe*." Sometimes when I was a teenager, I'd buy an album and I'd go, "I don't know if I like it." Then I'd listen to it again . . . and again . . . and again. And by the third or fourth listen, it's like, "Jesus Christ. That's a great album." It's those ones that take a while to grow on you, and they kind of last the longest.

ROGERS STEVENS: The thing that you're really talking about is *teenage energy*, right? That's what this is—it's whatever is the thing that captures that moment. That's what you're supposed to be looking at. We have nostalgia for this music, and we like it—the "rock 'n' roll era." It's what we remember as the representation of that feeling we had. But now, it's something different. But if you're looking to find this for teenagers now . . . I mean, maybe. Someday. Some variation of it. But they'll have their *own* thing—and it definitely won't be what we want it to be.

LORI BARBERO: I hope that rock 'n' roll will come back. Rock 'n' roll is kind of kaput. There really aren't those many rock bands. And a lot of people are leaving this planet—which is really sad. It seems like live music with instruments is kind of "*Eh.*"

CHRIS HASKETT: I was watching *Jurassic Park* with my kids the other day. And you've got Jeff Goldblum going, "Nature always finds a way." It's trite and it's stupid, but I think by analogy, there will always be a reaction to commodified culture. Music consumption at this point has become so spoon-fed . . . don't get me started on Spotify. Or TikTok, for that matter. What's happened there is this interesting phenomenon where . . . participating in TikTok, having your own Spotify playlist, the fact that you participate in this way has become part of the musical consumption process—in a way that buying an album as opposed to a cassette wasn't really meant as a statement. But now, there's this whole *ethos* around the way people engage with music. Which is different. And I think there will be a reaction to that.

KENNEDY: Spotify just recommends things. Which is great for me because I like to be lazy. But for people for whom the joy came from finding a bar in the East Village with an incredible jukebox where you could discover stuff that you never heard before . . . that was almost like a ride at Disneyland.

DARREN JESSEE: You don't have the same dynamic range streaming or listening on your phone as you did on the other formats. Even vinyl is being pressed from a digital file now. And that's fine—technology is amazing with what they're doing. Recording is amazing, really. It's all a little more similar sounding. The '90s was such *a time*. It was more than music. I don't know if we'll ever have that feeling culturally again.

ART ALEXAKIS: I would love something that is derivative of punk rock, hip-hop . . . anything that would piss the status quo off, could make an amalgam of itself and come out with something new and fresh. That would be wonderful. We've been waiting for that for a long time. Doesn't seem to be happening. We've reverted back to the pop era of singles because it's easy for labels to work singles and not commit to bands for a whole album. It's not creative, it's not genuine, but that's what works.

COREY GLOVER: There's going to be another movement of music. And I think it will probably be led by some hip-hop artist who decides they want to expand what they do and how they do it.

LOU BARLOW: The way people are cutting and pasting music now, I think there's really some amazing shit that's going to happen. I don't know when, I'm not sure how. I've been hearing a lot of this Brazilian pop music recently, where I'm like, "This shit is wild." It's really disjointed; it's really infectious. To me, what's going to happen is like . . . some cut-and-paste *rap/shoegaze band* that's going to blow everybody's head off.

SPEECH: Definitely. I think it's bound to happen again. If I had my way of thinking about it, it's usually every thirty years or so. So, we're long overdue for that now. I don't think it's happening right now, but I do think that human beings are designed to blossom when they're kept in a box. And in my opinion, music has been kept in a box for quite a while. I think people are going to blossom and explode out of frustration and love and further expression and rebellion—all the various reasons people start to create great things.

FRED SCHNEIDER: I don't know about in this country. They seem to want to shut down anything that is open-minded and fun and alternative—whether it's the lifestyle or beliefs or music. But things *could* change.

TANYA DONELLY: It could be happening right now for all I know. Yeah, absolutely. There's always renewal, rebirth, and regrowth.

MATT PINFIELD: It certainly wouldn't happen the way it did. Because what was beautiful about it was the people in Seattle were all isolated, doing their own thing. At the early shows of all those Seattle bands, the audience wasn't packed, and it was each other. So, because they were insular and isolated, it gave them the ability to be influenced by anybody from Zeppelin to the Ramones.

JASON PETTIGREW: Everybody with the internet, you can speak precisely into whatever echo chamber you want and do the stuff that reinforces you—whether it's politics, spaghetti sauce recipes, or whatever it is, you've got your own thing. You can give people infinite options on stuff . . . but they don't know what they want. I don't think there's a band that is going to unite people the same way these people we talked about did.

VADEN TODD LEWIS: The system is all different. Kids can crank out a song in their bedroom, and it's a hit on Spotify. I don't know what that does to the rest of the world. Terrestrial radio has a different meaning now.

GERALD CASALE: It would be interesting if there was a band whose foundation was in rock, who could be as original about it as the Rolling Stones were in 1965. It wouldn't sound like them; it wouldn't look like them. But it would be as exciting and shocking. The way Jimi Hendrix was in 1967. Nothing like that is happening now. Nothing comparable is happening. But there is interesting stuff happening—my wife, who is much younger than me, loves King Gizzard & the Lizard Wizard.

KEVIN MARTIN: It would never happen. The labels won't allow it. There are bands that could certainly do it, but it won't be mainstream. It won't ever reach what it did. It was a perfect time and a perfect storm for it. There is no "storm" allowed anymore.

JASON PETTIGREW: I turn sixty-three in a couple of months, and I was really looking forward to having that archetype moment like, "You kids call *that* music?!" and have the histrionic fingers-in-my-ears type of thing. And I'm not getting it. I'm like, "Oh, this is what you like . . . which is a combination of this thing from the '90s and this thing from the mid-'80s." What's the old line? "What do sausages and laws have in common? You never want to see how they're made." I think there will come a time when I go, "Hey, I think I'm done with new stuff. I'm going back to old stuff I may have missed—from '78 or '84."

THE REVEREND HORTON HEAT: Right now, there's a lot of things about AI—and we might be seeing new artists come on the scene who aren't real. So, the good thing to come of that is a little bit of the backlash. The backlash may mean bands that are absolutely 100 percent real, and the fans know and they can tell that. And they're saying, "This AI stuff is stupid. We like this guy because he can really play guitar well."

MOBY: My one criticism toward the more recent era—how apolitical a lot of alternative music has become. Because alternative music was always about overt politics, but also lifestyle politics. Nirvana being the perfect example of that—they were an incredibly successful band who *challenged* their audience. And they talked about politics, and they wrote about politics, and they talked about gender norms.

LES CLAYPOOL: There's always something going on somewhere, that old guys like me and you don't know about. And that's the shit. It's there. Nobody knew who the fuck Primus was or gave two shits in the music business—until there were a few of us out there starting to scrape and scratch. Then, all of a sudden, something percolates like Nirvana and takes over the world. So, something like that *will* happen again. Who knows where it will come from? That's just the way it is—whether it's music or literature or film. There's always something bubbling under that's going to surprise the shit out of everyone. I look forward to it.

FRED ARMISEN: Even as we're talking, we don't even know the name of it, and there's something happening in Chile or Miami or South Korea. All the time. It's the best thing about being alive—there's always a new movement. *What a dream!*

GERALD CASALE: Well, I'd be foolish to say nothing can happen again. But when it happens, it won't sound like it did in the '90s.

Trent Reznor with Nine Inch Nails, April 1994. "I think there is no time barrier in music or other art. It always holds up."—Naoko Yamano *Pictorial Press/Alamy*

24 TEST OF TIME

"There's nothing like it"

How does '90s alt-rock hold up today? Have changing tastes relegated it to the "oldies" category—or made it as relevant as ever?

GERALD CASALE: What's good is good. And the test of time shows you what sifts out the wheat from the chaff. Like, "These guys hold up. These songs hold up. They're as good as anything historically—but it just took a while to digest." And that's what I was admitting happened to me [with '90s alt-rock]—at first, I was put off by a lot of the lack of style and lack of visual presence. But then I got it.

Good art is good art—whether it's pop styling or Jackson Pollock or minimalism, you can see the intelligence and the originality behind it. And that's all I was ever looking for: the originality. That's what you hope for as an artist, whether I was trying to do it or whether somebody else did it. I would *appreciate* when somebody else did it. I wouldn't be jealous. I'd be like, "Wow. They did something I didn't think of."

LOU BARLOW: There was a period where people were like, "Oh, the '80s were awful. Only bad music was made in the '80s." And then each successive decade, as the "unearthing" begins . . . it's like the unearthing of the '60s is an incredible thing. How many obscure bands that you start to dig up and go, "Oh, my God. Who the fuck knew they were around?" So, to me the '90s were fascinating because there were so many math rock bands and weird pop bands—you don't really know all of it.

THE REVEREND HORTON HEAT: The '80s was when original music was wanted by the clubs and the local people. But the '90s was really the rise of the alternative venue—where those venues reinforced that they wanted a band that was very different, like Soundgarden or the Toadies or Nirvana. I think certain bands are going to be listened to for a very long time—decades and decades. I love Soundgarden—I think they're probably going to be listened to forever. And those songs by Nirvana—those are definitely a fabric of our civilization now. I think the music of the '90s is going to hold up well.

DARREN JESSEE: I think it holds up great. I heard Radiohead's *The Bends* the other week, and it sounded awesome to me. Those records have a big dynamic range. I heard My Bloody Valentine, and it sounded pretty amazing to me.

RUDEBOY REMINGTON: The early '90s, they didn't force themselves to be big—they just expressed themselves. You've got so many great records that you feel like, "That cannot be topped by anyone now." Today, I hear lackluster sounds, lame-ass people, characters that I don't have any connection with. Yes, sometimes it's very obvious. And some are great, actually.

Radiohead in Brussels, Belgium, December 5, 1995. Left to right: Phil Selway, Jonny Greenwood, Thom Yorke, Colin Greenwood, and Ed O'Brien. "I heard Radiohead's *The Bends* the other week, and it sounded awesome to me. Those records have a big dynamic range."—Darren Jessee *Gie Knaeps/Hulton Archive/Getty Images*

EVAN DANDO: It holds up just as well as the things we were trying to make it hold up to. Some of the Pixies songs, some of the Nirvana songs, a couple of ours . . . for me, Screaming Trees.

FRED ARMISEN: It always sounds great to me. I live in it. I will put on Stereolab and Dinosaur Jr. today. I saw Green Day recently. I saw Pearl Jam recently—I love it.

MIKI BERENYI: I suppose it depends on what you mean by "'90s alternative." It's such a broad spectrum. It could include anything from all the 4AD bands I love—Cocteau Twins, Throwing Muses, Pixies. Or does it mean Pearl Jam and Soundgarden? Does it mean Babes in Toyland? Does it mean Weezer? There's nothing really musically that similar to any of these bands. It was mostly about attitude.

MATT JOHNSON: I like the bands that I used to *not* like—more than I thought I would. When I was young, I fell into the whole idea that Stone Temple Pilots were not really authentic. I will listen to Stone Temple Pilots if it comes on, and I'm like, "Fuck, that's a *really* cool song! I like the vocal. I like the writing." So, I appreciate Stone Temple Pilots—where I didn't appreciate them before.

The caricatured, stereotypical [*mimics an Eddie Vedder impersonator*] voice? I don't miss that shit *at all*. I don't miss the affectation in the voice. I don't really think of Kurt Cobain's voice as being highly affected. There are other singers from that time that seem like it's more of a character and it's an affectation. But nonetheless, most of the main artists, I think, "They were writing cool songs." And that's the thing that I really miss.

CRAIG WEDREN: There's stuff then that I was not "hearing." I thumbed my nose at it—at the time—that I think is great music now. And I'm like, "What was I thinking?" I was just being young and snobby. But most of it was not remarkable, because most music that most people make isn't great, right? There's only a little bit of great music or art or film or literature at any given time. I'm really impressed by a lot of what has filtered through.

I'm aware of it because I have a fifteen-year-old son, so I hear what he and his friends are listening to. And again, because they're living in the digital age, and they're Spotify kids or TikTok kids—they listen to *everything*. The entire history of recorded music is right there. But there are certain things that literally everybody knows. And one of those things is Nirvana. And another one of those things is Radiohead. And another one of those things is the Ramones. So, you can't really argue with that. I think it's really good music.

FERGAL LAWLER: I still listen back to loads of '90s stuff that I'd never gotten sick of—like Dinosaur Jr., Pixies . . . Nirvana stuff is a little bit overplayed, but I still listen to it every now and again. Amazing sounds. My youngest child is eighteen and she's playing piano and drums, and I'm kind of introducing her to stuff she might like from back then. My daughter just got into the Breeders, and I'm trying to explain, "Kim Deal was in the Pixies, and then

FROM ALT-ROCK TO CHILDREN'S MUSIC

John Flansburgh describes how They Might Be Giants found a whole new audience.

After ten years with Elektra, we found ourselves in a weird vicious cycle—we were teetering on being broke and we would keep going on tour to earn money but come back with a little less money because we were touring on a scale that wasn't quite profitable. Facelessly, we started doing television work—incidental music for the *New York Times Television Network*, *Malcolm in the Middle*, *The Daily Show*. Except for the theme from *Malcolm in the Middle*, I don't think anybody knew we were involved.

And then the offer to do a kids record came through Rounder. It seemed like, "This is a way we can eke out a middle-class existence, maybe." The thing that really made our kids' album career take off was the continuity of Borders bookstores and their ability to do in-store performances on a really huge scale—for unpaid general audiences. It was like baby Beatlemania.

We would float from Boston to Providence to New York to Philadelphia to D.C. to Baltimore with just me, [bandmate] John [Linnell], and our drummer Marty Beller; and we would play these six o'clock shows at a Borders . . . and a thousand people would show up with their kids. Then they would buy two copies of everything, and we'd be signing. We'd play for a half-hour, and it was their kids' first show. That was really the "secret weapon"—they sold CDs, they had a kids' section, and because they had this in-store setup for book readings . . . you could make five phone calls and set up five shows.

she went on to form this band . . ." and the whole history. It's great to be able to pass that down to another generation.

KENNEDY: I think it holds up beautifully—and I know that because my daughters and their friends listen to a lot of it. Like, my fifteen-year-old daughter came back from the record store yesterday, and she was like, "Oh, I bought Fleetwood Mac *Rumours*, Nirvana *Nevermind* . . . and a Billy Joel record." But she loves '90s music, and I can't tell her how I used to dress and the extent of my job—because she would be *so* horribly embarrassed.

KEVIN MARTIN: It's still the best. There's nothing like it. Love or hate some of the bands that came out of that time, the freedom that we were allowed as musicians and artists by the labels and these great A&R guys that have all been fired by their jobs because they fought the presidents and whatnot, they allowed us to create some of the greatest music *ever*.

COREY GLOVER: It still holds up. It's some of the music that I listen to. I listen to a lot of different kinds of music, and it's not nostalgia-based, but I often feel good when it comes past my ears. It's the soundtrack to certain parts of your existence. Like, what were you listening to in high school just before you graduated—and that whole life-changing experience of being sixteen, seventeen, eighteen years old? And being in college on your own and finding your own voice within that context?

NAOKO YAMANO: I think there is no time barrier in music or other art. It always holds up.

VADEN TODD LEWIS: If you have an LP from '93 or '94 and something that's mastered today, it's just going to sound different. But as far as the structure and the music, I think it stands up.

JONN PENNEY: Production-wise, some things show their age a bit. But song-wise, I think a lot of the bands really hold their own. I'm going to DJ at a record fair in a few weeks' time—just for a bit of fun—and I've got an hour's worth without even blinking. Bangers all through. So, I think the quality of songwriting definitely stands up.

MATT PINFIELD: I think it's fucking great. That music is *so* good. I see young people discovering it all the time. Teenagers, college-age people, people who weren't into it when it came out but are actually going back and listening have given a reevaluation to a lot of it and found that they realize there were so many great songs there.

In the words of Noel Gallagher, "All the other bullshit won't really matter. Because what people care about is, 'Is there a great song?'" And there were great songs, and there were great performances. And that's why you had the Lemonheads, Dinosaur Jr., and Everclear and all these bands that were kicking against the pricks—it was great. In the words of Nick

The entire history of recorded music is right there. But there are certain things that literally everybody knows. And one of those things is Nirvana. And another one of those things is Radiohead. And another one of those things is the Ramones. So, you can't really argue with that. I think it's really good music.

CRAIG WEDREN

Cave, "Kicking against the pricks." I loved it. I'm very grateful. It's not wasted on me that I was able to be there in the center of one of the most creative explosions in music history and be at the center of platforms like *120 Minutes* to expose it to people.

KRISTIN HERSH: Timeless music is the *only* music. If you can't listen to something because it isn't in style anymore, it was never substantive enough to be actual music—it's just wearing a sound outfit.

PAGE HAMILTON: The bands from New York I think hold up really well. Sonic Youth sounds great. I haven't heard Live Skull or Rat at Rat R in a million years, but it's always a warm fuzzy place. We have a crew guy from Minneapolis who would play that music, and I'd be like, "Oh, man, I haven't heard this in a million years. This sounds cool!" And I don't know if it's because it reminds me of those days and that feeling, or if it's good. Is it nostalgia or is it really cool?

SPEECH: Me, personally, I think it's the golden age of hip-hop. I actually think it's the golden age of music *in general*—reminiscent of the '60s. The '60s revolutionized music—whether it was folk, rock, jazz, soul . . . you name it. And I believe that the '90s was it. The '90s overshadows anything that has happened between the '60s and the '90s, and anything that has happened since. *To this very day.* The '90s is the more creative, vibrant, diverse musical selections of Western culture since the '60s.

ROGER JOSEPH MANNING JR.: Quality songwriting is quality songwriting. A good hook, a good lyrical moment, a good sentimental emotionally charged moment . . . there's very few things I don't enjoy going back to. That would include Supergrass and Blur. And Soundgarden—those riffs were *so* intense and well-crafted and interesting.

LES CLAYPOOL: I think it depends on what you're listening to. Go down a rabbit hole of Fishbone on YouTube from the early '90s and it's unbelievable. Jane's Addiction, those records are spectacular. Bad Brains. [The Red Hot Chili Peppers'] *The Uplift Mofo Party Plan* is an unbelievable record. Soundgarden, of course.

VINNIE DOMBROSKI: About a year ago we were on the road, and I listened to a whole cross section of stuff on Spotify and listened with different ears. Everclear, Stone Temple Pilots—it's just well done. And I think it's got the right heart. Listening back to the Screaming Trees and Lanegan, it comes from the right place. Jeff Buckley is like . . . coming from outer space. It was unbelievable. And to have the opportunity to have *Grace* released on a major label back then, it's stunning. It didn't have any hit songs—there certainly are *memorable* songs, but not songs that we would call "hit songs." It was a wonderful time period of music—it's like the inmates ran the asylum.

THE FROGS GET (BARELY) PAID FOR BEING SAMPLED BY BECK

Jimmy Flemion recalls an unexpectedly low payday.

We had seen Beck twice before [his song "Where It's At"] came out. We saw him at the Rave in Milwaukee, and we gave him some tapes to listen to. And then the next time we saw him at the Rave again, he said, "I sampled 'I Don't Care If U Disrespect Me (Just So You Love Me)' and 'Hot Cock Annie.'" That's one we've never heard—his version, or whatever he did, with "Hot Cock Annie." I said, "Okay, that's cool"—and didn't think anything of it.

And the day before [the release of Beck's *Odelay*], [brother and bandmate] Dennis [Flemion] gets a phone call from Beck, and Beck says, "My new album is coming out tomorrow, and it's called *Odelay*. I don't know if you mind . . . I sampled your song 'I Don't Care If U Disrespect Me (Just So You Love Me).'" And he said, "Okay." On the underground local station, they debuted the song, and we were listening on the radio. We had no idea what it was going to sound like. And then, "Where it's at . . . that was a good drum break."

It was just a one-time payment for the sample. Which would be kind of like if you worked at a day job . . . "Here's your weekly wage." But at the time, you didn't know the video would be seen millions [of times] or the album *just blew up*. The record label we signed to, they owned 50 percent of the publishing. And that guy did the deal, and I don't remember he necessarily doubled it to get himself in the deal or if it was just the same payment. But anyway, here's the amount: It was $5,000. He got $2,500, and Dennis and I split—$1,250.

ROGERS STEVENS: I think like most things, certain things don't stand the test of time. But I do think Nirvana were better than everybody else in terms of just the songs. Not the performance of the song, it's not about how good they were as musicians—it's the *idea* of the song. That to me, there is nobody in the realm that we could have been on a bill with that was that good. Like, *consistently*.

I liked Soundgarden, the way they sounded when you'd see them live—particularly the way the later records sounded. Those hold up to me. But when I listen to what is probably my favorite record by them, *Badmotorfinger*, that album doesn't sound very good. But the band is so good it overcomes the production in my mind. And Alice in Chains had some great singles, but I don't really know the records.

MIKE EDWARDS: Superficially, probably not all that well. Certainly, the likes of me and many other people around me were simplistic songwriters. And I think songwriting over time has evolved and become a lot more complex and a lot more interesting.

PAUL LEARY: Because I wasn't a big fan of a lot of that stuff to start with, I can't really say how it held up—because I have the same opinion of it now that I did then. Things got a little different from the mid '90s to the late '90s, and I got to work with Sublime, and I got to produce a couple of their big radio hits—"Santeria" and "Wrong Way." I really love listening to that on the radio whenever it comes on.

PAUL Q. KOLDERIE: I feel like the early '90s, up to about '95–'96, holds up better than that next wave. Like, when you saw the rise of the Smashing Pumpkins and stuff like that, as it went on, things got a little bit formulaic. It turned into "grunge"—this kind of guitar sound and this kind of vocal sound. And ultimately, you get Nickelback. The best of any era is always going to hold up.

One thing that's interesting is, as good a record as *Nevermind* is, it's a little bit hard to listen to—because it's so "of a moment." And when you listen to it, you're like, "Oh, yeah . . . *that*." *Live Through This* got a posthumous "10" in *Pitchfork* because it's aged so well. Or when they talk about "Creep," for some reason that has aged well. You might not have thought it was gonna, but somehow it has. People find meaning in it. That song is getting over a million streams a day. *Every day.* And it's more than thirty years old. I don't know why, but it is. It's streamed more than any Beatles song!

STEVE ALBINI: The stuff that was super-popular—like most pop music—very low batting average. Hit records are hit records because they have sort of general appeal, not because they're outstanding. But the best records I think from that era are *really* phenomenal. I wouldn't say go to the radio hits and listen to them first. I would say, "Ask the fans of the band that you're interested in what's their best record." And then listen to that first.

MARY TIMONY: It really depends on what band. I like certain bands, and I don't like other bands—it's like I think about any era. The bands that I like, it's fun to listen to. I love Pavement, Sonic Youth, Unwound, Liz Phair, the Breeders, the Pixies . . . but there are other bands I don't ever have to hear again.

DANA COLLEY: Some bands I love. Screaming Trees—I love Mark Lanegan's solo work. I didn't really listen to Screaming Trees until right around the time he died [in 2022], I started listening again. And I was like, "*Holy shit.*" There was danger and power to it—and also an impermanence to the sound. And the permanence to the lifestyle—knowing you can't live like that, you can't sustain that. It's great when you're twenty, but at sixty it's a whole other thing. There was a resilience to being able to live and walk the walk.

I look back at it as pretty much a golden era in terms of music. Certainly, Nirvana to me, I'm constantly amazed at what I hear, even though it's been played to death, you know everything you've ever heard, you've heard it all. It's kind of like the Beatles in the way that if you stop and listen, you're going to hear something new you haven't heard before—the tonality, the fierceness, just the power of that band never ceases to amaze me. And the energy. I think there's a lot of opportunities to go back and hear some great music.

BILL GOULD: Aside from computer-generated music, I haven't really heard anything to replace it. I don't know if music has really changed much since then—except on a technical level. We're talking rock music, not R&B and pop, right? I haven't really seen a lot of progression since back then . . . actually, I take that back: some of the black metal stuff, Meshuggah. Some of the prog stuff is pretty out of control. That's happened, where it's kind of similar to what was happening then but became a little bit more extreme. But I haven't seen anything that has really diverted and taken me somewhere that's a completely different place.

MOBY: When I go back to some of that major label grunge—or even throughout the decade—it's amazing how well it was made. I went down a weird rabbit hole recently of watching some of that late '90s major label rock like Limp Bizkit and Kid Rock, and I was kind of stunned—just the days when they would spend a million dollars on a video and a million dollars making a record. I stood back and appreciated how phenomenally technically well made some of that was. And of course, Soundgarden: "Black Hole Sun" and "Fell on Black Days," pretty much every Nirvana song . . . it's so special. There's a reason why everyone in the world fell in love with it and why people still listen to that music constantly today.

MIKE WATT: fIREHOSE, those were hard, hard years. Because playing without D. Boon [who died in 1985], I didn't think anybody wanted to hear me without him. I've got to give [guitarist] Edward [Crawford] and [drummer] Georgie [Hurley] so much credit for playing with me then. I was really trying to get over the loss of D. Boon. I couldn't even write songs about him until the first opera, *Contemplating the Engine Room*, in 1997.

DANNY SABER: Somewhere along the line, what's biggest has become equated with what's best. Which is not always the case. In fact, if it's the biggest thing of the moment, it's probably not the thing that is going to be looked back upon as, "Oh, that was the thing that *really* had the most impact."

POE: As dark as those times were, there was enormous hope. There was never the idea that you were going to placate some commercial engine. Like, with these algorithms—"Oh, your song must conform to *this* length. It has to have a chorus at *this* point. Your face has to be positioned *this* way." There was this moment where radio had enough autonomy; DJs could play things on major radio stations with nobody's permission. You still had these *tastemakers*.

MIKI BERENYI: I think what's missing is the Perry Farrells of the future who want to make a Lollapalooza. It isn't with people like me who were making music God knows how long ago, or people who are getting shitloads of money being put behind them but are going to get six bands from Hull or something and do something ambitious with it. But also, that means people have to *go to gigs*. And I despair when I look at social media, people who I love and who should know better, the only time they post that they've gone to a gig is when it's a stadium. Because it's an event and, "Oh, look at me and twenty thousand people!" And yet, when there are bands playing literally around the corner from them, they won't go. If you go, I promise you, it's way better—as an *experience*. If you're not going to go, it's going to die.

SPEECH: I'm very grateful to be the age I was—to be able to witness the magic of that time. It was a *very* magical time.

JENNIFER HERREMA: As far as where I was from—DIY, punk rock, no budgets—I felt the '90s made a *big* mark.

EVAN DANDO: Who would have thunk that at this point in time, we would collectively be looking back so hard on it like it's the '60s or something? I'm happy to have been a part of it.

EDDIE "KING" ROESER: To have the music that was for total nuts, and people thought you were crazy to spend all your time playing this music—people thought it was "noise rock" or whatever—and to have it take over the world for a while, *was really kind of cool*.

MATT PINFIELD: There was so much great music coming out in the '90s. Every other week. Like any era that you're right in the center of, you're like, "This is never going to stop! This is the greatest! It's going to go on forever!" But then when all of a sudden, when there's a lull of exciting bands or music, you're like, "Oh, wow. *That was an important era.*"

25 HEADLINERS

"They had such impact and control over their environment"

A handful of '90s (non-grunge) alt-rockers certainly could put an immense number of fannies in seats . . . and their presence was constantly felt on the charts and airwaves.

R.E.M.

LOU BARLOW: R.E.M. were a *real* influence. And there are all kinds of incredible bands underneath them—Dream Syndicate, the Neats, True West.

ART ALEXAKIS: They came out about the same time as the Smiths. The distortion was turned down—which, at first, I didn't like because I was listening to X and punk rock, which was really aggressive. But after about two or three listens, that album *Murmur* just killed me. It was unique and American, and it was roots-based, but it had a level of psychedelia in there as well. I found it really compelling. And every album I think they progressed—they still sounded like themselves, but they sounded a little different record to record, which I think is important.

TANYA DONELLY: R.E.M. is one of my all-time favorite bands. I love every album and every incarnation of them. That live show [for the tour in support of *Monster*], in particular, was *mesmerizing*. They were in such a special space at that time. I know that they're not people that are naturally comfortable with fame and that level of attention. But they handled it *so* well. They were able to take being in a stadium, and the rock songs were big and it was loud and people were dancing . . . and then they could bring it way down and you could hear a pin drop in a stadium of sixty thousand people. They had such impact and control over their environment. It was amazing to watch.

Red Hot Chili Peppers, 1990. Left to right: Chad Smith, Flea, John Frusciante, and Anthony Kiedis. "It would be a different landscape without the Red Hot Chili Peppers."—Vinnie Dombroski *Avalon/Hulton Archive/Getty Images*

EVAN DANDO: I had *Murmur* and I know it's good, and I love "Catapult." And something about it was sounding a little too *delicate*—especially when they went all "U2" in "Follow me, don't follow me" [the song "Orange Crush"]. I wasn't able to follow that irony at that time. Obviously, they were making fun of themselves and shit. I think they're amazing, those guys. They did untold great things. They made the future what it was.

KENNEDY: I got to see R.E.M. in 1988 or 1989. It still felt small; it still felt like "your band"—even though they had been around forever. At that time, R.E.M. was my very favorite band. I really liked *Out of Time* and *Automatic for the People*—but it was almost like U2 on the Zoo TV Tour. Like, *it's a different band*. It inhabited something that almost got away from them. And who knew Michael Stipe was such a secret perv—years later, he was posting a lot of dick pics on Tumblr!

But pound for pound, four of the most talented people in rock. It's so ironic, because Michael Stipe was so shy but secretly absolutely *loved* fame. So, they had no choice—that's what you do: You push the limits, and you try new things. But it's scary doing what you do best, because at what point do you become a parody of yourself? So, I totally get the reflex to push it in certain directions. But you also risk like . . . Mumford & Sons sound like shit with a drummer.

RED HOT CHILI PEPPERS

ANGELO MOORE: I think what makes the Chili Peppers unique was they put funk into their rock. When they started out in Hollywood, they were some the funkiest white boys in the neighborhood with their music. And that's something you didn't see too often. They definitely turned a lot of people on to a lot of funky music they usually wouldn't hear in the Hollywood rock scene.

LES CLAYPOOL: With Primus, we never really had people we could play with in the Bay Area. We always had to do our own shows. We opened for the Swans and the Pop-O-Pies. There was never really anybody we could play with that was a good fit. And then all of a sudden, here comes the Red Hot Chili Peppers. But Flea basically kicked the door wide open for bass players to step out a bit. And his energy was *insane*. Especially them and Fishbone together were some of the greatest shows I've ever seen in my life.

One of the greatest albums of that era was two albums before *Blood Sugar Sex Magik*—*The Uplift Mofo Party Plan*. That album, to this day, is a monster of a record. I remember when that came out; it was like Zeppelin or something. An incredibly powerful record. Michael Beinhorn produced it, and the tonality of that record is incredible. That was the one that has always been the pinnacle Chili Peppers record. That thing is still a monster.

RUDEBOY REMINGTON: When [guitarist] Hillel Slovak died [on June 25, 1988, from a drug overdose], we were scared that they wouldn't survive. And they did. When we saw that John Frusciante was there, then we figured, "He fits in." We didn't know they were ready for *Blood Sugar Sex Magik*, but the other one, *Mother's Milk*, was no joke. We felt it was a pity that Hillel didn't experience that success, but the band at least survived. We weren't jealous; we just knew, "These guys are going to be extremely big" because of the record with Rick Rubin.

MIKE EDWARDS: Red Hot Chili Peppers always have their moments. Sometimes few and far between. But a track like "Give It Away," I love that. I thought that was fantastic.

VINNIE DOMBROSKI: I look at the Chili Peppers back in the day as one of the most important alternative bands. I'm certain they were influenced by Funkadelic. If I think about the Chili Peppers at any point in time—I remember them from the late '80s and early '90s—they were making their niche in alternative radio along with Jane's Addiction. It would be a different landscape without the Red Hot Chili Peppers

NINE INCH NAILS

AL JOURGENSEN: No! Not competition [between Ministry and NIN]. Trent started out as our roadie. And more power to him—he refined a sound. He's mentioned it—that we were an influence on his sound. And then he refined it to fit his own ideals. And I say, "More power to ya." There's no competition. I think the stuff he does is great. And I think it sounds more different than Ministry by the day as he found his own footing. *Go, Trent, go!*

COREY GLOVER: Their whole industrial bent was really sort of great. And watching them [on the first Lollapalooza] really put that out there and got a reaction. I remember there was a band back in the '80s called the Beatnigs, and their whole gig was they would have chainsaws and metal grinders—and they were making music with that. That was amazing. And that's what Nine Inch Nails reminded me of. But really honed and refined.

TRACY BONHAM: I liked Trent Reznor's writing. It was definitely his own thing, and it was *truly* alternative. And it was dark. A lot of stuff was dark back then, but it was dark and musical . . . and it was dark and emotional. And it seemed like he tapped into a really dark place. I look back now, and I really appreciate that he took a lot of chances—those songs would *not* be played on the radio these days if it was coming out new. He found his own niche, and it was unlike anything else I'd heard.

GERALD CASALE: They took what we did—which people accused us of being Disney-fied electronic music mixed with guitars—and he took it to a deeper, darker place. A psychological self-evaluation place. And the sounds that he was getting using synths and programming of sequencer lines were incredible. That was *so* cool.

RICHARD PATRICK (Filter singer/guitarist, ex–Nine Inch Nails guitarist): I constantly was like, "Dude, we're wearing black." When I saw the record cover for *Pretty Hate Machine*, I was like, "Why is it pink? Why isn't it more black?" That was kind of my thing. I was always the guy whispering, "Hey, make it meaner and heavier."

Then when *Broken* came out, that was the record where [Reznor] literally goes, "I'd like to thank my live band for influencing me into this direction." And that was the only credit I got: I was an influence. I was in his ear the whole time saying, "Mean. You're pissed. You're angry. That's what people want." And he was like, "Alright. I get it."

And that was my main contribution, really, to Nine Inch Nails. And jumping around the stage and just being completely dedicated. I mean, he would tackle me onstage, he'd throw beer at me, and I'd throw beer at him, and the audience just couldn't believe it. They're like, "These guys are out to kill each other!" Our shows were just over the top, so he got a little of that.

My alter ego became "Piggy." I was Piggy. And when I left, it wasn't necessarily the nicest way to leave. So, when I heard that song "Piggy" later on [on *The Downward Spiral*], I was like, "Oh, shit. Is that about me?" Because my nickname in the band was Piggy for three years. Now I go over to Trent's house and blow his speakers up with my records.

SONIC YOUTH

EVAN DANDO: Sonic Youth were unique because they were from a time where there was no star trip. They had a lot of dignity and really good taste. They brought bands out, and as soon as they did . . . Sonic Youth was like a "gold seal."

LOU BARLOW: I read about them before I heard them. For some reason in my small town in Massachusetts, there was a tobacco store that carried this magazine called *New York Rocker*. It was a paper, but it had the most insanely cool shit in it—that I couldn't hear. I was reading articles about this music called No Wave, and I'm like, "Oh, my God. This sounds like the greatest shit ever." I became obsessed with Sonic Youth just by reading about them. I finally got the *Confusion Is Sex* record, and that was it. It was the only band that I ever read about that lived up to what it felt like they might sound like—based on the writing. *Confusion Is Sex* to me is up there with the Ramones and the first Velvet Underground record.

MARY TIMONY: They were making music that no one had made before. Which people don't do as much now. It was good *art*—really exciting. The drummer, Steve Shelley, was really incredible; and he had a lot to do with it. I mean, every member of the band was great.

JOHNNY TEMPLE: *Goo* was a huge influence on so many of us. Also, Sonic Youth was not only musical predecessors to Nirvana, but Sonic Youth were at the forefront of carving out a space for bands to make deals with big record companies and retain creative control. So, that was also a nonmusical lasting impact. Sonic Youth really staked out, "We are going to sign to Geffen, but our music is still going to be as weird as we want it to be." And Sonic Youth sounds a lot weirder than Nirvana. Sonic Youth did some really wonderful business maneuverings that benefited all of us.

DAVE MARKEY: It's funny how for me, it was all these close connections with people that were my friends that I had worked together with—I had shot a couple of videos for Sonic Youth for the *Goo* album. I think that was the first major label video directing gigs that I got. I think that made the film [*1991: The Year Punk Broke*] possible: Thurston was able to talk his band and the management into incurring the expense of bringing me along with a suitcase of Super-8 film to document that tour.

LEE RANALDO: [Songwriting] with Sonic Youth, it was kind of a four-way street in a sense. We were all involved in the composition of the songs and in working them out. With Sonic Youth, it was almost as though arranging the songs *was* writing the songs, and we'd all contribute to what a song sounded like in a very concerted way.

SMASHING PUMPKINS

BUTCH VIG: Well, Pumpkins are a pretty amazing band. The first time I met them, I was taken by their appearance, just how they looked. With D'arcy [Wretzky], there's this cool-looking bass player, and James Iha being Asian, the second guitarist, and Billy [Corgan] was this tall gangly guy—he had long hair at the time. Then they came out and played this incredible psychedelic rock that was just crushing. And Jimmy Chamberlin, an incredible, incredible drummer. I love working with them.

KEVIN MARTIN: The musicianship was insanity. I remember the first time I saw them at the Off Ramp in Seattle, I had that first album [1991's *Gish*]; and I was absolutely floored by how great the band was. And Billy is a commanding guitar player. He was a metalhead, and you could see it in his playing. But he attached himself to this new style of writing. This landscape that he was painting musically was so beautiful and all-encompassing—it sucked you in. You couldn't avoid it. *It was magical.*

I have every record they've ever made. I'm not crazy about the last few records, but I love that Billy still does what he does and the way he does it. And I love Jimmy's playing as a drummer. I try to emulate his playing a lot when I write music and when I jam with my friends—I love his approach to playing Billy's songs. The Pumpkins were an incredible band.

MATT SWEENEY: They could play really well, and they had lots of guitar solos. They sounded really unbelievably tight, polished, and ready to rip. The drums were *so* unbelievable. Was there any other band that had as amazing a drummer? That made them really stand out, like, "Jesus. The guitar-playing and the drumming are really remarkable." They're so remarkable that people didn't seem to realize that the band was playing, like, *Fugazi riffs*. [*Laughs*] But they were an interesting band.

I sometimes think of "record store bands"—the guy who was in charge of that band worked at a record store and listened to a lot of records and also had '70s chops. I thought they were really cool when I first heard them because they were so *not* cool at the time. They weren't in step with a lot of other things—like a lot of the bands were trying to be like the Stooges or something like that. They really stood out.

CRAIG WEDREN: It was fascinating, that tour [Shudder to Think toured with the Pumpkins in 1993]. Smashing Pumpkins . . . whoever schemed that, devised it, and executed it—I assume Billy in conjunction with the record label and management—did a beautiful job. Because I couldn't possibly count the number of failed versions of that that I've seen. Where it's like, "We're really going to 'groom' this band. We're going to build it up and put out an indie album that's *sort of* an indie album . . . but it's sort of *not* an indie album. And then you're going to do the tour, and then we're going to do the 'big record.' And then you're going to break through, and you're going to be huge."

They invited us on tour with them—and we were thrilled. *Gish* did well—it was well known—but it wasn't like a pop radio hit. When we went out on tour with Pumpkins, it was right before *Siamese Dream* came out. The album came out in the middle of that tour, and I remember the first shows were maybe three to five hundred people. And the final shows we played with them—a month or two later—were like three to five *thousand* people. It was very significant, and it happened very fast.

DAVID PAJO: I never really listened to them. I saw them in Louisville when they played on a tiny little stage . . . and someone had brought a chicken to the show—total Kentucky vibe—and it was running around on the stage! I was the first band of the day on the side stage on one of the Lollapaloozas [the 1994 lineup]. I was playing drums in King Kong—and Smashing Pumpkins were the last band on the main stage. I would watch them side stage every night. But it was mostly trying to understand why everyone liked them so much. I guess I couldn't figure out their songs—what the appeal was.

I knew the "rat in the cage" song ["Bullet With Butterfly Wings"]—just that lyric part. You *had* to at that time, it was so huge. I don't know if it was ever a point of contention [when Pajo was briefly bandmates with Corgan in the band Zwan]—I think Billy thought it was funny. He'd be like, "'1979.' You don't know that song?" And I'd be like, "Can you sing the chorus? I'm sure I heard it." [*Laughs*]

GERALD CASALE: I remember the Smashing Pumpkins thing because I thought, "*Who's this whining brat? What the hell is he doing?*" He bummed me out. But then by the time he's doing, "Despite all my rage, I am still just a rat in a cage," I'm going, "Okay, okay. That's the right lyrics for that voice. I like that."

CHAD TAYLOR: What makes any musician great is their ability to channel this fingerprint into the art. Billy Corgan has this in droves.

RADIOHEAD

PAUL Q. KOLDERIE: My and [studio partner] Sean Slade's manager was friends with the guy who was running EMI at the time. Sean and I had been doing a lot of indie records that had been popular in England and Europe—Dinosaur Jr., Lemonheads. Our manager wasn't getting us jobs in America because we didn't have a platinum record yet. So, we said, "Why don't we go to England and take some meetings over there? They think we're cool because they read about us in the music press."

He gave us Nick Gatfield's contact info, and we set up a meeting with him . . . and he had a record on his desk—Clockhammer: *Klinefelter*—that he liked the sound of the guitars on. And he said, "You did this?" And we said, "Yeah. We did that." He said, "Well, we have this band. It's three guitar players, and we're having trouble getting the guitars to really 'happen.'" He played us a couple of songs, and we said, "Sure. We'd love to work with them." But we didn't meet them until we got to Oxford to start the record [1993's *Pablo Honey*], actually.

MOBY: Arguably the most remarkable, successfully creative, artistic band of the last thirty years. They live in a world unto themselves. They started off with "Creep" and "High and Dry" but then all of a sudden became so experimental, so interesting, and so revered that you really can't quite compare them to anything else.

TANYA DONELLY: I loved the evolution of that band. The experimentation, the fact that they put the healthy pressure on themselves to continue to evolve. Any new Radiohead record, you're like, "Okay . . . what's it going to be? What street will they walk down this time?"

JASON PETTIGREW: I don't understand why *OK Computer* did as well as it did. There was that aspect of the vulnerability, and the hardcore fans for some reason glommed onto *Kid A*, like, "We're going to make the weirdest possible record that we can . . . *because we can*." Well, that's contrived, too—because it's not sincere. But as far as *OK Computer* goes, it's kind of setting you up for *Kid A*, where it's not guitar, bass, and drums anymore. "Karma Police" and "Paranoid Android" tapped into some form of national psyche, the same way that Kurt Cobain was doing on the Nirvana records. Whereas Kurt's was very non-sophisticated, very in-your-face, and very minimal, *OK Computer* taps into that but with a greater sense of sophistication.

DARREN JESSEE: I heard a story that when they sent that record [*OK Computer*] out to the press, they glued the cassette in a personal Walkman!

KENNEDY: People didn't realize what was possible. And with *OK Computer*, they were moved.

PAUL Q. KOLDERIE: That's why we got [Hole's *Live Through This*]. Kurt and Courtney went to Butch Vig and said, "Will you produce Hole's record?" He had just finished a long stint doing *Siamese Dream* for the Pumpkins, and he said, "I want to do my own band"—which turned into Garbage—"and I can't take on another big production now." So, they basically opened the floor and said, "Well, who then?" And somebody said, "Why don't you get the guys who produced 'Creep'?" And Kurt said—and I know he said this because of the A&R guy who was there—"Yeah. *I like that sound.*" So the A&R guy said, "I know those guys. They're from Boston. Let's do a phone call with them." We did a phone call, and it led to us getting the record.

GREEN DAY

FAT MIKE: Green Day were opening for Bad Religion on the tour right when *Dookie* came out. And I was like, "Bad Religion, they're going to be the band that 'does it.'" Because they're a better band. But Green Day . . . they did it perfect.

MATT SWEENEY: Green Day was coming out of a whole other huge underground scene that was getting kind of ignored. There's so many bands out of the Gilman Street thing—this huge aesthetic there. There were pop-punk bands, but there were powerviolence bands and bands like Man Is the Bastard—huge underground swells that are just as interesting as the college rock thing. And then something like Green Day was the beginning of a whole thing—and then there were all these bands that sounded like Green Day.

MIKE JOHNSON: They come from the Bay Area punk scene, so they're actually a *real* band. Although, they're totally poppy. I wouldn't blame them [for all the similar-sounding "pop-punk" bands that followed], although I was never a fan. It does seem like it went in a different direction . . . but I wouldn't blame Green Day. [*Laughs*]

FRED ARMISEN: I love Green Day. I remember when I started to hear them on the radio, I was *so* happy because they sounded like all the bands that I loved—like the Descendents and ALL.

ROGERS STEVENS: That's one of the best shows I've seen in my life—Green Day, last year. I don't own any Green Day records or listen to them ever. But at Sea.Hear.Now, they *blew my fucking mind*. You listen to them, and there are *so many* hits—and they're all good. They're a great band.

FAT MIKE: *Dookie* and *Nevermind* are both incredible albums. It was Green Day's best album. And Nirvana changed everything. And they're simple songs, too—both of those bands have pretty simple songs.

OASIS

MATT PINFIELD: Oasis were such a breath of fresh air. When I heard "Supersonic," it had that snarl and attitude that we loved in rock 'n' roll. But it was also alternative rock because it was not so slick. It lived in that space. Noel Gallagher once said that when he heard *Nevermind* that he could take melodies—you can call them pop melodies or just good melodies—and play with distortion and do things that are different. And that's what happened.

Noel was a great songwriter—he had an arsenal of great songs. Those first two albums [1994's *Definitely Maybe* and 1995's *(What's the Story) Morning Glory?*] are undeniable. So are all the B-sides—that *Masterplan* B-side album is great . . . and it didn't even include all their best B-sides! He was *exploding* as a songwriter. And Liam [Gallagher] is such an interesting frontman because he doesn't do a lot onstage, but that delivery is somewhere between

Oasis at Nomad Studios in Manchester, England, November 1993. Left to right: Noel Gallagher, Paul Arthurs (aka Bonehead), Paul McGuigan, Tony McCarroll, and Liam Gallagher. "Nirvana had taken over the world, and Oasis was England's new savior of alternative music and rock when they came out."—Matt Pinfield. *James Fry/Hulton Archive/Getty Images*

John Lennon and Johnny Rotten. He incorporated "the Johnnies" when he delivered those vocals—with a snarl, but with melody . . . and a shitload of attitude.

Plus, the cool thing about that band was they really didn't give a fuck. It was some of the young naiveness of it and growing up in working-class-poor Manchester and being raised by their mom with their dad not around. And the thing about Oasis is they would play anywhere, drive up and fall asleep on each other in a beat-up car and van. They paid their dues early on. But it exploded much faster, I think, than anybody would have expected—just like Nirvana. Nirvana had taken over the world, and Oasis was England's new savior of alternative music and rock when they came out.

KENNEDY: I'll never forget, Lewis Largent got in a screaming match with Liam Gallagher—I think it was in the Paramount Hotel Lobby—because Liam's like, "We're better than the Beatles." And Lewis was like, "*YOU FUCKIN' SUCK!*" [*Laughs*] Of course, Liam just wanted to push anybody's buttons and destroy anyone's sacred cows. Lewis was furious. But he knew he had to play Oasis [on MTV]. And they did.

U2

MOBY: I had loved U2 from *Boy*, *October*, *The Unforgettable Fire*, and *The Joshua Tree*. Those are all phenomenal records. But from *The Joshua Tree* especially, it seemed like they were heading down the path of very roots-oriented rock music—the way they were dressing, the way they were playing, the way they were presenting themselves. And then—maybe this goes back to ecstasy, I'm not sure—but suddenly, they discovered dance music. And it's hard not to if you're in the UK. *Achtung Baby*, everything about it—the way they reinvented themselves visually, sonically. And it's still a U2 album—it's still guitars, bass, and drums—but you can tell Adam [Clayton] and Larry [Mullen Jr.] were really into for the first time focusing on the beats. Focusing on rhythms. Basically, making a Happy Mondays/Primal Scream–inspired album with beautiful melodies on top of it.

TANYA DONELLY: U2 is the only other band [besides R.E.M.] I've seen who are able to walk into a football field and control it in the warmest, loveliest way.

KENNEDY: I went to a bunch of those shows [on the Zoo TV Tour] with my friends, and it was so much fun. They really got it—they totally gave the fans what they wanted. They understood. And I would put Metallica and Nine Inch Nails in that category—they understand that the arena was an extension of the band and was an extension of their music. Soundgarden—God rest Chris Cornell's soul—they were one of the worst arena bands I've ever seen. It was *so* boring. They were not made for that. But U2 was made for these performative aspects.

Bono with U2 at the National Exhibition Centre in Birmingham, England, June 1, 1992. "Is that the tour Bono tried to call the White House?"—Jason Pettigrew *Trinity Mirror/Mirrorpix/Alamy Stock Photo*

That live show [for the tour in support of *Monster*] in particular, was mesmerizing. [R.E.M.] were in such a special space at that time. I know that they're not people that are naturally comfortable with fame and that level of attention. But they handled it so well.

TANYA DONELLY

And it's very difficult, because you can lose so much sonically—especially back then with technology. So, it's very difficult to connect your audience with the most important and poignant songs in your set. But they did that beautifully—because there was so much dynamic in that setlist. There were times where you're raging and singing at the top of your lungs, and then you're in tears when they play "One." And it's beautiful. That's why they were the first band to play at the Sphere [in Las Vegas]. There's obviously something so technical in their artistry, and that's how they have to push themselves.

They were kind of cheesedicks when they were doing the whole "rock star thing"—I know they thought they were making fun of it, but it's very difficult to distinguish that when you're a fan. And you're like, "Oh, wait . . . I thought you were an Irish punk band singing political ditties? What's with this sunglasses-and-leather-pants bullshit?" The arena shows were more important than the music at that point. And it's like, for my money, I was done being a U2 fan—I'm not sitting up at night reading the liner notes for *Achtung Baby*. But I sure loved the show. And that's how they grew. And I love Larry Mullen Jr.—he's my favorite drummer.

JASON PETTIGREW: There's a lot of good songs on *Achtung Baby*. The presentation was very steeped in irony . . . is that the tour Bono tried to call the White House? I didn't hate it because I thought that record was really good. I think the most disingenuous portion of U2 was when they were like, "Oh, we've discovered electronica" and made that *Pop* record, which I thought was really dismal. *Zooropa* came before—it was kind of like the harbinger of what was to come. After *Achtung Baby*, when they start getting murky with electronic stuff and thinking that they've reinvented the wheel, it's like, "Eh . . . *no*."

Beastie Boys, September 1992. Left to right: Ad-Rock, MCA, and Mike D. "Beastie Boys to me is one of the most influential, fantastic hip-hop groups of all time." —Speech *Fairfax Media Archives/Getty Images*

26 ARTISTS

"They left blood all over the stage"

Those who were interviewed for this book discuss some of their favorite—or most notable—'90s alt-rockers, and what made them so darn special.

10,000 MANIACS

MATT PINFIELD: You could get 10,000 Maniacs played on the same alternative radio station as Alice in Chains and Soundgarden. The late '80s and early '90s 10,000 Maniacs stuff, like *In My Tribe*, were amazing albums. Natalie Merchant was a unique vocalist, and the songs were really strong as well.

AFGHAN WHIGS

MATT PINFIELD: In many ways, the Afghan Whigs' *Gentlemen* was like the alternative *Quadrophenia* [by the Who]. It was a concept record about this relationship and period of confusion, pain, hurt, love, sex. I think *Gentlemen* is one of the most important records of the 1990s.

TORI AMOS

KENNEDY: Tori Amos was super-hot, and she was very theatrical. She reminded me of a musical theater nerd who lost her virginity at Lollapalooza and was never quite the same . . . and just spent the rest of her career trying to get back to that weekend.

FIONA APPLE

POE: The song "Criminal" is the one that won me over. "What would an angel say? The devil wants to know." I related to that so completely. She's grappling with this sense of power that she has, which was a very new story. It was like, *owning* your power—not wanting to abuse it.

BAD RELIGION

FAT MIKE: You know where Brett Gurewitz got a lot of his ideas? *From Jewish songbooks.* Bad Religion is one of the only bands that if you dissect it, a lot of their song structures are in 4/6—they're waltzes. [Note: Fat Mike likely meant 3/4, 3/8, or 6/8 time, which are common for waltzes.]

BEASTIE BOYS

SPEECH: Beastie Boys to me is one of the most influential, fantastic hip-hop groups of all time. And the reason is not because of their lyrical content per se—it was their spirit of creativity, experimentation . . . being willing to re-create themselves with almost every project they released.

CHRIS HASKETT: They don't get enough credit for what good musicians they were/are. Especially Mike Diamond's drumming. He has an amazing pocket, and he and Adam Yauch made some stupidly funky grooves together.

BECK

ROGER JOSEPH MANNING JR.: Everybody was like, "One-hit wonder" [after "Loser"]. But songs like "Pay No Mind" and several others on *Mellow Gold* were like, "No. This guy is a classic songwriter. He can decorate it any way he wants to decorate it." He absolutely had done his homework and has something to say. That's why I was so excited to see what he was going to do next. *Odelay* was his follow-up, and to me, that's one of the strongest follow-ups in the history of popular music.

BJÖRK

TRACY BONHAM: When I would see Björk and all of her creativity, I remember being *so* envious of that freedom. She must have had more support but also probably could stand up for her art that I wish I could have done. Her vocal style, for sure [made Björk unique]. But also, just the way that she expressed herself.

FRANK STALLONE INTRODUCES JELLYFISH TO THEIR FAVORITE ARTIST

Roger Joseph Manning Jr. recounts how Jellyfish met Harry Nilsson.

There were many strange and wonderful happenings during the Jellyfish journey, but one of them was in '93. Frank Stallone was really good friends with Harry Nilsson. Somebody told Frank Stallone that Jellyfish couldn't be more enamored with Harry. And lo and behold, Frank Stallone brings Harry Nilsson to our Los Angeles show in '93—at the Palace. We had a great show, and we had the honor of being introduced to him afterwards.

He's in his later years here, he's pretty soft-spoken, he's hobbling around on a cane. Word on the street was he wasn't doing too well physically. We were amazed that Frank Stallone even got him out of the house—so, it was a pleasant surprise. Somebody asked him, "Harry, do you still write with other people these days?" And he goes, "Sure. I love songwriting." Somebody said, "You should write with Roger and Andy when they get back from the road." And he said, "Nothing would make me happier."

We were like, "We're off the road in a few months . . . we're going to write with Harry Nilsson!" Because we had a brief writing exploration series with Brian Wilson—which was neat, but nothing panned out from it. But now, we're going to write with *Harry Nilsson*. Well, in the months that passed while we were on the road, he passed away [on January 15, 1994, at the age of fifty-two]. So, not only did we then cover the song "Think About Your Troubles" for the Harry Nilsson tribute record [1995's *For the Love of Harry: Everybody Sings Nilsson*], but to us, "He's My Best Friend" was always that big "thank you" to him, anyway.

BLINK-182

MATT PINFIELD: Blink-182 were direct descendants of the Descendents. Not only did Mark Hoppus have a Descendents tattoo, but it was obvious that they were carrying the torch of punk-pop with a sense of humor—which started with the Buzzcocks in the late '70s in the UK.

BUFFALO TOM

JOHN AGNELLO: With all the grunge stuff happening, Buffalo Tom weren't like that. They were more like Rolling Stones-y or punky or something. But they were American. Bill Janovitz's gravelly voice was different from a lot of other stuff. He wasn't like, "*EVENFLOOOW!*" He could belt, but it was more gravelly. On a certain level, they reminded me a little bit of Tommy Keene, but a little different.

BUILT TO SPILL

DARREN JESSEE: I kind of started getting into those "vibe-y" bands—it was a little melancholy. Built to Spill was just *fun*—it was so different than a mainstream alternative band. They were homespun in a way that was cool, and Doug Martsch is a great guitar player. They ended up writing a bunch of great songs. I think I would find those type of records that had a melancholy vibe about them and were unique.

BULLET LAVOLTA

PAUL Q. KOLDERIE: They were the coolest band in town for a minute there. Kurt Davis—who went by the name Yukki Gipe—was a charismatic singer who had lots of energy. Their guitar player, Kenny Chambers, had a bit of a Mike Bloomfield thing—he didn't want to be too concerned with success. I produced their record *The Gift*, and we had three days to record, overdub, and mix the record. It was moving quickly, but on the second day, I saw Kenny slumped against the wall with his head in his hands. He goes, "Man . . . why does it have to take *so long*?"

BUSH

MATT PINFIELD: Gavin Rossdale wrote great songs, and his vocal delivery was incredible. When they came onto the scene with "Everything Zen," it was such a great song; and *Sixteen Stone* is an incredible album. There were bands that would be accused of ripping off the Seattle thing. *Whatever, man.* Great songs is what it was about.

THE CARDIGANS

DARREN JESSEE: They had such cool-sounding parts. That record *Life* is just a great record. Great songs and a cool, charming recording—you can tell they're performing it. All those Swedish bands have a great sense of melody. They were just a charming, catchy band that had a good lyrical perspective.

COCTEAU TWINS

JOHNETTE NAPOLITANO: They had no words—which was amazing. You have this emotional reaction. You're in this whole different world. It was flowing from a place that you felt.

THE CURE

JONN PENNEY: They followed their noses and had gone whichever way they wanted to go. "If we want to bring a brass section in and sing about cats, we're going to damn well do that—and we'll do it well." And the mainstream will take it on.

DEPECHE MODE

MATT PINFIELD: How many people have covered "Personal Jesus"? From Johnny Cash to Sammy Hagar. If it's a great song, people will be able to deconstruct it and reconstruct it. That's the thing of great, timeless songwriting—and I think Martin Gore has that.

ELASTICA

MATT PINFIELD: The same reason I love the Breeders, even though they're not the same animal—it's still that same thing where it's not afraid to be an individual, strong woman who was not afraid to say what they're going through or what's on their mind. "Connection," their big hit, actually borrowed the music from the band Wire [the song "Three Girl Rhumba"], who came from the post-punk era.

THE FLAMING LIPS

JOHN AGNELLO: "She Don't Use Jelly" is such a poppy, great song with a really cool melody on a really weird instrument. They're all great musicians. I love Wayne Coyne's voice—he's a wacky dude. They're all weird, but great. All their records sound different. I love the big, roomy drum sounds that Steven [Drozd] gets.

FOO FIGHTERS

CRAIG WEDREN: [Dave Grohl] gave me a cassette of some demos he had been doing, which turned out to be the first Foo Fighters record. I remember listening to it, and Dave has this ability—it comes from punk and alternative—there's this accessibility or a classic rock-ness to it that, even on that first cassette when he gave it to me, I remember being like, "This is so fucking awesome. It's like 'punk Steve Miller Band.'"

GRANT LEE BUFFALO

FERGAL LAWLER: Grant-Lee Phillips' voice is amazing—a unique voice. And Paul [Kimble], the bass player, played piano as well. For a three-piece . . . I think it was the fact that Paul played chords on the bass—to try and fill up that sound. Because Grant had an acoustic guitar, but he had pedals with it. He had a distortion pedal, and he'd have this big wall of sound, and then Paul would play these chords to fill in the gaps. I remember watching them, thinking, "How do they sound so big for a three-piece?"

GUIDED BY VOICES

JOHN AGNELLO: They're the classic drinking band—where they have the keg of beer or the whiskey on the stage. When I saw them in Asbury Park, I think they played "I Am a Scientist" twice because halfway through the set, Bob Pollard was so drunk, he played it again. People were like, "You already played that." And he's like, "Fuck you! *I want to play it again!*"

HAPPY MONDAYS

MIKE EDWARDS: A band you have no idea why they sounded like they did. I enjoyed that. First and foremost, it's having a very highly stylized, individual singer/frontman. I mean, Shaun Ryder has his own way of approaching singing, words. You couldn't really understand him, which was great. [*Laughs*] That's the best thing—when you don't really understand what is going on.

PJ HARVEY

TRACY BONHAM: What I loved about PJ Harvey—and what I really tried to emulate—was the simplicity. Sometimes, she'd just have one chord—maybe two—and she'd make a song, and it would *rock*. You'd want to move your body and feel this visceral feeling.

JULIANA HATFIELD

EVAN DANDO: Juliana never hid the whole trashy, Olivia Newton-John, poppy side of herself. In fact, she threw it to the front to annoy people. She has all kinds of integrity, she's super-smart, super-talented. She writes great songs about things that really happened—amazing ones. She's an inspiration. She kept it together, and I don't know how she did it.

HOLE/COURTNEY LOVE

KENNEDY: Courtney Love, I haven't seen her for a while, but when I knew her, she was absolutely, 1,000 percent batshit crazy. She got a lot of heat because she always needed to collaborate with people. But it's like, so does every other popular singer nowadays. Like, Taylor Swift doesn't write anything alone. Courtney Love didn't write anything alone. But I think that the issue was that she wanted credit for it. Because she always said, to her credit, that she only wanted to compete with the boys. She did not want to tear down other women, even though she did—she spent a lot of time feuding with and tearing down other women.

And I always I thought that was interesting, that she was like, "I want to be better than Billy Corgan. I want to be better than Trent Reznor." And by "better than," I think she meant she wanted to have intercourse with them—neither here nor there. She still to this day . . . my fifteen-year-old daughter loves listening to her and loves hearing about her. She is so intriguing—she's tall, has massive eyes, this personality that comes *seeping* out of her. But she had some natural gifts and some natural demons that lined up for a few bright and crazy spots throughout her career.

JESUS AND MARY CHAIN

MIKE EDWARDS: They came through at a time when you expected rock music to be very produced and very slick, and not really very interesting. And they had huge squalls of feedback and that really weird mix of this 1960s styling—but done really wrong in a really right way. Again, another band that were really interesting that didn't fit.

JESUS LIZARD

STEVE ALBINI: I admired Scratch Acid, which was the band David Sims and David Yow were in, in Texas. The Jesus Lizard was kind of an elaboration on a lot of those ideas—a slightly less spastic or less frantic version. A little more graceful, but very much of a type.

MARILYN MANSON

DANNY SABER: When Trent [Reznor] signed them, he was probably like, "Yeah, you'll do good, you'll be a cult band, you'll sell half a million records." And they *eclipsed* Nine Inch Nails. They were huge. For a minute there, he was the real fuckin' McCoy. I saw him as our generation's Bowie—he had the potential to be that guy, in his own way. And he could change and evolve. But it didn't really work out that way artistically for him.

APRIL MARCH

FRED SCHNEIDER: In the '90s, I really liked April March. While I was doing my solo album [1996's *Just Fred*], I was listening to the college station in Atlanta at Emory in the '90s. She was real melodic, but her lyrics were different and fun. The guy who produced her, Bertrand Burgalat, I really got into his productions, so I bought Valérie Lemercier. It was mainly those two I really liked and bought all their CDs.

MASSIVE ATTACK

POE: They were using programmed drums and making beats that were *so* unique and interesting. You didn't feel like they were imitating a drumbeat. They were inventing out of this "soup." They had exquisite sonic taste. They had a brilliant minimalism—that is popular now, in a way. I feel like Massive Attack birthed artists like even Billie Eilish. And then they'd have these guest singers that were incredible.

MAZZY STAR

FERGAL LAWLER: They had a "dusty" kind of sound, and the singer [Hope Sandoval] had an amazing voice. I didn't realize they were American because they almost sound like the Cocteau Twins. A different sound to anything I'd heard before.

MIDNIGHT OIL

KEVIN MARTIN: A huge fan of Midnight Oil. I've always had a crazy affinity for Australia—the country, the people, and the music. And that was one of the bands that stood out for me. Candlebox is actually named after a Midnight Oil lyric—a song called "Tin Legs and Tin Mines." Peter Garett mentions the aboriginals being "boxed in like candles" and that you can't contain beauty like that in a simple little reservation. And I just loved the imagery of that—so I chose it as the band name.

MIGHTY MIGHTY BOSSTONES

PAUL Q. KOLDERIE: They were kind of a gang at first. They were younger—they were hard-drinking kids influenced by the Specials and the Clash. Back in those days at Fort Apache, you'd get assigned to a session—I was just one of the engineers on staff—and they would say, "These guys are coming in." I came in, and I was *really* hungover. And I made the mistake of trying to get sympathy and say, "Take it easy guys. I'm not feeling too good." And they were like, "Oh, yeah? *FUCK YOU!*"

ALANIS MORISSETTE

MATT PINFIELD: She was cool and confrontational. Any time someone brings that element of surprise and danger into new music—or speaking your mind and speaking for a group of people who feel that they haven't been represented—that is the essence of what alternative music was at that period of time. *Jagged Little Pill* was an incredible record because it was very introspective.

MORRISSEY

JASON PETTIGREW: I really should sit down with people who were immersed in hardcore in the early '90s and have them explain to me why Morrissey fits so big in . . . you see these guys who've got huge biceps, and they're mean and they're wearing a *The Queen Is Dead* T-shirt. And I don't understand where that comes from.

MUDHONEY

EVAN DANDO: We toured with Mudhoney in 1989, and I was like, "*This is godhead!* This is what I always wanted to hear from music. They're doing everything. They're perfect." We had to play after them sometimes, and it was the worst. It was *so* hard. They killed it—they left blood all over the stage. [Singer/guitarist] Mark Arm's a personal hero of mine—he's an amazing person.

MY BLOODY VALENTINE

MIKI BERENYI: I used to go and see them before Lush started. And at the time, they had Dave Conway singing for them, and they were a garage band. They used to play with the garage-scene bands: Purple Things, Stingrays, Vibes. They had nothing to do with what came later. I think it was when Dave left, Bilinda [Butcher] joined, and suddenly, it went a bit more jangly pop—and then it went into the whole *Isn't Anything/Loveless* sort of era. Which I do actually think was just a maturity in Kevin [Shields].

My Bloody Valentine, March 1992. Left to right: Debbie Googe, Colm O'Ciosoig, Bilinda Butcher, Kevin Shields, and Anna Quimby. "I keep waiting for somebody to top *Loveless*." —Bob Mould
Ian Dickson/Redferns/Getty Images

BOB MOULD: The biggest one to me was My Bloody Valentine. I keep waiting for somebody to top *Loveless*. There have been records since then that have gotten close to that level . . . but that was like a beacon of light of what can be done with this form. So, that would be the one that I would always go to.

NO DOUBT

MATT PINFIELD: Somebody at MTV told the record label we were never going to play it. But I know that I and a couple of other people disagreed when we heard "Just a Girl"—we knew it was a smash. It had those elements of ska that I loved—the Specials, English Beat, the Selecter. But I think we could see Gwen [Stefani] was special and the band was great, and it represented part of that new attitude of young women being individuals and having strong personalities.

SINÉAD O'CONNOR

JOHNETTE NAPOLITANO: I love Ireland—I've spent time there; I appreciate the Irish experience. And Sinéad O'Connor was *passionately* Irish. She was very unique as a performer. If you had the chance to see her live, you could hear a pin drop in that hall. I've seen a lot of great artists—Bob Marley, Sly and the Family Stone, Cat Stevens—and some people are just connected to something else. And Sinéad was connected to something else. She was connected to the source. She was a seeker all her life. She wanted to be close to God, and that's where her voice came from. Sinéad was a gift to the planet. She was amazing.

THE OFFSPRING

FAT MIKE: I had lunch with [Bad Religion's] Brett [Gurewitz] one day, and I said, "I don't understand it. The lyrics, 'I took her back and made her dessert' [from the song "Self Esteem"] . . . *what the fuck?!*" And Brett said, "Mike, have you heard the Red Hot Chili Peppers? Have you heard pop music? It's *all* stupid. People don't write lyrics like we do." I went to a disco one night in London and they knew I was there, so they played "Leave It Alone" by NOFX. People were like, "That's pretty cool." And then they played "Self Esteem." Everyone got into it. But I heard it in a club next to our song, and I went, "Oh! I get it now! They fucking rock. The Offspring *are* a great band."

PAVEMENT

DAVID PAJO: It was the conversational singing style. It was kind of loose—like Jonathan Richman. I don't really remember hearing that style back then. It had a "youthful enthusiasm" to it—and I don't think that's something you can bottle and sell. You either have it or you don't.

PEARL JAM

CRAIG WEDREN: It seems to me that Fugazi has had a big influence on the way Pearl Jam does business—there's an enormous amount of "DIY integrity" and familial value in that crew, which I think is pretty rad. Sort of anti–rock stars, in a way. This may sound negative, but I actually mean it as a compliment: They're a rock band like the Who. There's something "meat and potatoes" about them that was wonderful live. And not that common for that era. Like, there was something *classic* about them.

LIZ PHAIR

MATT PINFIELD: Even though she didn't cross over as big in the pop market, I think *Exile in Guyville* was another record . . . songs like "Fuck and Run" and a song that was a hit in the alt world called "Never Said," it's another record that takes people on a journey and speaks for women who should have a stronger individual resolve.

JEFF BUCKLEY'S POSTHUMOUS NO. 1

Drummer Matt Johnson describes an eventual classic cover song.

I came into Studio B at Bearsville Sound Studio, and I remember hearing [Jeff Buckley's rendition of Leonard Cohen's "Hallelujah"] coming off the speakers at one point. I certainly remember some playback and being like, "*Holy shit.*" The images that I had were kind of like, stained glass . . . sun coming through stained-glass imagery—particularly through the guitars. I guess its reverb and delay combination—and probably a Fender Twin and a Telecaster.

A lot of times it was [a moving experience when the song was performed live]. But for me as a drummer, it made it hard for me to interrupt the flow of the show. Because a lot of times—especially at that time in my life—I felt that I needed to "play, play, play" to stay within my game. I remember being really amazed by the song but also feeling a bit nervous about interrupting the flow of the drumming in the set. Which, I realize is absurd.

Jeff's version of the song might be considered the ultimate version of it—at least I know that it is considered the best version of it by a bunch of people. It's totally subjective—I just mean to say his version had a huge impact on people. And it did live. I remember seeing that and being really amazed at his ability to work a room full of people. His skill set was totally a level from which I had ever seen.

When I was on tour with Rufus Wainwright and he was doing it, I remember laughing, like, "I've toured this song more than any other song . . . *that I've never played*." [Note: Buckley's and Wainwright's renditions were performed with a vocal and one instrument, which was not drums.]

I didn't really know that [Buckley's rendition of "Hallelujah" was released as a single for the first time in 2007, topping the digital charts and peaking at No. 2 in the UK]. I'm impressed about it in a similar way to [Guns N' Roses'] "November Rain." Because "November Rain" is seven minutes long. I'm like, "How do you get a song like 'Hallelujah' to be a hit?" It doesn't have a bass line . . . it's basically a guy with a guitar. And similarly, I'd be like, "I have a challenge: Somebody write a seven-minute song, don't do a radio edit, and make that shit go to No. 1."

PIXIES

GAVIN ROSSDALE: "Where Is My Mind?," "Debaser," "U-Mass," "There Goes My Gun" . . . it goes on and on. *Surfer Rosa* and *Doolittle* are my two favorite records. I just love the sound of the band. I love the balance with Kim Deal. I love her voice. I just love the songs, I love the lyrics, I love the nihilism, and I love the tunefulness. They had all the elements that I love. They still do.

PORTISHEAD

KENNEDY: Beth Gibbons' voice, she sounded like a "beautiful hostage." Her voice was very haunting and transportive. There was something about her that is so remote, but you want to save her . . . but there is still a great deal of strength and almost rage—which is so effective with that style of music.

PRODIGY

JASON PETTIGREW: If the early stages of the industrial rock scene were just too wild and overmodulated, the Prodigy understood that people like to go to clubs to dance—and also the concept of punk and heavy metal. *People like loud guitars.* They really amped those things up. And I guess you've got rave culture in there, too.

RAGE AGAINST THE MACHINE

SPEECH: Their take on politics was potent and in your face. It educated a lot of communities that normally wouldn't have gotten that information. I think that that was extremely powerful.

COREY GLOVER: It was really the first incorporating of hip-hop into what was going on—to me. It begat that whole rapcore kind of thing. I don't think Limp Bizkit would exist if Rage wasn't around.

RANCID

FAT MIKE: What made Rancid great was Tim Armstrong wrote great lyrics. Heartfelt. He's the only one of us that ever won a Grammy—for producing a Jimmy Cliff album [2012's *Rebirth*]. . . . *And Out Come the Wolves* by Rancid is so fucking consistent. And then he wrote songs for Pink—he's a crazy-great songwriter.

RIDE

MIKI BERENYI: When Britpop came along, a lot of these bands were like, twenty-eight, twenty-nine, thirty. When us [Lush] and Ride were starting, we were like, twenty. We were *very* young. We didn't want to have our faces on our record sleeves—the early Ride stuff is quite obscure and these one-word titles that we all used to love. We had a similar vibe to that. Ride were a lot better rehearsed than us—better at playing their instruments, for sure. I just thought of Ride as a bunch of sweet stoners. If they were weed, we were alcohol. [*Laughs*]

ROCKET FROM THE CRYPT

KENNEDY: Rocket from the Crypt is still my all-time favorite band, and they always will be. That's the only band logo that I have tattooed on my body. They combined rockabilly with skate-surf culture in San Diego. That was such an incredible sweet spot.

ROLLINS BAND

CHRIS HASKETT: We worked *really* hard. That band rehearsed and played so much. I was lucky to be in a band with that rhythm section. I've almost always been the weakest element in whatever band I've been in because I just happened to play with some absolutely phenomenal people. So, you take the rhythm section of Andrew Weiss and Sim Cain and you put Henry with that dynamism and that fury out front and just let me do my thing in the corner . . . we had a drive to be great.

SLEATER-KINNEY

FRED ARMISEN: They're my favorite band, ever. I love them. They're a perfect band—their instrumentation, vocals. *The Hot Rock* is my favorite album of theirs.

ELLIOTT SMITH

DARREN JESSEE: There was this "loud angry movement" going on. There were bands that were almost rapping a little . . . and being annoying, I thought. And Elliott Smith showed up and was really sweet. His lyrics were so smart and really beautiful. I always felt like Elliott informed Beck because he went from *Odelay* into *Sea Change*. I feel like Elliott Smith was the person in music who opened that up for all of us to be more thoughtful and to play slower tempos.

SOCIAL DISTORTION

THE REVEREND HORTON HEAT: Mike Ness has gone on the same route that I went, but their band sounds totally different than the Reverend Horton Heat. But he understood that the vintage styles of music—of the early rock 'n' roll—translated to what was going on with the punk rock thing. So, he basically borrowed a lot of stuff from the era that the Reverend Horton Heat borrows a lot of stuff and made it modern and made his own thing with it.

SOUL ASYLUM

MATT PINFIELD: Starting out on Twin/Tone Records out of Minneapolis, and then they got signed to A&M. But it wasn't until they made the jump to Columbia Records and things exploded with *Grave Dancers Union*. Which song after song were hit alternative songs—"Somebody to Shove," "Black Gold," "Runaway Train."

SOUNDGARDEN

BILL GOULD: Soundgarden were very complex because they had all these ironic trappings of classic, institutional rock—but in a very subtle way, you could see that they were twisting the concept around.

EDDIE "KING" ROESER: For a second there, Soundgarden was the biggest band on earth . . . *and probably the best band on earth*.

STEREOLAB

MATT JOHNSON: I know their sound changed a lot from record to record. But a lot of the stuff we listened to had a slightly overdriven keyboard sound and really interesting melodies and a very hypnotic, driving beat that you would almost associate with not in terms of fashion but in terms of this primal drive of the music—it wasn't that far from the Doors.

STONE ROSES

JASON PETTIGREW: It was that groovy, funky thing that was undercutting everything. They'd play something like "Fools Gold," where a seven or nine-minute version of that would have you in the clubs, all tripped out. But then they would have that great melodic thing, where they'd do "She Bangs the Drums" and all the Anglophiles would go, "Oh, this is the most amazing thing! I'm going to go buy some really baggy pants!"

SUEDE

MATT PINFIELD: Suede's debut album [1993's self-titled] not only was a really cool record, I loved Brett Anderson's gay overtones and suggestive . . . it was not asexual, but it was androgynous. It had that thing that people were interested in about David Bowie and a lot of artists that came out in the glam era. But also an element of what made Morrissey and the Smiths interesting. And I think that's why that first record—with "Animal Nitrate" and "The Drowners"—was such an important record at the time.

SUGAR

MATT PINFIELD: When Hüsker Dü broke up and Bob Mould made the solo records *Workbook* and *Black Sheets of Rain*, they were really incredible records; and Bob was showing his diverse taste in music. I felt like it all came together on Sugar's *Copper Blue* album—another one of the best records of the '90s, which is a pretty perfect album.

SUNNY DAY REAL ESTATE

KENNEDY: I had a short-lived talk show called *Get Late with Kennedy*, and one of their songs ["Seven"] was the theme of the show. That is one of the few bands that for their fans, they got to remain theirs. They were on sort of the tail end of the Northwest swing, but *so* good—and the fact that not everyone knows who they are is very pleasing for their longtime fans.

SWERVEDRIVER

BOB MOULD: Swervedriver being up there at the top, as well. The way that Adam [Franklin] and Jimmy [Hartridge] approach songwriting and putting stuff together and the sounds of their records was really brilliant, as well. It was just the guitar interplay, Adam's voice, the songwriting was really complex . . . but it stayed really catchy. And I knew about those guys from like, '88, when they were called Shake Appeal—because they sent me the demos that became *Son of Mustang Ford*. I go way back with them, and I'm a huge fan. I always sing their praises.

TEENAGE FANCLUB

EVAN DANDO: Teenage Fanclub is one of my favorite bands. Their first album, *Catholic Education*, has some of my favorite songs: "Everything Flows" and all that stuff. And it's really Stones-y . . . and you've got some *Zuma* [Neil Young's 1975 album] and Todd Rundgren in there, too. That unholy mix. And when you need to break it out, Black Sabbath always comes in handy . . .

TOOL

LES CLAYPOOL: I remember when I first heard [singer] Maynard [James Keenan], I was like, "Dude, you sound like Micky Dolenz when you sing!" I don't know if he liked that. Grunge and that dirge-y sound was popular then, but then Tool added more textures to it, and the time signatures were less straightforward. *Ænima* to me is the most classic Tool record.

VERUCA SALT

MATT PINFIELD: Veruca Salt—named after the character from *Willy Wonka*—broke out of Chicago. Nina Gordon and Louise Post captured the free spirit of women in rock and alternative music—breaking through with their single "Seether," which debuted on MTV's *120 Minutes*. The Foo Fighters' biggest song of their early years, "Everlong," was inspired by Dave Grohl's relationship with Louise.

THE VERVE

MATT PINFIELD: Richard Ashcroft looked like a rock star from the get-go. But it was *Urban Hymns* that solidified their place in British alt-rock history. Hailed and loved by Oasis, Noel Gallagher wrote "Cast No Shadow" on *(What's the Story) Morning Glory?* about the Verve lead vocalist. It yielded three emotional classic '90s singles: "Bittersweet Symphony," "Lucky Man," and "The Drugs Don't Work," about watching his father deteriorate from cancer.

WEEN

LES CLAYPOOL: I remember when I first heard Ween, I heard "Push th' Little Daisies." *And I absolutely hated it.* Then I started getting into some of their other stuff. *The Mollusk* is one of my favorite albums ever—it's a spectacular piece of art. Obviously, there's the humor element, but they write incredibly compelling, catchy songs. And Mickey [Melchiondo, aka Dean Ween] is a monster guitar player.

WEEZER

KENNEDY: Weezer is awesome because it's one of those bands where they play the same three chords. I love Rivers Cuomo's lyrics—they're goofy and nerdy and funny, and they make fun of themselves. And they know exactly who they are. It's like, they're nerdy and they're kinda snobs, but they also want to have a good time.

WESLEY WILLIS

JIMMY FLEMION: His keyboard . . . it was not on repeat, but the songs were similar. He had to find his way, and he painted [Willis was also an artist, who was diagnosed with schizophrenia] to work out what was going on in his head. You'd always see him writing at the bar and probably writing lyrics down, or "rock you like a magic kiss" or whatever he was writing about. God bless him that he was able to take the stage and find an outlet and people took to him and enjoyed him. Because I'm sure he had a tough life that way, and maybe when your mind is like that, you don't really know what you're going through.

THE YOUNG GODS

BILL GOULD: It was probably around 1992, we had a night off in Berlin and went to their show not knowing what to expect. Their heavy, beautiful arrangements blew us away as we realized that they were bringing sampled music to an entirely new level. One of the few bands that I can say that we all loved unanimously. And it was this admiration that led to bringing Roli Mosimann in as producer for *Album of the Year*.

KU1123 EVENT CODE
15.00 PRICE & ALL TAXES INCL.
3.50
G.A. SECTION/BOX
G.A. GEN ADM
GEN ADM ROW SEAT
All Taxes Incl.
SMASHING PUMPKINS
ROSELAND
239 W 52ND ST./NYC
TUE NOV 23, 1993 7:30P

D0713 EVENT CODE
32.50 PRICE & ALL TAXES INCL.
FIELD SECTION/BOX
GEN ADM
QVN139W
22MAY9
FIELD GEN ADM ADULT
ROW SEAT All Taxes Incl. If Applicable ADM $ 32.50
WATERLOO FIELD
WHEREVER U GO, THERE U R
LOLLAPALOOZA '93
PRICE INC.PARKING + TAX
WATERLOO * STANHOPE, NJ
WATERLOO * CHARITY*RAIN/SHINE
.50 TO CHARITY*RAIN/SHINE
TUE JUL 13 '93 GATES NOON

G.A. SECTION/BOX GEN ADM ROW SEAT ADULT
GEN ADM All Taxes Incl. If Applicable ADM $ 15.00
21 + OVER TO DRINK
MORPHINE
IRVING PLAZA
17 IRVING PLACE/NYC
SAT JUN 3,1995 8:30PM

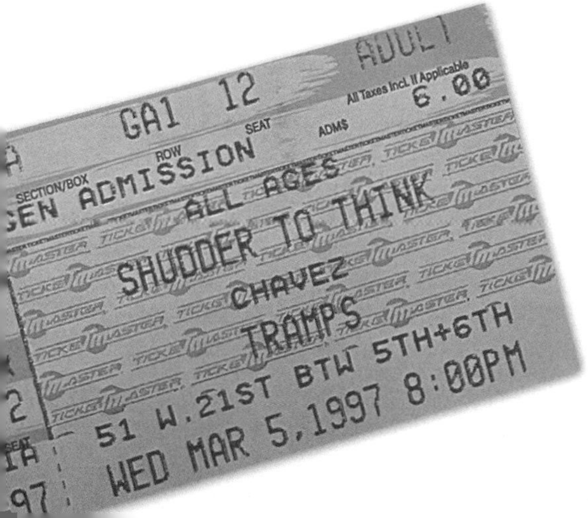

GA1 12 ADULT
ROW SEAT All Taxes Incl. If Applicable ADM$ 6.00
SECTION/BOX GEN ADMISSION
ALL AGES
SHUDDER TO THINK
CHAVEZ
TRAMPS
51 W.21ST BTW 5TH+6TH
WED MAR 5,1997 8:00PM

27 SONGS

"It sort of captures an aspect of what people would say about that era"

The stories behind some of the greatest alt-rock songs—and in a few cases, videos—of the '90s. (Helpful hint: They make one dandy playlist!)

ARRESTED DEVELOPMENT

"Tennessee" [1992]

SPEECH: "Tennessee" was the last song we recorded for our album. We had everything done and, unfortunately, I got a call that my grandmother had passed away. She was by far one of the most pivotal people in my life. We all went down to her funeral in Tennessee and celebrated her life. And the next week, my brother, who was twenty-nine at the time, he had just become a doctor, and he died from an asthma attack. And the last place I saw him was at her funeral in Tennessee. I was crushed as a brother, grandchild, and just as a person. I wrote that song as a prayer because I didn't know how to get out of the pain that I was feeling.

THE B-52s

"Good Stuff" [1992]

FRED SCHNEIDER: Our ex-manager sleazily gave us a whole box full of porno. So, we're watching one of them, and in one of them, the starlet is obviously stoned out of her gourd, and she goes, "Hey, give me some of that good stuuuff." And the way we think, we were like, "Hey . . . that's a good line for a song!" And the video was crazy, because the "foam thing" was big in Europe, so I think at one point the foam started going up over our heads—so we had to stop. But it really burned if it got in your eyes.

Fugazi at Rock for Choice Benefit, The Palladium, Hollywood, California, January 24, 1992. Left to right: Ian MacKaye, Brendan Canty, and Guy Picciotto. "We obviously listened to a lot of different music, but we were *really* blown away by Public Enemy at that time and what the Bomb Squad production team was doing. Those records were just *revolutionary*." —Ian MacKaye *Kevin Estrada/MediaPunch/Alamy*

BABES IN TOYLAND

"Bruise Violet" [1992]

LORI BARBERO: I remember making the video at CBGB's in New York City. We had a live audience at CBGB's, which was one of the greatest rock clubs of all time. And then we got to close down the Brooklyn Bridge for a few hours to film the end of the video. I bet we're one of the only people that got to shut down the Brooklyn Bridge. [*Laughs*]

BEASTIE BOYS

"Sabotage" [1994]

MATT PINFIELD: It's a great video [directed by Spike Jonze]. It's an incredible video. It's funny—Mike D and I, for years, would always talk about blaxploitation movies from the '70s that we loved. In that period of time, you didn't have DVDs; so the only way you could get those movies was if you were buying them [on videocassette] on 42nd Street at one of those "karate movie shops."

So, they and I used to talk about them and collect that stuff—we were fascinated with all that '70s culture. And the band was obviously, too. So, it made perfect sense for them to do a *Starsky & Hutch*/Quinn Martin homage. Quinn Martin was a TV producer who did all these cop TV shows, like *Cannon* and all these other things. So, it made absolute sense.

Once again, it showed a band's sense of humor and playfulness and not being afraid to have a good time. It was a change of direction as far as the song goes. It was full-on rock inspired, that '70s rock feel on that song. I felt there was a lot of Zeppelin in it. That's why I think it's such a great takeoff on all those great '70s cop shows and those blaxploitation movies.

BELLY

"Feed the Tree" [1993]

TANYA DONELLY: It's a funny song, because I could say it's about demanding rather than earning respect. And sort of really laying down a line of, "If we are moving forward, this is what I need." There's a lot of death in there because that's my go-to imagery. "Feeding the tree" is about, "I need your fealty until I die." It's a big ask, y'know?

FRANK BLACK

"Headache" [1994]

FRANK BLACK: I know the studio that we were at: It was Dave Stewart's studio, a place called the Carriage House. He built a carriage house studio out behind his property there in

L.A. And I can't remember if "Headache" was in the first batch, but it was the new song that showed up one morning, right as we were wrapping up that session.

But that was certainly the song that was going to usher in the next wave of creativity, if you will. We had done the eleven or twelve songs, and "Headache" showed up, and it was this kind of . . . Creedence Clearwater kind of a vibe or something. We really liked it. We just loved the vibe of the track, and [producer] Eric [Feldman] and I were excited about it.

And it didn't sound like any of the other tracks that we had recorded up until that moment, so that was our signal that "Oh, no . . . this is not done. We're continuing." It represented a new breath of air or something. It was like, "Oh, this 'Headache' song showed up . . . what's behind *that*?" That song dictated that we would continue.

BLACK GRAPE

"Reverend Black Grape" [1995]

DANNY SABER: They had a batch of demos, and "Reverend Black Grape" was one of the demos. The "doot doot doot doot"—that was actually on a Casio keyboard. And they went to a pub and came back with this harmonica player—Shaun had an amazing eye for talent. There's a bunch of samples in that song, and there's a sample of the lady in the Parliament—"Order, order, order." I literally put on the television and recorded shit. Stuff like that was on TV live when I grabbed it.

BLIND MELON

"No Rain" [1992]

ROGERS STEVENS: That song was really personal for [bassist] Brad [Smith]. It didn't strike me as being as universal as it ultimately became. But I guess everybody feels introspective at times. It has a melancholy to it, and I think it sort of captures an aspect of what people would say about that era—the people who were young in that era.

TRACY BONHAM

"Mother Mother" [1996]

TRACY BONHAM: The lyrical inspiration came from, I was writing about my early twenties and how I had moved away. I had moved to the East Coast—from growing up in Eugene, Oregon, and then going to school in Los Angeles. Things really changed because I was out of my comfort zone, and I had gotten involved in a *really* destructive and abusive relationship with a guy. I had been doing drugs with him, and my life was on the wrong path. I was going to Berklee College of Music . . . but I was *really* in a dark place.

So, I'd call my mom, and this depicts the kind of relationship I had with my mom—and also many relationships in my life where I didn't want to tell the truth. I didn't want to share how bad it was. I didn't want her to worry. I think we had a lot of codependency. And I'm afraid of confrontation—so, it was natural for me to just shove everything under the rug, really.

THE BREEDERS

"Safari" [1992]

TANYA DONELLY: We recorded it in New York—Kurt Cobain was there for a few of the days while we were recording, just hanging out. At one point, we were recording at Philip Glass's studio [Looking Glass Studios], and Philip Glass came in to listen to it and had a couple of suggestions about a multilayered harmony part me and [bassist] Josephine [Wiggs] were working on.

[Black Sabbath's] "Paranoid" is a favorite song of both mine and Kim's. There was a point where we were talking about actually covering it. We played that song a couple of times in practice—it's a perfect song. So, that's what Kim wanted to base the look of the video on [a popular video featuring Black Sabbath performing the tune on the German TV show *Beat-Club* in the early '70s]. Why were we in pantsuits? I think Kelley was coming straight from work, and I was like, "I'll wear a pantsuit, too." I loved that video.

JEFF BUCKLEY

"Last Goodbye" [1994]

MATT JOHNSON: There is a song called "Cherry-Coloured Funk," which is a Cocteau Twins song off of probably their most well-known album, *Heaven or Las Vegas*—and there are some other songs on that record that have cymbal swells into a verse, and then it comes into the verse. I know "Cherry-Coloured Funk" was probably an influence—the way I was thinking about it. Jeff was influenced by the Cocteau Twins, and I was influenced by the Cocteau Twins the way I approached tracking the drums to that song.

BUSH

"Everything Zen" [1994]

GAVIN ROSSDALE: One band that really inspired me at the time—and always, forever—was Jane's Addiction. I had seen a show of theirs, and they have that line "sex is violent" [from the song "Ted, Just Admit It . . ."]. I thought about that line, and it always struck me as a powerful lyric. I was thinking about that, and I was thinking about where I was living and where I had grown up and some of the more violent aspects of that life and of those kids. I really hated that violence growing up. I was a little bit lost and didn't know where I was going, what I was doing; and I was committed to music, with no chance of having any success. I had been struggling for years. And that line, "sex and violence," that is a common thread through art. I just decided to put it in the context of, "There's no sex in your violence." It's sort of a personal belief, a personal mantra.

BUTTHOLE SURFERS

"Pepper" [1996]

PAUL LEARY: I'm guessing that it did, but I don't remember hearing that song until we did "Pepper" [in response to being asked whether Beck's "Loser" influenced "Pepper"]. I think a lot of why people say that is because of the drums—they're mostly electronic drums. We came up with the song, the chord structure, and the lyrics; and then [producer] Steve Thompson had brought in somebody to work on drum loops. And that guy came up with the drum loop for "Pepper." I can assume he'd been listening to Beck.

Gibby did his vocals and then kind of disappeared. We went to New York and we were working on overdubs and mixing at Steely Dan's studio in Manhattan. Gibby was off doing whatever, and Steve Thompson and I worked on that song, and brought in Mark Eddinger to do some keyboards. We got it all worked up and it was pretty fancy. Finally, Gibby came in and we played it for him. We were all excited about it . . . and Gibby hated it. "Well, sorry, but you weren't around. And this is what it is now."

The album came out and "Pepper" started climbing up the charts. I remember saying, "OK Gibby, we're on the charts now. Do you like the song now?" And he's like, "No." Next week, "Gibby, we're in the top ten now. Now do you like the song?" "No." "Gibby, it's number five now. Now do you like the song?" "No." "Gibby, it's number one this week. Now do you like the song?" "No. *It should have been number one-half.*"

CANDLEBOX

"Far Behind" [1993]

KEVIN MARTIN: That was about [Mother Love Bone singer] Andy Wood. The initial lyric was, "Now Andy, I didn't mean to treat you bad." It was written from the perspective of the heroin that killed him. I wanted to pay homage to somebody that I really respected. I met him when I was sixteen years old, working in Fluevog Shoes. Susan Silver—who managed Soundgarden, Alice in Chains, and Screaming Trees—was my manager, and she would make the flyers for the bands, and Andy came in one day to pick up some flyers.

We started talking about music, and I said, "Man, I love everything you do." We chatted for hours and hours, and he would come in and just hang out. We had a connection. And when he died [on March 19, 1990, at the age of twenty-four], I was devastated by the loss. The video was about that loss that we all feel when something passes. That kind of being alone. And a lot of the people in that video are dead . . . which is fuckin' weird—they died shortly after we made the video, or not too long after. Two of them to heroin, sadly.

CHAVEZ

"Break Up Your Band" [1995]

MATT SWEENEY: The lyrics were sort of about what it's like to be in a band you don't want to be in. I wonder if I was thinking of the same stuff as [Pavement's] Stephen Malkmus was with "Cut Your Hair." That was sort of a lighthearted thing of like, "There are too many bands. It's not great to be in a band." [*Laughs*] While, of course, ironically, fully enjoying being in a band. The video was so much fun. Clay [Tarver] and Scott [Marshall] did it. The whole idea was like a dreamy scenario: "I had the weirdest dream. I was playing on a TV show, and there were male strippers, and the audience was all intellectual women who were not feeling it at all. And then something went wrong with props, and then the whole thing fell apart."

Johnette Napolitano with Concrete Blonde at Borderline in London, May 19, 1990. "The closer you get to the truth or are vulnerable with it and express it, the more universal it is."—Johnette Napolitano *dpa picture alliance/Alamy*

CONCRETE BLONDE

"Joey" [1990]

JOHNETTE NAPOLITANO: [Producer] Chris Tsangarides was really instrumental in our success. I remember doing the demo of "Joey" at Bad Religion's studio in Hollywood, and [bassist] Jim [Mankey] didn't like it at all. That was the last song I wrote lyrics for on the album because it was an emotional song. I remember every day when we were in London, we'd go to the studio and Chris would say, "Do we have lyrics for 'Joey' yet?" Chris knew that was "the one" from the very beginning. So, one day, everything gelled in my head. In a black cab on the way to the studio, I wrote down the lyrics and went ahead and cut it. I was flooded with mail after "Joey" about everybody who had known that story, lost a buddy, or had a relationship with an alcoholic. It was a big lesson—the closer you get to the truth or are vulnerable with it and express it, the more universal it is.

THE CRANBERRIES

"Zombie" [1994]

FERGAL LAWLER: That song had actually been written even before our first American tour. I remember playing it when we were touring Europe with an Irish band called the Hothouse Flowers. And that tour was just before we came to the States for the first time. So, that song was a year-and-a-half old before it was recorded. We had played it live a lot and got great reactions from people. It was about a horrible incident that Dolores had read about in the paper, where two boys lost their lives because of a terrorist bomb; and it was her imagining what it must be like for the parents. And how frustrating it is that people have to resort to violence to try and get their point across—you can't just sit down and talk to somebody. It's futile the violence of war, really.

DINOSAUR JR.

"Feel the Pain" [1994]

MIKE JOHNSON: Ah, the "golf video"! They blocked off streets in New York City to film parts of it. I got cut out of a little of that video because at the end I got sick—that's why somebody stood in for me. Our A&R guy stood in for me. I remember listening to the basics of the song with J [Mascis] driving back from the studio and thinking, "This one's cool. It's kind of 'new wave' sounding." You could tell it was going to be a hit. It seemed like it was different and catchier than the other tunes.

EVERCLEAR

"Santa Monica" [1995]

ART ALEXAKIS: Before we went into the studio, Perry, my A&R guy, flew up to Portland, sat in my basement, and I played him songs. When I played him "Santa Monica," he said, "Wait a minute. Play that song again." I played it again. He said, "That may be the most promising song I've heard from any band in a long time. *But it doesn't feel finished.*" I said, "It's finished—we'll record it; you'll get it." We recorded it. He's like, "It's not done yet." I said, "Let me mix it. You'll hear it." I mixed it, and he's like, "*It's not done yet.*" We got into a verbal "Fuck you," "Go to hell," this and that. He thought it should be longer. I said, "I'll go in and try to make it longer . . . but I'm going to write a song just for you, called 'You Make Me Feel Like a Whore.'"

We went in the studio, we tried to record it, but it just didn't have that "thing" that we had had. So, we took the last chorus and actually recorded it to another twenty-four-track and then spliced it onto the end of the tape, recorded some more guitars, some more vocals where I'm going higher, and just vamp another chorus and a half. Cut the intro off and put it on the end of that extra chorus and a half. Mixed it and played it for Perry. He said, "There it is. *Now it's done.*"

FAITH NO MORE

"Easy" [1992]

BILL GOULD: [A cover of Black Sabbath's] "War Pigs" is what we were really known for. This is during the Real Thing Tour, and we're doing shows with Metallica, Voivod, and bands like that. They started knowing us as "the band who played 'War Pigs.'" We kind of did it in a tongue-in-cheek way in the beginning. So, the irony was catching up to us. We were sitting in some hotel bar, and "Easy" [by the Commodores] came on the speakers. It hit me like a bolt of lightning. I looked over at [singer Mike] Patton, we both looked at each other, and it was like a spontaneous thing: "*This is our next cover song.*"

I think we filmed the video in Britain on a day off. We were in London. On a really cheap budget—like five thousand bucks or something like that. The record company there was thinking of getting a bunch of girls for the video. And we were like, "That sounds pretty 'hair metal.' We'll tell you what—we'll do it . . . *but the girls have to be trans*. They can't be hetero girls. If you can do that, we'll do it." And they said, "Yeah, no problem." We said, "Okay. *Let's go.*"

FILTER

"Hey Man, Nice Shot" [1995]

RICHARD PATRICK: "Hey Man, Nice Shot" was the "aha moment," where you're like, "That was so easy." Coming up with the riff and chorus was one of those things like, "Well, how the fuck hasn't anyone ever done this?" Like, in the last five hundred years of music, how in the hell has someone never just pieced this together? Because it makes so much sense, such a perfect little never-ending riff that you could just play forever and ever and ever, and it would never get old.

fIREHOSE

"Down with the Bass" [1991]

MIKE WATT: "Down with the Bass," see, I'm trying to relate myself to [singer/guitarist] Edward [Crawford]. But the bass . . . it was "right field in little league." So, this idea, like, "[Bassist] Richard Hell writes his songs? He's the bandleader? *Whoa!*" So, I made a song about being the bass player, and you guys want him to be with you.

FISHBONE

"Sunless Saturday" [1991]

ANGELO MOORE: Spike Lee directed that video—before Spike started to really blow up. I remember I hit my head really hard on the gate. They took me to the hospital and I had to get stitches in the middle of my forehead. There's a part when the band is in a really big cage and I hit my head on the screw on a latch. Kendall Jones wrote that song—a song of hope. Almost like it's a blues song—at least the lyrics are.

BEN FOLDS FIVE

"Brick" [1997]

DARREN JESSEE: When Ben and I met, even back then, I was writing songs. One of the first times we got together, we were sharing ideas we were working on. And I showed him the chorus of "Brick" that I had written. We didn't really talk about it much, and we started touring. Then he realized it could sort of work with the verse ideas for "Brick" that he had. So, we put the two ideas together, and that's how that song ended up coming together.

FOLK IMPLOSION

"Natural One" [1995]

LOU BARLOW: The film [*Kids*] was finished, and one of the instrumentals we had come up with was called "Dr. Dre's House." It was just us imitating the L.A./Dr. Dre production style of the early '90s. Which was really cool—it incorporated a lot of live instruments. So, we made this instrumental track, and they were like, "Why don't you guys go back and do something with this instrumental?" I immediately had a vision for it and stripped it all down—brought it down to bass and drums—and added some sparse guitar, the basic synthesizer of the track . . . and it sounded fuckin' great. And I made up lyrics about the movie, basically.

THE FROGS

"I Only Play 4 Money" [1997]

JIMMY FLEMION: That song is from 1985—the "I only play for money" part. And then in 1993, I wrote a song called "Prick." Billy [Corgan] had heard that song in a hotel, and he liked that—"I don't do interviews/I won't sign autographs/Don't you love the star when he's a prick?" Then he suggested, "Why don't you combine that tune and go right into 'I only play for money'?" And that part at the end, Billy came up with that chord progression. He said, "*That sounds like a Rush song.*" I don't know any Rush songs. At the end, I do all this "rock talk" that you can't make out. It's just one guitar solo, and Billy smashed all the guitar pedals while I was playing guitar.

FUGAZI

"Repeater" [1990]

IAN MacKAYE: We obviously listened to a lot of different music, but we were *really* blown away by Public Enemy at that time and what the Bomb Squad production team was doing. Those records were just *revolutionary*. And it was really inspiring in terms of what you could do with sound. So, when we were recording "Repeater," it was sort of this idea of approaching . . . not to mimic it, or it wasn't supposed to sound like hip-hop, but to think of using sounds and guitars in a way that was almost like a sample or something.

And the lyrics—in the late '80s in Washington, DC, we had a tremendously high murder rate. It was what they refer to now as the "crack wars." Crack had come into Washington, and there was a lot of gunplay—people were fighting for their sales territories. And a lot of young men died—hundreds and hundreds. It was appalling. I was very sensitive to the reaction that *The Washington Post* and the media in general had because it was so dismissive of these people who were being killed. So, the song was really about these young men and looking at the situation from their perspective.

GARBAGE

"Stupid Girl" [1995]

BUTCH VIG: "Stupid Girl" started when Steve [Marker] sampled a drum loop by the Clash ["Train in Vain"]. We started putting down this bass groove over it to try to get something kind of groovacious. And then Duke [Erikson] started playing that little [*sings melody*], and Shirley [Manson] started singing, and the whole song was written in about thirty minutes.

GIRLS AGAINST BOYS

"Kill the Sexplayer" [1994]

JOHNNY TEMPLE: "Kill the Sexplayer" is kind of about delivering on a fantasy. Lyrics like, "This song is so hip right now/I'm going deaf/I want to kill the singer"—he [Scott McCloud] is, of course, the singer; but it's not suicidal ideation. It's like he wants to obliterate the "real world me" and be able to live a fantasy. Also in the song, he has lyrics like, "That music really turns me on, maxes me out." So, you can look at it as suicidal ideation, but why would someone who was suicidal say, "That music really turns me on, maxes me out"?

THE REVEREND HORTON HEAT

"Bales of Cocaine" [1993]

THE REVEREND HORTON HEAT: I wanted to write a funny song about cocaine—kind of showing how stupid and "redneck" cocaine was. It wasn't a song to glorify cocaine. My idea was to make "Bales of Cocaine" like *The Beverly Hillbillies* struck oil. But instead of hitting oil, [a farmer] found some bales of cocaine that fell out of a plane that flew over, and he goes and sells them and becomes a millionaire. It's stupid, I know. But sometimes, you've got to write stupid songs.

HELIUM

"XXX" [1994]

MARY TIMONY: That is more of a pop song that was deconstructed by the other two band members at the time and made it more dirge-y and grungy-sounding. It was sort of a riot grrrl thing [lyrically], I guess. A feminist song. The guitar solo was me deconstructing what I learned on guitar and going, "I'm just going to do a solo on one string with one finger. I'm not going to try and make this sound good—I'm going to try to make it *weird*." That video we shot with David Kleiler, and it was in an abandoned building—in the middle of winter in Boston. It was like, *ten degrees*. I had never been so fucking cold in my whole life.

HELMET

"Unsung" [1992]

PAGE HAMILTON: I was living with my now ex-wife and a friend in a railroad flat between Avenue B and C on 11th Street [in New York City]. We had a bathtub in the kitchen, our room was in the front of the place, and there was a little room that faced an airshaft. You'd walk through that room to get to our friend's room, and then the toilet was in the back. That little room became my workroom. So, I was in there writing—staring at this pigeon shit airshaft—and I was really fascinated by a rhythmic displacement. Which is, "Here's a rhythm. I'm going to move it around in the measure." So, you're playing the same two notes—it's an answer.

HOLE

"Doll Parts" [1994]

PAUL Q. KOLDERIE: The basic track is edited together from a couple different takes of the song. And as the song goes on, there's a part where it really takes off at the end—there's a big snare roll, and you can hear that the snare is completely different from then on. Because it was the track that was the best and the sound didn't match. But we just said, "Fuck it." I always enjoyed that part. But a lot of work on the vocals on that one—trying to get her to sing at different times of the day and different moods and pull it all together.

JANE'S ADDICTION

"Been Caught Stealing" [1990]

MATT PINFIELD: The thing about the "Been Caught Stealing" video [directed by Casey Niccoli] is it shows the sense of humor and playfulness and the complete lack of fear that the band had. Like, "Let's have a good time. Let's do something that's crazy." It's a classic video from that period of time. There wasn't much like it—although a lot of people definitely have tried to use some of those ideas.

JELLYFISH

"He's My Best Friend" [1993]

ROGER JOSEPH MANNING JR.: That was another colossal songwriting experiment that we were very excited to have on that record. Very different from anything we'd done. That song was when [drummer/singer] Andy and I were forming that idea together; it was always this optimism or faith in it. Every time we tried an arrangement idea, a vocal idea . . . it just worked. I wish songwriting was always that easy. That was a song we always had great faith in and couldn't have been happier when people gave us a compliment about that song.

JESUS JONES

"Right Here, Right Now" [1991]

MIKE EDWARDS: The inspiration was watching the Berlin Wall coming down. Which was something monumental. Having grown up in the '80s kind of thinking there could be a nuclear war at any moment—like in the next minute, nuclear bombs could be going off—to find the Berlin Wall coming down was something that I didn't think *my grandchildren* would witness. And there we were, seeing it on telly. I looped a bit of [Prince's] "Sign O' the Times" and played it round and round, and I played some guitar over the top and added bits and pieces in. The whole thing took me a matter of hours. I usually struggle with lyrics, but the lyrics came quickly. It was a pleasure to write. "Right Here, Right Now" is still a song I enjoy listening to and playing.

MARK LANEGAN

"Ugly Sunday" [1990]

MIKE JOHNSON: "Ugly Sunday" was written as kind of a "Lee Hazlewood pastiche" in a way—or tribute. Mark was like, "I'm going to a do a thing that's going to be like the Lee Hazlewood albums we love." We went for it and pulled it off, somehow.

THE LEMONHEADS

"Mrs. Robinson" [1992]

EVAN DANDO: If you can't get a hit, then get one by mistake, upside down, backwards, in three hours! We literally got it on the first try to record it. We'd never played the whole song. So, that was a big helper in it sounding fresh. We didn't know it and played it once. Martin Scorsese saved the fucking day—it's just that perfect, annoying, druggy, uptight, ecstasy, early-'90s vibe *so* perfectly. It was such an honor to have the song in *The Wolf of Wall Street* like that at the end—*the whole song*.

LIVE

"Selling the Drama" [1994]

CHAD TAYLOR: I wrote the first refrains to "Selling the Drama" sitting in the living room of my first apartment in York [Pennsylvania]. I knew it was a remarkable idea when I played the first guitar bend. I had a cassette tape recorder, but when I hit record, I discovered the batteries were dead. Fearing I would forget the idea before presenting it to [singer] Ed [Kowalczyk], I jumped in my car. I drove to his house—an apartment inside an old barn in nearby Lancaster, Pennsylvania.

I hummed the tune as I went, refining the chordal melody as I drove. Thankfully, Ed answered his door enthusiastically and showed his lyrical brilliance within minutes of our first run-through. Ed sang along to my guitar part in the chorus, and this unification of sound hadn't happened in any other Live song. He also added the chords to the pre-chorus, and our collaborative skills shone through. Like "Operation Spirit" for *Mental Jewelry*, I had somehow birthed "Selling the Drama," which became the first single to the new album, *Throwing Copper*.

LIVING COLOUR

"Type" [1990]

COREY GLOVER: I think for [guitarist] Vernon [Reid], it was kind of stream-of-consciousness Dadaism. R.E.M. had that one tune, "It's the End of the World as We Know It (And I Feel Fine)," and it was that kind of thought experiment. To say, "What would work with that? What would work with this?" And "Minimalism . . . what goes with that? What moves on from there?"

LOCAL H

"Bound for the Floor" [1996]

SCOTT LUCAS (Local H singer/guitarist): I had a tiny apartment on the top floor of this house in Zion [Illinois]. I would hang out all day playing guitar and watching stolen cable on a cheater box. I had come across stacked fifth chords from learning to play Police songs, and I was fucking around with this moving bass line thing that I was trying to perfect because of my guitar setup. I figured I'd mash them together. That basically took care of the riff.

I love words that nobody uses anymore. That crops up over and over in our songs. Phrases and words that have been tossed on the scrap heap of linguistics. "Copacetic" was a word I'd heard in war movies about Vietnam. Also, Velocity Girl had a record called *Copacetic*. So, it was a way to reintroduce a dead word and give a shout-out to Velocity Girl. Plus, it rhymes with "pathetic."

LUSH

"Sweetness and Light" [1990]

MIKI BERENYI: [Producer] Tim Friese-Greene spent many days with us in a rehearsal room, tweaking and refining the drums with slightly different accents and rimshot positions, rearranging the parts and introducing the whooshing break section, et cetera. It was a bit daunting, especially for Chris [Acland]; but it was good discipline and gave real impact and precision to the track. There were forty-eight tracks in all, I think, and *a lot* of experimenting with guitars and sounds. I do know what the song was about, but it's [singer guitarist Emma Anderson's] lyrics, and I don't know how comfortable she is about having the exact source revealed. Her generic answer was generally, "It's about a relationship."

MEAT PUPPETS

"Backwater" [1994]

CRIS KIRKWOOD: I thought the video was great. The guy Rocky [Schenck] who did it, he had cool ideas. Like, the way they did the flower scenes—he mounted a camera, and he had these clear plastic boxes built, stacked, filled them with water, and then floated crap on them. Flowers and other shit. We lay down underneath those, and I remember him above, shooting down through it. It was pre-CGI and all that. We used a troll mask in it; I've got on a *Wallace and Ladmo Show* badge at one point, which is a kids' show from here [Phoenix, Arizona] that was famous. And it actually got on MTV!

MINISTRY

"Jesus Built My Hotrod" [1991]

AL JOURGENSEN: [Butthole Surfers singer] Gibby [Haynes] came to the studio I was recording at—*completely* shitfaced. I didn't like my lyrics on my song—the song was already recorded, and I didn't like what I was doing on it. So, I said, "Gibby, give it a try." He was just wasted out there. He fell off his stool two times, I think he puked two or three times, I think he broke the mic stand at one point. And came up with this gibberish: "Ding a ding dang my dang a long ling long." But it sounded *really* good . . . even though I had no idea—nor did he—what he was singing about. So, I spent a couple of weeks editing together what I could decipher of what he was saying. And spliced it together to make it sort of make sense. And the rest was history.

MOBY

"Natural Blues" [1999]

MOBY: "Natural Blues" was simply the product of me not being a great singer. In the early '90s, I realized if I wanted to have beautiful voices on my records, I had to work with great singers, or I had to find great vocal samples. I heard Vera Hall's "Trouble So Hard" vocals and fell in love with them. So, really, the music I created around her vocals, it's just a tribute. It's an homage to her phenomenal vocal performance.

ALANIS MORISSETTE

"Hand in My Pocket" [1995]

MARK KOHR: I had a conversation with Alanis, and I said, "Do you have any ideas of what you'd like the video to be?" And she said, "I'd like it to be a parade where I'm driving the car that the beauty queen is sitting in." I sent out the art director on that job to get some different books of street photography. And one book I think was called *Close-Up*—it was all shots of people. But the way they did it was people were crowding every frame and deep into the frame—just faces and all the little nooks and crannies. It was wonderful. And we were like, "*That's* what we're going to do. Let's make it where every frame is compact with people." I really wanted to make it about the "warts and all" of the parade of one's life.

MORPHINE

"Honey White" [1995]

DANA COLLEY: That song is very reminiscent of early rock 'n' roll. Kind of like Chuck Berry, Fats Domino, or Jerry Lee Lewis—that kind of vibe. To me, it was always an homage to an early rock song by any one of those guys.

NED'S ATOMIC DUSTBIN

"Grey Cell Green" [1991]

JONN PENNEY: My intention was to try and say that the human race was extremely selfish. So, a lot of people think "Grey Cell Green" was a love song because I sing the word "desire" a lot in it. And that's a perfectly good conclusion to come to. But what I'm singing about is the fact that we don't, as a race, seem to realize or recognize or care about the damage we do until we've done it. So, as long as we get what we desire, it doesn't matter afterwards—we're off. "We're far away from the mess, who cares?"

NINE INCH NAILS

"Head Like a Hole" [1990]

RICHARD PATRICK: Oh, the filming of the "Head Like a Hole" [video] was fun. I had just bought my new little amp. That little GK amp. And Trent was trying to knock it over. You can see me holding it up with my butt, trying to hold it up. And Trent was pissed. He was like, "Dude, let it fall over!" I'm like, "But I just bought this thing. I just spent six hundred dollars on this, man." He said, "We're making a fuckin' video, Rich." I'm like, "I know, but I had to ask my mom for six hundred bucks. I don't have six hundred bucks."

They put fake painting on us and stuff. I was bummed because I got sent home early. He got to hang out with Al—the night Al Jourgensen hung out—and I was this little bummed out, hurt kid that was like, "Awww, man, I had to go home with the gear, and you guys got to fly back because you're doing special effects?" It was fine. It was a key time in my life. I remember just thinking to myself, "One day I'm going to be the leader of my own band." Good times.

NO DOUBT

"Just a Girl" [1995]

MARK KOHR: Gwen [Stefani] and Tony [Kanal] said, "Imagine how we load [the equipment] into a show. Let's say instead, we load into bathrooms. And then the guys play in the men's room and the girls play in the girls' room, and then somehow, the guys cross through into the ladies' room at some point."

NOFX

"Leave It Alone" [1994]

FAT MIKE: There was some "Kurt Cobain"—because that song is a little bit more poetic than I normally write. The same with "Linoleum." And like most NOFX songs, there's no chorus and the lyrics don't rhyme. And then the chord progression was a very strange chord progression—it's F to A to D to A sharp. I wrote "Linoleum" and I was like, "Shit . . . this is a cool progression!" And then I wrote "Leave It Alone," and it's almost the same progression—but it's up a half step. And I put those songs next to each other!

POE

"Hello" [1995]

POE: That was one of the first songs that I recorded for *Hello*—that still continues its own weird legacy, because I'm friends with some of the hackers that the song was a shout-out to. I was into these early BBSs [bulletin board systems], and there was this group of kids who were sort of the "cool kids" in the dial-up modem Commodore clan that I just worshiped as a kid. And they had hacked into the Telco servers in Queens. The song was a shout-out to their group, The Masters of Deception, "M.O.D. are you out there?/I can't see your face/But you left a trace on a data back road/That I almost erased."

PRIMUS

"My Name Is Mud" [1993]

LES CLAYPOOL: I had this whole notion of this guy, his name is Mud—who's all tweaked out and ends up killing one of his friends for some trivial thing, like he stepped on his shoes. The reason being is because I grew up with a lot of tweakers—and shit like that escalates very quickly. As far as the video, that's what I wanted to convey.

RADIOHEAD

"Creep" [1993]

PAUL Q. KOLDERIE: When we finished the rough mix in the studio, Thom [Yorke] turned to Jonny [Greenwood] and said, "What do you think?" And Jonny said, "It's the best thing we've done." And at the time, it was. I'm not saying it still is, but it's the most successful song they've ever done—it's at a billion and a half streams. "Smells Like Teen Spirit" has four billion streams, but . . .

RED HOT CHILI PEPPERS

"Give It Away" [1991]

MATT PINFIELD: That video [directed by Stéphane Sednaoui] is a work of art. It was another way to introduce another one of the most important records of the 1990s. I remember there was one radio programmer telling the record label that the song wasn't a hit and shouldn't be a single. Which, obviously, proved to be way wrong. [*Laughs*] That was a breakthrough record for them.

The thing that was so unique and adventurous about the Chili Peppers was they wanted to make their videos very artistic. They were having fun, but there was certainly so much thought put into what was going on. Those guys had all the paint all over them—you can imagine people seeing them for the first time, going, "*Who the fuck are these guys?*" That was when they really broke through to the mainstream. But I loved the video—it said so much about the character of the band members.

ROLLINS BAND

"Liar" [1994]

CHRIS HASKETT: I remember coming up with that riff. That was when Andrew [Weiss] was in the band, and it's a variant on a Lou Reed riff—it's either "Kill Your Sons" or "NY Stars." And it had been kicking around in my head for ages. We had originally jammed on that in Atlanta when Tool were opening for us—it was the last night of the tour; we played at a place called the Cotton Club. At that point, it was just a ride-out—the King Crimson chorus and the R&B verse/vamp, none of it was there. The ride-out came first.

The "Liar" video was Anton Corbijn. Since he only shoots in natural light, it was shot near Twentynine Palms out in the desert. They were doing all the Henry [Rollins] setups . . . and then all of a sudden this freak storm came and destroyed the set! That's why there's almost no band in there—the band is shot from a distance, with what they could salvage. In terms of making videos . . . it was less awful than most. [*Laughs*]

ROYAL TRUX

"The Spectre" [1993]

JENNIFER HERREMA: Neither one of us are religious or have been religious but just trying to find something that helps to guide. "The Spectre" is basically all that we had been through at that time . . . but it has to stay there. Basically, never forget—whether it was positive or negative. That was kind of our higher power or whatever they say in twelve-step meetings. It's the only thing that nailed us down to our past—so we could not repeat it.

SEBADOH

"Rebound" [1994]

LOU BARLOW: I had come out of my "Soul on Fire" thing—my girlfriend had split up with me and ran off with my lawyer. I hooked up with a new girl—which was great. So, I wrote a song about my "rebound relationship." I had come up with the riff on four-track kind of long before that. This multilayered, almost psychedelic thing, repeated over and over again on cassette and layered a bunch. We threw the video together with footage we shot on tour—footage that I shot with a Super-8 camera that Sub Pop had given us.

SHONEN KNIFE

"Tomato Head" [1993]

NAOKO YAMANO: When we toured the UK in 1992, I drank a lot of tomato juice for my health. A band member from BMX Bandits who supported us said that if I drink tomato juice too much, I could be a tomato head. The lyrics came from this.

Shudder to Think in New York City, 1998. Left to right: Stuart Hill, Craig Wedren, and Nathan Larson. "Here ya go. Thanks for taking the ride."—Craig Wedren
Bob Berg/Archive Photos/Getty Images

SHUDDER TO THINK

"X-French Tee Shirt" [1994]

CRAIG WEDREN: [The song's title] is one of those things that gave me an image. If you went to the merch table of an alt-rock show in the '90s, they would sell these things called baby doll T-shirts—they were little, tight, short-sleeved T-shirts that mostly girls were wearing, that were really cute and sexy. At least we thought so at the time. And there's something about a French T-shirt that made me think of those shirts. And then "X," it just made it sexier—if you put an X on something, it just *does*. We weren't really writing choruses then. But that one, there was something exciting about putting the hook at the end—just a big ol' "Here ya go. Thanks for taking the ride."

That was a big-budget MTV video. Epic Records really plunked down for it. We flew out to Los Angeles, we had a big-time director [Pedro Romhanyi] who wrote a treatment, and we responded to the treatment about the elevator and the voyeurism. And there was going to be wardrobe and makeup, and they hired this wonderful makeup woman and really discovered some radical looks for the mid '90s for us. Y'know, boys weren't wearing makeup then. And we flew out, they put us up at a hotel, we shot for a couple of days—they built a whole elevator set. It was a construction and our first foray into "making movies"—which Nathan [Larson], Adam [Wade], and I are still in that world.

SLINT

"Breadcrumb Trail" [1991]

DAVID PAJO: The open riff is just an open A and then some harmonics—and a little arpeggiated thing. But the arpeggiated thing, I would play a descending melody, and Brian [McMahan] would play an ascending melody. But we'd do it at the same time, so it would sound kind of blurry. Like, you couldn't tell who was doing what. And little things like that I thought was cool, because I think a lot of bands wouldn't do things like that. Lyrically, it was written together by both Britt [Walford] and Brian—which is why they do vocal parts. I remember hearing them talk about the lyrics at band practice. Britt would say, "This part kind of feels like an amusement park ride," and Brian would chime in.

SONIC YOUTH

"Superstar" [1994]

DAVE MARKEY: Kim [Gordon] had written the song "Tunic (Song for Karen)." But in the music video, they had a bunch of Carpenters imagery that they had gotten from some Carpenters video release—like Karen running through Disneyland. And as it turned out, they had to obscure all of that for the release—Geffen couldn't get the clearance. So, here it is just a few years later, and now Sonic Youth are taking on this song [for the 1994 tribute album, *If I Were a Carpenter*], and we were granted access to the Carpenters' archives to use any footage we wanted!

SOUL ASYLUM

"Runaway Train" [1992]

KENNEDY: "Runaway Train" is not about missing children. But they threw pictures of missing children up there [for the video], and it had this great utility. If I were those parents, I'd be like, "Oh, thank God." It's so hard getting your kid's face on TV when they're missing. So, that was great. And then, of course, the band got to go to the White House . . . and Bill Clinton showed them the cigar room, probably.

SPONGE

"Plowed" [1994]

VINNIE DOMBROSKI: It was a song that was written during the day in Detroit. I was out there shoveling snow, this melody came to me, I went in the house, grabbed a guitar, and started writing the words, and knocking out the chords. I called my buddy, Tim Patalan, with a studio [The Loft] up in Saline, Michigan, and said, "I've got this song I want to record." I drove out there that night and we recorded "Plowed." Mike Cross came up with the iconic guitar solo, which we use for the intro, as well. What you hear on the record is what we recorded that night. The mess of what was Detroit [was the song's lyrical inspiration]. "Plowed" is about the crumbling of me, the people around me, my city, and my memories.

STONE TEMPLE PILOTS

"Vasoline" [1994]

ROBERT DeLEO: On "Vasoline," we had so many ideas [for the video], and we were coming up with them on the spot. We had so many different ideas that I think we made three different versions of that video. But I really like that video. It's got a vibe to it. And I got to dress up like a clown in it! A lot of cool stuff in there.

SUBLIME

"What I Got" [1996]

ERIC WILSON (Sublime bassist): It's a true Sublime song. It seems to be like an anthem-type thing. Actually, that song was produced by David Kahne. And then we ended up doing that one again with Paul [Leary]. I was fortunate to meet [Jamaican reggae singer] Half Pint—he's a legend and an inspiration. And it turns out that Brad [Nowell] had gotten parts of that song from one of his songs that was like a B-side ["Loving"]. I thought I'd heard all his stuff, but I found out it was one of his songs but not one of his hits. Brad turned that song into something totally different than what it originally was. Half Pint wanted to get paid for it, so then we got a relationship through that. And when we did the Dub Allstars, Half Pint went on the road with us for a summer, and I got to know him really well and play with him every day. That was a blessing in itself.

SUGAR

"Your Favorite Thing" [1994]

BOB MOULD: Real super riff, super catchy. I don't think that one took long to write. That might have been like, a half hour song. Which, a lot of the good ones are. But I just thought it was a really cool signature riff. It's sort of in that classic "Sugar tempo"—y'know, the 120s to 130s. Just those sort of hard-driving four on the floor pop songs. The lyrics, there's nothing revelatory in the words. But hopefully the way that they were constructed is interesting. Good song, though.

THEY MIGHT BE GIANTS

"Birdhouse in Your Soul" [1990]

JOHN FLANSBURGH: As the track was coming together for the album, there really wasn't a role for the guitar in this song. On a practical level, I was like, "Am I going to get 'Andrew Ridgeley'd' out of the picture on this project?" Very smartly, as it came along, [co-producer] Alan [Winstanley] realized the bass line of the song was kind of the hook. So, if I just did a unison guitar part to the hook on the guitar, it would actually bring out a very cool thing. We rented a Marshall cabinet, and he totally did a "Hendrix" on the volume—you just swipe your hand across the top of all the knobs, and it turns everything on full blast.

THROWING MUSES

"Counting Backwards" [1991]

KRISTIN HERSH: "Counting Backwards" refers to hypnosis—trying to regain lost memories due to dissociation. Katherine Dieckmann made the video—she directed *The Adventures of Pete & Pete* series for Nickelodeon, and she's a beautiful soul. She won't let women make either of the two faces we're allowed to make at cameras: the fashion face and the fuck-me face. I was always alone in my refusal to do this, asserting that men aren't idiots and women aren't idiots, et cetera, that maybe we're all humans. Anyway, Katherine's going to heaven for taking this stance against sexist product.

TOADIES

"Possum Kingdom" [1994]

VADEN TODD LEWIS: I was dating this girl who was fucking out there—just nuts. It was kind of exciting . . . but also scary. And I had a dream that she invited me to this party, and I'm walking into this party and as I get there, the party is that you come in, you join our cult, you self-immolate, and then you become a different person. I woke up and I thought, "I need to break up with this person"—so I did. But I wrote "I Burn" based on that dream. Then, I love characters and continuing their stories, so I thought, "Suppose this guy did it and he's just smoke—this spirit. What would he do?" And that's where I went with the rest of "Possum Kingdom." This guy goes out to do the same thing—to lure somebody to be his companion.

U2

"One" [1991]

MARK PELLINGTON (music video director [Pearl Jam, U2, Foo Fighters]): I had done a lot of stuff for them for their Zoo TV Tour. So, the video was just the projections for the song, and I ended up making a single-screen video for them. They had made a video for the song already—that Anton Corbijn had done—of them in drag, and they weren't really crazy about it. So, they released mine, and it was out there for a while. It was a very "anti-video": no band, a slow art piece.

And they made a third version of the video with Bono singing in a bar. It always was interesting to me to have more than one video for a song. I don't know why bands don't do that more. I've made videos, and sometimes they end up being two different versions.

But they are great people, and I've done stuff for them over the years [including directing the 2007 feature film, *U2 3D*]. I think people just responded to it because it was weird and different. It wasn't the singer . . . my version wasn't like any video anybody had ever made. It's just an out-of-focus buffalo!

URBAN DANCE SQUAD

"Deeper Shade of Soul" [1990]

RUDEBOY REMINGTON: DJ DNA used to have these records by Ray Barretto, and he used to come up with a thing he used to play [Barretto's song, "A Deeper Shade of Soul"], and we looped that. Every morning when I started to shave or something, I'd put that little thing on. One of the last days, I wrote the song. It deals basically about the five persons in the crew; that symbolizes basically what the world should be like—different types of people with different types of ideas and maybe even different mentalities, but still, we connect because we think in a different way about certain things.

URGE OVERKILL

"Girl, You'll Be a Woman Soon" [1992]

EDDIE "KING" ROESER: We had agreed to do an EP [1992's *Stull*] and we were basically out of songs. And it happened to be a thrift-store find that we had picked up a couple of weeks earlier and had listened to it enough that we started playing it as just another thing to do. It was such an easy song that we didn't even have the record there [while recording their version]—we didn't reference it or anything. We played it just from memory.

MIKE WATT

"Big Train" [1995]

MIKE WATT: The song was not mine. It comes from the Kinman brothers, who had a band Blackbird. But they come from a band called the Dils, who was a big influence on the Minutemen. Seventies Hollywood scene. I loved the song. And Dave Grohl played drums on that. An *incredible* drummer, man. We did it up in Seattle. I did two songs: "Big Train" and "Against the '70s." And right away, Dave Grohl—an intuitive musician—just picks up on what you're doing. You play it for him, and he's right along. And then started piling stuff on—I got my old friends from the Meat Puppets, Cris and Curt, to play on it. I think Cris played banjo! It was like that—*let your freak flag fly*. And then that big guitar solo dueling between Curt Kirkwood and J Mascis. That was intense.

WEEZER

"Buddy Holly" [1994]

MATT PINFIELD: The idea of taking a song like that and using the *Happy Days* TV show as a background, that was one of the first times anybody had done something like that, although Nirvana did the same kind of thing with "In Bloom" when they were looking like a '60s band. As you've seen Weezer's career go on, it really summed up who they are.

Whoever came up with the actual idea of putting that in a *Happy Days* video [Note: It was probably the video's director, Spike Jonze], it made total sense. Because *Happy Days* is one of those shows people still knew about in the '90s because it was back in the '70s and people remembered watching not only when it was new but in repeats that were on so much in that period of time. It was an absolutely brilliant idea—especially in a song that is only a little over two minutes long. It was perfect.

28 ALBUMS

"We definitely want to take this ride together"

The stories behind some of the greatest alt-rock albums of the decade.

ARRESTED DEVELOPMENT

3 Years, 5 Months and 2 Days in the Life of . . . [1992]

SPEECH: Initially, I was writing that album in my bedroom—with an ASR-10 Ensoniq sampler and an HR-16 Alesis drum machine, primarily. And I would record it on a Tascam four-track initially, then an eight-track cassette recorder. Basically, recording the album on four-track, then I would get enough money to get an eight-track and re-record the album on an eight-track in my room. Then when we got the deal, we were able to go to a studio called Trax 32—and that would be the *third time* that I'm recording this album. And then the whole group was able to come in that time and record parts that initially had been recorded by me or recorded by me and Headliner.

BELLY

Star [1993]

TANYA DONELLY: I did those demos with Joe Harvard at Fort Apache, and Kim Deal actually plays on the demos for what ended up being *Star*. And then I went back to Rhode Island, and I formed Belly. 4AD signed me as an individual because they were interested in that bunch of songs. We recorded the bulk of it in Nashville. We had reached out to Gil Norton to produce the album—he was interested, but he was working on something else, so he couldn't produce the full album. So, we ended up saying, "Can you do four or five songs?"

Blind Melon, 1993. Left to right: Rogers Stevens, Shannon Hoon, Glen Graham, Brad Smith, and Christopher Thorn. "It was *ferocious*—you can really hear a bunch of angry young men." —Rogers Stevens *Lynn Goldsmith/Corbis Historical/Getty Images*

FRANK BLACK

***Frank Black* [1993]**

FRANK BLACK: For the first time in my career, the head of the record company—a nice guy called Ivo Watts-Russell—he decided to visit me on my recording session in Los Angeles. They were all the way back in London, but he said, "I'm coming over for a visit to check out what you're doing." And while we were plenty proud of what we were doing musically, we knew that we had momentum. We had some "thing" that we were exploring. When I say *we*, I mean Eric Feldman, my producer, and I. But we hadn't recorded the so-called "libretto." We had not put any vocals down.

So, for people listening to music, when you hear rock 'n' roll music without the singer, it doesn't really make sense to them. It isn't finished; it's not even a song if you don't have the guy singing on it. And Eric and I understand this kind of dynamic, so we were in a bit of a quandary because, "Holy fuck! The guy is showing up tomorrow! He's flying in, and he wants to check out the stuff."

And so, I ran down to the delicatessen there in Burbank, and I ordered a matzo ball soup that I could sit with for a very long time. And I proceeded to write lyrics to several of the songs, including, I think, "Los Angeles" and maybe "I Heard Ramona Sing" and maybe a couple of other songs, like "Ten Percenter." Whatever were my "A-list" from that record. And I finished some of the material just in a mad dash for this guy's arrival. And I ran back to the studio after my soup, and I sang the songs, and it seemed good. And he showed up, and he went, "Wow, sounds great!"

BLACK GRAPE

***It's Great When You're Straight . . . Yeah* [1995]**

DANNY SABER: I remember before I went to the session, I was going around saying, "Hey, I'm going to work with this guy, Shaun Ryder." And they're like, "*Shaun Ryder?!* Don't do it, man!" Which only made me want to do it more. We went in a room—it was some little dumpy studio in South London. I didn't speak Mancunian. They all had this slang—"Fookin' 'ell, mate." I could barely understand half the shit he was saying. And he shows up and he's got a black doctor's bag. He whips out this bottle of cough syrup—in those days, you could buy kaolin and morphine cough syrup—but it was like a gallon of this shit. So, he's guzzling it. And he goes, "Fookin' want some?"

Then we got this groove going—he'd brought in this idea—and he looked at the back of the bottle, and he's like, "Shake well before opening." And that was the first song we wrote together ["Shake Well Before Opening"]. And the vocals from that session are on the album. It was magical. Him and Kermit [Paul Leveridge] would face each other, and I would just get a loop going, and I would let them go. And then I would tape it and, "Okay. *Here's* the verse. *Here's* the chorus."

BLIND MELON

Blind Melon [1992]

ROGERS STEVENS: That, more than the other ones, was collaborative. And it has the moments that establish "the sound." It has a more organic presentation. We were at the very beginning, so it was like the place we were from. And the next one [1995's *Soup*] was like, "Okay. Now we're leaving this place *and going somewhere*." I did hear recently the first record—on a really good-sounding system—for the first time in probably twenty years. From front to back, without stopping. I was driving out in the desert. But goddamn, it was fucking good. It was *ferocious*—you can really hear a bunch of angry young men.

TRACY BONHAM

The Burdens of Being Upright [1996]

TRACY BONHAM: "Mother Mother" was maybe the second song I ever completed. So, this handful of songs, they came from the first batch of me sitting down and trying to write songs. I've played them recently as per request of my audience, and a lot of the songs were premonitions—"One Hit Wonder," "30 Seconds" is about having thirty seconds of fame. Those two, in particular, when I look back, I realize I saw the writing on the wall already. I knew that the music business was changing, and I was already writing about it.

THE BREEDERS

Pod [1990]

STEVE ALBINI: That was their first record as a proper band. Britt Walford was the drummer on that—he's one of my favorite drummers. He's the drummer from Slint. That record was made in a residential setting—it was a studio built into an old manor house. So, the acoustics of the studio were very "home-y." Like, the drums were recorded in what would have been a dining room, and the guitars were recorded in what would have been a bedroom. The acoustics in the rooms were very familiar—they sounded like natural, normal spaces. They didn't have super-dead studio acoustics, and they didn't have big, cavernous auditorium-type acoustics. It was a great experience all around. Kim [Deal] is a genius, and I would take a bullet for her.

JEFF BUCKLEY

Grace [1994]

MATT JOHNSON: I remember being able to set up an extra drum kit in my little shed or shack where I was staying [in Woodstock, New York]—I remember practicing drums to this record by Cameo. And I remember Jeff being in his own shack that was in the back of this property where they used to house us—which was separate from the studio [Bearsville]. And Jeff would have his . . . I don't know if it was patchouli, but it was little oils that he liked. And probably some candles and some mementos that were meaningful to him. He'd be a little messy—I was only out there once or twice—but it was "creative chaos" out there with some interesting items. Definitely a sense of some introspection was going on.

BUSH

Razorblade Suitcase [1996]

STEVE ALBINI: That record was spread out over a longer period of time. They had been on a very intense touring schedule—for two or three years, had been playing nonstop, around and around. Gavin [Rossdale] had been writing songs all along, and they had rehearsal sessions to arrange the music. But their principal experience as a band was playing onstage. So, I tried to set it up in the studio so they could have exactly that experience—they could play normally, as onstage. Everybody playing at the same time.

BUTTHOLE SURFERS

Electriclarryland [1996]

PAUL LEARY: That was quite a different experience—going from John Paul Jones to Steve Thompson. They were super hands-on producers—which I really appreciate, and I learned a lot from both of those guys. Steve Thompson was just meticulous. We thought we had all the songs we were going to do, ready to go. So, we got up to Bearsville Studio up in New York, and they rented us a nice, old house to stay in. We were recording our songs, and Steve Thompson said, "You guys need one more song." We were looking at each other dumbfounded, like, "Well . . . what do you want?" And finally, he tells me to "Play a riff." So, I said, "What key do you want?" He says, "G." So, I played a riff on the guitar in the key of G, and he recorded it. That was the basis for the song "Pepper."

CANDLEBOX

***Candlebox* [1993]**

KEVIN MARTIN: It was fast, easy, a complete joy. We had the best time in the studio. We loved our rehearsal space. We were a young group of guys that really wanted something to happen. And we were very excited, and we loved working with [producer] Kelly Gray. The front cover photo was by Kevin Westenberg. That was on Whidbey Island or Vashon Island—it's a tulip festival that happens every year. We had walked out there not knowing that that was highly protected soil and ground. He got two or three shots off before this guy came out of his house from across the street with a shotgun and said, "You get out of my fuckin' tulips right now . . . *before I shoot you*."

CONCRETE BLONDE

***Bloodletting* [1990]**

JOHNETTE NAPOLITANO: I spent a lot of time in New Orleans at the time, writing. I was really into *The Vampire Diaries* by Anne Rice. The New Orleans atmosphere to me wasn't a party atmosphere—*it was very dark*. I didn't hang out with musicians—I hung out with the psychics at the Bottom of the Cup Tea Room . . . and then I turned [the album] into the label, and [label head] Miles [Copeland] goes, "I don't hear a single on it. Go back and record six more songs." I'm like, "I don't think so. I'm going to London; you won't be able to find me." And I took off for a couple of months—until they *had to* put it out.

THE CRANBERRIES

***No Need to Argue* [1994]**

FERGAL LAWLER: We recorded it in Oxford—in the Manor Studio, where Mike Oldfield did *Tubular Bells*. It was this old manor house that had a studio in it, and you could stay there. I think we did about a month there. It was incredible because we had a lot of the songs written, and we had actually played a lot of them live on the previous tour. So, we were really tight and really focused and knew exactly what we wanted. And didn't feel any pressure.

Unfortunately, we went on a skiing trip toward the end of that, and Dolores broke her cruciate ligament in her knee—so she was in the hospital laid up for a few months. That put a bit of a damper on everything. We had moved to London by that point to finish it off, and we did as much as we could without Dolores. Then once she got her health back, she came into the studio; and we finished off the album.

Faith No More in England, 1993. Left to right: Bill Gould (kneeling), Jim Martin, Mike Bordin, Roddy Bottum, and Mike Patton (kneeling). "We were immature kids, I have to admit—so, we did it the way a bunch of peckerheads would do it."—Bill Gould *Mick Hutson/Redferns/Getty Images*

DEVO

Smooth Noodle Maps [1990]

GERALD CASALE: That was our last record before Mark [Mothersbaugh] was out the door with both feet. It was for Enigma Records, very low budget, very do-it-yourself—the whole thing. In the end, we had Jeff Lord-Alge do some mixes of the record. But it was doomed. Enigma Records had the right name—*they were an enigma, alright*. They were mismanaged from the top down and blew all their money—I think they got a fifty-million-dollar cash infusion from Capitol Records and just pissed it away. There was no marketing or promotion for that record at all. Nobody went to radio with it. I think there were some really good songs on that record: "Stuck in a Loop," "Post Post-Modern Man," "Morning Dew."

DINOSAUR JR.

Where You Been [1993]

MIKE JOHNSON: I got a phone call—I think it was [Sub Pop's] Megan Jasper—saying, "J [Mascis] wants to talk to you." And she had told me, "I think J is going to ask you to join the band." And he just asked me to join the band, and I was like, "Well, I never played bass." And he said, "It's two less strings than guitar." [*Laughs*] I went out to Massachusetts for a month or something and practiced. A lot of practices were just me and Murph—bass and drums—getting the parts together. Then, we went up to outside of Woodstock at Dreamland Studio and did the basics there. It went smoothly and did overdubs in L.A. J had a pretty great set of songs, too. I remember thinking at the time, "This is going to work out good."

EVERCLEAR

Sparkle and Fade [1995]

ART ALEXAKIS: I flew to Madison, Wisconsin, and looked at Smart Studios and found this punk rock guy who recorded some indie punk rock records [Michael Douglass]. We went in and spent three weeks there and recorded *Sparkle and Fade*. Then this guy who I had a production deal with earlier that year mixed it in New York, and I sent it to my label.

FAITH NO MORE

Angel Dust [1992]

BILL GOULD: [Mike Patton] went through a transformation from the beginning of *The Real Thing* to the end of touring. Musically, I think even the guys in Mr. Bungle—the guys he was hanging out with—were even going through some transition stuff as well. Like, they moved to San Francisco from the woods [Eureka, California], and they were absorbing a lot of "San Francisco stuff." And a lot of just getting turned on to new music. And Patton was headed in that direction.

We booked a different kind of studio than we had before. *Introduce Yourself* and *The Real Thing* were done in the same studio—Studio D, in Sausalito. And it had a really big, nice drum room. Really great-sounding place. But a lot of that air sometimes takes away some impact and punch, and we wanted to find something that was a little more deader and compact. We wanted to sonically go in a different space. And Patton had his own place for the first time. He was doing experiments like staying up for three or four days in a row. I mean, *everybody* was doing crazy stuff. We were immature kids, I have to admit—so, we did it the way a bunch of peckerheads would do it.

fIREHOSE

Flyin' the Flannel **[1991]**

MIKE WATT: That was a hard record because my pop was dying of cancer. He died during that recording—he was only fifty-three. And the Gulf War was going on—the first one. That's what I was thinking of—more than my major label debut. A Boston guy mixed it, Paul Kolderie. I recorded it in Venice [California]. We used to put out records—back to SST—and they were like flyers. It was opposite—you didn't tour to promote records; you put out records to promote your gigs! Because people would forget about you. So, you put out a record every six months.

FISHBONE

The Reality of My Surroundings **[1991]**

ANGELO MOORE: *The Reality of My Surroundings* had a lot of genres of music. That's all Fishbone does—we stick our foot into a lot of different genres of music, because it's all music, it's all challenging, it's all funky and danceable, it's all aggressive. And a lot of our lyrics ended up being pretty intellectual—paying attention to social commentary and real-life experiences.

BEN FOLDS FIVE

Whatever and Ever Amen **[1997]**

DARREN JESSEE: We took the budget we were offered and soundproofed Ben's house he was living in at the time. It was not a big house—it was like a 900-square-foot, two-bedroom rental house. That's where we practiced. His dad soundproofed it for us, and we recorded the album there in the house, which made for some challenging sound things.

But that album, I was in the back bedroom, and Ben was in the living room, and [bassist] Robert [Sledge] was in Ben's room. We had a headphone monitoring system, and we were one of these bands that would play a lot of takes—we would play songs *so many* times. It's ridiculous to think about now, but we would sometimes play something twenty times, and then we were asking [producer] Caleb [Southern] to parse through that and find "the version." After we made the record, we got Andy Wallace—who just had *the touch* in that era—to mix that album. That was really amazing for us and really brought out the best in that record.

THE FROGS

Starjob [1997]

JIMMY FLEMION: We had started *Starjob* in January 1994, and it would have been ready by January of 1995, but that album was such a delay—it took until May of 1997 to come out. And they were talking about the song "Lord Grunge," but "Lord Grunge" had been written in 1993 after we had seen Mudhoney in concert. We did some shows with the Smashing Pumpkins, and Billy Corgan said, "Let me hear some of the songs you have," because we knew Billy; and James [Iha] and D'arcy [Wretzky] had their label, Scratchie. And they said, "We want to put out a record on our label." So, we did some shows with them, and then in between, we played some songs for Billy, and he said, "Yeah." [Note: Corgan produced *Starjob* under the alias "Johnny Goat."] It was kind of his choosing which songs and even the order of the record. D'arcy and James would say, "Are you done with the artwork for it?" But we were on the road, so Dennis [Flemion] brought this star and a goat on the road, and eventually he mocked it all up and got it all together.

FUGAZI

Repeater [1990]

IAN MacKAYE: Guy [Picciotto] had just started playing guitar in the band. We were writing like crazy. We practiced *a lot*. Something about Fugazi was if we were home, we would probably practice four or five days a week—for three to five hours. We spent a lot of time together. In the beginning of the band, I was the only person playing guitar and writing most of the music. Joe [Lally] wrote a little bit of music. But when Guy started playing guitar, then all four of us really started writing. And it changed everything. It was a new era for the band. I can remember we were really psyched about the songs.

It was fast—we were in and out of the studio. We recorded the whole thing in probably less than a week. We recorded in Don Zientara's basement [Inner Ear Studios] on a half-inch sixteen-track. I started recording there in 1980 with the Teen Idles, but a tiny little room in a small brick house in South Arlington. And the room that we played in was the children's rec room, so there were children's clothes and toys around. And the control room was in the boiler room, so you had to sit next to a water heater and a furnace. And it was tiny.

PJ HARVEY

Rid of Me **[1993]**

STEVE ALBINI: That was a great experience. The three-piece band [Harvey on vocals and multiple instruments, Steve Vaughan on bass, and Rob Ellis on drums] was operating on all cylinders. I thought that three-piece band was probably my favorite expression of Polly's music—just because on that record they played together so well. A very intuitive connection between the guitar playing and the drum rhythms and everyone was sort of "breathing" well at the same time. I had an occasion to listen to it not long ago, and I was impressed by how great they sounded. There's an aesthetic to her music where she likes big dynamic changes. Like, she'll have a very quiet verse that builds up a big head of steam when it gets into the chorus. I always enjoyed that about her music.

THE REVEREND HORTON HEAT

Smoke 'Em If You Got 'Em **[1990]**

THE REVEREND HORTON HEAT: A lot of those songs were ones I had been playing for four or five years. We got the deal with Sub Pop, and we recorded at a couple different places, and we decided to come back to Dallas and do the songs live in the studio. One thing about that album is I did the liner notes . . . all the songs that we did live in the studio, that were going to be the album. But then Sub Pop came back and said, "We want to put 'Psychobilly Freakout' on there." That was *not* recorded live—that was [recorded by] Jack Endino in Seattle. So, it was a lie—a lot of those songs were just us going straight to two-track in a studio in Dallas, but there is other stuff that's not live to two-track.

HELIUM

Pirate Prude **[1994]**

MARY TIMONY: We'd been touring a bunch on the East Coast, and we went and recorded it in Boston. I was really depressed at the time—I was going through a *major* depression—so I don't remember a lot of it. I had this whole thing about destroying what I already learned on guitar, so I tried to like . . . play things only on one string and make weird, crazy sounds. Sort of like trying to deconstruct what I knew about music. I wasn't really trying to write catchy songs—it was more, "Seeing what happens."

HELMET

***Meantime* [1992]**

PAGE HAMILTON: We already had songs written—"In the Meantime," "Unsung," "FBLA II." So, when we signed the deal [with Interscope], I had a conversation with Jimmy Iovine, and I was thinking, "We'll make an album sometime next year." And he's like, "You're going to make an album *now*!" That was before Christmas in '91. So, wrote the rest of the songs and we wanted to work with Wharton Tiers, and it was a comfortable place. I remember talking to Kim Gordon about Wharton's studio, she said, "You're in the 'womb' at Fun City—that cozy basement with the pipes over your head." People from the record company would stop by periodically. Ted Field, who was the owner of Interscope, we were working on "Give It," which starts off in 5/4, this weird intro, and then goes into this heavy swing, Miles Davis kind of part. And Ted goes, "This sounds like another 'Teen Spirit.'" And I was like, "*What?!* This could not be further from 'Teen Spirit'!"

HOLE

***Live Through This* [1994]**

PAUL Q. KOLDERIE: We were working in Atlanta—which wasn't home for any of us. In those days, I used to go jogging a lot—just to clear my mind and get going for the day. I'd go running down along the Chattahoochee. I'd psych myself up—it was kind of psychological warfare. But I think we came out on top. I'm not saying we won the game—I'm saying we got through it and made a good record. Courtney had a lot to prove because her husband's record had gone, like, *fifteen times platinum*. She wanted a platinum record, too . . . and she got one. It ultimately wasn't that much more difficult than working with anyone else. There were some times when things were a *little* crazy, but she wanted to make it happen—she had a lot to prove.

She had done one record [1991's *Pretty on the Inside*] that was really noisy and didn't really catch on, and then she saw what Kurt did with *Nevermind* and was like, "I can do that, too." We didn't talk about it like that, but I think she had a strong interest in getting a record out. She was on Geffen, this was an opportunity to make it happen, and she did it—they had videos on MTV, and it sold millions. That album got a posthumous "10" in *Pitchfork*—that's the only time I'll get a "10" in *Pitchfork*.

Kurt was there for a couple of days, and they didn't spend that much time in the studio. She wanted him to sing harmonies, and he said, "Play me the song. I don't know the song." So, obviously he didn't write it, or else he would have known it. There are a few little bits of him in there. He didn't really do much that we ended up using. And he certainly didn't play on it. We had a jam session at one point in the studio, which I don't think was even recorded. But he didn't write the songs—other than he was married to her and I think they were bouncing the songs off of each other. But she was quite competitive with him—she wasn't going to let him write the songs for the record. Her whole point was to prove that she could write some songs, too. So, to say that Kurt wrote those songs, it's not true. Some of them were actually written and finished in the studio right in front of me—she had bits of lyrics and things and was like, "Let's put this in." They didn't need him to do it.

JELLYFISH

Spilt Milk **[1993]**

ROGER JOSEPH MANNING JR.: *Spilt Milk* was, thankfully, another opportunity for Andy and I as songwriters to further and complete the statement that we initially tried to put out there with *Bellybutton*. Which, we feel we arrived at in many ways. But we always felt that the idea wasn't complete. So, we were hellbent on this next collection of songs being more completely expressed. Of course, we'd learned things—what to do, what not to do—on the first record. Just trying to hone our craft, which was both incredibly challenging and a level of focus and hard work that I don't think either of us had any experience with, but it's also something we wanted to do. So, we were committed.

JESUS JONES

Doubt **[1991]**

MIKE EDWARDS: It was a funny album to make, because it wasn't done in the typical way of, "I've written a bunch of songs. Let's spend three weeks in a studio recording them." It was more a case of, "It's February 1990. I've written a song. Let's record it." And in two months' time, it's released as a single . . . things like "International Bright Young Thing," "Right Here, Right Now," "Real, Real, Real"—there were *months and months* between those. But they all ended up on the same album. It was also quite a schizophrenic album in that you had these well-produced pop singles and the appallingly badly produced—that would be my part—rock songs on the album, too. There's very little of it that I like. I don't listen to it for years and years at a time.

MARK LANEGAN

The Winding Sheet **[1990]**

MIKE JOHNSON: Mark asked me if I'd help him with this solo record he was going to make. Of course, I was more than psyched to do that. I remember driving up to Seattle and staying at his house, and he played me some four-tracks of songs he had: "Mockingbirds," "Ugly Sunday," and some of the other songs from the album. I added some guitar parts, and he wanted me to flesh them out because he was insecure about them all being the same three chords. So, I inserted some breaks and intros . . . or got him to change the key maybe on one. Then, I went back to Eugene and came back a month later or something, and had time booked with Jack Endino at Reciprocal. We went in and it was like three days; we did everything—it was Mark Pickerel playing drums, me playing guitar, and then Jack overdubbed his bass later.

THE LEMONHEADS

It's a Shame About Ray **[1992]**

EVAN DANDO: It was a cool phase of my life, where the record company went, "Oh . . . *we've got one of those*"—like Nirvana. "Let's strike while the iron's hot." People weren't ready for *Lovey*, like, "Let's hit 'em with the most difficult record first." I went to Melbourne—I had a few weeks off, and I got really depressed. It said "Rudderless" on the front of a newspaper. I had the music already, so I wrote the words there in Melbourne. I went back to Sydney and took speed for a long time, and we stayed up—one day we started writing, and we didn't stop. Then I got home, got depressed, got straight, and wrote "Allison's Starting to Happen," "Hannah & Gabi," "Ceiling Fan in My Spoon," and "My Drug Buddy." I needed to reconnect with it, and I wasn't going to be able to do it with drugs. I went to my shrink from high school, and he said, "Dude, stop drinking, don't smoke pot, take care of yourself, and you'll be fine." And I was.

LIVE

Throwing Copper **[1994]**

CHAD TAYLOR: When we returned to Milwaukee for preproduction in 1993, our band had been transformed by the road and endless touring. A newfound punch and fire from my guitar playing altered the band's sonic footprint. If *Mental Jewelry* was defined by the explosive rhythms of [drummer Chad] Gracey and [bassist Patrick] Dahlheimer, then *Throwing Copper* was all about the guitar—especially when coupled with the growing capacity of Ed [Kowalczyk]'s vocals. We found our sound in those hot, sweaty nightclubs fueled by the passion of the early fans.

After preproduction, we moved to Cannon Falls, Minnesota. We recorded at Pachyderm Studio, where Nirvana had just finished recording *In Utero*. I stayed in Kurt's bedroom. Jerry Harrison was back producing, and we added audio engineer Lou Giordano to the team. These are our most extraordinary recording sessions—at least in terms of band purity. We tracked live, straight to two-inch tape, and truly captured the raw essence of the band. Gracey's drum performances were epic, as there was tons of pressure for the "perfect performance." I don't think we ever played a song more than three times. We recorded the entire album in only ten days.

INSPIRING A HIT TV SERIES

Fred Armisen reveals the alt-rock foundations of *Portlandia*.

Our first episode of *Portlandia*, we talk about the "dream of the '90s." We [Note: Armisen and Sleater-Kinney's Carrie Brownstein were the show's creators and main actors] were born of it, we lived it, and even throughout all our seasons, *we addressed it*. So, it was very much about that. We were already making sketches—we were putting stuff online, and it was an easy sell [to make *Portlandia* a TV series]. But whereas you and I can talk about how it's a direct reference to the '90s, that's not how it was sold. The idea was that it was sketches that were hopefully funny. I don't think in our pitches we ever even said "'90s" or "alternative."

There's two sketches that are a little more direct. One is Jello Biafra wakes up from a coma. He was in the Dead Kennedys, and he missed a lot of the '90s because he was in this coma, and he calls everyone around him "yuppies." And in the '90s, that was a real sticking point. That was a real issue—"Ugh. Look at all those *yuppies*." And the notion of it disappeared after a while. Now, everyone's sort of a yuppie, and we accept it. But that is a direct reference to what the '90s were about.

And then there's this other one where I play this guy who has a home studio, and I feel like the '90s—in Chicago—the recording studio scene was *really* thriving. It was the best. I loved that about Chicago—people were making their own studio with a real seriousness. They were really trying to make great recording studios. That's something I don't remember from the '80s. And because of technology, I don't see it as much now. But boy, in the '90s . . . "Guess who has a studio?!" And you'd go to another city, and like, "*Whoa!*" That was its own culture.

The "Riot Spray" episode was about the physical body as punk gets older: How does it match up with what our bodies are doing? And it came from a weird place of older people like to look in windows—bookshop, antiques, furniture. And as I was getting older, I was like, "Yeah, sometimes when you're on tour, you do tend to stop a little more and look at stuff." Whereas when you're in your twenties, you're like, "*Who cares?!*" It came kind of from that.

And then we wanted to get more into the idea of what is a band's message like compared to physically how they are and what they want to do. How much time they want to spend on the road. But it was toward the end of our run, and I think we just wanted to have a good time with our friends—Krist Novoselic, Brendan Canty, and Henry Rollins. So, it was a combo of talking about how we grow older and also, let's make some fun music.

LIVING COLOUR

Stain **[1993]**

COREY GLOVER: *Stain* we did up in Massachusetts in this barn—Long View Farm. It was like a horse farm—they had horse stables in the back. And the song "Nothingness" . . . there was this giant, twenty-foot satellite dish on the property that didn't work. So, we had no television. But every time we walked past it and talked into it, the sound would reverberate in a very strange sort of way. We were like, "We've got to find a way to use that!" It's on "Nothingness." That's why you can actually hear crickets on the track. I think we wanted something a little darker. In our minds, we were like, "This record has to be slightly darker than the last. And the themes have to be slightly more sinister." I think we were on our way to doing that whether Muzz was there or not. [Note: Bassist Muzz Skillings left the band prior to the album, replaced by Doug Wimbish.]

LUSH

Spooky **[1992]**

MIKI BERENYI: It was a little bit fraught because of the way we signed with 4AD. Basically, all the songs we had got used up on many EPs that eventually came out as *Gala* in America. But we used up *all* our fucking songs. So, to be able to write *Spooky*, we had to write it all from scratch. Whereas usually a band's first album is, "Here you go, these are the songs we had for the best part of however long we've been formed," we had to write it very quickly.

MEAT PUPPETS

Too High to Die **[1994]**

PAUL LEARY: They wanted John Paul Jones to produce their album [who was producing the Butthole Surfers' *Independent Worm Saloon*]. They asked me if I would contact John Paul Jones and ask him. So, I did. I played the Meat Puppets for John Paul Jones quite a bit when we were working on our album—so I fully expected him to say yes. He said no. I produced an album called *Delusions of Banjer* [by the Bad Livers], and the Meat Puppets liked that record. They were like, "Well . . . do you want to do it?" And I'm like, "*Hell yeah I want do it!*"

MINISTRY

Psalm 69 **[1992]**

AL JOURGENSEN: At that point, relationships had frayed in the band, and it was difficult. And we all were fuckin' junkies. The first budget Warner Bros. gave us went up our arms and up our noses . . . and we had nothing to show for it. So, they had to decide, "Do we want to double down and give these knuckleheads more money? Or do we want to cut them off now?" So, it was a difficult album to make. But it seemed the right music to make for that period of time in the '90s.

MOBY

***Play* [1999]**

MOBY: That was made in my bedroom with a bunch of cheap equipment. And at that point, '97–'98, my career had essentially ended. I had been dropped by my American label, and I still had a deal in the UK—only because my label boss, Daniel Miller, had never dropped anyone. I think he released that record because he felt sorry for me. I thought it was going to be my last record, and I was going to go back to school and get a PhD and teach philosophy at community college. Whenever I've expected success, it hasn't worked out. And whenever I've expected failure, it surprises me with success.

MORPHINE

***Cure for Pain* [1993]**

DANA COLLEY: We had been playing quite a bit at that point and just got back from California. [Drummer] Jerome [Deupree] had decided that he wanted to leave the band. We decided to record what songs we had before he left the band. We went into Fort Apache with Paul Kolderie. I remember laying it down pretty quickly. When it was finished, I had a mixed tape in my hand, and I was painting houses. I put the cassette into the boombox as I was rolling a wall and just thinking to myself, "For the first time, here's something that I could *really* be proud of."

NED'S ATOMIC DUSTBIN

***God Fodder* [1991]**

JONN PENNEY: A lot of the songs were road-tested. We'd been playing a lot of shows from '89 to '90—we were playing every night, sleeping on floors, doing as many shows as we possibly could. I think it was a time in everyone's lives, especially mine, where there was a lot of change going on. So, there was a lot of influence and inspiration. I was forced to leave home at that time, and you're twenty-one—you're becoming an adult, so there's so much to rally against. It was very much an album of the time, very much a bunch of nineteen, twenty, twenty-one-year-old kids starting to vaguely eloquently express ourselves. Well road-tested, because we'd seen what people liked and what people didn't like on the road.

NIRVANA

In Utero [1993]

STEVE ALBINI: Another scenario where the band was just operating at peak efficiency. A lot of people in my position get attention for records that were good because the band was at their peak. Like, my job as an engineer was quite simple in that setting: just get it on tape in a way that sounds good and don't interfere with them. So that was a very straightforward, easy session. We got a lot of work done in a relatively quick period of time. Everybody was happy with everything.

There was a big political thing with the label after it was done [Scott Litt remixed two songs], but that's all water under the bridge—when you listen to the record now, it seems kind of insane because it sounds like a good record. It doesn't seem *that* adventurous—it just seems like a good record. But at the time, the record label found a lot of stuff to complain about. It boils down to that political nature of the power structure within the record label.

Like, the record label wanted to be in control of their product, and here this band went off on their own and made a record for half of what they were supposed to spend. And then they turned this record in and said, "We're done." The record label couldn't allow that to stand as a new paradigm. Because then they would be ceding control to the artists on all the records they released. And they didn't want that to be the case. They wanted to be able to take authorship of everything that came out. The fact that they didn't get their say in how things were done was really offensive to them.

NOFX

White Trash, Two Heebs and a Bean [1992]

FAT MIKE: That was our first *good* record. Two years before that, my vocals were horrendous—so out of key. But we got our sound—and it's good to get your own sound. And *White Trash* pulled it off. It's one of our best-sounding albums. And that's really when we broke the rules—we had jazz and ska. That's when we kinda got big.

POE

Hello [1995]

POE: I was living with RJ and Dede Rice in Southfield, Michigan. RJ and his wife were both producers, and they had a mixing board and a tape machine in their living room. They had become sort of a local "hub" for a lot of the creative talent in that neighborhood—who just happened to be insanely gifted. J Dilla, who was a teenager then, and Amp Fiddler, who gave J Dilla his first MPC [Music Production Center], were part of that scene. It was an informal but incredibly creative environment. Everybody was speaking in rhyme all the time and obsessively hunting for loops. Working with J Dilla on my first demos, and later on my album *Hello*, was a highlight of my life to this day. Another thing that influenced the recordings on *Hello* was technology. It was the beginning of the internet, and I had the only laptop in the neighborhood that could go online—through an ethernet cable.

PRIMUS

Sailing the Seas of Cheese **[1991]**

LES CLAYPOOL: Our whole thing has always been—and sometimes to a fault—we wanted to go against the grain and do our own thing. So, all of a sudden we were on a major label [Interscope]. We were going to be marketed right alongside all these other bands—like the Bon Jovi's—and I just said, "Y'know, we're going to be *sailing the seas of cheese*. We're going to sink or swim—we're going to be in this cheesy world."

We had a blast making that record. Ler and I were probably stoned every minute of recording it. We went into Fantasy Studios in Berkeley, and Herb shows up with this brand-new drum kit from Pork Pie . . . *that he had never set up, ever*. And here was [A&R director] Tom Whalley and Interscope wondering, "What are these guys going to do?" And the first thing Tom sees when he shows up is me and Ler in the studio [recording "Sathington Waltz"]—I'm playing clarinet and Ler is on banjo, and we're just making these weird noises!

The other big standout is we had saved "Tommy the Cat" for our major label release. We didn't want to put it on *Frizzle Fry*—because I wanted to do something different with it, because it had been such a popular song on the live record [1989's *Suck on This*]. I said to Tom Whalley, "I want to get somebody to do the voice of Tommy the Cat. Someone like . . . Tom Waits." And he goes, "Well, *let's get Tom Waits*." So, I wrote him this letter and sent it off. We were recording one night, I went home, I hit the phone voice recorder, and I hear this voice: "Hey, Les, this is Tom Waits. I got your letter. It would be a wonderful thing. *Let's do this thing.*"

RADIOHEAD

Pablo Honey **[1993]**

PAUL Q. KOLDERIE: Chipping Norton was a famous studio outside of Oxford—it was a residential studio, so it made sense for everyone to go there. It was a good studio—it was state-of-the-art for 1992. All analog, of course—Studer Tape Machines. And they had a cool drum room which I used for "Creep" but I decided not to use for the rest of the album—to my regret today. And a guy told me, "You should use the drum room." And I was like. "Thank you . . . *I'll do it my way*." He must have muttered under his breath, "*Stupid Yankee.*"

I don't really get nervous in the studio, but I think they were a little bit nervous. They were just trying to make sure they made the most of their opportunity, basically. They're all smart guys, but they didn't know what was going to happen. The thing was that "Creep" happened right away—like an explosion. And all of a sudden, their whole status as a band changed at EMI because they had a song that was successful. Making the record, it took a little pressure off, because there was a song already done that everybody was excited about. That's not the way things usually go.

ROLLINS BAND

***Weight* [1994]**

CHRIS HASKETT: The Chili Peppers had recorded *Blood Sugar Sex Magik* in a mansion [The Mansion in Los Angeles]. And they were sleeping there, eating there, and recording there. We were like, "Oh, we'll do that!" Then, at the last minute, whatever building they had used became unavailable. So, we had to scramble and find something else and found a residential conference bungalow thing outside of Lake Tahoe. And that was with our soundman Theo [Van Rock] producing.

The material was pretty much done—we didn't write much there. We did get a little bit stir crazy because it snowed and we couldn't go anywhere. There was nothing to do except watch TV or sit in your room and read. I remember doing guitar overdubs at night with my cabinets set up in a bay window. And while I'm tracking . . . a fucking bear walks by the window and goes into the dumpster!

ROYAL TRUX

***Cats and Dogs* [1993]**

JENNIFER HERREMA: *Cats and Dogs* was the first time we had a drummer and a second guitar player. Neil [Hagerty]'s pretty proficient on all the instruments, but we came together as a band—but with two strangers, from totally different parts of the United States. We were rehearsing at a farm in Virginia, and we made it work. I remember them saying they had the board from the Beach Boys' *Smile*. We really made an effort to include more than just our own ideas—we didn't tell [guitarist] Mike Kaiser or [drummer] Ian Willers exactly what to play at all. Neil wrote the music, but those guys didn't read music, so it was just play and play . . . and then stop. The whole rehearsing and writing was three weeks, which seemed like a year. It gave time for our lyrics and melodies to find a background of music.

FRED SCHNEIDER

***Just Fred* [1996]**

FRED SCHNEIDER: When I first met Steve Albini, I think he was really bemused about the fact that I asked him to produce it. And my ex-partner encouraged me to ask him. I was in Chicago, met Steve and Tom Zaluckyj—who was working with Steve a lot and was also in the band Tar—and Steve liked the B-52s. So, he said, "Sure." I let him take control and the way he liked to work, he put me in touch with different bands—Six Finger Satellite, Shadowy Men on a Shadowy Planet, Jon Spencer Blues Explosion—and I really enjoyed working with them. I think I wrote some of the best lyrics I ever wrote—way different from the B-52s.

SEBADOH

Bakesale [1994]

LOU BARLOW: Eric Gaffney was a big part of the band—he wrote over half the songs. He finally quit. He used to quit every couple of months. He finally was like, "For the next Sebadoh record, I want to receive one-third of all of the advances, and I want to record entirely by myself, and I'm not touring." I'm a person pretty much without any boundaries, and I was like, "That's it! *You crossed the boundary!* You're out of the band!" We hired this really good friend of ours—my pot connection—Bob Fay. We had him play drums, and we immediately started recording *Bakesale*. And luckily, I had already recorded three or four songs with Eric on drums.

SHONEN KNIFE

Let's Knife [1992]

NAOKO YAMANO: *Let's Knife* is the first album which had a contract with a major record company in Japan and in the US: MCA Victor and Virgin Records. In the UK, it was for Creation Records. We re-recorded eleven songs and made three new songs for this album. We started to work with a management in Tokyo in 1991, and they got us the major label record contract. We wanted people who didn't know our songs to hear us. This was a good chance to let people hear our early songs. We invited Craig Montgomery—who was a soundman of Nirvana—as a recording engineer. We were always having fun!

SHUDDER TO THINK

Pony Express Record [1994]

CRAIG WEDREN: *Pony Express Record* was great because we had these songs and we got signed on this collection of songs. In no uncertain terms, we made it clear, "Okay. You understand *this* is the album we're going to be recording. So, if you're into that, we definitely want to take this ride together." And Michael Goldstone and Epic Records were down. It was the first time we had a budget, and we had a month or two in the studio to really lock it down. So, there is a precision to *Pony Express Record* that I think suits Shudder to Think—which, we had never had the time or experience to fully realize the music that we were making in the studio. We always tended to write a little bit beyond our abilities, and we didn't have enough studio experience to know how to properly serve the songs in the studio—until *Pony Express Record*.

SLINT

***Spiderland* [1991]**

DAVID PAJO: The writing was really intense in hindsight. At the time, we didn't even think about it as being intense. It became part of our daily routine—after everybody was off of work, we had band practice. And we did that in pretty much isolation . . . for I think it was longer than a year. And it's funny, because we would play our old songs, and then we would be writing mostly, and just wrote and wrote and wrote. It wasn't uncommon to spend like a week on a three-second bass transition to the next riff!

We recorded pretty much everything live in a weekend—Friday night to Monday morning. We had a limited time, and we had to bust it out. So, we didn't think at the time that we had spent all this time practicing and then no time recording. And then we broke up . . . it feels like it was within a couple of days of sending in the finished artwork for *Spiderland*. I remember getting the test pressings of *Spiderland* and not listening to them. [*Laughs*]

SMASHING PUMPKINS

***Siamese Dream* [1993]**

BUTCH VIG: *Gish* was fairly easy to do, but *Siamese Dream* was probably the hardest record I've ever recorded, just because of the sheer intensity—Billy and I really set the bar high in terms of how we wanted it to sound. There was a lot of pressure on them to make a great record, and the band was really starting to fall apart at the time—a lot of drugs and they just weren't communicating. We spent five months recording the record in Atlanta, basically recording every day, almost seven days a week.

Then we came to L.A., and we mixed for six straight weeks, every day, including Sundays. I was mentally and physically completely wiped out when the record was done, but I'm really proud of how that record sounds. I think it's because of the amazing dynamics: The songwriting is really ambitious, and the band was playing at the peak of their powers. Even though Billy ended up doing a lot of the guitar and bass overdubs, the band, when we would cut a song, they would all play live in the studio with Jimmy. And D'arcy and James contributed to the record also by just being there, talking about the arrangements and the performances and stuff. So, it was a very intense experience.

I kept a journal making that record. I started to go back and read it, but it was a little too hard for me to go back, because I immediately went back into the zone that we were in in the studio, and there were some dark days in there when we were making that record. But I'm really pleased with how it turned out.

That's true [that Corgan and Chamberlin played the majority of everything on *Siamese Dream*]. They would go into the big room and cut the song live. But what I was really trying to keep was Jimmy's drums. And then we would go back and overdub everything.

Billy probably played 90 percent of the guitar and bass parts. Someone played some keyboards, and Billy played Mellotron, and we had a cello player come in and play. A couple of string players came in for "Disarm."

James is a great guitarist, and D'arcy was a good bass player, but Billy Corgan is just technically better. He's better than both of them, and the band knew that, and I knew it. So, it was like, "Well, if we want this to be as good as it's going to be, we want the best possible performance out of it." So, Billy ended up doing probably over 90 percent of the overdubs on the record.

But he had a "feel thing" with Jimmy. He really understood Jimmy's drumming. Jimmy had this push/pull thing. He wasn't like a metronomic drummer, you know. He wasn't like a perfect 4/4 click track drummer—I think we used a click track on one or two songs on *Siamese Dream*. It moves around a lot, and Billy really understood Jimmy's playing. It was like a thick fence, almost, but he was really able to lock in with Jimmy, which is not always easy to do when you have to come back and overdub, when you're not playing live with someone.

STONE TEMPLE PILOTS

Core **[1992]**

ROBERT DeLEO: I think the first record [the band was "firing on all cylinders"]. It was all or nothing. That record and the energy we put into that, it allowed us to make another record. When you get signed to a major label, it's scary, and you don't know what's going to happen next; so it was great that that first record allowed us to make a second one and a third one. I look at that as a really good time right then. Ambitious.

SUGAR

Copper Blue **[1992]**

BOB MOULD: After that record [1990's *Black Sheets*] ran its course and I parted ways with Virgin Records, the goal in 1991 to me was to just start writing what I was hoping would be the best record I could possibly write. I was on the road, constantly doing solo acoustic shows.

I would play for three weeks and try out new material. I'd go home for a couple weeks, write more stuff. I'd go back out for another three weeks. And this was all sort of planting seeds for what was to come. This is the working out the material in front of the people to gauge what's good and what's not. And then by the end of '91 it became clear to me which record companies would be interested, what kind of structure would work.

And January '92 is me and David Barbe and Malcolm Travis—the three of us rehearsing and learning thirty songs in the back of a tire shop in downtown Athens, Georgia, with the intent of making the third Bob Mould solo album. And we got asked to do a show at 40 Watt the night before we started heading up to suburban Boston, to record the album. And decided we should give it a band name, and we came up with the name Sugar. That's sort of how that all started.

THEY MIGHT BE GIANTS

Flood [1990]

JOHN FLANSBURGH: We were afforded this luxury of time and of working with these British producers, who were just complete gentlemen. Clive Langer and Alan Winstanley were really the guys behind Madness—that was their original production. Up until then, we only worked on eight-track recorders, and the worlds of MIDI and sampling were really coming together. It was a really interesting moment for us professionally. We basically had spent eight years fully "DIY."

THROWING MUSES

The Real Ramona [1991]

KRISTIN HERSH: We lived in an apartment house in L.A. with the Pixies and a bunch of hookers who called themselves models and a bunch of metal guys who called themselves musicians. We only had enough money to eat dinner once a week, but we drank lots of cheap champagne in the hot tub outside our apartment building.

TOADIES

Rubberneck [1994]

VADEN TODD LEWIS: I had been writing a ton of songs. My process was to write a bunch of songs and then melt them down into less songs. Like, combine them into songs. The song "I Burn," for example, was the bridge from another song. It was a very long bridge, and I liked it better than the song—so I lifted it out, scrapped everything else, and ran off with it. "I Come From the Water" was probably the very first song that I wrote for the Toadies. "Backslider" was the one that I wrote right before we went in the studio. It's a nice document of where I was as a songwriter.

TORTOISE

Millions Now Living Will Never Die [1996]

DAVID PAJO: *Millions* was recorded when I was living in Chicago at the Tortoise loft. It was sort of like a commune there—*a Tortoise commune*. Part of it was recorded at Idful Music. It was Brad Wood's studio—Brad did Liz Phair and Veruca Salt. The opening track, "Djed," there was this transition, and we couldn't figure out how to get this one part of the song to the other part. So, John McEntire was doing all these tape edits, and we were like, "Yeah, that's cool"—but nothing was really blowing us away.

And then, I think out of frustration, he got all the pieces of tape that were in the garbage next to the tape machine, spliced them all together, and put that on there. We listened to it, and were like, "*Oh, my God!*" It was so random and fucked up—it sounded like a CD skipping or something was wrong with the recording. And we loved that. That's still one of the key moments on the record—when he spliced it.

TRENCHMOUTH

Inside the Future **[1993]**

FRED ARMISEN: There's something about it that was just space and weird. The album cover, they misprinted it, so it came out really pink—and then we wound up loving it. We were at a stage in our career where . . . you know where the middle stage of everyone's career is so fun and exploring what you want to do? I *really* liked that record.

URBAN DANCE SQUAD

Mental Floss for the Globe **[1990]**

RUDEBOY REMINGTON: For two years, we didn't want to make a record. Then we took the challenge. The problem was that within the group, people had the idea to make certain songs that normally we would do in a very heavy way, to do it more mellow. It became a strange thing, because when the record came out and they heard "No Kid" acoustic, certain people were disappointed. It depended on who you were. I think that element made it more difficult for us. I always liked "Brainstorm" because I liked the idea and the effects we used to do live—we were *ferocious* live back then. I like "Piece of Rock" because of the strange "atmospheres"—talking about drugs and stuff like that.

URGE OVERKILL

Saturation **[1993]**

EDDIE "KING" ROESER: The guys who worked on that record had been known Philly-based producers who were largely doing hip-hop for years. And the guy that signed us for Geffen, we have to give him credit for hooking us up with the Butcher Brothers, who were dying to get back into more traditional recording, more traditional instruments, or a rock-type thing. Where they had been sampling beats.

That was really a sort of brilliant thing—it was sort of like Beck hooking up with the Dust Brothers. This was going to be sort of a similar thing. I think what makes that record stand out is they were more than happy to use a few unconventional things—drum machines, interstitial music, and things that were probably not going to happen if we worked with Butch or Steve.

MIKE WATT

***Ball-Hog or Tugboat?* [1995]**

MIKE WATT: The title is a test, right? If the bass player knows the song, maybe anybody can come in and sing, play drums, guitar. I used a metaphor, *The Wrestling Record*—that's what I called it. So, nobody practiced. The only guy who practiced was [guitarist] Nels Cline and his drummer friend, Michael [Preussner]. Because I thought *I* should have a backbone.

So, three or four tunes are like that, but all the rest of the tunes, I'd go in there, show them the songs, and see what they do. And whoever's available at the time—it was three days in Cherokee in SoCal, three days in Robert Lang Studios in Seattle, and three days in Baby Monster in New York City.

I just gave people the thing on the bass and then they brought to it. In a way, it was kind of like bebop—a jam session where people don't have a lot of time to practice and just come together. Y'know, Bruce Willis—probably not your favorite actor, either, but Quentin Tarantino put him in that *Pulp Fiction* thing . . . hey, that makes sense! That's kind of what I got to with that record. Great little worlds. "Petri dish rock." I didn't use any managers—I just called guys up.

VARIOUS ARTISTS

***Kids Motion Picture Soundtrack* [1995]**

LOU BARLOW: Harmony Korine had some really specific innovative ideas about the soundtrack and culturally how he wanted to match indie rock or lo-fi with urban culture. He wanted the two to be together, because I think he understood that a lot of times really disparate music and scenes can bring out emotions in them. He mostly wanted me to do lo-fi acoustic stuff in it, but then I thought it was a really good opportunity to use a studio and incorporate some of the other influences I'd been experiencing in the '90s—like trip-hop and rap. I wanted to fuse my sensibilities and [bandmate] John Davis's sensibilities with that.

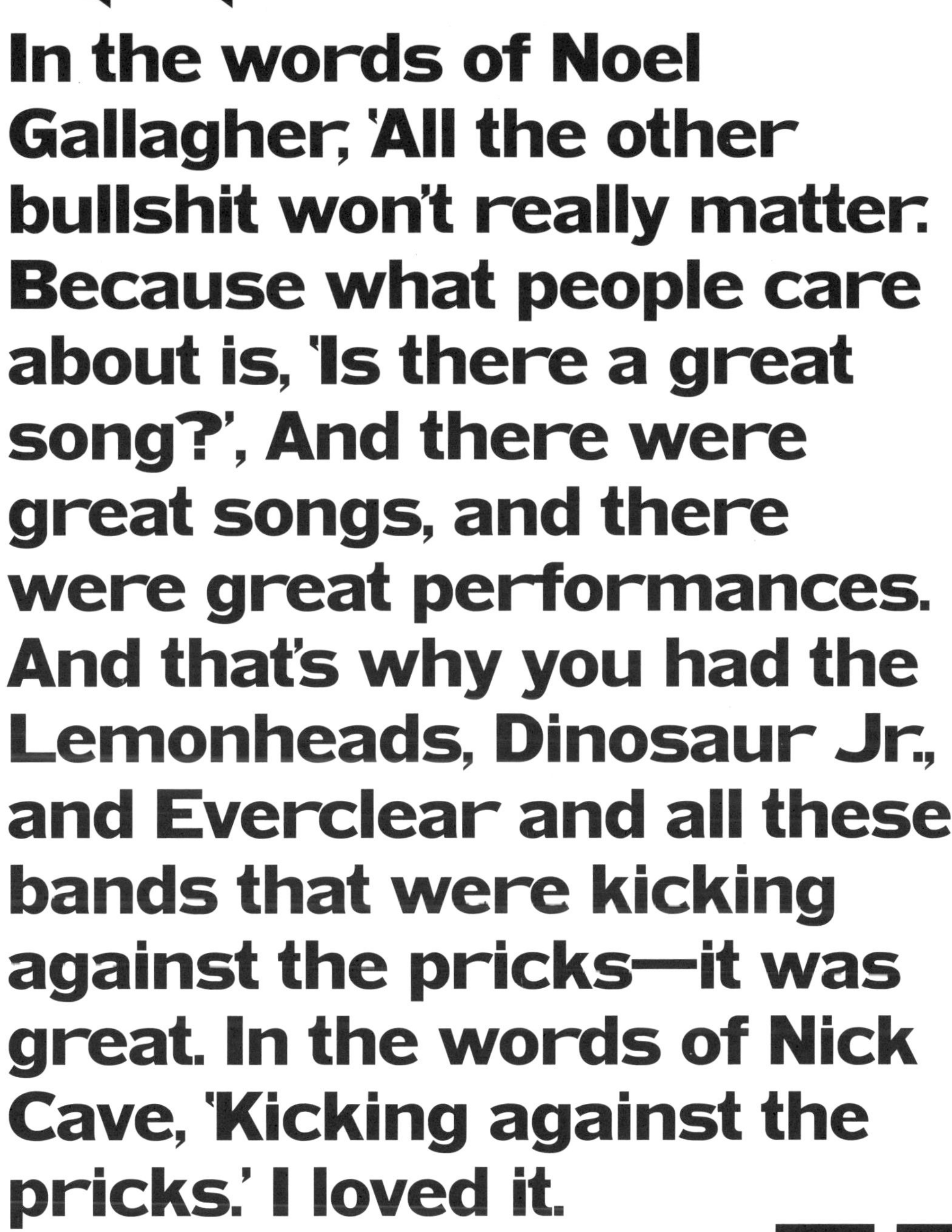

"In the words of Noel Gallagher, 'All the other bullshit won't really matter. Because what people care about is, 'Is there a great song?', And there were great songs, and there were great performances. And that's why you had the Lemonheads, Dinosaur Jr., and Everclear and all these bands that were kicking against the pricks—it was great. In the words of Nick Cave, 'Kicking against the pricks.' I loved it."

MATT PINFIELD

SOURCES

(all interviews conducted by Greg Prato)

CHAPTER 1

Bob Mould: "Mid-tempo, super . . . specialty, I guess." (AllMusic—February 4, 2025); Bob Mould: "There were a . . . in South Jersey." (AllMusic—February 4, 2025); Bob Mould: "If I look . . . was Black Sheets." (AllMusic—February 4, 2025); Frank Black: "The compact disc . . . the financial connections." (AllMusic—January 8, 2025).

CHAPTER 3

Joey Santiago: "I had no . . . became a surprise." (AllMusic—February 6, 2023); Bob Mould: "Well, I had . . . hand in building." (AllMusic—February 4, 2025); Fat Mike: "Books are important . . . bands a career." (Songfacts—March 29, 2023); Frank Black: "['Smells Like Teen . . . do it ourselves." (Songfacts—August 22, 2019); Joey Santiago: "For me, it . . . at the time." (AllMusic—February 6, 2023); Butch Vig: "Well, that record . . . changed my life." (Songfacts—June 18, 2013).

CHAPTER 4

Bob Mould: "So, that late . . . to that point." (AllMusic—February 4, 2025); Bob Mould: "I did not . . . was pretty exciting." (AllMusic—February 4, 2025); Bob Mould: " I think I . . . yeah. That's right.." (AllMusic—February 4, 2025).

CHAPTER 5

Gavin Rossdale: "I like that . . . elements to them." (Songfacts—November 22, 2017).

CHAPTER 8

Eric Kretz: "Brendan O'Brien's records . . . were putting together." (*BONZO: 30 Rock Drummers Remember the Legendary John Bonham* book—2020); Butch Vig: "Well, Kurt [Cobain] . . . Billy's work ethic." (Songfacts—June 18, 2013).

CHAPTER 12

Robert DeLeo: "I think people . . . It really was." (Songfacts—June 22, 2021).

CHAPTER 13

Lee Ranaldo: "Well, I was . . . guitar or whatever." (Songfacts—March 7, 2014); Lee Ranaldo: "Everybody in New . . . a sound maker." (Songfacts—March 7, 2014).

CHAPTER 14

Cris Kirkwood: "[Mike Watt and . . . of bass monsters." (*The 100 Greatest Bassists* book—2018); Mike Watt: "There are some . . . them get weird." (*The 100 Greatest Bassists* book—2018).

CHAPTER 15

Frank Black: "And also the . . . kill for now." (AllMusic—January 8, 2025).

CHAPTER 16

Bob Mould: "MTV, in general . . . question about it." (AllMusic—February 4, 2025); Frank Black: "To give you . . . little fucking clip!" (AllMusic—January 8, 2025).

CHAPTER 19

Robert DeLeo: "I think that . . . it was 'grunge.'" (*I Love Grunge: 'Grunge Is Dead' Outtakes* book—2023); Bob Mould: "I remember going . . . who they were." (AllMusic—February 4, 2025); Robert DeLeo: "I always go . . . to that record." (*I Love Grunge: 'Grunge Is Dead' Outtakes* book—2023).

CHAPTER 20

Robert DeLeo: "I think that . . . go to jail." (Songfacts—June 22, 2021); Robert DeLeo: "People think drugs . . . in the way." (Songfacts—June 22, 2021).

CHAPTER 22

Frank Black: "So, there was . . . and the MP3s." (AllMusic— January 8, 2025); Bob Mould: "I think [Sugar's] . . . Naturally, I think." (AllMusic— February 4, 2025).

CHAPTER 23

Frank Black: "I don't think . . . era of abundance." (AllMusic—January 8, 2025).

CHAPTER 25

Richard Patrick: "I constantly was . . . with my records." (Songfacts—July 19, 2013); Lee

Ranaldo: "[Songwriting] with Sonic . . . very concerted way." (Songfacts—March 7, 2014); Butch Vig: "Well, Pumpkins are . . . working with them." (Songfacts—June 18, 2013).

CHAPTER 26

Bob Mould: "The biggest one . . . always go to." (AllMusic—February 4, 2025); Gavin Rossdale: "'Where Is My . . . They still do." (Songfacts—November 22, 2017); Bob Mould: "Swervedriver being up . . . sing their praises." (AllMusic—February 4, 2025).

CHAPTER 27

Matt Pinfield: "It's a great . . . those blaxploitation movies." (Songfacts—July 11, 2018); Frank Black: "I know the . . . we would continue." (AllMusic— January 8, 2025); Gavin Rossdale: "One band that . . . a personal mantra." (Songfacts—November 22, 2017); Butch Vig: "'Stupid Girl' started . . . about 30 minutes." (Songfacts—June 18, 2013); Matt Pinfield: "The thing about . . . of those ideas." (Songfacts—July 11, 2018); Scott Lucas: "I had a . . . rhymes with 'pathetic.'" (Songfacts—February 12, 2018); Richard Patrick: "Oh, the filming . . . band.' Good times." (Songfacts—July 19, 2013); Matt Pinfield: "The video [directed . . . the band members." (Songfacts—July 11, 2018); Robert DeLeo: "On 'Vasoline,' we . . . stuff in there." (Songfacts—June 22, 2021); Eric Wilson: "It's a true . . . blessing in itself." (Songfacts—August 14, 2015); Bob Mould: "Real super riff . . . Good song, though." (AllMusic— February 4, 2025); Mark Pellington: "I had done . . . out-of-focus buffalo!" (Songfacts—July 27, 2018); Matt Pinfield: "The idea of . . . It was perfect." (Songfacts—July 11, 2018).

CHAPTER 28

Frank Black: "For the first . . . 'Wow, sounds great!'" (AllMusic—January 8, 2025); Butch Vig: "*Gish* was fairly . . . live with someone." (Songfacts—June 18, 2013); Robert DeLeo: "I think the . . . right then. Ambitious." (Songfacts—June 22, 2021); Bob Mould: "After that record . . . that all started." (AllMusic—February 4, 2025).

ADULT
All Taxes Incl. If Applicable
HM0805 MEZZ1 GA4 320
26.5
EVENT CODE
SECTION/BOX ROW SEAT ADM$
GENADM/SEATING
$ 26.50
METROPOLITAN PRESENTS
PRICE & ALL TAXES INCL.
THE VERVE
CONVENIENCE CHARGE
MEZZ1
311 WEST 34TH ST, NYC
SECTION/BOX
HAMMERSTEIN BALLROOM
GA4 320
ROW SEAT
AT THE MANHATTAN CENTER
10N600A
WED AUG 5, 1998 8:00PM
17JUL98

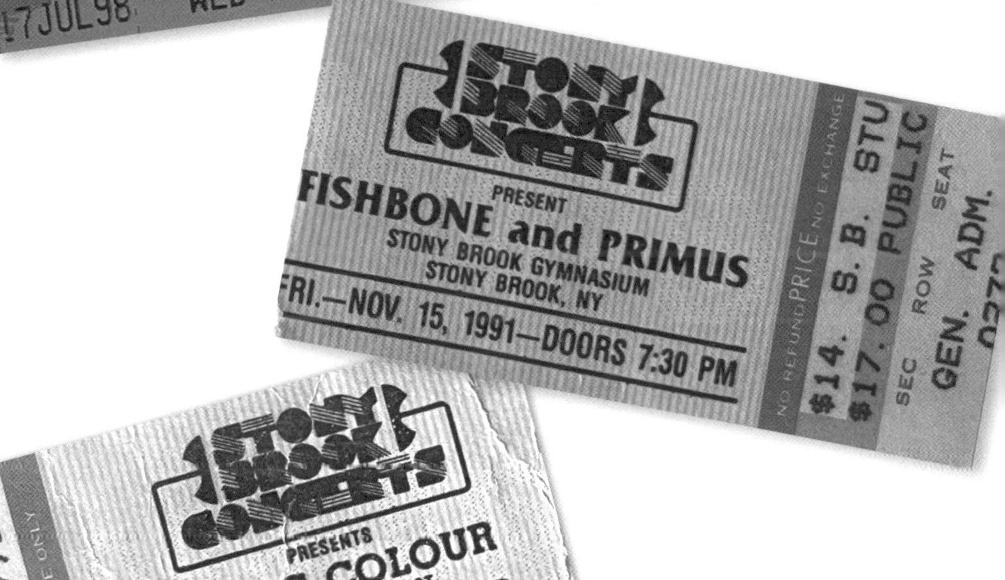
STONY BROOK CONCERTS
PRESENT
FISHBONE and PRIMUS
STONY BROOK GYMNASIUM
STONY BROOK, NY
FRI.—NOV. 15, 1991—DOORS 7:30 PM
NO REFUND PRICE NO EXCHANGE
$14. S. B. STU
$17.00 PUBLIC
SEC ROW SEAT
GEN. ADM.
STONY BROOK CONCERTS
PRESENTS
LIVING COLOUR
WITH SPECIAL GUEST
URBAN DANCE SQUAD
STONY BROOK GYMNASIUM—STONY BROOK, NEW YOR
SAT.—FEB. 23, 1991—DOORS 8:00 PM
SEC ROW
GEN. ADM.
FEB 23, 1991
ADMIT ONE THIS DATE ONLY

OTHER BOOKS BY GREG PRATO

MUSIC

A Devil on One Shoulder and an Angel on the Other: The Story of Shannon Hoon and Blind Melon

Touched by Magic: The Tommy Bolin Story

Grunge Is Dead: The Oral History of Seattle Rock Music

No Schlock . . . Just Rock! (A Journalistic Journey: 2003–2008)

MTV Ruled the World: The Early Years of Music Video

The Eric Carr Story

Too High to Die: Meet the Meat Puppets

The Faith No More & Mr. Bungle Companion

Overlooked/Underappreciated: 354 Recordings That Demand Your Attention

Over the Electric Grapevine: Insight into Primus and the World of Les Claypool

Punk! Hardcore! Reggae! PMA! Bad Brains!

Iron Maiden: '80 '81

Survival of the Fittest: Heavy Metal in the 1990s

Scott Weiland: Memories of a Rock Star

German Metal Machine: Scorpions in the '70s

The Other Side of Rainbow

Shredders! The Oral History of Speed Guitar (and More)

The Yacht Rock Book: The Oral History of the Soft, Smooth Sounds of the 70s and 80s

100 Things Pearl Jam Fans Should Know & Do Before They Die

The 100 Greatest Rock Bassists

Long Live Queen: Rock Royalty Discuss Freddie, Brian, John & Roger

King's X: The Oral History

Facts on Tracks: Stories Behind 100 Rock Classics

Dark Black and Blue: The Soundgarden Story

Take It Off: Kiss Truly Unmasked

A Rockin' Rollin' Man: Bon Scott Remembered

Avatar of the Electric Guitar: The Genius of Jimi Hendrix

BONZO: 30 Rock Drummers Remember the Legendary John Bonham

John Winston Ono Lennon

Shannon

Iconic Guitar Gear

A+ Albums: The Stories Behind 50 Rock Classics (Vol. I), 1970–1982

A+ Albums: The Stories Behind 50 Rock Classics (Vol. II), 1982–2000

Lanegan

The 100 Greatest Songs of Heavy Metal [e-Book]

The 100 Greatest Songs of Punk Rock [e-Book]

I Love Grunge: 'Grunge Is Dead' Outtakes

50 Rock Lists + Surprise Twists

World Infestation: The Ratt Story

Led Clones: The Led Zeppelin Imitator Craze of the '80s . . . and Beyond

Bang Your Head, Feel the Noize: The Quiet Riot Story

SPORTS

Sack Exchange: The Definitive Oral History of the 1980s New York Jets

Dynasty: The Oral History of the New York Islanders, 1972–1984

Just Out of Reach: The 1980s New York Yankees

The Seventh Year Stretch: New York Mets, 1977–1983

Butt Fumbles, Fake Spikes, Mud Bowls & Heidi Games: The Top 100 Debacles of the New York Jets

Hapless Islanders: The Story Behind the New York Islanders' Infamous 1972–73 Season

ABOUT THE AUTHOR

Greg Prato is a Long Island, New York–based author and journalist, who has written a veritable smorgasbord of books. Maybe you're familiar with such titles as *Grunge Is Dead* or *MTV Ruled the World*. Or perhaps you read his writing for *AllMusic* or *Songfacts*. If not, then hopefully you've at least heard him being interviewed on *Eddie Trunk Live* or *The Howard Stern Wrap-Up Show*. At any rate, Greg remains comfortable in his own skin.

INDEX

Quarto.com

First Published in 2025 by Motorbooks, an imprint of The Quarto Group,
100 Cummings Center, Suite 265-D, Beverly, MA 01915, USA.
T (978) 282-9590 F (978) 283-2742

EEA Representation, WTS Tax d.o.o.,
Žanova ulica 3, 4000 Kranj, Slovenia.
www.wts-tax.si

29 28 27 26 25 1 2 3 4 5

ISBN: 978-0-7603-9842-5

Digital edition published in 2025
eISBN: 978-0-7603-9843-2

Library of Congress Cataloging-in-Publication Data

Names: Prato, Greg interviewer
Title: Alternative for the masses: the '90s alt-rock revolution – an oral history / [interviews by] Greg Prato.

Description: Beverly, MA : Motorbooks, 2025. | Includes bibliographical references and index. | Summary: "Alternative for the Masses: The Oral History of the '90s Alt-Rock Revolution offers insights, opinions, and memories from an incredible cast of musicians and producers who created the music"—Provided by publisher.

Identifiers: LCCN 2025017637 (print) | LCCN 2025017638 (ebook) | ISBN 9780760398425 hardcover | ISBN 9780760398432 ebook

Subjects: LCSH: Alternative rock music—History and criticism | Rock music—1991-2000—History and criticism | Rock music—1981-1990—History and criticism | Alternative rock musicians—Interviews | LCGFT: Oral histories

Classification: LCC ML3534 .A463 2025 (print) | LCC ML3534 (ebook) | DDC 782.42166—dc23/eng/20250414

LC record available at https://lccn.loc.gov/2025017637
LC ebook record available at https://lccn.loc.gov/2025017638

Book Cover & Layout: Landers Miller Design
Cover Image: Ebet Roberts/Redferns/Getty Images
Printed in Malaysia